New
Nations
in a
Divided
World

New Nations in a Divided World

The International Relations
of the Afro-Asian States

Edited by KURT LONDON

Published for
THE INSTITUTE FOR SINO-SOVIET STUDIES
The George Washington University

FREDERICK A. PRAEGER, *Publisher*
New York · London

327
Li847n

FREDERICK A. PRAEGER, PUBLISHER
64 UNIVERSITY PLACE, NEW YORK 3, N.Y., U.S.A.
77–79 CHARLOTTE STREET, LONDON, W. 1, ENGLAND

Published in the United States of America in 1963 by
Frederick A. Praeger, Inc., Publisher

Manufactured in the United States of America

Contents

Introduction   *Kurt London*   vii
Neutrality—Utopia or Reality?   *Panayotis Kannelopoulos*   xiii

ONE

COLONIALISM AND COMMUNISM

Colonialism Yesterday and Today   *Rupert Emerson*   3
The Communist Attitude Toward Colonialism
     (to 1941)   *Jane Degras*   19
"Neo-Colonialism"—the Soviet Concept   *Walter Laqueur*   34
The Communist View of Colonialism—An
     African Interpretation   *B. G. D. Folson*   45
"National Democracy" and the Post-Colonial
     Revolution   *Richard Lowenthal*   56
Soviet Doctrines on Developing Countries: Some
     Divergent Views   *Herbert S. Dinerstein*   75
Some Factors in the Communist View of
     Neutrality   *Masao Onoe*   90

TWO

NEW NATIONS IN TRANSITION

Notes on Democracy and Leadership in the New
     Afro-Asian States   *Wolfgang H. Kraus*   101
The Social and Political Role of the Intelligentsia
     in the New Countries   *Klaus Mehnert*   121

v

9806

The Role of a Constitution in Developing Political
    Systems: The Nigerian Example   *Kalu Ezera*   134
The Idea of African "Neutralism" and "Non-Alignment":
    An Exploratory Survey   *Edward W. Blyden, III*   146

THREE

COMMUNIST POLICIES IN NON-ALIGNED COUNTRIES

The Soviet Union Seeks a Policy for
    Afro-Asia   *David T. Cattell*   163
The U.S.S.R. and Ethiopia: A Case of Traditional
    Behavior   *Sergius Yakobson*   180
Soviet Economic Policies Toward Afro-Asian
    Countries   *G. Warren Nutter*   193
Soviet Economic Aid to Non-Aligned Countries and the Soviet
    Program in South and Southeast Asia   *Tetsuji Yasuhira*   205
Leadership Cohesion in Communist China and Under-
    developed Asian Countries   *Roderick MacFarquhar*   222
Communist China and the Non-Committed Countries:
    Motives and Purposes of Communist
    China's Foreign Policy   *Franz Michael*   236
Communist Tactics in Non-Aligned Countries and the
    Ideological Quarrel Between Moscow
    and Peking   *Ernst Kux*   256
Communist Polycentrism and the Underdeveloped
    Areas   *William E. Griffith*   274
Communist China's Economy and Its Impact on
    Afro-Asia   *Choh-Ming Li*   287

Notes   301

Notes on the Contributors   337

Introduction

In 1956, an international conference of Sovietologists was held in Münstereifel, West Germany, under the auspices of the Deutsche Gesellschaft fur Osteuropakunde (German Society for East European Studies), of Stuttgart. It was concerned exclusively with Soviet affairs. The usefulness of this conference was recognized by Austrian specialists, and as a result the newly established Austrian Arbeitsgemeinschaft Ost (Work Association on the East), organized a second international conference, at Bad Aussee, Austria, in 1958. Its theme was "The Soviet Union—A Model for Asia?" At the end of that conference, during which Sino-Soviet relations were all too briefly discussed, the writer suggested organizing a third meeting that would concentrate specifically on this crucial issue. The idea came to fruition, and the conference took place in September, 1960, at Lake Kawaguchi, Japan, under the auspices of Óa Kyokai (the Japanese Society on Communism in Europe and Asia). Twenty of the thirty-six papers presented there were published in February, 1962.[1]

By early 1961, preparations had already begun for a fourth international gathering, to be held in September, 1962. The topic was to be "The Non-Aligned Afro-Asian Countries in a Divided World." Relations of these states with the Communist bloc and with the West were to be examined and discussed. The Pantios School of Political Science in Athens, Greece, agreed to be the host for the conference and recommended that it be held at the Mount Parnes Hotel, some 20 miles from Athens. Various subsidies, including the facilities and hospitality extended by the Pantios School, finally enabled the organizers to schedule the meeting for the week beginning September 17, 1962.

Thus, more spontaneously than by design, the conferences developed into a series. Having established an international reputation for high academic standards and the participation of first-rate experts, they are now recognized as important opportunities for the presentation of academic research, for mutual educational impact, and for contacts among scholars from all over the world. Owing to the natural growth of the series, there has been no need for an international secretariat. Each conference, once assured of funds from foundations and learned societies, has obtained the support of a host organization in sponsoring its meetings. The preparatory work for the Athens meeting was conducted by a Steering Committee that consisted of Dr. Klaus Mehnert of West Germany, Mr. Yoji Hirota of Japan, Professor John Georgakis of Greece, and the writer, who directed the organizing American secretariat, which is attached to the Institute for Sino Soviet Studies at The George Washington University in Washington, D.C.

The Athens Conference

The Athens conference lasted a week. An agenda was issued in advance, broadly outlining the program and specifying the material to be discussed at the individual sessions, each of which was to be presided over by a different chairman. Each participant was expected to submit a scholarly paper within the framework of the program, to be coordinated by the writer. These papers formed the background for the discussions. They were not read during the proceedings, but were circulated before the conference so that the participants could study them. At the beginning of each session, previously designated reporters briefly summarized and analyzed the papers that pertained to the topics of the day.

In addition to the sixty participants from twenty-two countries of Africa, Asia, Australia, Europe, and North America, there was, as in the previous conferences, a group of observers, consisting mainly of diplomats, government officials, specialists, and journalists. The observers took no active part in the plenary discussions, but were free to speak in the informal meetings. The conference, like its precursors, was closed to the public.

The participants' expertise ranged over a wide field. This was not, properly speaking, a Sino-Soviet conference; Sovietologists and Sinologists were present, to be sure, but there were also experts on non-Communist Asia, Africanists, specialists on the Middle East, and men familiar with Western affairs. The social sciences were well represented by scholars, some of whom are also active as government officials or consultants. As at the conference held in Japan in 1960, most participants had a practical acquaintance with the impact of the East-West rivalry on the non-aligned world of Asia and Africa. The convention was by no means held in an ivory tower.

THE CONFERENCE PROCEEDINGS: PIVOTAL ROLE OF THE AFRICANS

The proceedings were opened by the Honorary Chairman of the Conference, Professor Panayotis Kannelopoulos, Deputy Prime Minister of Greece. Perhaps as a result of the strong position taken by the Deputy Premier against non-alignment as a viable political and ideological concept—a position that caused a strong reaction among the non-aligned participants—the meeting became animated immediately. It was highlighted by a confrontation of the Western scholars with the Africans, whose attitudes and reactions had a strong and stimulating impact on the entire proceedings, and from whom both Western and Asian scholars learned a great deal. At the same time, the West's concern with problems of Communism became more understandable to the Africans as the conference progressed. Indeed, during the last two days of the meeting, some of the Africans stated frankly that they felt they must begin to study these problems more intensively.

Emotional outbursts punctuated the discussion of such basic concepts as non-alignment, neutralism, nationalism and imperialism, colonialism and neo-colonialism. The atmosphere at the outset was so tense that on the second day a British delegate submitted that the conference was deadlocked. The writer felt, on the other hand, that this exchange constituted a healthy escape valve necessary to clear the air. The conference had been convened not to arrive at specific conclusions or formulas, but rather to enable different schools of thought to learn from each other. Several European, Asian, and African participants shared the view that, in a forum of this nature, disagreements did not constitute a deadlock.

From then on, the conference remained on an even keel. Initial suspicions and resentments, particularly on the part of the African delegates, gradually gave way to recognition that all the participants were seeking to approach the topics under discussion with objectivity and understanding. The resulting rapprochement became evident not only in the plenary sessions but also in personal contacts among the participants.

The Africans' initial wariness was understandable against the background of the prime concerns of the new countries on the African continent: (1) the maintenance and consolidation of national sovereignty, and with it *human dignity*; and (2) the need for *rapid* economic development. The desire for dignity is overwhelming; the anxiety to move speedily toward economic independence is pervasive. It was natural, therefore, that the question of the applicability of principles of Western-style democracy in Africa should become the focal point of numerous conversations and the topic of one of the extracurricular evening meetings.

Considerable disagreement developed over the Common Market, the theme of another informal gathering. Most of the Africans and some of the Asians regarded the European Economic Community with suspicion, considering it a monopolistic attempt to dominate the world market. They feared that both its political and its economic impact might create obstacles to their efforts to establish political independence and economic viability. The French participants, assisted by German scholars, tried to dispel such misgivings and suggested that a strengthening of the European economy would ultimately redound to the benefit of the Afro-Asian states. It is doubtful, however, that they succeeded in fully reassuring either the Africans or the Asians. Interestingly, there were similar doubts on the part of some Greek scholars.

The concept of "neo-colonialism" was clearly congenial to the representatives of the former colonial and semi-colonial countries. Their embrace of the concept was qualified, to be sure, by a tendency to reject Moscow's one-sided identification of the neo-colonialist villains and to cast both East and West in the role of latter-day imperial powers. Nevertheless, they spoke as if it were an undeniable fact that the imperialists, having relinquished their political rule, were now trying to return through the back door of economic domination. They expressed the natural sentiments of former colonials toward their erstwhile masters—mixed sentiments of attraction and repulsion—and, in so doing, pointed up the dilemma faced by their countries: While relying on the West for tangible economic help and expert advice, these countries are mortally afraid that the acceptance of such aid will open the door to the reintroduction of a quasi-colonial domination. Some Western scholars tried to assuage such fears, with manifest lack of success. Other Westerners agreed with the Africans that neo-colonialism existed, citing the Philippines and pre-Castro Cuba as examples.

There was no indication of how the dilemma could be resolved, how Western help could be accepted without fear of hidden encroachment. An American plea for an effort to forget past bitterness against the former colonialists fell on deaf ears. It will take time and patience to dispel these grievances.

Thus there seems to be no hope for the quick disappearance of the antagonism toward the former imperial powers that has accumulated among Africans and Asians over the years. Whether this formidable barrier can be removed by future generations will depend largely on the policies and attitudes of the Western powers, as well as on the growth of Asian and African awareness of the far greater dangers inherent in Communist aid than in such "strings" as may be attached to help from the West. Events such as the Athens conference can help to eliminate existing prejudices on both sides, and the writer believes very strongly that this confrontation should be the first of many such sessions.

Forums of this sort, it must be understood, can be successful only if the principles established in the first four international conferences are carried forward. One of these principles is the steadfast rejection of Communist participation. This issue was raised in Athens by an African delegate who considered the exclusion of Communist representation deplorable. The writer, having polled organizations and individuals who have encountered Soviet delegates across the conference table, and himself keenly aware of the importance of free discussion, explained that Communist participation would not permit an objective procedure. Even if tolerable personal relations could be established, Communist contributions, both written and in plenary sessions, would necessarily tend to parrot the Party line and thus cloud the issues we strive to clarify. The other members of the Steering Committee and an overwhelming majority of the participants concurred.

THE CONFERENCE PAPERS: ESSAYS, ARGUMENTS, ANALYSES

The fifty-seven papers submitted dealt with a wide range of problems. They reflected not only the thinking of the individual authors, but in many instances also the positions of their countries. It was, of course, impossible to publish them all. A selection had to be made that would reflect, as much as possible, the scope of the conference within the framework of a thematic and topical breakdown. As a result, a great many contributions, some of them very deserving, had unfortunately to be omitted. Lack of space further contributed to the need for limitation, causing the editor to forego the addition of his own projected epilogue.

Nevertheless, the reader will find a great variety not only of topics but of treatment in this volume. The level of scholarship is not consistent; some of the essays are position papers rather than academic analyses, and there are considerable differences in interpretation. This is not a disadvantage. On the contrary, the symposium in its present form mirrors the intellectual climate of a conference at which discussion that was sometimes heated developed around subjects of crucial importance. It offers significant samples of the thinking of Asian, African, European, and American scholars on some of the most vital issues with which the new nations are concerned.

ACKNOWLEDGMENTS

This symposium would not have been possible without the financial assistance of the Pappas Charitable Fund in Boston; the American Council of Learned Societies in New York City; the German Society for Eastern European Studies in Stuttgart and Aachen; the Japanese Society on Communism in Europe and Asia in Tokyo, and the Pantios School of Political Science in Athens. It is difficult to express adequately the gratitude of the participants to the people and organizations through whose interest and understanding this costly and complex international gathering came into being. A special word of thanks is due Professor John Georgakis, who, on behalf of the Pantios School, extended such generous hospitality to the members of the conference, and to Mr. Walter Hassler, the general manager of the Mount Parnes Hotel, who made the conference participants feel at home in his beautiful and unique establishment.

As editor of this volume, my thanks go first of all to Mrs. Tybel Litwin and Mr. Carl Linden of Washington, D.C., whose invaluable editorial assistance greatly contributed to the present shape of the book. I am also grateful to my wife, Jean, for her help in solving major and minor problems and to Mr. Byron L. Hallsted who successfully found his way through the maze of footnotes.

KURT LONDON

The George Washington University
Washington, D.C.

Neutrality — Utopia or Reality?

—*PANAYOTIS KANNELOPOULOS**

From the beginning, opposing concepts have vied for supremacy on earth. This is proper, for conflict is the essence of life. The Creation itself resulted from a clash of opposing forces—in metaphysical terms, the cosmological zero and being, *l'être et le néant*. The creation and development of man were the result of a succession of dramatic divisions and clashes—the human spirit at odds with the physical realities of the world, logic and thought in conflict with matter, male in conflict with female, older generations resisting the ideas of the new, one family opposing another.

Was there ever throughout the life of mankind a moment of universal *détente*, of neutrality? Neutrality in the legal sense is an abstract concept and a useful one; without the ability to reason from abstractions, human thought would be sterile and meaningless. But it would be a tragic mistake to confuse an abstraction with a basic reality. It must be remembered that neutrality is a concept, a product of the mind of man; it does not reflect truth deriving from experience. This is equally true of the concept of peace. From Heraclitus to Thomas Hobbes, voices have been heard defining conflict, and more specifically war, as the only true reality and even as the source of life and creation. And it is certainly true that always, in one way or another, we are at war: When we are not fighting with lethal weapons, we are fighting with ideas, impelled by material or moral aspirations, by egoism, by altruism.

Since the days of Hobbes, man's view of the world has changed, and man's concept of the forces of history has changed accordingly. The most important change has been the progressive development

* *Professor Kannelopoulos, then Deputy Prime Minister of Greece, was Honorary Chairman of the Fourth International Conference on World Politics, held in Athens in September, 1962. The following observations are taken from his opening remarks.*

of a total concept of the ebb and flow of human affairs as affecting the whole world; there has been less concentration on episodic small wars and clashes in the various spheres of life. Thus, it became natural that history should, for the first time, concern itself with global, all-encompassing considerations, as Marx and Engels pointed out in their "German Ideology," a brief essay that is among the most significant of all their works. With the spread of the concept of the world as an entity, it was equally natural that opposing concepts seeking to define universal law should emerge and find proponents on a world-wide scale. The source of the major cleavage of the world was a social revolution, but its substance was political, psychological, and geographical. If this schism had not been sparked by the October Revolution, there would have been some other cause.

But can we, in fact, say that the earth is divided into only two worlds? Is there not a "third world" made up of those countries in Asia and Africa aligned with neither the East nor the West? I do not doubt that the enlightened men of the Afro-Asian countries—and there is much enlightenment in those countries—are animated by living and dynamic concepts of moral greatness. Yet I seriously doubt that these concepts offer the promise of practical solutions to the problems created by the basic division of the world into opposing ideologies. I truly believe that there is a core of great moral value in the "non-aligned" world, which adheres neither to the East nor to the West. But in the exercise of politics, this attitude of neutrality, reflected in passivity, represents adherence to an abstraction that is in fact utopian.

Let me put the matter in another way. Is it not possible that this "neutrality" is in practice useful to one side at the expense of the other in this divided world? Neutrality, if it is really to merit the name, must be advantageous to neither side or to both. A middle position that directly or indirectly favors only one of the two sides by definition cannot be called neutrality. I believe that the neutrality, or non-alignment, of the Afro-Asian "third world"—despite the intentions and hopes of those who espouse it—cannot be a true neutrality. For neutrality implies a lack of resistance, and such passivity can only serve the aggressor. In the present confrontation between the two major forces dividing the world, I do not believe that the West is the aggressor. I would hasten to add that I do not believe that any nation has aggressive intentions; unfortunately, however, some ideologies are aggressive. Countries that are founded on the basis of aggressive, totalitarian ideologies may profess to be peace-loving and may even call for world-wide congresses in favor of peace, but the meetings they sponsor are, in the final analysis, designed to achieve the moral disarmament of those countries dedicated to democratic ideals. This fact is of profound meaning for the would-be neutrals. For the aim of the aggressor is not only to gain active allies, but, failing that, to neutralize potential allies of the opposing camp. If Communism were to neutralize the entire non-Communist world, it would itself dominate the world. And what would neutrality mean then?

History may prove which side is right and which wrong. But we cannot sit back and let history take its course unassisted. There would be no future for us if we were to surrender to indecision and fail to fight for what we think is right. Our responsibility as human beings dictates that we be ready at any moment to take a stand for or against. History may reconcile elements which are today in conflict. Its dialectic is inscrutable, but as a moral being man must take a clear position at every stage.

COLONIALISM AND COMMUNISM

Colonialism Yesterday and Today

—RUPERT EMERSON

The processes now called "colonialism" have been, beyond question, the most beneficent, disinterested, and effective force which has ever been brought to bear on Africa in all its history. That it might have been better, that it has its blemishes and faults, does not alter that plain statement of fact.—*Sir Philip Mitchell, ex-Governor of Kenya.*

Colonialism regards poverty, disease, ignorance, brutality, treachery, the bondsman's chains, and the hangman's rope as its allies in Africa. —*Moscow broadcast.*

In the earlier stages of this war when my country was grimly fighting a vastly stronger foe, it was only the existence of our African Colonial Empire . . . which saved us from defeat. And if we had been defeated at that time, very likely none of us would be sitting here today. . . . And the same I know is true of the French territories which rallied to General de Gaulle and of the Belgian Colonial Empire. These colonial empires in fact were welded into one vast machine for the defense of liberty. Could we really contemplate, as the conscious aim of our deliberations, the destruction of this machine or its separation into its component parts?—*Lord Cranbourne, at the United Nations Conference on International Organization, at San Francisco, June 20, 1945.*

Colonialism today is the basis of all the fears and tensions which now afflict the world. . . . Colonialism has created fear, and fear has led to the armaments race, thus the problem of disarmament is closely connected with the eradication of colonialism from Africa.—*President Nkrumah of Ghana.*

The General Assembly
. . . Convinced that the continued existence of colonialism prevents the development of international economic co-operation, impedes the social, cultural and economic development of dependent peoples and militates against the United Nations ideal of universal peace . . . Declares that:

3

1. The subjection of peoples to alien subjugation, domination and exploitation constitutes a denial of fundamental human rights, is contrary to the Charter of the United Nations and is an impediment to the promotion of world peace and co-operation.

2. All peoples have the right to self-determination. . . . —*Declaration by the United Nations General Assembly.*

I

The era of colonialism has moved toward its grave accompanied by jubilant celebrations and almost no mourners—or, at least, almost none prepared to display their mourning in public. So far has the wheel turned that the once proud boast of exercising imperial sway over great domains is now expected to give way to an embarrassed apology for the delay in accomplishing full decolonization. Yet only a short while ago the colonial regimes that embraced so large a part of mankind were accepted as part of the established order of things, and the supremacy of the Western European powers in all spheres was a central fact of the international system. Before World War I the only effective challenges to the supremacy of these powers came not from the hundreds of millions directly under their rule, or from countries like China that were more loosely subordinate to their imperial designs, but from the United States and Japan, the powers that were rising on the periphery of the system.

A highly oversimplified version of the progression of history might pick out the following salient events. In 1884–85, the Berlin Conference gave official European blessing to the scramble for Africa and, with a pious nod in the direction of improving the conditions of native moral and material well-being, laid down the ground rules for partition. At the close of World War I, when national self-determination was the reigning doctrine for European peacemaking, virtually no attention was paid to occasional proposals that the doctrine might also be applied to the Asian and African colonies. The members of the League of Nations, in an obscure clause of its Covenant, went no further than to "undertake to secure just treatment of the native inhabitants of territories under their control," save that in the territories taken over from defeated Turkey and Germany the mandate system was applied. The latter established a tenuous but praiseworthy measure of international control over the colonial spoils that were parcelled out among the victors, but only in the case of the Arab lands was there any suggestion that independence was the goal. By the time the

Charter of the United Nations came to be written, a great leap forward was under way but it still fell far short of the headlong rush toward the dismantling of the whole colonial structure that was about to start. In the Charter as composed at San Francisco, colonialism was on trial but not yet condemned. The principle of equal rights and self-determination of peoples was recognized, all non-self-governing territories were placed under international scrutiny in a somewhat ambiguous fashion, and the colonial rulers pledged to develop self-government and free political institutions; a strengthened trusteeship system added independence to self-government as a possible goal.

The transformation that was overtaking the old order came out in full clarity when the Asian and African countries met at Bandung to declare among other things that "colonialism in all its manifestations is an evil which should speedily be brought to an end." Here, for the first time, the underdogs rose up to take their own stand in the world in a fashion that would have been inconceivable a decade or two earlier. Their partisan action at Bandung won a substantial measure of international recognition when the General Assembly in December, 1960, with no opposing vote, adopted a Declaration on the Granting of Independence to Colonial Countries and Peoples that denounced colonialism and demanded immediate steps, wherever colonialism still survived, toward the grant of independence without any conditions or reservations. Following the language of Bandung, the Declaration found the subjection of peoples to alien domination and exploitation a violation of fundamental human rights and of the Charter.

Aside from the actual accomplishment of independence only one further step was perhaps possible, and it can be found in some of the claims and justifications put forward at the time of India's takeover of Goa, which were also drawn upon in relation to Indonesia's drive on West New Guinea–West Irian. Here was to be found an assertion that all colonialism was so iniquitous and so repugnant to the nature of man and human society that rights established under it had no proper claim to international recognition. In particular, it was contended that a higher law justified the overriding not only of such rights but also of the Charter's injunction against the threat or use of force. Goa, it was argued, was merely being reincorporated in the country that it had never rightly left, and West Irian had always been a part of an indivisible Indonesian nation.

What is missing in any such recital of the formal stages by which colonialism has moved from the status of world policeman and tutor to that virtually of outlaw is the passion with which the colonial relationship is regarded. The contemptuous overtones that the term "native" has taken on betray the nature of that relationship as seen by the alien rulers from the heights of their superiority. This is the essence of the colonial situation against which the subordinate peoples have risen in anger, prepared to settle for nothing less than full respect for their equality, dignity, and membership in the human race. The white man often finds it easy to persuade himself that the abuses of colonialism had best be forgotten as lamentable lapses no longer relevant to the contemporary scene. Once the colonial status is ended he sees no occasion to look back to it—save, perhaps, to record the good things which colonialism has brought. For those just coming out from under colonialism the story is very different: for them it was a searing experience, pressing down upon them an intolerable sense of inferiority, and it will be long before the vivid consciousness of the past that they have successfully repudiated subsides into the background.

II

In the present climate of opinion, the temptation to reduce the colonial relationship to simple terms of good and evil is great. What is in reality a most complex matter, to be understood only if its intricacies and nuances are explored, is brought to the level of a straightforward clash between the good colonial peoples carrying on a heroic struggle for independence against the implacable resistance of the sinister forces of domination and exploitation represented by the imperial power. The selfless oppressed masses combat the greed of the self-serving overlords. Even where the latter give the appearance of yielding gracefully, it is only because they have been forced to their knees or because their Machiavellian calculations convince them that they can exploit more efficiently by withdrawing from some of their more exposed positions.

Such a simplistic view is not of course wholly false, but it conceals as much truth as it reveals; and the more complex version has the merit not only of being more accurate but also of being more interesting.

The subtleties of the problem may be illustrated by pointing out that it has by no means always been the case that the rising leaders among the colonial peoples have repudiated the imperial power that has imposed itself upon them. On the contrary, in many instances it is clear that the men who were coming up within the colonial system had, if anything, an undue regard for their rulers. This was occasionally true for those who came later, but it most frequently concerned the earliest generations of those who secured a Western type of higher education, or an approximation of it, and found themselves dazzled by the new vistas opened up to them. Thus the distinguished Indian leader, Sir Surendranath Banerjea, wrote that the nationalist extremism of the first decade of the present century in Bengal was of recent origin, whereas

> Our fathers, the first fruits of English education, were violently pro-British. They could see no flaw in the civilisation or culture of the West. They were charmed by its novelty and strangeness. . . . Everything English was good—even the drinking of brandy was a virtue; everything not English was to be viewed with suspicion.[1]

The counterpart of the endorsement of the British and Allied position in World War I by the Indian National Congress may be found in the resounding backing given Great Britain in World War II by Africans in the Sierra Leone Legislative Council. Thus, in a debate on September 8, 1939, on a motion expressing shock at Germany's attack on Poland and giving full support to Britain and France in declaring war on the aggressor, the Honourable the First Urban Member, Dr. H. C. Bankole-Bright, a leader among the nationalists of the time, said that Sierra Leone like all British possessions had good reason to pray for England at this hour of trial because that colony was based on the principle of protection for the weak.

> The heart of Sierra Leone throbs today towards England the motherland; her prayers are sent to the Great Architect of the universe that England be protected from the adventurous wiles and the unscrupulous propensities of a pugilistic grabber. Unshaken in her loyalty, unswerving in her devotion, she will contribute her quota, however small, towards the emancipation of England from the thralldom of this great revolutionary act.[2]

Speaking on a motion to give £100,000 to the Imperial War Fund, Bankole-Bright's successor as First Urban Member said on July 2, 1940, that his people regarded this sum "as a token of their everlasting devotion and loyalty to the British Crown and nation," and he was followed by Chief Albert George Caulker who declared that

we feel that we are in Heaven so to speak. The British Government
has no distinction of race, colour or creed, and the British law, the
law of England, without doubt, I say, is next to the law of God. . . .
By the grace of God it will not be long when His Majesty's Government will rule in peace throughout the world once more.[3]

That expressions such as these were not a vagary solely of those
subjected to British rule is established by the similar sentiments
which may be culled from the records of the French African colonies. Thus, in 1922, Blaise Diagne, Deputy from Senegal, wrote to
Marcus Garvey, disclaiming any aspiration to see French Africa
turned over exclusively to the Africans as demanded in unauthor-
ized fashion by American Negroes for whom Garvey claimed to act
as spokesman. "We French natives," Diagne asserted, "wish to remain French, since France has given us every liberty and since she
has unreservedly accepted us upon the same basis as her own European children."[4]

Much the same evaluation of the relationship with France was
made thirty-five years later by Félix Houphouet-Boigny, leader of
the Ivory Coast and member of several French cabinets, who proclaimed with pride his preference for continued association with
France as against Nkrumah's demand for full independence from
Britain for the Gold Coast. To the *mystique* of independence and
nationalism Houphouet-Boigny opposed what he regarded as the
loftier and more up-to-date *mystique* of interdependence and fraternity, although, as the situation changed and the tide of anti-
colonialism mounted ever higher, he later insisted on independence
for his own country. In a speech on January 7, 1957, in the United
Nations, where he appeared as a French delegate, he sang the
praises of France:

> Is there a single country in the world which would offer to an African
> of my color, race, and stage of civilization, the liberty, equality, and
> fraternity we can find within the French community? . . . Yes, I
> am a mystic fervently devoted to brotherhood. And because I believe
> in brotherhood, I believe in the final triumph of the French-African
> community, inasmuch as we want it to be humane, equalitarian and
> fraternal.[5]

Such statements as these are not cited with any thought that they
represent, now or in the past, the opinion of any very large body of
people, but they certainly indicate that the anti-colonialism, now so
fervently taken for granted, is a sentiment of fairly recent origin.

In the earlier stages of the colonial impact, the few who underwent a process of assimilation to the culture of the alien rulers were often immensely attracted to it and impressed by the power that it represented. Their aim in the ordinary course of events was not to overthrow the colonial regime but by good behavior and rational argument to persuade their alien betters that since they had succeeded in rising above the mass of "natives" and had mastered the white man's ways they deserved both to be accepted in the social life of their rulers and to be given a share in government. Frequently, it was only when this polite request was rebuffed and they continued to be excluded from both government and European society that they began to turn toward political agitation that in due course often developed into a mass movement under the leadership of the new Western-oriented nationalist elite.

Even in later generations, a few people are likely to retain a strong attachment to the imperial center, but as nationalism becomes the wholly dominant theme it becomes increasingly hazardous for them to give any public expression to their views. Two groups might be cited as falling in this category. One is the handful of people who have become so completely assimilated to the alien culture that they no longer feel any significant identification with the one into which they were born, a handful that contains some aristocrats and magnates of great wealth who feel their position and possessions threatened by the nationalists. Another group consists of those who found attractive the kind of order and authority established under colonial auspices, and in particular the civil servants who rose to prominence and some measure of authority in the colonial regime and who deplore the political machinations of the new party bosses and their hangers-on—machinations that interfere with orderly and impartial administration.

There is, of course, an easy means of disposing of the kind of proposition I have been putting forward, and that is to denounce the persons involved as Uncle Toms, running dogs of the imperialists, corrupt betrayers of what their people must evidently want. This line of attack is the counterpart of the equally easy assertion that all the colonial civil servants sent out by the imperial power, from governors general down to the most junior officers, are, like those who man the Colonial Office at home, hirelings of the capitalists who cannot deviate, even if they should want to, from the essential aim of exploiting the natives for home profit.

Both these attacks on colonialism and the people concerned with it suffer from the fatal defect that they are not true. Colonialism had its appalling sins, brutalities, and corruptions, but it had also much which must be brought into the reckoning in other terms than these. It is a fact not open to honest dispute that colonial administrators have often been devoted to the task of increasing the well-being of their charges, and have given their lives to it to the best of their ability and understanding, even though it is also evident that imperialism is not an enterprise that has in any era been undertaken for the purpose of improving the lot of those who were overrun. It is equally a fact that some of the colonial victims at some stages have with full sincerity held views sharply at variance with the passionate detestation of colonialism that later became dominant.

III

Colonialism—in the sense of primarily European domination over peoples separated from them by salt water and generally differing from them in race and creed—is coming to the end of its days. What evaluation is it possible to make of it, so close upon the heels of its days of grandeur? Many answers, sometimes flatly contradictory, are possible, and I know of no objective ground on which it may be determined that this answer or that embodies "truth." The values from which one sets out, the facts that one selects from an almost infinite array of material, and the emphasis that is placed on different aspects of these facts—these are in whole or very large part the elements that determine, indeed predetermine, the conclusions.

The most radical approach to colonialism, leaving room neither for argument nor inquiry into particulars, springs from acceptance of the basic principle that any alien rule imposed on others is beyond the moral pale. If this be taken as the fundamental starting point, all controversy whether this colonial system is better than that or whether a particular colonial policy represents net gain or loss is eliminated by blanket condemnation of the whole. The position is the same as that of the total pacifist for whom debate as to whether one war is better than another is senseless.

It is this position to which Asian and African opinion has been tending, backed in words if not always in operating policy by the Communists who delight in exposing the sins of their imperialist rivals. President Sékou Touré of Guinea has declared that no distinction is to be drawn between domination by one or another European power or between military, political, economic, or cultural

domination: "We consider domination in itself as a criminal policy, contrary to the universal right of peoples to self-determination.
No argument true or false, no circumstance, can restrict this right,
postpone its application, or modify its content."[6]

The same doctrinal principle inspired the Declaration on the
Granting of Independence made by the U.N. in 1960, since it not
only provides that immediate steps shall be taken to transfer all
power to the peoples of trust and other non-self-governing territories but also adds that "Inadequacy of political, economic, social
or educational preparedness should never serve as a pretext for de-
laying independence." Since colonialism in all its manifestations is
seen as evil, the abandonment of colonial rule cannot be made conditional on the achievement of goals or standards of any kind.

The position diametrically opposed to this is presumably the
unqualified assertion of the right of the stronger to impose himself
as he can and reap whatever his strength yields him. This is a position so remote from the accepted mores of the contemporary scene
as not to be worth examining in detail; but Margery Perham in her
recent survey of the end of British imperial rule in Africa rightly
stresses the fact that the present global sweep of anti-colonialism
is a very recent phenomenon, since men through the ages have
gloried in the extension of their imperial power.[7]

For the most part, insofar as any effort has been made to cast up
a balance sheet of empire, neither of the extreme positions, wholly
condemning or wholly accepting, has been taken. Those who have
been concerned to examine colonialism in terms of a more pragmatic ethic have generally set off from some variant of the criterion
laid down by John Stuart Mill in his *Representative Government*.
In the case of dependencies whose people have not attained a sufficiently advanced state to be fitted for the high calling of representative government, he defended their being kept under alien rule on
the ground that: "This mode of government is as legitimate as any
other if it is the one which in the existing state of civilisation of
the subject people most facilitates their transition to a higher stage
of improvement."[8]

This is a statement that evidently bristles with debatable issues,
the full exploration of which could occupy many volumes. What
is the justification for the opening assumption that the ability to
manage representative government should determine the right to
self-government? Can one with such clear-eyed confidence assume
the existence of a higher stage of improvement? On the available

evidence, is it plausible to think that imperialist regimes can be trusted to facilitate advancement with any serious devotion to the task; and, if so, which of the various types of colonial policy is most likely to achieve the goal under the particular circumstances? How are the stages of advancement to be measured, and by whom? Can either the imperial power or its agents on the spot, even assuming them to be benevolent but paternalistic, be counted on to relinquish control at the appropriate time? Throughout, there runs the question whether it is proper that the colonial authorities should be judge and jury in their own case, despite the fact that they are supposed to be acting in the interest of the subordinate people.

These are, however, questions not exclusively directed to Mill but also, with minor variations, to anyone who is prepared to entertain the possibility that colonialism can do good as well as evil. The measurement of the good must surely be in the improvement of the condition under which the dependent peoples live, as determined by some reasonably identifiable standard,[9] that will almost certainly, though perhaps not necessarily, include an increase in the ability to manage their own affairs without outside intervention. An alternative approach would be merely to seek to establish what consequences had actually flowed from colonial rule, but it seems virtually inescapable that there should be an attempt at evaluation as well.

I have suggested elsewhere that, if it is allowable to impute missions to history, the mission of the characteristic imperialism of the last centuries might be seen as the spreading to the rest of the world of the great revolution that was taking place in the West, a revolution of enlightenment and reason, of science and industry, of the organization of human affairs in war and peace.[10] At all events, the practical effect of Europe's imperialism, and particularly of colonialism, was to force almost all of non-European mankind to start the process of adaptation to the new and irresistibly powerful forces that had their origin in Europe.

One of the most striking features of the response to colonialism has been the uniformity with which the rising nationalist leaders, themselves almost always men with an intimate acquaintance with the West, have recognized the need for their people to master the new ideas and techniques. Vehemently repudiating the West's imperial domination, they have at the same time regarded the West as furnishing a model for many aspects of the future of their own societies. They have wanted in greater or less degree to preserve the distinctive traditional attributes of these societies, endowed with a new prestige in the era of nationalism, but they have generally been even more concerned to win for them the fruits of what the West had already achieved. The eagerness with which the economic and technical assistance of the advanced countries, including the Soviet bloc, has been sought is ample evidence that what is desired is much less a return to the old than an advance into new spheres.

A few of the major items that must be taken into account by anyone who would attempt the impossible task of drawing up a balance sheet of colonialism may be spread on the record. At the present day, the item in the account which is likely to be given the greatest weight is the almost universal detestation of colonialism by those who have experienced it and the jubilation which accompanies its disappearance. But it should not be forgotten that a vast number of people have lived in colonial subordination without appearing to find it more intolerable most of the time than the other regimes under which they have lived throughout the ages. Until a relatively late stage, the mass of the people, indifferently accepting their colonial status, were not susceptible of being mobilized for political action by their aspirant leaders, and, as has been seen, some of these leaders themselves looked with admiration on their colonial masters. Yet before long the scene began to change drastically, as the mounting nationalist fervor embraced increasing numbers of the populace.

How is the change to be explained? It would be a simple matter to ascribe it to intensification of exploitation, growing brutality of the colonialists, and increasing misery of the masses. Again, the barrier to such simplicity is its evident lack of truth, since what has actually been going on is generally just the reverse. Far from tightening the screws in the last couple of decades and more, the colonial powers have been loosening them: the imperial conscience has become decidedly more tender, responsibility for the promotion of colonial advancement has found growing acceptance, and, with the exception of Portugal, European colonial powers have acknowledged the goal of independence as determining the immediate agenda of colonialism. The many elements that combined to bring about this frame of mind, involving such matters as the rise of liberal and socialist movements, the spread of democracy, and the effects of two world wars, have been reviewed too often to need examination here. The net effect has been both to ease the pressure on the dependent peoples and to weaken the imperial will to fight to preserve empire.

On the other side of the fence, the nationalist pressure for independence has constantly increased, not because conditions have grown worse but rather because they have improved. In undertaking the development of their territories the colonial powers have brought into being a new set of political demands that they were in some instances unable, and increasingly often unwilling, to resist. Where the West made its greatest contribution to its own overthrow was in undermining traditional societies that had lost their forward drive and creativity and in prodding them into a new mood of social and political dynamism. It could present to the rest of the world no more distinctive and revolutionary gift than the restless concept of progress, the working idea that people of their own volition and by taking thought can change the structure of their lives and the environment in which they live.

Usually less as a matter of intent than as an inescapable by-product of its colonial presence and activity, the West furnished its overseas subjects with tools and models they could use in the attack upon colonialism. When the traditional societies, no longer endowed with the mandate of Heaven, rose to defend or to reassert their old ways, they were regularly beaten back by the imperial forces. Victory became only a matter of time, however, when the new generation of Western-trained leaders challenged the West in its own terms, asserting that they spoke on behalf of nations, and enlisted substantial segments of the masses into modern types of political organizations. Their new strength was magnified by the declining confidence of the imperial powers in themselves. In the forefront of this anti-colonial struggle stood not the most oppressed of the colonial subjects, but those who in a sense had profited most from the imperial connection in that they had almost always had close contact with the West and had become deeply imbued with its lore and its standards. Yet, in terms of felt grievances, perhaps these were precisely the people most oppressed since they were the ones who, spurred on by Western-inspired ambitions and expectations, were most exposed to the rebuffs and racial discrimination inherent in colonialism.

The colonial territories that the nationalist leaders moved to take over differed vastly among themselves, but in comparison with the advanced countries they had some fundamental similarities. In all of them development along modern lines had only just begun, desperate poverty enveloped the whole population, except for a few at the top, and illiteracy was the rule and not the exception. The colonial powers had undoubtedly conferred some benefits and brought some improvements, but when the dependencies were contrasted with the metropolitan countries there was an immense gap in both the actual conditions and the standards that were applied. Nowhere in the colonies did the same all-out drive for education, health, welfare, and prosperity take place as was assumed to be essential in the imperial center. Conditions that would have been found intolerable in a European capital or countryside were found far more easy to tolerate in Asia or Africa. Under imperial auspices, economic development was carried forward only in a partial and hesitant fashion, with a lingering presumption in favor of the old *pacte coloniale* under which the colony supplied unskilled labor and raw materials while the mother country monopolized manufacture, transport, and upper level services. In varying degree, some of the essential foundations for survival in the modern world were established in the different colonies, but not much had been built upon them.

IV

The territories that still retain their colonial status today are only a small fraction of the colonies that were in existence at the close of World War II, but some of them threaten to become trouble centers of the first order.

In number, by far the largest group of presently non-self-governing territories is made up of small colonies (particularly those of the British) scattered over the face of the globe, many of them with tiny populations.[11] Of these, only a few seem at all likely to cause difficulties reaching significantly beyond the territory itself. For the bulk of them, the puzzling issue is to devise formulas that will satisfy their desire for self-government and development without multiplying the number of miniscule sovereign states and further cluttering up the United Nations. The solution that was found for Puerto Rico in terms of autonomy and continued close association with the mainland United States may furnish a model that could be adapted to meet the varying needs of a number of other territories. What is required is a large measure of political and constitutional ingenuity, breaking away from the assumption that the only valid alternatives are full "national" sovereignty or colonial subordination. The demand of small peoples for equality and self-rule is as legitimate as that of their more numerous brethren, but the international community should also have the right to protect itself against debasing the coinage of membership.

The two sets of territories that appear to have the potentiality of causing major trouble are the two large Portuguese possessions of Angola and Mozambique and, to a lesser extent, the two Rhodesias with their white settler problem.[12] For a realistic view of the prospects of trouble, it is necessary to add South Africa and its own dependent territory, Southwest Africa. South Africa is obviously not in the conventional sense a colony, but its internal colonial problem cuts so sharply across the African drive for liberation and unity that it cannot be eliminated. Indeed, it may become necessary to consider the whole of the vast southern portion of the African continent from the northern frontiers of Angola, the Rhodesias, and Mozambique to the Cape of Good Hope as constituting in a sense a single bloc in which white supremacy of different varieties seeks to maintain itself against African advance.[13]

The mere existence of these white-dominated countries is a constant provocation to the militant Africans to the north who continue to fear a resurgence of colonialism and who feel their own freedom incomplete if other Africans remain unfree. If violent interracial conflict flares up again in southern Africa, as it seems sure to do, whether in the form of more Sharpevilles or of an intensification or spread of Angola's revolt, the effect will be to lend new inspiration to the pan-African movement and to anti-colonialism.

That hundreds of millions of people have achieved independence since World War II, and that former Asian and African dependencies now form a large part of the membership of the United Nations, is no adequate guarantee to the enemies of colonialism that the danger is past. Addressing the U.N. General Assembly on September 30, 1960, President Sukarno, branding imperialism and the struggle to maintain it as the greatest evil of our world, warned that: "imperialism is not yet dead. It is dying, yes. Still—mark my words well—dying imperialism is dangerous, as dangerous as the wounded tiger in a tropical jungle."

For the Marxists, particularly, it is a basic assumption that the capitalist-imperialist states can never, short of revolution, shake off their evil ways. If the old-style overt imperialism is barred to them, they turn to a neo-colonialism in which they maintain their supremacy by more subtle methods such as Balkanizing the newly freed countries, the adroit manipulation of puppets, and economic controls. Chief among the neo-colonialists is the United States, manipulator of the NATO imperialist coalition. In this view, the real nature of the imperialists is demonstrated not by the independence of the Philippines and India, of Ghana, Nigeria, and the French African colonies, but by the continued economic predominance of the former colonial powers; by the colonial warfare that blocked the freeing of Indonesia, Indochina, Algeria, and Angola; by the Anglo-French attack on Egypt in the Suez crisis; and by Western intervention in the Congo affair.

Undoubtedly some of the heirs to power in the ex-colonial countries are seriously afraid that imperialism will again swallow them up, and all have good reason for concern about the extent to which their economies are controlled by alien interests, impinging on the substance of their new-found sovereignty. Undoubtedly also, however, they have other significant reasons of a different order for their emphasis on the dangers of imperialism and neo-colonialism. In their victory over the colonial regimes, they gained a new prestige but in losing at the same moment their overt and ever-present enemy they lessened their ability to rouse popular enthusiasm and keep dissident factions in line. Because of the success of the nationalist movement the necessity to maintain the united front that the prior struggle had demanded was dispelled. In countries whose national unity is often slight and where the loyalty of the people to the government is uncertain, the need to produce rallying cries that would evoke the widest possible support was a matter of the first importance. The discovery of the threat of neo-colonialism, added to the fear of a reversion to outright imperialism, reinstated the old enemy and justified pressure to curb divisive groupings and interests. As hostility to the colonial regime was the cement that had held the nationalist movement together, what could serve the present need better than a return to the same theme, adapted to the changed circumstances?

In this realm, the new countries and their former masters are likely to differ sharply in their interpretation and evaluation of what has been going on. For the imperial powers, it is a point of pride to establish wherever possible that they granted independence freely and from good will; for the nationalists it is important to make it clear that independence was not granted but was won through a hard-fought struggle. The ex-imperialists are persuaded that they have left imperialism behind them and now aim only at equal and friendly intercourse with peoples whose development they wish to aid; the new political leaders may feel a necessity to persuade their people that they must unite to combat the unrelenting imperialist menace. Least of all can the nationalists cheerfully accept the often justified claim of the imperial power that it literally created the country, and hence the assumed nation that has come, or is coming, to independence. Yet in all sub-Saharan Africa, in the Arab world, and in the case of Malaya, Indonesia, and the Philippines in Asia, the historical record is clear: it was the imperialists who drew the lines on the map that now divide the countries from one another, and the colonial regimes that began the process, carried further by the nationalists, of endowing the people within these lines with some sense of common identity.

The Communist Attitude Toward Colonialism (to 1941)

—JANE DEGRAS

In Communist writings, it is difficult to detach the concept of colonialism from the related concepts of nationalism and imperialism. And at first colonialism as such was only rarely examined by Communist writers. Marx scarcely dealt with the subject, although he was deeply interested in both India and Ireland. Lenin treated it largely within the context of imperialism, of which he considered it was one characteristic feature; for the rest, Communist interest in colonialism was polemical, political, and pragmatic in character. Doctrine was shaped by interest, assumed or real.

In the correspondence between Marx and Engels, there are a few casual references to the problem, but no analysis. But Marx was well aware of the immense importance of the changes that were bound to follow from the impact of economically and socially advanced countries on the economically backward parts of the world. In a number of articles in the *New York Tribune* on British rule in India, Marx, while unsparing in his condemnation of the greed and hypocrisy of the imperial power, nevertheless wrote that "whatever may have been the crimes of England, she was the unconscious tool of history" in bringing about the revolution that was to break up India's stagnant society and draw her into the modern world. By training a modern army, by building roads and railways, by starting industries, Britain was creating the conditions for India's self-emancipation and future progress.[1]

In these and other writings, Marx provided the elements that were later to be drawn together into a theory designed to explain the connections between the labor movement in capitalist countries and the movement against the imperial power in colonial countries, summarized in his remark that no nation that oppresses another nation can itself be free. He came to the conclusion that liberation was of benefit not only to the oppressed nation, but to the working class of the country from which it was liberated. "It is in the direct and absolute interest of the English working classes to get rid of their present connexion with Ireland. . . . The English working class will never accomplish anything before it has got rid of Ireland." "Irish history," Engels wrote in 1869, "shows how disastrous it is for a nation when it has subjugated another nation. All the abominations of the English have their origin in the Irish Pale."

"I have come to the conclusion," Marx wrote to Meyer in April, 1870, "that the decisive blow against the English ruling classes (and it will be decisive for the workers' movement all over the world) cannot be delivered in England, but only in Ireland." Ireland was the means by which the English aristocracy maintained its domination in England, while the English worker disliked the Irish worker as a cheap-labor competitor, and thus a tool of the capitalists, and the dislike was reciprocated. "This antagonism is the secret of the impotence of the English working class. . . . It is the secret by which the capitalist class maintains its power."[2] The English worker would have to learn that the emancipation of Ireland was the first condition of his own emancipation.

The 1905 revolution in Russia was the first in a series of upheavals that shook the more advanced of the backward countries in the years before the outbreak of World War I. The stirrings of revolt in Persia, Turkey, and China drew Lenin's attention, and he wrote of the millions in the East who would join the world-wide struggle; although led by the middle classes, they were the potential allies of the socialist revolution in the West.

The size and importance of colonial empires had expanded enormously since Marx's time, and played a far greater part in the economy and trade of the metropolitan countries. Lenin attributed this (in his *Imperialism*) primarily to the more intense competition between monopolies, anxious to bring all the processes of manufacture under their direct control, and to the falling rate of profit at home:

> The capitalists partition the world . . . because the degree of concentration which has been reached forces them to adopt this method in order to get profits. . . . Colonial possession alone gives a complete guarantee of success to the monopolies against all the risks of

the struggle against competitors. . . . The more capitalism develops, the more the need for raw materials is felt; the more bitter competition becomes and the more feverish the hunt for raw materials throughout the world, the more desperate the struggle for the acquisition of colonies.[3]

The search for colonies was also stimulated by the need to export capital, and their acquisition served a further purpose in keeping the workers contented. Lenin quoted Rhodes: "If you do not want civil war, you must become imperialists."[4] Monopoly profits, based partly on colonial exploitation, enabled the capitalists to bribe part of the working class and "so created the bond between imperialism and opportunism." This was the origin of Lenin's theory of the "corrupt labor aristocracy," which was content with gradual reforms paid for by colonial profits instead of seeking the revolutionary overthrow of capitalism. Hence the fight against imperialism was a sham unless it was accompanied by a fight against opportunism in the labor movement. Colonies also provided an outlet for the frustrated, the impatient, the under-employed who would otherwise be a menace to public order. An opening abroad averted an explosion at home.

As fewer and fewer areas remained to be taken over, empires could no longer be expanded by direct acquisition, as in the nineteenth century, but only by the seizure of colonies belonging to other states, or by encroachment on nominally independent states. Relations between states were established "on the basis of the territorial division of the world, of the struggle for colonies, of the 'struggle for economic territory.'" It was this rivalry, inherent in the very nature of modern capitalism, that was the primary cause of war. "Is there, under capitalism, any means of eliminating the disparity between the development of productive forces and the accumulation of capital on the one side, and the partition of colonies and spheres of influence by finance capital on the other side, other than war?"[5]

The growing restlessness in the colonial countries in the course of World War I brought home to the Bolsheviks the potential scope and significance of the anti-colonial movement, and when they established their government it was natural for them to regard it as an integral part of the world-wide struggle to overthrow imperialism, in which their own seizure of power was the first successful step. The "Manifesto to Moslems of Russia and the East" issued by the Soviet government in December, 1917, announced that

> Russia is not alone. . . . The mighty call to freedom sounded by the Russian revolution has been taken up by all the toilers in the East and West. . . . Moslems of the East! Persians, Turks, Arabs, and Hindus . . . Overthrow these robbers and enslavers of your country. . . . You must be masters in your own land. . . . We inscribe the liberation of the oppressed peoples of the world on our banners. . . . We look to you for sympathy and support in the work of regenerating the world.[6]

Practical considerations reinforced this attitude. The Bolshevik Government was weak, its position highly precarious; if it could not count on direct allies, it could at least seek indirect support by weakening and distracting its enemies. What were the forces that could help to redress Russia's weakness in face of the West? What movements gave promise of changing the balance of forces, and should therefore be encouraged? Of these, colonial revolts were second only to proletarian revolution in the industrial countries in the prospects they opened for holding off the enemy.

At the Eighth Congress of the Russian Communist Party, Bukharin made no attempt to hide the considerations underlying this policy:

> If we propound the solution of the right of self-determination for the colonies . . . we lose nothing by it. On the contrary, we gain. . . . The most outright nationalist movement, for example that of the Hindus, is only water for our mill, since it contributes to the destruction of English imperialism.[7]

The program adopted at the congress reverted to the unity of the two movements against imperialism, and Lenin took up the same theme in speaking to a congress of Moslem Communists:

> The socialist revolution will not be only or chiefly a struggle of the revolutionary proletarians in each country against its bourgeoisie— no, it will be a struggle of all colonies and countries oppressed by imperialism, of all dependent countries, against international imperialism.[8]

It was in this way that the three conflicts—between Russia and its opponents, between labor and capital, and between the imperialist and the dependent countries—were merged into one in Communist theory, and it was in line with this reasoning that the Soviet Union gave such support as it could to the far from socialist or proletarian King Amanullah in Afghanistan and to Mustapha Kemal in Turkey. The newspaper published by the Commissariat for Nationalities wrote (September 2, 1920):

> It is necessary to break and to destroy the capitalist front by organising the revolution and the revolutionary fighting forces behind the capitalist lines. This means calling to revolutionary life the peoples and countries which have so far been the prey of capitalist vultures . . . striking a blow in the rear of the rapacious Entente, and this in turn will clear the way for the triumphant march of the proletariat of the West.[9]

The dispute between London and Moscow in the autumn of 1921 was concerned with Soviet violations of the "no propaganda" clause in the Anglo-Soviet agreement of March, 1921, by "alleged activities of the Russian government and its representatives and agents in Eastern countries directed against British interests."[10]

The importance attached to colonial movements at this stage is clearly reflected in the earlier pronouncements of the Communist International, founded in March, 1919. Its first manifesto, written by Trotsky, included the following passages:

> The last war, which was not least a war for colonies, was at the same time fought with the help of colonies . . . Indians, Negroes, Arabs, and Madagascans fought on the European continent—for what? For their right to remain the slaves of England and France. Never before . . . has the problem of colonial slavery been posed so sharply as it is today. Consequently there has been a series of open insurrections, revolutionary ferment in all colonies. . . . The emancipation of the colonies is possible only in conjunction with the emancipation of the metropolitan working class. The workers and peasants . . . of Annam, Algiers and Bengal . . . will gain their opportunity of independent existence only when the workers of England and France have overthrown Lloyd George and Clemenceau and taken power into their own hands. . . . Colonial slaves of Asia and Africa! The hour of proletarian dictatorship in Europe will also be the hour of your own liberation.[11]

The theme was taken up in greater detail at the Second Comintern Congress in 1920, which adopted theses on the national and colonial question drafted by Lenin. These, and the speech in which Lenin introduced them, were designed to explain the relation between the colonial and the proletarian revolutions against imperialism, two aspects of one and the same struggle. They took up the argument that imperialism diverted the industrial workers from revolution by bribing them with the profits of colonial exploitation, and therefore only an alliance between the two movements could overthrow the enemy. (The difficulties in the way of proletarian support for colonial revolution were hinted at by the British representatives, who said that the majority of English workers would regard such support as treason to their country.) For imperialism, Lenin went on, the main enemy was Russia, and it was therefore in the interests of the colonial peoples to ally themselves with Russia against the common enemy. Once liberated, they would not necessarily have to pass through the capitalist stage of development but, aided by the victorious proletariat of the West, could move forward on the road to Communism.

Here, as in the first Comintern manifesto, colonial liberation is made dependent on successful proletarian revolution in the West. In those early years Soviet hopes of revolution in Europe ran high, and it was natural to conclude that it would precede the colonial revolution. There were in fact over the years continual changes in the order of priority given by the Communists to these two movements, reflecting expanding and shrinking hopes as capitalism "entered a period of relative stabilization" or "approached a new series of revolutions and wars." No definitive conclusion was reached until —as Communists would say—"life itself answered this question."

Shortly before the Second Congress, the Comintern had issued a statement on the Congress of Eastern Peoples to be held in Baku in September, 1920.

> Peasants and workers of the Near East, if you organise, if you arm yourselves, if you unite with the Russian workers' and peasants' Red Army, then you will be able to defy the French, English, and American capitalists, then you will be free of your oppressors, then you will have the opportunity in free alliance with the workers' republics of the world to take care of your interests.[12]

At Baku Zinoviev said: "We are ready to help any revolutionary struggle against the English government. . . . Our task is to help the East to liberate itself from English imperialism. . . . Our task is to kindle a real holy war against the English and French capitalists." Radek made the alliance a life and death matter: "We are bound to you by a common destiny; either we unite with the peo-

ples of the East and hasten the victory of the western European
proletariat, or we shall perish and you will be slaves."

When events failed to conform to the Leninist laws of history,
and the Russian Revolution did not develop into the world revolution, the emphasis in Comintern activities began to shift more to
the East. This had indeed been implicit in the theses submitted by
Roy and adopted at the Second Congress, in which he argued that,
since the metropolitan working class was diverted from revolution
by colonial profits, it was only with the success of the colonial
revolution that there could be a successful proletarian revolution:

> One of the main sources from which European capitalism draws its
> basic strength is in the colonial possessions and dependencies. With-
> out control of the . . . colonies, the capitalist powers of Europe
> would not be able to exist even for a short time. . . . It will not be
> easy for the European working class to overthrow the capitalist order
> until the latter is deprived of this source of super-profit.

At Halle, later in the same year of 1920, Zinoviev said he had
learned at Baku what was missing from the concept of proletarian
revolution—it was that "the oppressed masses of the East must
awaken."[13] The change in emphasis may be placed roughly in the
spring of 1921, with the New Economic Policy (NEP) in Russia
and the collapse of the "March action" in Germany; the recognition that Russia could not rely for support on Communist triumphs
in Europe was reflected in the series of treaties concluded with its
neighbors and with Britain. More and more, Moscow turned in its
foreign policy to cooperation with Eastern nationalists to redress
the balance of power.

It was in this situation that the inherent incompatibility of a
genuinely revolutionary colonial movement with the policies of "a
state among other states" came to the surface. (It was this which
induced the Tatar Communist Sultan Galiev to propose a "Colonial International" quite separate from the Communist International; imperialist or red, the metropolitan countries would continue to exploit the colonies.) The dilemma was unmistakable but
could not be admitted, and it explains the self-contradictions and
equivocations of Communist attitudes and policies. On the one
hand, in the absence of Communist successes in Europe, which
would by definition liberate the colonies, Russia might be confronted with a situation in which the leaders of a national libera-

tion movement, while asking and expecting support from Moscow, were determined to suppress social revolutionary movements in their own country. Anti-imperialist movements were not necessarily well-disposed to agrarian reformers and socialist agitators. On the other, the anti-imperialist movement itself might at times run counter to Soviet interests. As an instance of the first situation, we may take Soviet relations with Turkey in 1920–22. Britain and France were hostile to the Kemalist Government, which, for its part, severely persecuted Turkish Communists. Nevertheless, in the war between Greece and Turkey, Russia supported Turkey, while Britain and France gave aid to Greece. "Everything that strengthens the Eastern peoples, oppressed and exploited by international imperialism," Radek wrote, "also strengthens Soviet Russia, which is threatened by the same danger."[14] And, at the Fourth Comintern Congress, after the Turkish delegate had recounted the tale of Kemal's persecution of the Turkish Communists, Radek said: "We do not for a moment regret telling the Turkish communists that their first task . . . was to support the national liberation movement." In the following spring, at the Twelfth Congress of the Russian Communist Party, Bukharin said that, though it persecuted Communists, "Turkey plays a revolutionary part, since in relation to the imperialist system as a whole it is a destructive instrument."

For the second aspect of the dilemma, I would like to give an illustration that takes me beyond the period of this essay. This is the policy adopted by the Indian Communist Party after June, 1941. While the leaders of the Indian Congress Party—being consistent in their anti-colonial policy—were imprisoned, the Indian Communist Party did what it could to persuade the Indians to give full support to the policies of the imperial British government, at that time the ally of the U.S.S.R.

Implicitly, of course, the incompatibility was acknowledged in the assertion that the interests of the Soviet Union were the supreme law, that defense of these interests was the primary and overriding duty of every Communist, and the power of the U.S.S.R. was the best guarantee of the final triumph of the world revolution. If the Soviet fatherland were weakened or defeated, the workers' movement throughout the world would suffer a severe setback; therefore, in the final analysis, there *could* be no incompatibility of interests.

Stalin, who was regarded as something of an expert on the national and colonial question, summoned the authority of Marx to justify Soviet policy. To the students of the Sverdlov University in April, 1924, he said that the national question was "part and parcel of the general question of the proletarian revolution."[15] He spoke of "utilizing" the colonial revolutionary movements for the proletarian revolution, transforming them into "a reserve of the revolutionary proletariat" and making them its ally. Where a national liberation movement tended to weaken imperialism, it must be supported, but where it came into conflict with the interests of the proletarian movement, no support could be given. The rights of nations were only part of the proletarian revolution, and as a part were subordinate to the whole. That was why Marx had not supported the national movements of the Czechs and South Slavs, because they were backed by Czarism, the enemy of the revolutionary movement, whereas Afghanistan's struggle against Britain was objectively revolutionary, notwithstanding the monarchical and feudal character of the country, because it weakened imperialism.

This was the period of united front tactics; in relation to the colonial world, they took the form of cooperation between Communist parties and non-Communist, anti-imperialist movements. India had no Communist Party; in Indonesia, where there was one, an attempt was made to work with Sarekat Islam, because it embodied the struggle for national emancipation, and was therefore progressive and anti-imperialist, despite its religious character. The outstanding instance of such cooperation was in China, where from early 1923 until the spring of 1927 the Communist Party collaborated with, and attempted to direct, the Kuomintang. (China, of course, was not a colony in the strict sense of the word; its government—or rather governments—was Chinese; it fell into the "semi-colonial" or "dependent" category.) The disputes about Communist policy in China in the nineteen twenties deserve full-scale treatment. For it was not only the divergent needs of the Soviet state and the colonial revolution that bedeviled Communist policy there; the question became inextricably entangled with the disputes within the Soviet Communist Party itself, and to analyze those would go beyond the scope of this paper. Official Comintern policy —that is, Stalin's policy—was elaborated in a series of resolutions and theses at successive meetings of the Comintern Executive.

At this point, it is no longer possible to avoid reference to the concept of the "national bourgeoisie." For anti-imperialism was not a simple and uniform movement. Its composition, structure, and aims gave it a complexity that from the very outset baffled the Comintern, and the behavior, actual and potential, of its leaders was the subject of endless analysis and debate, a vexing and intractable problem that still survives to perplex the Kremlin.

Before World War I, Lenin regarded the colonial struggle as essentially economic—the bourgeoisie, petty bourgeoisie, and peasants of the colony against the bourgeoisie of the imperial power. In this struggle, the proletariat—in the absence of acute social tensions—would fight alongside the bourgeoisie. (This was one of the points on which the dispute with Rosa Luxemburg turned; she thought the workers should not be seduced by the national movement to fight alongside the bourgeoisie, whereas Lenin argued that, while the national struggle was always subordinate to the class struggle, it embodied demands that could rally the workers and facilitate their organization.)

But 1917 had introduced a fundamental change. The colonial revolution, Lenin said, like the Russian, was still part of the bourgeois-democratic revolution, but it could not be left to the bourgeoisie to accomplish; it was now part of the world proletarian revolution. What, then, should be the Communist attitude to the bourgeoisie of a colonial country that, though hostile to imperialism, both as its oppressor and its competitor, would with the development of industry, find itself challenged by the proletariat? At the Fourth Comintern Congress where this was discussed, Roy opposed close cooperation with bourgeois nationalist movements, as he had done at the Second Congress, whereas Malaka, representing Indonesia, thought it should be extended. The resolution adopted evaded the issue, saying more or less that it all depended on circumstances. (It also evaded the question of why the colonial bourgeoisie should accept the help of those who, once victory was won, would turn against them.)

The argument in fact was not (and could not be) resolved, for the situation was inherently contradictory so long as it was believed that it was the Communists who would have to make the bourgeois revolution in the colonial and semi-colonial countries, and carry it forward to the socialist revolution. This meant that, while it was necessary to seek alliance with the bourgeoisie and petty bourgeoisie, the allies of today would become the enemies of tomorrow. That the alliance could not be lasting was recognized in the theses adopted at the Second Congress:

The Communist International has the duty of supporting the revolutionary movement in the colonies and backward countries only with the object of rallying the constituent elements of the future proletarian parties . . . in all the backward countries and educating them to a consciousness of their special task, namely, that of fighting against the bourgeois-democratic trend in their own nation.[16]

It therefore became necessary to distinguish between the different kinds of colonies, according to their stage of economic development. Stalin undertook this in a speech to the students of the Communist University for Working People of the East in May, 1925;[17] in this he followed the scheme worked out by Roy in 1920. In colonies where the workers' movement was growing, such as India, the national bourgeoisie would split, one part, the petty bourgeoisie, continuing the struggle against imperialism, while the big bourgeoisie would make a bloc with imperialism. To win hegemony in the colonial revolution, the proletariat would have to isolate the big bourgeoisie, rescue the masses from their influence, and so make it easier to link the national struggle with the proletarian struggle in the advanced countries. "The treachery of the big bourgeoisie must be exposed."[18] They were already in alliance with imperialism.

In the most backward countries, without an industrial proletariat, Communists must create a united front against imperialism, and in the course of the struggle build up a Communist party. In between were countries like China and Egypt, where a bloc with the revolutionary petty bourgeoisie (such as the Kuomintang) and with the bourgeoisie, in so far as it was anti-feudal and anti-imperialist, was permissible.

The rupture between the Kuomintang and the Chinese Communist Party precipitated by Chiang Kai-shek signified the collapse of Stalin's policy, and was one of the reasons for the change in Comintern tactics from "united front" to "class against class." (This corresponded to an analogous change in the U.S.S.R. itself from a "soft" to a "hard" line—that is, from NEP to forced collectivization and industrialization.) There was to be no collaboration with the national bourgeoisie; Communists everywhere were to compete with them for the support of the masses. This was the period in which Gandhi and his followers were described as agents of imperialism, prepared to betray Indian independence and the interests of the Indian masses. In China "the counter-revolutionary

Kuomintang" had entered into an alliance with imperialism. "Only under proletarian leadership," said the Executive Committee of the Communist International in May, 1928,

> will the Chinese working masses defeat the counter-revolution inside the country and win independence for revolutionary China. Only the power of the workers and peasants organised in Soviets . . . will with the help of the world proletariat lead the national revolution to victory and open a broad road to socialism.[19]

Shortly afterwards, the Sixth Comintern Congress adopted an immensely long set of theses on the national and colonial question. The first great movement of anti-imperialism in India, it was said, "ended with the betrayal by the Indian bourgeoisie of the cause of national revolution. The chief reason for this was the fear of the growing wave of peasant risings, and of the strikes against native employers."[20] Distinctions were still made between the attitudes of the different sections of the colonial bourgeoisie and petty bourgeoisie to the colonial revolution—some were more vacillating and inclined to compromise than others; while their opposition to the imperialists and feudalists was reformist, not revolutionary, it could accelerate the political awakening of the masses, and their conflicts with imperialism, though in themselves insignificant, might serve as the starting point for revolutionary mass action. But "what is important about [bourgeois-reformist opposition to imperialism] is that it obstructs and retards the development of the revolutionary movement."[21] There could be no bloc between the Communist Party and the national-reformist opposition; temporary cooperation with petty bourgeois revolutionary movements was permissible, but on no account must the individuality and rights of the Communists be compromised.

It was in connection with these theses that the debate on "decolonization" occurred—the last debate in the Comintern on which there was open disagreement on an important question. It represented an attempt to re-examine the facts, to analyze the relations between metropolis and colony in the light of the changes which had occurred since Hobson, Hilferding, and Lenin had studied the question. Implicitly, Marx had foreshadowed decolonization in its industrial sense, and Lenin had noted that the export of capital, an essential feature of imperialism, accelerated the development of capitalism in the countries to which it was sent. Logically, of course, the decolonization theory would have fitted very comfortably into the "class against class" framework, since it would have given a solid economic foundation to the rejection of cooperation with the bourgeois nationalist movement. But the theory had grave disadvantages, for, said Kuusinen, "if it were true that British imperialism had really turned to the industrialization of India, we should have to revise our entire conception of the nature of imperialist colonial policy,"[22] and Remmele added that this would mean "revising Lenin." It is significant that it was the British delegation (with one exception) that advanced the theory (the Indians were divided), arguing that it was nonsensical to contend at one and the same time that Britain was destroying industry in India and that the Indian proletariat was moving forward to independent class action. Their arguments carried no weight, and the theses stated that Britain was "reverting to its policy of hindering India's economic development." Everywhere

> the specific colonial forms of capitalist exploitation . . . in the final analysis hinder the development of the productive forces of the colonies. . . . The colonial country is compelled to sacrifice the interests of its independent development and to play the part of an economic (agrarian raw material) appendage to foreign capitalism.

But, since the effect of capital exports could not be entirely ignored, the theses went on to say that capital "invested in production does to some extent accelerate industrial development, but this is not done in ways which promote independence."[23]

The program of the Comintern, also adopted at its Sixth Congress, reverted to the unity of the two main revolutionary forces, the workers of the capitalist countries and the "popular masses" of the colonies, to the bribery of certain sections of the proletariat by the imperialist bourgeoisie, and to "the treachery of the national bourgeoisie in the colonial and semi-colonial countries who are frightened by the revolutionary movement." Once foreign imperialism was overthrown, however, and "the democratic dictatorship of the proletariat and peasantry on the basis of Soviets" had been established, "the bourgeois-democratic revolution, consistently pursued, will be transformed into the proletarian revolution in those colonies and semi-colonies where the proletariat acts as leader."[24]

There are few matters of interest to record in the years between the Sixth Congress and the tactical turnabout to a "popular front" policy in 1934–35. At the meeting of the Comintern Executive Presidium in February, 1930, Manuilsky once more emphasized the importance of proletarian leadership of the national revolutionary movement—the crucial question was simply who would lead the peasant masses, the bourgeoisie or the proletariat. For the proletariat to lead, a Communist Party was essential, and this the workers did not have even in India, not to speak of other colonies. Hostility to the "bourgeois nationalists" was reaffirmed in the theses on the fifteenth anniversary of the establishment of the Comintern.

> In all the colonial and semi-colonial countries, national reformism plays the same role of the chief impediment to revolution as the Second International plays in the imperialist countries. The KMT paved the way for the partition of China among the imperialists. The National Congress in India, the Wafd in Egypt, the Arab Executive Committee in Palestine, and the African National Congress are following in the footsteps of the KMT. By exposing their treachery, the communists are undermining the influence of these organisations on the masses.[25]

An article on India, written shortly before the theses, made the same point:

> The bankruptcy of Gandhism is rapidly accelerating the process of disillusionment among the revolutionary sections of the petty bourgeoisie. . . . National-reformist practice has revealed the treacherous attitude of the Indian National Congress toward the struggle for independence.[26]

Safarov, the Comintern expert on Eastern affairs, wrote at the end of 1934:

> For many years bourgeois nationalism has exploited the humiliated and downtrodden state of the enslaved people of India . . . in order to emasculate and destroy the mass anti-imperialist struggle by betraying the struggling masses at every stage. . . . The vicious circle of the national-reformist policy of capitulation and conciliation consists in the fact that the bourgeoisie of a colonial country cannot give anything worthwhile to the masses. . . . Hence the necessity for the systematic deception of the masses. Hence the constant fabrication of illusions which exploit the thirst for national emancipation.[27]

The "popular front" policy, adopted as it dawned on the Kremlin that Hitler's government was something more than just "the open rather than the indirect dictatorship of the bourgeoisie," necessitated a change in every sphere of Soviet and Comintern policy, including the attitude to colonial movements. The League Against Imperialism, a subsidiary organization founded to promote and recruit support for Communist policies, was allowed to fade quietly out of existence; in China, the Communist Party, after protracted negotiations, entered into an agreement with the Kuomintang for joint action against Japan, although the Central Committee of the Chinese Communist Party had declared earlier that "the condition of success in the war against Japan is the overthrow of the KMT."[28]

The long resolution on "the struggle against fascism" adopted by the Seventh (and last) Comintern Congress in 1935 paid scant attention to the colonial question—it was of little importance at the time to Moscow, then concentrating on the acquisition of allies against Germany; but it did exhort the Communists in the colonies to establish an "anti-imperialist people's front," for which it would be necessary to "take an active part in the mass anti-imperialist movements headed by the national reformists and strive to bring about joint action with the national-revolutionary and national-reformist organizations on the basis of a definite anti-imperialist platform."[29]

Understandably enough, the conclusion by the U.S.S.R. of the pact with the Nazis in August, 1939, and the outbreak of World War II one week later, necessitated a reversal once more, though the Communist parties remained unaware of this until reminded by Moscow. This, after all, *was* the fight against fascism for which they had been agitating for some years, and it was a shock to be told by their superiors in the Comintern that it was nothing of the kind, but just another war between rival imperialisms. The Communist ranks in the West were thinned, but on the whole discipline prevailed and the confusion was quickly overcome. Communist tactics were once more reshaped, this time to hamper the conduct of the war. This was not necessarily unpalatable to the Communists in the colonies themselves, who could claim the Sinn Fein in Ireland in World War I as their model. It must have been rather more difficult to turn into reverse once again less than two years later, when the Soviet Union was forced into the war by the Nazi attack. Never since the early years of the Soviet regime was Communist propaganda tuned to such a high pitch. The war was not an imperialist war after all, but a war for democracy and freedom, and merited the support of every true anti-imperialist; after all, wasn't that what the colonial revolution was about?

"Neo-Colonialism" — the Soviet Concept

—WALTER LAQUEUR

There is an anti-colonial tradition in the West going back to the Middle Ages, as old as the idea of colonialism itself. Palafax de Mendoza, the Spaniard, writing about the virtues of the Indian, is in this tradition, so is La Bruyère with his essay on the equality of nations. Voltaire (*Lettres d'Analect*), Condorcet, Jean Baptiste Say, all thought colonies a nuisance if not positively harmful. According to Turgot, colonies were like fruits that clung to a tree until they were ripe, then detached themselves and produced new trees.[1] Comte expressed the hope that the Algerians would one day expel the French if they did not leave of their own volition.[2] In England, Charles James Fox and Richard Cobden were links in the anti-colonial chain; Cobden thought that it would be a happy day when England ceased to possess one acre of land on the continent of Asia. This anti-colonialism was by no means always humanitarian and democratic in inspiration; its source was often pure self-interest. Mussolini (until comparatively late in life) regarded colonialism as a folly, and German Nazism considered overseas colonies a dangerous aberration from the true vocation of German foreign policy.

I

Socialist anti-colonialism was the offshoot of the anti-colonial leanings of radical liberalism in the nineteenth century. German and Austrian Social Democracy came to deal frequently with colonial problems after 1900, and there were debates at the meetings of the Socialist International with the Dutchman van Kol acting as the spokesman for the pro-imperialist minority.[3] For the Russian Socialists, colonialism was not exactly one of the most pressing problems, although Lenin devoted some time and energy during

34

World War I to a study of the policy of conquest pursued by finance capital in the struggle for markets, raw materials, and areas for the investment of capital. Soviet attitudes to colonialism in the nineteen twenties and thirties are the subject of the preceding paper; the present study is devoted to an analysis of Soviet views on "neo-colonialism." During the late nineteen forties and nineteen fifties, there was no change in the traditional Soviet attitude. Stalin believed in the existence of two sharply antagonistic camps and was firmly convinced that there was no room for a third. He largely ignored the emergence of a group of neutral and unattached countries outside Europe after World War II; at seventy he was not alert enough to take cognizance of these developments and to adjust his policy accordingly.

From 1951–52, there had been some appreciation among the Communists of the growing importance of the national movements in Africa, Asia, and Latin America, but it was not until about 1955 that a somewhat belated reappraisal of the world situation and of Communist strategy was made. This delay was not all Stalin's fault; conditions for close collaboration between the Soviet Union and territories in Asia and Africa did not ripen until the late nineteen forties. A new, and happier, concatenation of circumstances arose only after the great majority of Asian and African colonies had become independent states.

Khrushchev and his colleagues did not fail to draw the obvious conclusions. They were in favor of assisting the movement toward neutralism in Asia, Africa, and Latin America, even if it involved assisting movements that were by no means Communist-controlled or that were even actively opposed to the local Communist parties. They were confident that, in the long run, Communism would prevail in the newly independent countries as the result of the inner momentum of social, economic and political developments, and of the incompetence of the "national" leadership of those countries that had achieved national independence but would be unable to cope with their urgent social and economic tasks. The Soviet blueprint provides for a gradual transition from the rule of the "national bourgeoisie" to "national democracy," and ultimately to full Communism.

This, in briefest outline, is the gist of the changes in the Soviet orientation vis-à-vis the neutral world.[4] The development of this orientation involved, for instance, a temporary retreat from the concept of the hegemony of the proletariat in the national movement, and in consequence a rediscovery of the progressive role of the "national bourgeoisie." It also implied a re-examination of the Soviet view of colonialism, its changing character and various manifestations. Once the broad outlines had been fixed on the highest level, the working out of the details could be left to the experts.

II

"In the late forties our economic journals refused to publish [my] articles under the title 'The Disintegration of the Colonial System,'" complains one prominent Soviet author.[5] It certainly is true that those concerned were slow to adapt themselves to the far-reaching changes on the world scene; the fact that hundreds of millions of Asians had gained independence in the years following World War II passed almost unnoticed, and Professor Varga ran into considerable trouble for having suggested that Indian and Pakistani independence was of more than symbolical significance. The situation in this respect has, of course, greatly changed, and present-day Soviet studies of colonialism do not omit to mention the fact that at present (1961–62) only about 80 million people continue to live under colonial rule. Soviet writings on colonialism (or "neo-colonialism") are, however, by no means restricted to an analysis of Western policies in the few remaining colonial areas. On the contrary, the term "neo-colonialism" embraces Western policy in Asia, Africa, and Latin America in general, whether the Western country in question ever had colonies or not. For—the Soviet argument runs—the West still wants to subjugate the newly independent countries, and if the old-fashioned colonial methods can no longer be applied in view of the changed world situation, a new, more refined, but even more dangerous approach is used.

In the economic sphere, according to Soviet doctrine, liberation from domination by foreign capital is the prerequisite for overcoming economic backwardness. Once this has been achieved, the level of productive forces and labor efficiency can be increased, living standards can be raised, etc. In this context, Soviet authors invariably emphasize the decisive importance of industrial development and emphatically reject the view that economic progress can be achieved in any other way. Western suggestions that in many countries equal attention should be given to the development of agriculture are interpreted as a calculated effort to retard the economic development of these countries and are denounced as an imperialist intrigue.[6]

This, needless to say, is not the only accusation leveled against the West.[7] According to Soviet doctrine, the last decades have witnessed an intensification of the exploitation of the workers and peasants in the colonial world; American monopolies in their chase after high profits are said to have revealed a "feverish activity" and stepped up enormously the economic invasion of the formerly colonial world. While the colonialists may not be able to continue their policy of open robbery directly, they are said to continue to achieve the same aim by more sophisticated methods such as causing inflation and thus depriving the population of the newly independent country of its gains, by paying low prices for imports of raw materials from Asia and Africa, and demanding stiff prices for their own industrial exports to these countries.

This Soviet critique is a mixture of correct observation and outright falsification. It is correct, for instance, that falling prices for raw materials on the world market have a very detrimental influence on the economy of many underdeveloped countries, and that it is urgently necessary to find ways and means to stabilize these prices. Unless this is done, the Western projects for economic aid cannot possibly fulfill their aim. (It has been calculated, I believe, that a very small rise in the price of coffee in the United States would cover about half the budget of the Alliance for Progress.) The anarchy of the world market is not, however, entirely the fault of the Western powers; the Soviet bloc, too, has appeared as an exporter of raw materials, and Soviet exports of crude oil, for instance, have contributed to a fall in the income of the Arab countries, Persia, and Venezuela.

To choose another illustration: according to the orthodox Leninist version, monopolistic capital streams into the colonies or ex-colonies because these offer opportunities for the quickest and most profitable returns; this is the so-called "law of maximum profits." Only recently, Soviet authors have discovered that practice does not conform with the theory, that a far greater part of American capital streams to Western Europe, and that Western governments find it in effect extremely difficult to induce private investors to become interested in Asia, Africa, and Latin America.[8] It is now admitted that this alleged law no longer functions as far as the ex-colonial countries are concerned.

Many other "laws," it would appear, have also ceased to function. According to Lenin, imperialist conflict for the redivision of colonies made war a virtual certainty—this was the so-called law of "uneven development." By 1961, it was admitted that circumstances had changed and that a new war for the redivision of colonies and spheres of influence had become unlikely.[9]

If so many of its old characteristics have changed out of recognition, a redefinition of colonialism (or neo-colonialism as it is now frequently called) has obviously become imperative. In Communist eyes, colonialism now uses different methods on the political and the economic as well as the ideological level to ensnare the unsuspecting ex-colonials. In the so-called second phase of the crisis of the capitalist system (World War II and its aftermath), colonialism was not able to prevent the liberation of these peoples, but it still wants to maintain its positions by different ways and means. As one Soviet author has put it: "The old troubadours of imperialism such as Rudyard Kipling and Claude Farrère called the people of the metropolis to engage in colonial expeditions; nowadays they try their luck by influencing the national bourgeoisie and the national intelligentsia in the former colonies."[10]

To the critique of the "neo-colonialist" ideology and practice much time and effort has been devoted in recent years, and some of the main arguments used in these polemics should be mentioned here. Soviet economic aid and assistance are said to be radically different from Western aid, inasmuch as no political strings are attached to them. Western aid, it is argued, is designed to tie the new countries, to impede them in their economic growth and political development; Communist aid, on the other hand, is completely altruistic, merely intended to strengthen the sovereignty and the dignity of these peoples. In this context, Communist spokesmen advocate the extension of the state capitalist sector; true enough, they regard this merely as a transient phenomenon but they are fully convinced of the advantages of state intervention in comparison with private enterprise. They reject the concept of interdependence as harmful and misleading; interdependence, they argue, presupposes a division of labor within the (capitalist) world market. But this will only tend to perpetuate the new countries' dependence on the West. In order to gain full independence the new countries need a truly national economy. "The successful economic development of any country is possible only by way of industrialization."[11]

The idea of "political interdependence" is attacked no less sharply. According to the Soviet credo, there are fundamental conflicts of interest between "Western colonialists" and the "national bourgeoisie." Admittedly, Soviet leaders did not always think so; both during the "third period" (1928–35) and in Stalin's last years (1947–53), a very different approach prevailed. Since Stalin's death, however, it has been argued time and again that the national bourgeoisie would betray its own class interests by collaborating with the West. A modified and more reserved appraisal on these lines has become general. As Chairman Khrushchev recently reminded Asian and African national leaders, it was only by relying on the working class that victory could be achieved and correct solutions found to vital social problems; otherwise "other people would come after them who would better understand the demands of life."[12] This referred in particular to home-grown ideas of Asian or African socialism—which, according to Khrushchev, cannot possibly replace scientific Communism. At present, the official Soviet doctrine distinguishes between three different layers of the national bourgeoisie, namely the big, the middle, and the small bourgeoisie, and affirms that the differences between them become more marked as time goes on. Under imperialist rule, the whole national bourgeoisie fulfilled a "progressive role," but after independence has been achieved only certain groups of national entrepreneurs are capable of taking a resolute anti-imperialist stand.[13] This three-tier analysis of the national bourgeoisie resembles (as L. Labedz has pointed out) a similar analysis of the Soviet peasantry during collectivization; the label kulak was affixed to all those who, regardless of their social station, refused to join the kolkhoz. In a similar way, the national bourgeoisie is progressive (regardless of its actual economic and social position) when it joins the national democratic front; it is considered reactionary when it refuses to follow Communist instructions.[14]

This modified approach to the present national leadership of the Asian, African, and Latin American countries presents interesting political possibilities for the future. Meanwhile, however, Soviet doctrine vastly prefers to deal with neo-colonialism rather than with such a ticklish and politically explosive topic as the class character of the African and Asian national liberation movement. There are many variations, but by and large the following characteristics of neo-colonialism are usually enumerated: it substitutes a new, streamlined, collective colonialism for the old-fashioned, national colonialism. For a long time past, Soviet authors have been almost exclusively preoccupied with the study of "American colonialism," and have neglected, as is now admitted, the growing impact of

West German and Japanese "colonialism." Much attention is also now being given to the combined impact of the Common Market, and the various schemes for Eurafrica are frequently quoted as a perfect example of the new "collective colonialism." The late Dag Hammarskjöld was sharply denounced at the time for trying to establish a "collective colonial regime" in the Congo under the auspices of the U.N.[15]

On the ideological level one of the main charges against the West is "cosmopolitanism"—its alleged attempt to belittle the importance of national sovereignty. Western sociologists and political philosophers are criticized for maintaining that "national sovereignty" has become outmoded; in the Soviet view it still fulfills a progressive political function. Some Western writers are taken to task for sympathizing with moderate, enlightened, constructive nationalism in Asia and Africa but disavowing its less attractive features; the Communists are, for obvious reasons, more interested in what the West regards as destructive and aggressive nationalism. Lastly, Communist spokesmen do not accept the Western reservations with regard to the definition of African nations and nationalism. This, however, is a field where Soviet Africanists prefer to tread warily; for the present African states do not really fit into their traditional scheme of nations and nation-states; they also prefer to talk about the "national liberation movement" rather than "nationalism" in Africa. Nor have they ever made it clear whether the old (colonial) frontiers should be preserved, whether ethnic borders or perhaps the "emerging national consciousness" (which may transcend ethnic borders) should be decisive, whether linguistic classification should be of any relevance in this context, etc. Soviet speakers and authors emphasize the right to national sovereignty, which is not without a certain risk from their own point of view, for it is precisely on this ground that the various national Communist schools have developed and are likely to sprout even more in future. A major balancing act will be needed to combine support for unrestricted national independence with the condemnation of national Communist "deviations."

A whole host of accusations refers to "cultural neo-colonialism." This includes the propagation of cultural interdependence and interchange (which, according to Communist doctrine, have replaced the old concept of the civilizing mission), the preaching of "neo-Malthusianism," "psycho-racialism," and the American way of life. Some of these notions may need further clarification: According to the Soviet view any intensification of cultural contacts between the new countries and the West is undesirable because it is likely to strengthen "imperialist positions" in those parts. Hence they follow with great suspicion and utter lack of sympathy the activities of those who advocate close cultural cooperation between the West and the ex-colonial world and who believe that these civilizations complement each other.[16] Neo-Malthusianism was one of the great bogies of the early nineteen fifties and is still rejected today.[17] It is said to be both factually wrong (since the cause of poverty is not the population increase), and reactionary in political character. Since 1953, some second thoughts seem to have prevailed; neo-Malthusianism is still opposed, though both China and Russia no longer encourage an unlimited growth of population. The socialist organization of agriculture is advocated as a panacea; unfortunately socialist agriculture throughout the bloc has not been overly successful in recent years.

Psycho-racialism is explained by Soviet authors as a new, more sophisticated form of the old racialist theories about the superiority of the West. In practice, however, this charge is leveled largely at Western sociologists and psychologists who may not be guilty of racialism at all but merely of what is called in Soviet jargon the "psychologization of social processes." If, for instance, Mannoni has found certain neurotic trends in the psychological make-up of the Malagasy, or if Kardiner has discovered among many Indonesians a certain urge to become victims of aggression, such findings are immediately branded as part of the arsenal of Nazi race theories—notwithstanding the fact that similar or even more damaging discoveries may have been made with regard to Western nations.[18] At the same time, Soviet authors have admitted that feelings of national or racial superiority are found in the newly independent countries, too: the "idea of national superiority does exist . . . it is not at all impossible that the idea of national exclusivity will appear even more strongly in the not-too-distant future in Asian and African nationalism."[19]

Yet another accusation is that of "social imperialism," and the Socialist parties of Western Europe are among the main culprits in Soviet colonial demonology. They are charged with having gladly accepted the "White Man's Burden" (beginning with the famous Van Kol speech in favor of colonies at the Stuttgart Congress of the Second International in 1907, and extending up to the present day). They are accused of having supported Western colonialism in every possible way, of having denied the right of self-determination of the colonial peoples, of having opposed the rights of individuals to the rights of nations, of having offered harmful economic advice, and of having developed misleading theories about an alleged transformation of the character of imperialism (Strachey).[20] French and British, Belgian and Dutch socialists are said to be wholly responsible for the colonial policies (and the colonial wars) of their governments. The picture that emerges, to put it very mildly, is somewhat one-sided. The war in Malaya or the suppression of the Mau Mau in Kenya is mentioned, but the fact that under the Labour Government of 1945–51 the greater part of the British Empire became independent is passed over in silence. The attitude towards the British Labour Party is of some interest in this context: though the leadership is "social-imperialist" and the left wing "philanthropist" in inspiration ("permeated with the spirit of Uncle Tom"), there is, we learn, in the last resort no basic difference between Fenner Brockway and Aneurin Bevan, on the one hand, and the official Labour leadership, on the other. On the contrary, the activity of the left wing is, if possible, considered even more dangerous than that of the official leadership; Mrs. Barbara Castle's anti-NATO stand and neutralist theses are thus interpreted as an imperialist intrigue to lure the neutrals away from following the Soviet lead.[21] Generally speaking, the activities of the Socialist parties in Asia and Africa are sharply attacked, for obvious political reasons; their "fetishization of bourgeois democracy" and their belief that important changes may be accomplished following mere reforms is thought to be nonsensical and very harmful. Western trade unions, on the other hand, are charged with "deflecting the proletariat (of these countries) from active participation in the political life of the society."[22] In these circumstances, the conclusions seem fairly obvious: Marxist-Leninists cannot permit the slightest ideological concession to the socialists on the colonial question; on the contrary, the "unmasking of the social-chauvinist attitudes of the Labourites is the most important task on the ideological front."[23]

According to Soviet doctrine, anti-Communism is another weapon of neo-imperialism. It is used in an attempt to poison the friendly relations between the former colonial countries and the Communist world, and to subvert and split the national anti-imperialist front. However, the Communists themselves have frequently expressed concern about the political unreliability of the national bourgeoisie, and doubts about the durability of the national front.

They believe that the national anti-imperialist front as it was under colonial rule will be subject to drastic changes once independence has been achieved. According to Communist doctrine, the nationalist leaders are ultimately to be replaced by Communists; the charge of anti-Communism in this context probably reflects the fear that the national leaders may decide to act before their predestined successors are ready to take over. Both Communists and anti-Communists are, broadly speaking, in agreement that a break between Communism and its radical nationalist rivals is unavoidable in the long run, but Communism, not unnaturally, wants this break to occur at the date most convenient to the local Communist parties. "Anti-Communism" in Communist terminology presumably means encouraging and promoting the break before the time is ripe.

Although these are the most prominent and the most frequently cited features of "neo-colonialism" according to contemporary Soviet doctrine, there have been dissentient voices in the Communist camp. The Chinese, for instance, have often recorded more radical views. They have stressed that the anti-imperialist struggle should be stepped up relentlessly, without inhibitions and undue fears about sparking off a new world war. They have also, on occasion, sharply attacked the "national bourgeois leadership" in some former colonies, such as India—especially if that leadership happened to disagree with Peking on matters of common interest. But elsewhere (notably in Africa and Latin America), Peking has been quite willing to collaborate with neutralist forces, regardless of their class character. China is, for a great variety of reasons, in a more intransigent frame of mind than the Soviet Union, but it has not really developed a body of doctrine essentially different. Such militancy and radicalism in a perhaps even more pronounced form can be found in the Communist parties in some former colonies; they are often coupled with latent nationalist pan-African or pan-Asian deviations. An analysis of these stirrings, which are in part of the centrifugal, polycentric, trends in world Communism, is outside the scope of this paper.

On colonialism, there has been a wide area of agreement between Communism and the national movement throughout Asia, Africa and Latin America. Colonialism, in one form or another, was not a Communist invention, but, until about fifteen years ago, a reality for roughly one-third of mankind. True enough, colonialism had changed its character to a very great extent since its early days; during the late stage of colonialism the colonies were more often than not a cause of financial loss rather than a source of gain to the metropolis. The loss of the colonies has not caused the economic ruin of any Western country; in many cases it had very favorable results not only for the ex-colony but also for the ex-metropolis. However, colonialism stifled legitimate aspirations towards political independence and was therefore as bitterly resented in its late and comparatively mild period as in its earlier and less inhibited phases. In these circumstances, the Leninist theory of imperialism (the theoretical foundation of Communist anti-colonialism) found many adherents among Asian and African nationalists.

A colony, according to an authoritative Soviet definition, is "a country or a region that is deprived of political and economic independence, oppressed and exploited by an imperialist state."[24] This raises a number of interesting questions; could there be a post-capitalist imperialism just as there has been a pre-capitalist imperialism? Mr. Panikkar believes that in classical colonialism the element of distance is involved; a big country swallowing some smaller neighboring state or territory and assimilating it politically and culturally may be guilty of aggression but not of colonialism. It is debatable whether this thesis provides a satisfactory explanation for events that have taken place in the past, but it may well be correct in present world conditions. Old-fashioned colonialism is a thing of the past; less than 3 per cent of mankind is now living under colonial rule; soon the number will be even less. This, needless to say, does not mean that anti-colonialism will automatically die out; it may be an important political factor until the last vestiges of old-fashioned colonialism have disappeared—and it may persist, like a conditioned reflex, for a considerable time thereafter. So long as it does, the concept of neo-colonialism will have its advocates in both the Soviet Union and the former colonies.

The Communist View of Colonialism — An African Interpretation

–B. G. D. FOLSON

There is, on the surface, a large measure of agreement between Africans generally and the Communists on the nature of colonialism, imperialism, and "neo-colonialism"—a convergence of views that has been exploited by the Communists in their efforts to associate themselves with the interests and aspirations of the new and developing nations of Africa. The similarities, however, begin rapidly to dissolve under a close scrutiny of the connotations attached to these terms by the two groups, and particularly under an examination of the meaning of these terms in the Communist lexicon.

THE "WORLD SYSTEM OF CAPITALISM"

"Colonialism" and "imperialism" have become almost interchangeable in Communist usage. They are viewed as overlapping and interrelated facets of monopoly capitalism, although colonialism tends to connote primarily the political, and imperialism the economic, aspect of the domination exercised by one nation over another in the "world system of capitalism." Lenin wrote in 1920 that "capitalism has grown into a world system of colonial oppression."[1] And Communist writings have drawn an almost complete equation between capitalism and imperialism. Profit is the sole aim of this imperialism, and profit in Marxist economics can only be obtained through exploitation. Communist discussions of colonialism and imperialism are, accordingly, preoccupied with dissecting the economic mechanisms of exploitation and exposing their effects. The underdeveloped countries saddled with one-sided "colonial economies" emerge, in this presentation, as mere raw-material appendages of the imperialist-colonialist powers upon whom they are dependent for economic survival.

The Communists wax indignant at the system that breeds such exploitation. Their moral outrage knows no bounds. Demanding the total eradication of the system, they argue that the accomplishment of this goal is the more urgent in the nuclear age because of the intrinsic tendency of imperialism to produce wars. Exploitation of one people by another, the Soviet argument runs, leads inevitably to revolt, and revolt calls forth repression from the imperialist power, repression that is met by further resistance and further conflict that could escalate into a major conflagration. Such "local wars" in Africa have included the Mau Mau revolt in Kenya, the uprising in Angola, and the "heroic struggle of the people of Algeria." An even greater source of war is the inevitable conflict among the imperialist predators themselves—and on the inherently aggressive nature of imperialism there is no quarrel between the Soviet Communists and their Chinese rivals.

THE COMMUNIST REMEDY: THE "WORLD SYSTEM OF SOCIALISM"

The elimination of this breeder of exploitation and war is synonymous, in the Communist view, with the advent of "socialism." Colonialism does not end simply when independence is achieved, for, as in Africa, the newly independent country may be led by the "national bourgeoisie"—a group that is sincere in its anti-colonialism but capitalist after all, and hence concerned primarily with gaining control over the national market. The class interests of the national bourgeoisie preclude an overriding concern to carry through the revolution. The bourgeoisie is vacillating and cannot be trusted.

Thus it is only socialism, Marxist style, that can displace imperialism once and for all on the stage of history. Other, competing brands of socialism—the reformist and "revisionist" types, "Afro-Marxism," African socialism—can have no lasting future. To the African who asks why only the establishment of socialism under Communist auspices can wipe out all traces of imperialism, the Communist replies with the teaching of historical materialism: imperialism, in effect equated with monopoly capitalism, is essentially an economic phenomenon; historical materialism teaches that it is the socialist revolution that does away with the economic foundation of the bourgeoisie and, *ipso facto*, with imperialism; only the working class, led by the Communist Party, can bring to fruition the socialist transformation ordained by the Marxist-Leninist "laws of history."

The Communists, stressing the international character of this revolutionary movement, hold that it is impossible to fight imperialism or build socialism successfully outside the framework of the "world socialist system." Each party is a detachment of the world movement, subject to its disciplines of ideological unity and doctrinal conformity. By "socialism" the Communists mean first of all a system of government and a set of economic arrangements approved by the international Communist movement, and a "socialist" country must be unequivocally within the "socialist camp." Only when a country satisfies these conditions is its break with imperialism full and final.

THE PHENOMENON OF "NEO-COLONIALISM"

The picture is not yet complete, for of the large number of colonial and semi-colonial countries that have achieved independence since World War II, the vast majority remain outside the "camp." Is it to be concluded, then, that these countries are still colonies or still under imperialist domination? The Communist answer is: "neo-colonialism." Here, the Communists explain why the disintegration of the colonial system does not really dispose of imperialism. The imperialists, according to this concept, are forced to concede independence in the face of the rising tide of national liberation movements, but they grant it solely for tactical purposes and without abandoning their fundamental aims. They grant only political independence, without the economic independence that is the basis of true independence. This is the essence of "neo-colonialism." The threat of this sham grant of independence is said to emanate not only from the traditional colonial powers, but from such relative newcomers as the United States and West Germany that have joined the "new scramble for Africa."[2] Neo-colonialism, in short, means in the Communist vocabulary "an effort to attain the usual imperialist aims by indirect control of the countries that have formally won their independence."[3]

The insidious nature of this neo-colonialism is exposed by the Communists in elaborations of its methods of "indirect control":

1. First and foremost is the economic weapon, in the form of retention of control over major sectors of the economy and in the form of aid with strings attached. The latter form is said to pose the more serious threat. "Imperialist" aid is always used to ensnare the victimized country in political and military alliances and is

always calculated to increase the dependence of the recipient country on the dispenser of the aid.

2. Another major weapon is military aid and the building of military bases that tie the country to the imperialist war machine. In Africa, the efforts to establish military bases in Tunisia, Kenya, the former Belgian Congo, and the former French territories in West and Central Africa are cited as examples of neo-colonialist uses of military methods to sustain imperialism.

3. Neo-colonialism also foments international and inter-tribal hostility, capitalizing on the communalistic or tribalistic strife that erupts in many former colonies in the wake of independence. Examples may be found in Ghana, Nigeria, Uganda, Kenya, Rwanda, and, of course, the Congo. Attributing these outbreaks to the "machinations" of the "imperialists," the Communists conveniently fail to recognize that such disturbances may be perfectly natural manifestations of fears among minority ethnic groups about their fate at the hands of the majority once the imperialist power has released its hold, or that they have their roots in traditional hostilities and historic oppression.

4. The new colonialists nurture a middle class consisting of capitalists and entrepreneurs and an educated elite, using these groups as indigenous allies. In countries of pure African stock, these middle-class elements are, of course, black. In the multi-racial countries of East, Central, and South Africa, it is the white minorities that are the principal middle-class elements and collaborators in the system of neo-colonialism; but here, too, the necessity to make neo-colonialism acceptable to the black majority leads to the search for a black middle class to act as the ally of the white minorities.

5. Finally, say the Communists, a neo-colonialist fifth column— citizens of the former colonial power—remains in most of the new countries after independence, and its members occupy highly important posts as judges, civil servants, technicians, advisers, and so on. Again charging "imperialist machinations," the Communists conveniently overlook the fact that these people occupy such positions because the number of qualified indigenous candidates is insufficient.

The Deceptiveness of Semantics

Superficially, all of this has much in common with the Africans' own views on colonialism. Many Africans feel that the essence of colonialism and imperialism has always been exploitation. They believe it has bequeathed a legacy of underdevelopment to the newly independent countries. Africans also have experienced oppression, sometimes intolerable oppression, under imperial and colonial rule and agree with the Communists that the metropolitan powers have not granted independence out of the goodness of their hearts. Indeed, independence has been wrested from the colonial powers in hard-fought battles, bloody or peaceful according to the time, the place, and the particular metropolitan power involved.

More importantly, there is a close parallel between the African and the Communist view of neo-colonialism. As more and more African territories become independent, the struggle shifts increasingly to those subtle and covert forms of domination that make up the pattern of neo-colonialism (or as some, especially in East Africa, prefer to call it, "neo-imperialism"). Thus, African contemporary thought and writing on colonialism, like that of the Communists, concentrates heavily on the subject of neo-colonialism. Scarcely an African speaks or writes on politics today without mentioning neo-colonialism. At African conferences especially, neo-colonialism comes in for much abuse.

This should not be interpreted as evidence of Communist infiltration into African nationalism. The theory of neo-colonialism seems to have been developed independently, although concurrently, by the Communists and African nationalists. We generally feel that there is much truth in the Communist depiction of the devices of neo-colonialism, but we do not agree with the Communists that economic aid, the creation of a middle class, the posting of experts, and the rest are always and by definition weapons for achieving the aims of neo-colonialism. Indeed, it seems sheer nonsense to argue that whenever a middle class is created under colonial rule, dark designs of neo-colonialism must be lurking in the background. The middle class in an underdeveloped or colonial territory is not primarily a property-owning class. It is essentially a professional and educated class without whose services the country cannot be modernized. Such a middle class, in other words, is indispensable. Moreover, even if one were to regard the middle class in an underdeveloped country as essentially a property-owning class, it still would not make sense to view the mere existence of such a class as evidence of neo-colonialist machinations. For to do so is to ignore the immensely beneficial role that this class has played in the past and can play in the future in the development of society. Even Marxist historiography recognizes that at a certain stage in the development of society such a class plays an immensely important role. As *The Communist Manifesto* put it long ago:

> The bourgeoisie, during its rule of scarcely one hundred years, has created more massive and more colossal productive forces than have all preceding generations together. Subjection of nature's forces to man, machinery, the application of chemistry to industry and agriculture, steam-navigation, railways, electric telegraphs, clearing of whole continents for cultivation, canalization of rivers, whole populations conjured out of the ground—what earlier century had even a presentiment that such productive forces slumbered in the lap of social labor?[4]

However unrealistic it may be to expect the middle classes in the underdeveloped world to repeat such wonders today, they can still make a real contribution. It is the masses that suffer if the middle class is completely proscribed on a priori grounds.

THE THREAT OF "BALKANIZATION"

Significantly, the Communists obscure one colonialist legacy which Africans consider very important. This is the threat of "Balkanization." Many Africans are profoundly disturbed by the large number of states that are seeking to lead independent lives on the African continent. As many of these countries are not viable—a large number of the former French colonies still seek subsidies from France to balance their ordinary budgets—they are bound to become pawns in the hands of those once imperialist countries of Europe that help to maintain their economies. Hence the pressing need for unity of states in Africa is recognized by all African nationalists. The differences that exist on this score among some African leaders boil down to differences of approach and not of principle. We know that our salvation lies in our unity. With Africa united, not only will our voices be heard in the highest councils of the world, but Africa will cease to be a counter on the chessboard of power politics. We know that this is why some European powers actively sabotage efforts at unity in Africa,[5] a unity that would deprive them of the use of this continent as a springboard for the realization of their ambitions.

To Africans, therefore, such unity is a most important condition of complete independence and of the complete defeat of imperialism and neo-colonialism. To Africans, a complete break with imperialism means a united Africa aligned to no power bloc either politically or economically. Yet to the Communists, as we have seen, a complete break with imperialism means precisely the opposite: it means joining the Communist bloc. Here, then, lies the crux of the difference between the ostensibly similar African and Communist views. In the last analysis, African nationalism and Communism are at loggerheads on the question of imperialism. The crucial significance of this fact warrants a closer examination.

SOURCES OF THE IMPERIALIST THREAT

At every African conference where imperialism and colonialism are discussed, it is always imperialism "in any shape or form" or "in all its manifestations" that is condemned. The Communists choose to interpret this as applying only to imperialism from the West. But imperialism, or neo-colonialism, can also come from the East, as has already been recognized by some African leaders.[6] We have seen that the Communists consider imperialism and Marxist-Leninist socialism to be mutually exclusive, having arrived at this conclusion by the simple device of identifying imperialism with capitalism. But this is a semantic trick. Hobson had shown that there was a close connection between the monopolist financiers and the new burst of imperialism that took place in Western Europe at the turn of the last century, in that they were the people who really benefited from the system of exploitation that lay at the root of imperialism. Lenin got hold of this theory and said, "You must not draw any distinction between monopoly capitalism in Western Europe and the system of exploitation and domination abroad. The two are the same thing."

Although Lenin's presentation thus made it appear self-contradictory to speak of Communist imperialism or Communist neo-colonialism, history since Lenin tells a different story. It is not at all absurd to speak of Communist or Soviet imperialism in Central Asia; nor is it absurd to describe the relationship that exists between the Soviet Union and the satellite countries of Eastern Europe as neo-colonialist. There, complete economic dependence on the Soviet Union exists. There, are not only military bases, but governments whose main prop, as Hungary proved in 1956, is the Soviet Army; and there is the invisible arm that secures a surprising unanimity among the Communist countries in the United Nations, a unanimity that does not obtain between any of the former colonies and their former metropolitan masters.

All this is not absurd because there is no simple identity between capitalism and imperialism, as Lenin and the latter-day Communists would have it. The two phenomena must be distinguished. Even if one grants that monopoly capitalism inevitably gives rise to a system of domination and exploitation abroad, it does not by any means follow that another economic system cannot produce the same result. It is clear in the writings of Communists themselves that colonialism, in the strict sense, existed before monopoly capitalism and that the aim of this "old colonialism," no less than that of imperialism, was exploitation. John Eaton,[7] for example, openly acknowledges this. R. Palme-Dutt, again, admits[8] that British colonialism is older than British capitalism, and he is able to give us a broad outline of the history of the development of colonialism from the latter half of the sixteenth century to the period of "modern" imperialism in the latter half of the nineteenth century. Moreover, we know without consulting Communist writings that there were imperialisms in the ancient world before the era of capitalism. Africans are more concerned with the *fact* of domination and exploitation than with any theory about an economic system that arose in Europe.

Capitalism, to adapt A. C. Pigou, is an economic system in which the main instruments of production are owned or hired by private persons, who operate them with a view to selling at a profit the goods or services that they help to produce.[9] Imperialism, on the other hand, to quote Léopold Senghor, is "political and economic dependence of one people on another."[10] There is, therefore, no intrinsic incompatibility between socialism and imperialism. Simply repeating the claim that socialism and imperialism are mutually exclusive will not make Africans cease to be vigilant against imperialism in *all* its forms and varieties.

THE PITFALLS IN "SOCIALIST" AID

An analogous conclusion emerges from a dissection of the Communist picture of foreign aid. We have seen that, according to the Communists, the single overriding aim of all Western aid to newly independent countries is to ensnare the recipient countries in the Western net. The lesson the Communists would have us draw from this is that the newly independent countries should turn to socialist aid. Socialist aid, they claim, has no strings, political or military, and is directed wholly toward the development of independent industrialized economies in the new states. Its purpose, they say, is neither "investment" nor "profit."

Whatever the validity of these claims, the African may be pardoned if he discerns neo-colonialist motives in the advice to plump only for socialist aid. If we Africans were to accept only socialist aid, we would tie ourselves inextricably to the economy of the socialist bloc. This is surely none other than a neo-colonialist situation. By tying the economies of the newly independent countries to the economy of the socialist bloc, Communists seek to draw these countries into the socialist system and thus "free" them from imperialism. The more aid these countries obtain from the West, the farther this Communist aim is from realization. Here, then, lies the true explanation for the indignation with which the Communists view major Western aid to the newly independent countries. This is why Palme-Dutt, for example, condemns the Volta River Project in Ghana as "a typical example of modern imperialist colonial development."[11]

THE NEW COMMUNIST IMPERIALISM

The semantics thus disentangled, it is not unreasonable to argue that the real goal of Communist thought and writings about colonialism is the supersession of Western imperialism by Soviet imperialism, or the supersession of capitalist imperialism by Communist imperialism. This new form of imperialism is more dangerous than the one that we in Africa have known in the past. Western imperialism never had any consistent state-enforced theory behind it. Various justifications for Western imperialism were invented at various times and by various people. Sometimes the justification rested on sheer self-interest, as in the case of Cecil Rhodes; sometimes it was based on security considerations;[12] sometimes, too, it was founded on high—and impudent, not to say hypocritical—moral grounds, expressed in slogans such as "pax Britannica," "the white man's burden," and "efficiency and progress."[13] But this type of imperialism always had some saving features that were immensely important for Africa. The fact that opponents of imperialism could always be found in the metropolitan countries themselves, and were ready to aid the African fight against imperialism, was always of vast help to the African liberation movement. Citizens of the metropolitan countries could also oppose the imperialist policies and activities of their own countries without offending the canons of orthodoxy and courting charges of anti-state activities.

The new Communist imperialism is of a different order, in that it is buttressed with a theory of history—part of a general theory of reality—and maintained with all the might of the Soviet (and Chinese) state. There is no escape from such an imperialism. Since its theory is maintained with the power of the state, anyone who dares dispute the theory needs support from the power of another state. To speak against the theory, he must be protected against the power behind the theory. It therefore becomes impossible for a colonial territory trapped within this new imperialist system even to voice dissent or to appeal to the conscience of the new imperialist power. It is treasonable to fight the new imperialist master, for to do so is to reject the whole basis of the state. Thus it is impossible to call upon the aid of that element that, in the era of the old Western imperialism, was of such help to colonial territories seeking self-determination: the anti-imperialist citizens of the metropolitan country.

THE EURO-CENTRIC VIEW OF AFRICAN HISTORY

Nor is this all. The general theory on which the new Communist order is based is rooted in imperialist conceptions. While the theory of historical materialism is a generalization based on the experience of Europe, it purports to explain the historical process as a whole and not merely the course of development of particular societies: the histories of particular countries must fit into the general pattern of the historical process.[14] According to the theory, this historical process takes its cue from the most advanced class and since the most advanced class must come to the fore in a particular country, the theory reduces itself in practice to the proposition that the historical process takes its cue from the most advanced countries. At any particular moment in history, the world has to follow the trail of its most advanced country. This takes us back beyond Marx to Hegel. According to Hegel, "in the history of the World the *Individuals* we have to do with are Peoples; Totalities that are States,"[15] or, "each particular National genius is to be treated as only One Individual in the process of Universal History."[16] At any particular moment in history, there is one such people or state or union

> to which is ascribed a moment of the Idea in the form of a natural principle [and which] is entrusted with giving complete effect to it in the advance of the self-developing self-consciousness of the world mind. This nation is dominant in the world history during this one epoch, and it is only once that it can make its hour strike. In contrast with this its absolute right of being the vehicle of this present stage

in the world mind's development, the minds of the other nations are without rights, and they, along with those whose hour has struck already, count no longer in world history.[17]

There is no doubt that in the minds of the believers in "scientific socialism" the "peoples" or "nations" or "states" that are the bearers of history's purpose have been and are located in Europe. From the vantage point of the modern Soviet Communists in particular, there is no doubt, as we have noted above, that the leading country whose path the world is destined to follow is the Soviet Union. Moreover, the possibility of another country superseding the Soviet Union in the leading role is denied in Soviet theory: the classless society to which the Soviet Union aspires and leads the way is decreed to be the end of the various stages of history. There can be no further unfolding of the dialectic beyond this point.[18]

An important consequence of this theory is that it denies an independent history of Africa. It adheres firmly to a Euro-centric view of African history. Perhaps deep down in the Communist mind there is an admiration for Hegel's statement that Africa "is no historical part of the world."[19] Needless to say, this is a view that Africans have condemned as the hallmark of imperialist thinking about Africa. Both African scholars and nationalists have united to wage war on this attitude toward Africa. Among scholars it is indeed generally admitted, especially since Dr. Dike published his *Trade and Politics in the Niger Delta*, that the great need is to interpret Africa and its history from the African standpoint. Africans are determined to overturn the view that a history of Africa must be a mere appendage of another continent's history. As Tom Mboya of Kenya has put it, "the one great reality about our continent [is] that Africans are neither pro-West nor pro-Russian; they are pro-African."[20] This stems from a deep-seated belief that over and above the normal interdependence of countries and peoples in the world, Africa too has an identity that is as distinct as the identity of Europe, America, or Asia; that Africa, in the words of Dr. Nkrumah, "is not an extension of Europe or of any other continent."[21] This is what the Communists have not assimilated and cannot assimilate into their theory of colonialism. Fundamentally, there is an irreconcilable gulf between the Communist and African views of colonialism.

"National Democracy" and the Post-Colonial Revolution

—RICHARD LOWENTHAL

In the declaration adopted by the Moscow Conference of eighty-one Communist parties in December, 1960, a new formula for Communist strategy in ex-colonial, underdeveloped countries made its first appearance. The Communists working in these countries were told to work for the creation of "an independent state of national democracy," and to rally the broadest possible national fronts to achieve that goal.

The declaration defined the new type of state as follows:

> A state that consistently defends its political and economic independence, that struggles against imperialism and its military blocs, against military bases on its territory; a state that struggles against the new forms of colonialism and the penetration of imperialist capital; a state that rejects dictatorial and despotic methods of administration; a state in which the people enjoy the broadest democratic rights and liberties (freedom of speech, of the press, of assembly, of demonstrations, of forming political parties and social organisations), in which they have the possibility to strive for land reform and for the implementation of other demands for democratic and social transformations and for participation in shaping public policy. The rise and consolidation of national democratic states gives them a chance to advance quickly on the road of social progress and to play an active role in the struggle of the peoples for peace, against the aggressive policy of the imperialist camp and for the complete liquidation of the colonial yoke.[1]

A closely similar catalogue of "priority tasks for national rebirth" was listed a few paragraphs before in the same declaration as capable of solution only if "all patriotic forces of the nation join in a national, democratic United Front." Here it said:

Strengthening of national independence, land reforms in the interest of the peasantry, abolition of the remnants of feudalism, extirpation of the economic roots of imperialist rule, limitation and ousting of foreign monopolies from the economy, foundation and development of a national industry, raising of the standard of living of the population, democratization of public life, an independent, peace-loving foreign policy, development of economic and cultural cooperation with the socialist countries and other friendly countries—those are the all-national, democratic tasks for the solution of which the progressive forces of the nation may and indeed do unite in the countries that have liberated themselves.

Finally, the relation of the new concept to classical Leninist doctrine is summed up in this formula: "The Communist parties struggle actively for the consistent completion of the anti-imperialist, anti-feudal, democratic revolution, for the formation of a national democratic state and for an effective raising of the standard of living of the masses of the people."

In the course of 1961, the new formula was authoritatively interpreted and elaborated in Soviet theoretical journals, notably by Boris Ponomarev[2] and G. Gafurov[3] from a political and by A. Arzumanyan[4] from an economic point of view. When the draft program of the Communist Party of the Soviet Union was published at the end of July,[5] its section on "The National Liberation Movement" was found to center on the same tasks to be fulfilled after the winning of political independence, tasks that were now equated with the choice of a "non-capitalist road of development." Again, it was laid down that "the political basis of a national democracy is a bloc of all the progressive, patriotic forces fighting to win complete national independence and broad democracy, and to consummate the anti-imperialist, anti-feudal, democratic revolution," and the Communist parties were specifically instructed to struggle for this consummation and for the establishment of a state of national democracy. At the Twenty-Second Congress of the CPSU, these passages were adopted without change.

Because the document in which "national democracy" made its first appearance was the outcome of a conference dominated by the dispute between the Soviet and Chinese Communist parties, it was perhaps natural that Western students should at first have tended to interpret the new formula in the context of that dispute as a "semantic compromise" between Soviet and Chinese views on strategy towards the ex-colonial, uncommitted countries.[6] Evidence of different Soviet and Chinese reaction to the introduction of the concept does indeed exist and will be examined further on. But it is the contention of this paper that the concept of "national democracy" was devised primarily not as a reaction to the Sino-Soviet dispute, but in response to the real problems facing Soviet and Communist strategy in the ex-colonial nations, and that some new strategic formula of this kind would have had to be invented by the Soviet leaders at the present stage even if no dispute with Peking existed. In this view, a new strategy was required because the classical Communist two-stage theory of the revolution in colonial and ex-colonial countries had proved obviously inadequate to the situation in the growing number of former colonies emerging into independence, and "national democracy" represents an attempt to revise this classical theory in order to lay a foundation for a more realistic Communist policy.

The classical two-stage theory was based on Stalin's interpretation of the theses on the national and colonial revolution propounded by Lenin at the Second World Congress of the Comintern. It assumed that the subject peoples would achieve their liberation from imperialist domination and from their "feudal," i.e. pre-capitalist, domestic rulers by a revolution that would be at once national and "bourgeois-democratic." The "national bourgeoisie," i.e., the patriotic and modern-minded part of the upper class of those countries, comprising in the typical Communist view not only industrialists and some of the traders but also nationalist officers, bureaucrats and intellectuals, would take part in this revolutionary movement along with the workers, the peasants and the urban petty bourgeois, and would normally even lead it; but because the revolution against imperialism and feudalism could win only as a movement of the popular masses, this first, national and "bourgeois-democratic" revolution would also lead to the rise of powerful class organizations of the workers and peasants, including a battle-tried Communist Party. It would thus create ideal preconditions for the second revolution in which the Communist-led workers and peasants would overthrow the rule of the "national bourgeoisie" and, with the help of the Soviet Union, inaugurate a "non-capitalist development" (the phrase is Lenin's)[7] leading ultimately to the construction of a "socialist" order.

The theory was elaborated by Stalin on the occasion of the Chinese revolutionary crisis of 1924–27; and even there it broke down completely, because the "national bourgeoisie," represented by Chiang Kai-shek, proved its ability to consolidate its power, subject the workers and peasants to its control, and suppress the Communists. But as Stalin had been attacked for his earlier support of Chiang by Trotsky and had staked his authority on the correctness of his theory, he could not admit that it was wrong; he merely argued that Chiang had "betrayed" the revolution and gone over to its imperialist-feudal enemies, and that therefore the first stage —the national and "bourgeois-democratic" revolution—had not yet been victoriously completed either. On this basis, Mao Tse-tung, having assumed sole leadership of the Chinese Communist Party in 1935, undertook a first revision of the theory in 1939:[8] he claimed that the Communist Party must already assume sole leadership during the first stage of the revolution, and create a "new democracy" that would be socially based on the "classical" coalition of four classes, including the "national bourgeoisie," but would dispense with the need for a corresponding political coalition with independent non-Communist parties. Of course, once this kind of "new democracy" had won, the transition to the second stage of the revolution would amount to no more than a change of policy by the ruling Communist Party—the shedding of its consideration for its erstwhile bourgeois allies.

When the Chinese Communists finally conquered the whole mainland in 1949, this Maoist version of the two-stage theory was at least tentatively accepted by the Soviets and the international Communist movement.[9] National liberation of colonial and semi-colonial countries was considered by both Moscow and Peking, in the teeth of all contrary evidence, as possible only under Communist leadership, with the corollary that a number of great Asian countries that had emerged into national sovereignty, beginning with India, were held to be still ruled by imperialist stooges and to be suitable objects for Communist-led "liberation movements." Yet these attempts proved uniformly unsuccessful. Only in Vietnam, where the stubbornness of a shortsighted colonial power coincided with the presence of a strong and well-led Communist Party, did the latter in fact achieve leadership of a revolutionary movement for national liberation according to the Maoist prescription, and succeed in founding a Communist dictatorship on that basis.

After the death of Stalin, and particularly after the Geneva settlement for Indochina and the formation of SEATO, the doctrinaire denial of the independence of the ex-colonial, uncommitted nations was abandoned by both Moscow and Peking: the Communist powers now understood that these emerging nations were becoming a major new factor on the world scene, and that it was vital to keep them at least neutral. But the remarkably quick transition of the Communist governments to the diplomatic realism of the *panch shila* and the Bandung Conference left the Communist parties of the ex-colonial countries in a kind of theoretical void, without clear guidance for their strategy.

If the new nations were really independent, they had presumably achieved national liberation without benefit of Communist leadership, and the Chinese example was not universally applicable. But Stalin's older version did not seem to apply to them either, because hardly any of the new nations fitted the Communist vision of a revolutionary democracy—even of one under bourgeois leadership. In fact, more and more of them were achieving independence without any kind of revolution; and those regimes that could justly be described as emerging from national revolutions tended to be led by non-Communist dictators who, while gladly accepting the economic aid of the Communist powers and their diplomatic support against the "imperialists," insisted on limiting or altogether suppressing Communist activity at home, and on themselves controlling any class organizations of the workers and peasants. In either case, with independence achieved and the new nationalist regimes firmly in the saddle, the Communist parties were still in fairly weak positions in almost all the new countries—far too weak to attempt a frontal attack on the nationalist regimes in order to inaugurate the "second stage."

At the same time, some of the revolutionary nationalist leaders were setting out, with no Communist prompting, to tackle further tasks of the "bourgeois-democratic revolution" beyond the winning of national sovereignty. They endeavored to reform land tenure and to liquidate feudal or tribal positions of power; they embarked on a planned development of industry, using both Communist and Western help but looking in fact for a road which, in accordance with the conditions in their countries, was neither capitalist nor Communist. In doing this, some of the new nationalist regimes came into conflict with Western capitalist interests and with one or more of the major Western governments. It looked as if in these countries the national, anti-imperialist revolution was going on *after* the achievement of "formal" independence; all that was needed was for the Communists to use the opportunities of the post-colonial phase of the "first stage" to gain the influence and organized strength that they had failed to gain in the struggle for independence!

It was, in fact, the rise of a number of such nationalist revolutionary regimes in the second half of the nineteen fifties, and the opportunities, successes, and setbacks that rise brought for the Communists, that prompted the renewed discussion of Communist strategy from which the concept of the "independent national democratic state" has emerged. The relevant events include President Nasser's turn from marked pro-Soviet orientation in the pre-Suez and immediate post-Suez period to conflicts with the Soviets, first over their unsuccessful opposition to the union of Syria with Egypt in 1958 and then over their successful opposition to a similar union with Iraq in early 1959; the persecution of the Communists in the U.A.R. and the development of an ideology of "Arab socialism"; the Iraqi revolution of the summer of 1958, the growth of Communist influence in support of Kassem's struggle against the Nasserites, and the setback of the summer of 1959; the secession of Guinea from the French Community in an atmosphere of bitter conflict in September, 1958, and the subsequent quick growth of Guinea's ties with the Soviet bloc; the victory of Fidel Castro's movement in Cuba at the beginning of 1959, its growing conflicts with the United States, and increasing reliance on Soviet and Communist support; and the development of President Sukarno's "guided democracy" in Indonesia in steady conflict both with Dutch interests and with moderate domestic elements, leading to a general restriction of party life but to a growth of Communist influence on the government.

Serious Communist discussions of the lessons of these events seem to have started early in 1959. One of the first public signs that they were taking place was an international debate on the role of the "national bourgeoisie," held in May of that year in Leipzig, in East Germany, extracts from which were subsequently printed in *Problems of Peace and Socialism*.[10] The debate started from the common assumption that the national and democratic revolution —the first stage according to the classical theory—was not completed with the achievement of "formal independence" by the ex-colonies, and also remained on the agenda of the "semi-colonies" of Latin America; the struggle for real independence from imperialist economic control and for internal emancipation from the rule of foreign monopolies and feudal landlords through democratic and agrarian reforms remained the immediate task in all those countries. It followed that the classical four-class alliance, including the "national bourgeoisie," was still needed to fulfil that task. But as the contradictions inherent in the nature of that class were leading to more pronounced waverings once independence was won, and the further the national and democratic revolution proceeded, it followed that the completion of that revolution would henceforth depend increasingly on the ability of the working class, led by the Communists, to rally the peasants to its side and, together with them, exert effective pressure on the national bourgeoisie in favor of a consistent revolutionary policy. In other words, the Communists, while seeking to hold together a broad united front, including the national bourgeoisie, with a "national democratic" program, must begin the struggle for leadership within that front—not necessarily, and indeed not normally, in the sense of seeking to overthrow the governments headed by popular nationalist leaders, but in the sense of seeking to force their own policy on them.[11]

Throughout the discussion, in which no Chinese Communist took part, the Soviet policy of economic aid for uncommitted governments of the "national bourgeoisie"—including those that suppressed their own Communists—was not called in question; on the contrary, the importance of close economic relations with the "socialist countries" as a factor helping to keep the national bourgeoisie on the right path was stressed by several participants. But the new element in the discussion was not this endorsement of Soviet realism; the emphasis was rather on the point that Soviet diplomatic and economic support for the ex-colonial countries, however vital, was not in itself enough to ensure the completion of the national and democratic revolutions without the presence of skillfully led Communist parties within them. Egypt had shown the dangers of Communist weakness, Iraq the risks of rashness, Cuba and Indonesia seemed to indicate the gains that could be reaped with flexible tactics, while Guinea posed the problem of a revolutionary regime with a pronounced pro-Soviet orientation in a country where no Communist Party as yet existed. It was only logical that this increased concern with the Communist role in the emerging nations should soon afterwards be reflected by the publication —in October, 1959—of the first issue of the *African Communist*, a magazine nominally issued in the name of the South African Communist Party but clearly designed as a policy-making organ and a "collective organizer" for the whole of tropical Africa. Right from the start, the new journal left no doubt that one of its principal purposes was to help overcome the backwardness of the dark continent in the formation of Communist parties and to stimulate their creation in all the new African states.

By June, 1960, the new emphasis on the Communist task was clearly expressed in the resolution on the "struggle against colonialism" adopted by the Peking session of the General Council of the World Federation of Trade Unions (WFTU). It will be recalled that this session witnessed a major Chinese Communist attack on the Soviet concepts of peaceful coexistence and disarmament, and the rejection of the Chinese criticism by a large majority of the delegates. No similar clash, however, was reported over the resolution that called on working class organizations in the colonial and ex-colonial countries to increase their activity in the movements for national liberation, and to "assume the leading role in forming and consolidating a united national front, based on the alliance of workers and peasants and rallying all other anti-colonial forces."[12]

The declaration of the eighty-one Communist parties adopted six months later in Moscow, while giving a more detailed analysis of the role of the different classes in the "national, democratic united front," is actually less explicitly emphatic about the "leading role" of the working class: it paraphrases the idea by describing the working class as the most consistent force demanding the full consummation of the national, anti-imperialist, democratic revolution, and by saying that the degree in which the national bourgeoisie will join in the liberation struggle will depend largely on the strength and solidity of the alliance between the working class and the peasants. But the more cautious language used in this document intended for mass propaganda—and also in the program of the CPSU adopted in 1961—does not express a less definite claim to leadership. This is clearly shown by Khrushchev's report on the conference, which states bluntly that:

> the correct application of Marxist-Leninist theory in the liberated countries consists precisely in finding the forms that . . . will make it possible to unite all the healthy forces of the nation and to assure the leading role of the working class within the national front in the struggle to eradicate imperialism and the remnants of feudalism and to clear the way for a movement that will ultimately lead to socialism.[13]

With this hint that the strategic meaning of the new slogan of "national democracy" was to open the road for the transition to "socialism"—which, in Communist language, is synonymous with the transition to Communist Party rule—in the ex-colonial countries, Khrushchev had gone beyond the text of the declaration of the eighty-one parties. Subsequent Soviet comment on the declaration was further to elaborate that hint. In February, 1961, A. Arzumanyan concluded an outline of the conditions needed for completing the democratic, anti-imperialist revolution in those countries by asking: "But is that equivalent with socialism?" and replying: "It is not yet socialism, but a transitional stage on the road to socialism. It is the road to a state of national democracy."[14]

A few months later, Boris Ponomarev, head of the department for relations with non-governing Communist parties in the Central Committee of the CPSU (who has since been promoted to membership of the Central Committee Secretariat), explained that the transitional function of the new type of state consisted in starting its country on the "non-capitalist road of development."[15] When the draft program of the CPSU was published shortly afterwards, it equated the choice between the capitalist and the non-capitalist road now facing the ex-colonial countries with the choice between capitalism and socialism. In introducing the draft at the Twenty-second Congress of the CPSU, Khrushchev was still more outspoken:

> The seething underdeveloped countries of Asia, Africa, and Latin America, pursuing to the end the national liberation, anti-imperialist revolution, will be able to carry out the transition to socialism. In the present era, practically every country, irrespective of the level of its development, can take the path leading to socialism.

And, having repeated that "only the unification of all democratic and patriotic forces in a broad national front can lead the peoples on to this path," he summed up: "Marxist theoretical thought, profoundly studying the objective course of development, has discovered the form in which the unification of all the healthy forces of a nation can be most successfully achieved. This form consists in the national democratic state."[16]

We are now in a position to see the new concept of the "independent, national democratic state" in its strategic context. In the first place, it is the interim goal the Communists propose as a common objective for a united national, democratic front in ex-colonial or semi-colonial countries. It is identical with the full consummation of their classical first stage of the colonial revolution—the "national, bourgeois-democratic revolution" against imperialism and feudalism. In other words, *"national democracy" calls for a post-colonial extension of the first stage of the colonial revolution.*

Secondly, this post-colonial extension has become necessary because experience has shown that most former colonies are attaining independence without having passed through a first stage of the classical type, and therefore without having acquired the preconditions for the second, "socialist" stage of the revolution. The struggle for "national democracy" is to create these preconditions by breaking the new country's economic ties with the "world system of imperialism" and creating in their place economic links with the "socialist states," by destroying its pre-capitalist ruling class through agrarian reform, and by giving the Communists the chance that they may not have had under the colonial regime to organize the working class and the peasants under their leadership. *The demand for an "independent national democratic state" is thus a transitional slogan on the road to the second, "socialist" stage of the revolution.*

Thirdly, because the demands summed up under this slogan still form part of the classical first stage, they call for a continuation of the classical four-class coalition, of a broad national united front including the national bourgeoisie and the nationalist leaders representing it: "national democracy" is *not* a "new democracy" of the Chinese type in which the Communists themselves claim to represent all four classes; it is only used as a slogan where independent nationalist political forces have to be taken into account. But because these demands are at the same time intended to put the country firmly on the "non-capitalist road of development," to create the precondition for the second "socialist" phase, they can be clearly and consistently formulated only by the Communists. *The struggle for "national democracy" is a struggle for Communist leadership within the united national front,* for the extension of Communist influence on the nationalist government, and the Communist occupation of key positions in the political, military and economic state machine; it is, however, conducted wherever possible within the framework of the existing nationalist regimes— without aiming at the overthrow of popular nationalist leaders at this stage.

Finally, because in the period of the struggle for "national democracy" the Communists are seeking to build up their influence and to win leadership of the united national front, the struggle is accompanied by an open ideological attack on all native varieties of nationalist or populist socialism in the name of Marxism-Leninism. In campaigning for "national democracy," the Communists reject their left wing nationalist allies' description of the united front program of planned industrialization and agrarian reform as socialist; they call such a term "demagogic" and premature, and seek to reserve it for their own second-stage program of complete nationalization of industry and forced collectivization of agriculture. *Adoption of the slogan of "national democracy" for the united national front goes with the reassertion of the dogma that, contrary to the view of the Yugoslav "revisionists" and of many radical nationalists, the achievement of socialism in the ex-colonial countries* (as in all other countries) *will only be possible once state power is in the hands of a Communist Party.*[17]

Inasmuch as the strategy of "national democracy" means a reassertion of Communist political and ideological independence from the "national bourgeoisie" and a more militant bid for Communist leadership of the new nations, the Chinese Communist critics of Soviet policy might have been expected to welcome it. In fact, however, the resolution of the Chinese Communist Central Committee approving the Moscow declaration of December, 1961,[18] makes no mention of the new formula, and Chinese Communist propaganda has not used it since. While Peking has made no direct attacks on the new concept, an authoritative article published in mid-1961 on the corresponding phase of the Chinese experience[19] indicates its dissent by sticking to a different terminology throughout: where Soviet and international Communist documents now speak of a "national democratic front" completing the democratic phase of the revolution by means of an "independent state of national democracy," the Chinese attribute that function to a "people's democratic united front" and a "people's democratic dictatorship." Nor is the difference purely verbal: the Chinese concept, taken from Mao's theory of the "new democratic revolution," requires the conquest of full power by the Communists (though in the name of a four-class coalition) as a condition for completing even the "democratic" phase of the revolution; the new Soviet concept, as we have seen, implies a real if transitional sharing of power between the

Communists and their "bourgeois-nationalist" partners in the "national democratic" regime.

What makes the change unacceptable to the Chinese is above all the Soviet view that in favorable conditions, both the "national democratic" transition from bourgeois-nationalist to Communist leadership of the united front and finally of the government and the later transition from a Communist-directed "democratic" to a "socialist" revolution may be carried out peacefully. In the words of Ponomarev,

> there can be no doubt that the state of national democracy offers prospects for a transition to a higher type of social order, as the objective and subjective conditions for it are brought to maturity by the struggle of the peoples of those countries. For achieving a socialist order, revolutionary changes in one or another form are necessary. But it is not excluded that the road to a non-capitalist development will lead in some countries through the state of national democracy.[20]

The Chinese are willing enough to admit the peacefulness of the change from the "democratic" to the "socialist" phase of the revolution once Communist power is complete, but they deny that the original achievement of full Communist power in the course of the democratic revolution—the wresting of power from the hands of the nationalists—can be peaceful: they cling to their recently restated dogma that no transition from a bourgeois-led government to a Communist-led workers' and peasants' government is possible without the violent destruction of the old state machine.[21]

Closely linked to this difference between Soviet and Chinese views is a second major difference that concerns the usefulness of extending the economic power of "national democratic" governments, even when still led by bourgeois nationalists, by nationalization measures and the development of state-owned industries. In the Soviet view, as expounded by Ponomarev, these are important steps along the "non-capitalist road":

> The experience of the development of states that have recently liberated themselves from the imperialist yoke shows that, as a result of the nationalization of foreign banks and monopolies and of the creation of state-owned factories, banks, etc., on this basis, there arises a more progressive form of ownership than private ownership—the state ownership of the means of production.

He also argues that the growth of the public sector in a state of "national democracy" offers the "progressive forces" an opportunity to occupy important economic positions and thus to increase their political influence. But in the view of the Chinese, the growth of the public sector under a bourgeois government may only pave the way for "bureaucratic capitalism, which is an ally of imperialism and feudalism."[22] By this they mean the use of the state's economic power made by political officeholders and their families to accumulate private fortunes and privileged economic positions, a practice familiar under the Kuomintang regime, and not unknown in other underdeveloped countries today.

Between 1954, when they turned to diplomatic courtship of the newly independent countries, and about the end of 1958, the Soviets gave the impression of relying for their influence in those countries almost entirely on good will between governments—on the importance of their backing the new states in all conflicts with the imperialists; on the attraction of their anti-colonialist policy; on the value of their offers of credit and trade; and on the prestige of their own example of successful forced development without Western help. In discussing the future of the ex-colonial nations, they had long presented it in terms of completing political independence by the achievement of economic independence from the "imperialist world system" and had never tired of pointing out that the existence of their own "socialist world system" would enable the new nations to cut their economic ties with the West and rely increasingly and, in the end, exclusively on Communist aid and trade. Thus, the chance of the former colonies to follow a "non-capitalist road" of development appeared to depend only on the growing political and economic strength of the "socialist camp."

As the problems of Communist strategy within the new nations came again to be discussed by Soviet writers from 1959 onwards, it was increasingly emphasized that the use of these international chances, the choice of one or the other road of development by the former colonies, depended on the internal decisions of the peoples concerned. While solemnly disclaiming any intention of interfering with the free choice of the ex-colonial peoples, Soviet writers began to show an undisguised interest in the outcome of that choice. States that, in the Soviet view, showed by anti-imperialist orientation and nationalization of foreign capital assets that they were moving towards "national democracy"—notably Cuba, Guinea,

Ghana, Mali, and Indonesia—were freely praised and promised generous support. More and more frequently, the examples of the once backward republics of Soviet Central Asia and even of the Mongolian People's Republic were cited[23] as proof that even fairly primitive peoples could now avoid capitalism and "take the path leading to socialism"—provided they cut all ties to the capitalist world market and relied exclusively on Soviet bloc aid and guidance. There are indeed indications that the Soviets regard the pre-socialist republics of Khorem and Bokhara, founded in 1920, and the Mongolian People's Republic as the classical models of a "national democratic" development carried to its logical conclusion.

At the same time, nationalist governments that showed by measures taken against their native Communists that their internal development was tending in an "anti-democratic" direction—notably Nasser's Egypt and Kassem's Iraq—were now as frankly criticized by authoritative spokesmen from Khrushchev downwards, and were warned that such "despotic" methods, by undermining the unity of their nations, might ultimately even jeopardize their hard-won independence from imperialism. But to the new sharpness of the ideological distinction between "progressive" and "reactionary" regimes in the new states, there corresponds no similarly clear-cut contrast between the promise of Soviet aid to the incipient "national democracies" and its refusal to emergent "nationalist despotisms." On the contrary, substantial amounts of Soviet aid have continued to be granted to the latter—to the evident dismay of Peking.

In fact, the Soviets clearly consider that their diplomatic and economic practice towards the new countries must continue to be governed by their *actual*, diplomatic independence from the "imperialists"—not by internal developments that might, according to Communist theory, *potentially* endanger that independence. They have decided against making their loans conditional on the increase of Communist influence in the recipient countries, not because they are opposed in principle to interference in their internal affairs, but because they cannot afford to impose such conditions, owing to their intense competition with the West for the good will of these countries—just as the Western countries cannot afford to make their own aid conditional on the abandonment of military neutrality. In reply to Chinese criticism, the Soviets have defended their policy by saying that they are "granting economic and technical assistance to the former colonies on an inter-governmental basis, rendering it to nations and not to some classes within them," claiming that the struggle there was "not solely or chiefly" an internal class struggle, but a joint struggle against imperialism.[24]

While the above statement antedates the adoption of the formula of "national democracy"—it was published in June, 1960—the latter has made no difference to the policy expressed therein. The promises of Soviet aid for all countries striving to consolidate their newly won independence from imperialism remain unqualified by references to the internal development of those countries both in the 1960 Moscow declaration and in the new program of the CPSU. The reason is hinted at once again in Ponomarev's authoritative comment on the concept of "national democracy": "What matters here is not to classify all liberated countries and to say: these belong to one category, those to another. Such an approach would be schematic and harmful." In other words, the Soviets are aware that the development of most of the new countries is still in flux, and while they seek to analyze its direction in each case, they bear in mind that it may still change. The concept of "national democracy" is intended as a signpost for Communist strategy within the ex-colonial nations, not as a classification for the disbursement or refusal of Soviet credits.

As a strategic concept for the Communist parties of the ex-colonial countries, "national democracy" has a significant European model in the concept of "people's democracy" as used between 1945 and 1947. Today, the word is used only for the Communist states of Eastern Europe, and the program of the CPSU describes it as "a variety of the dictatorship of the proletariat." But it was originally intended as a slogan for the West European democracies freshly emerging from World War II and from the occupation by Nazi Germany, and as a description of a state of affairs in some Eastern European countries, which, while evidently brought about by Communist initiative, still seemed to fall short of a full-fledged Communist Party dictatorship in important respects.

"People's democracy," as then described, mainly with reference to the example of Czechoslovakia, was the rule of a coalition of progressive, democratic forces—basically the same coalition that had conducted the anti-fascist liberation struggle. That struggle had, according to the Communists, assumed the character of a democratic revolution—a revolution that was not completed with the expulsion and defeat of the German armies. To complete it, the fascists and their collaborators had to be eliminated from the political and economic life of the nation, their parties suppressed, and their property nationalized, while radical land reforms had to create the basis for a lasting democratization of public life. According to the Communists, those were democratic and not specifically socialist demands, and it was premature and demagogic to talk of socialism at that stage; but, since the implementation of such a program required the growth of the state sector at the expense of some forms of private property, the patriotic sections of the bourgeoisie were beginning to waver at that stage and completion of the democratic revolution depended increasingly on the leading role of the working class and its close alliance with the peasants. Accordingly the Communists, while striving to maintain the unity of a broad anti-fascist front, had to put forward an independent program of fighting for its leadership, and the slogan of "people's democracy" summed up that program. Wherever they succeeded, they would establish close co-operation with the Soviet Union, and by completing the democratic revolution would create a political and economic basis on which the later construction of a socialist order with Soviet help would be possible without violent upheaval.

When this concept of "people's democracy" was put forward by Communist propaganda, strong Communist parties were sitting in the governments of France, Italy, and Czechoslovakia in coalitions that were formally quite similar, though the facts of ultimate military power, and also of control of the police and communications media, differed fundamentally on either side of the post-war military demarcation line between Russia and the West. Even so, the political shape of post-war Europe was still in flux as late as 1947, and it was neither a foregone conclusion that Czechoslovakia must become a Communist dictatorship nor that no Western European country would turn Communist. Only when the announcement of the Marshall Plan and its rejection by the Soviets led to the break-up of the French and Italian coalitions and to a serious rift in the Czech government was the era of fluidity doomed; and only after the success of the Prague coup of February, 1948, and the failure of the Communist bid for power in the Italian elections in April did "people's democracy" finally lose its value as a transitional slogan, because the transitional situation in post-war Europe was at an end. In the West, the anti-fascist democratic revolution had failed to achieve its pre-ordained consummation, and the bourgeois state, backed by United States imperialism, was back in power; in Eastern Europe, the consummation of "people's democracy" had been attained, and it turned out to be "a variety of proletarian dictator-ship"—formally distinct from the Soviet system by its retention of the trappings of parliamentary government and of a sham coalition with satellite parties deprived of the last vestiges of independence, but substantially identical with it in being subject to total control by the Communist Party.

From what has been said, the similarity of the two strategic con-cepts appears too striking to be unconscious. The attempt to extend a broad movement of national liberation beyond the fact of libera-tion, to inspire it with more far-reaching revolutionary aims with-out proclaiming straight Communist demands, to maintain a com-mon front with bourgeois elements but to struggle to assume its leadership, even to use examples from inside the Soviet orbit as models for countries in apparently similar situations outside it—the present use of "national democracy" has all this in common with the original use of "people's democracy." But it does not follow that the prospects of the new slogan can be deduced from the results of the old, for the situation and problems of the ex-colonial nations are quite different from those of post-war Europe. On one side, the situation in most of these nations is far more truly "revolu-tionary" in the sense of requiring radical changes in the economic and social structure, than in most of post-war Western Europe; on the other, the Communist parties in most of them are far weaker, and the prospects of indigenous and undoctrinaire movements com-bining nationalism with a passion for radical social change, corre-spondingly stronger.

Much of the immediate economic and social program proposed by the Communists for the underdeveloped countries—whether ex-colonial or not—reflects the genuine problems of those countries, even if in a doctrinaire and one-sided form. It is true, for instance, that in many of those countries a radical reform of land tenure is urgently needed, that none of them can achieve a harmonious and all-round economic growth without state planning of investment and a more or less pronounced growth of the "public sector," and that in many cases these measures cannot be achieved without hurt-ing the interests and therefore provoking the resistance not only of the traditional native oligarchy or upper class, but also of some major Western business firms enjoying a privileged position in-herited from the colonial or semi-colonial past. The road of na-tional independence and development for these countries must indeed be to some extent a "non-capitalist road," not in the sense that it would be incompatible with an important contribution by capitalist private enterprise, both domestic and foreign, but in the sense that such a contribution can be fruitful only in the framework of a national plan. They cannot follow the road of classical *liberal* capitalism once travelled by the old industrial countries of the West.

But it is not true, as experience increasingly shows, that the developing countries have only the choice between the roads of doctrinaire liberal capitalism and doctrinaire Communism—that a "non-capitalist" road in the above, realistic sense must be a "socialist" road in the Communist sense of complete nationalization of industry and forced collectivization of agriculture. Nor is it true that a policy of state-controlled national development that conflicts with the interests of some important Western capitalist firms will necessarily be resisted by the Western powers, or that "capitalist" countries like the United States are bound to refuse aid for such a policy of planned development, leaving the nationalist planners with no option but one-sided dependence on the Soviet bloc. In general, the best chance for these countries lies in choosing a road of economic development that is neither the classical capitalist nor the Communist road, and a foreign policy that does not lead to one-sided dependence on either the Western or the Soviet bloc.

Here is the fundamental flaw of the strategy of "national democracy." The true interests of the developing countries do not require a policy that calls for Communist leadership and exclusive reliance on Soviet support, but are served best by a policy of nationalist planning and independence from either of the major power blocs. Where the nationalist leaders adopt such a policy, which they frequently describe as their own home-grown variety of "socialism," the Communist chances of gaining mass influence and ultimately achieving the transition to their "second stage" revolution are correspondingly reduced: hence the growing ideological fury of the Communist attacks on such eclectic socialist doctrines,[25] not only in the case of Nasser but even of such erstwhile candidates for the "national democratic" label as Sékou Touré. Whenever a non-Communist leader uses the term "socialist" to describe his own policy, he indicates his confidence in his ability to find his own road of development and his refusal to see his regime as a mere transition to Communist rule.

To this increasingly typical situation, the strategy of "national

democracy" provides no answer.[26] It tells the Communists to seek
nationalist allies and to press for influence on the nationalist governments while striving to avoid premature conflict with them; but
it leaves them at a loss as to what to do if the intended allies refuse
to accept them as partners, as in Morocco and Algeria, and if the
nationalist rulers will not permit Communist parties, as in Egypt
or even in Guinea. They may attack Nasser as a despot, but they
hesitate to go to the same length in the case of Touré—and Soviet
credits continue to reach both. In fact, by continuing to support
uncommitted countries even if their governments show no willingness to accept Communist guidance for their road of development,
the Soviets tacitly admit that a third road between classical capitalism and Communism is possible for those countries. But as we have
seen, the doctrine of "national democracy" presupposes the denial
of that possibility. Soviet diplomacy towards the new countries and
Communist strategy within them thus appear to be based on
premises that stand in flat contradiction with one another.

Soviet Doctrines on Developing Countries: Some Divergent Views

—HERBERT S. DINERSTEIN

Soviet doctrines on developing countries are of great interest because they help us to understand how the Soviet leaders expect the world to change in the next few decades. Soviet expectations of rapid progress within the Communist camp must have been reduced in recent years. The tragic failures in the Chinese economy and the continued unsatisfactory performance of Soviet agriculture mean that the fruition of many cherished hopes for improvement within the two largest socialist countries must be postponed. The main centers of capitalism hardly seem to be disintegrating. Western Europe seems to have survived the loss of its colonies without the cost to its stability predicted by the Communist theoreticians. On the contrary, it seems to have developed into a center of world capitalism comparable with the United States. Parts of the Communist world seem far more worried than the United States about the possibility of economic disintegration.

The reader of Soviet discussions of the American scene finds some expressions of satisfaction over American economic setbacks, when they occur, but he finds only the most generalized predictions of the ultimate collapse of capitalism, and no detailed analysis of weaknesses in the American system that might produce important political changes in the coming decades. Only when the subject is the underdeveloped countries, does one discover a spirit of optimism. As this paper will seek to demonstrate, the optimism is becoming increasingly tempered and moderate. Despite this qualification, however, the fact remains that the highest hopes of the Soviet leaders for the territorial expansion of Communism rest upon the underdeveloped areas of the world. It is for this reason that the full range of Soviet views on the underdeveloped areas invites attention.

75

Divergent opinions on matters of theory now occupy a different place in Soviet life than at an earlier time. In Stalin's day, if an unorthodox opinion on a matter of major importance did not swiftly become official opinion, its author was fortunate to escape with a forced public confession of his error. Hence views diverging from or contradicting the official line were rarely, and then only circumspectly, expressed. After Stalin's death, when different factions within the Communist Party were jockeying for position, the exponents of various views often reflected the distinctive policies of factions within the Party. The different formulas expressed by experts on the proper balance between light and heavy industry reflected divergent policies within the Party. Today, the style of discussion and debate seems to have undergone still another modification. It seems that discussion, at least the discussion reported in this paper, does not necessarily indicate a dispute over policy in the Party. A debate may be just what it purports to be: an exploration of differences of opinion by experts who hope that the cogency of their arguments will impel Party leaders to retain or modify official policies.

Some experts on the underdeveloped countries approve the present policy and recommend its continuation with perhaps modest changes; others seem genuinely critical and seem to argue for important modifications. If the Party leaders themselves are already dissatisfied with the results of their policy, the experts may now examine various possible alternatives. If the Soviet leaders are employing their specialists in this sensible way, then an essential (although not sufficient) condition of flexibility in policy has been established.

Obviously, if there were no need for improvement felt there would be nothing to discuss. As we shall see, the discussion on underdeveloped countries is part of a larger discussion on the allocation of resources to foreign and domestic programs, and the choices have not been easy. But difficult as the resolution of these problems is, one must not forget that they are what might be called pleasant problems. The problem of how much financial aid to give to Castro's Cuba may be troublesome, but the very fact of its existence means that Communism now has prospects in Latin America, whereas a few years ago it seemed to have none. It must be unpleasant and irritating that Nasser is so grudging with his thanks for Soviet economic aid, and that he treats Egyptian Communists so harshly. Yet the fact remains that now the Soviet Union plays a genuine role in the Mediterranean—an area where Russia has sought a *point d'appui* since the eighteenth century.

The Soviet Union may find it difficult to choose between so many new opportunities. The situation is a little like that of a man who has become rich rather quickly. He incurs many obligations, and many claimants for assistance flock to him. He is overcommitted and perhaps even in debt, yet he does not long for the days of his poverty. That the Soviet Union has *problems* in the underdeveloped areas should not suggest that the Soviet position in these areas represents a loss instead of a gain.

Soviet policy toward the underdeveloped countries has reflected two underlying assumptions, now in the process of modification. The first was that the twentieth century would see the world divided into two political camps and that competition between them would become so intense that non-alignment could be only a transitory stage. Stalin's successors believed that the transitory stage might be lengthy and that the newly independent countries might be controlled for a significant period neither by one camp nor the other.

The second underlying assumption of Soviet policy was that international politics is, as game theorists would put it, the zero-sum game. In other words, whatever one side loses, the other gains. Accordingly, the creation of new independent states from old empires was thought to be an automatic loss for capitalism and a gain for socialism. But, according to Soviet theory and experience, capitalism can regain some lost positions, even though it cannot reverse the general trend of history. An important concern of Soviet theory is the consolidation of gains so as to preclude such reversals. Consolidation takes time, so that the "final victory" of socialism in the Soviet Union was not proclaimed until the Twenty-first Congress of the Communist Party of the Soviet Union in 1959, twenty-three years after the country was declared a "socialist state."

In the Soviet view, capitalist resurgence is not merely a theoretical possibility; actual cases have occurred. Until 1947, Communist parties were represented in governmental coalitions in Italy and France, but Western policy stiffened. Instead of progress towards "peoples' democracies," Western Europe has witnessed the military and economic consolidation of capitalism.

The problem of maintaining gains won in the underdeveloped world is only part of a larger Soviet problem. The Soviet Union is unquestionably in a better military position than it was ten years ago. Now, it is a power with an intercontinental military capability, whereas formerly it could only exert pressure outwards from its borders. But this improved position is costly to maintain. It is expensive to be a member of the same military club as the United States.

Many foreign and Soviet observers agree that in the Soviet Union a moderate but unmistakable optimism about the future has supplanted the widespread apathy of Stalin's day. Improved popular morale is considered a necessity for the rise in labor productivity on which Soviet plans are based. The new atmosphere of hope derives from the relaxation of police controls and increased attention to the production of consumer goods. Soviet successes in science are, understandably, a cause for self-congratulation, but like consumer goods they cost money. Soviet leaders are constantly facing choices among economic goals, and decisions about maintaining one or another of the gains already made. What is the political cost of a reduction in the urban standard of living? Will resources diverted from some sector of the economy really stimulate the peasants to greater production by increasing their share of its rewards? How much economic assistance should be given to foreign countries, and how should that quantity be divided among socialist and non-socialist countries? What gains can be maintained even if investment does not continue, and what gains may be lost without continued expenditures? This is the background against which policy toward the underdeveloped world is discussed in the Soviet Union.

A powerful motive in the formulation of Soviet policies toward developing countries is, as we have seen, the consolidation of the gains believed to arise from the decline of colonialism. The policy followed is largely pre-emptive, in that its success is measured in terms of opportunities denied to the capitalist world rather than gains for Communism. It is for this reason that Soviet military aid has so often been added to economic loans. Soviet sales of modern military equipment to Afghanistan, Indonesia, Egypt, and Cuba have the common purpose of further separating these countries from the United States and its allies. Military aid to Afghanistan intensifies bad relations with Pakistan over Pushtoonistan. Arms sales to Indonesia were expected to give the Indonesians the wherewithal for a military conflict with the Dutch over western New Guinea, a conflict that fortunately did not materialize. Military assistance to Egypt was intended to decrease Nasser's dependence on England and France, and it emboldened him to attack Western interests in the Middle East.

The direct role of Soviet military aid in preventing new countries from improving relations with older capitalist countries is not often mentioned, but the very size of Soviet arms sales (probably almost as large as the economic loans) testifies to their importance in Soviet planning. Soviet writers prefer to describe how the might of the Soviet Union protects new countries: "The imperialist powers now cannot have recourse to large colonial ventures without meeting the most determined opposition of the united forces of socialism . . . and without the threat of plunging the whole world into the bloodbath of a new world war."[1] "Now the world system of socialism has come forward as a guarantor of the national independence of the young sovereign states."[2] This reassurance is also repeated by a Latin American Communist: "The support of the Soviet Union . . . can serve as a shield for the independence of even quite small countries and can make the imperialists refrain from aggressive plans and local counter-revolutionary wars."[3]

Military aid is only part of the first stage of Soviet policy toward underdeveloped countries. It is intended to help them hold the ring against imperialist intervention while indigenous social forces proceed to make irreversible social changes. How to induce such changes is the most discussed topic in the pages of Soviet books and articles devoted to the developing countries. Must the new countries go from pre-capitalist relationships, through capitalism, to socialism, or can the capitalist stage be compressed or even sometimes skipped? And what are the opportunities open to the Soviet Union to influence this process?

The generally accepted Soviet theory is well known: State capitalism in underdeveloped countries is objectively a progressive phenomenon, because it strengthens the economic independence of new countries and thereby makes their independence genuine, rather than formal. State capitalism is essentially the program of the bourgeoisie of the new countries, but it can create the conditions for the transition to socialism even though that is not the purpose of the bourgeoisie. This theory is familiar enough: help the newer and weaker bourgeois forces against the old entrenched ones, because the latter are the major enemy and the former are open to socialist influence once the centers of capitalism are weakened or destroyed. This policy, proposed by Lenin in 1920, failed in its application to the Turkey of Mustapha Kemal and the China of

Chiang Kai-shek in the nineteen twenties, but as Soviet writers never tire of repeating, the nineteen sixties are not the nineteen twenties and the balance of forces has changed. It will not be as easy, they say, for present-day leaders who accept Soviet military and/or economic aid to turn on their benefactors and ally themselves with capitalism.

The validity of this simple assertion, however, has been questioned by other Soviet writers on the following grounds:

1. State capitalism in the underdeveloped countries has led to more and not less foreign investment, and somewhat surprisingly the capitalists are not rushing to re-establish their power over these countries by thrusting capital upon the new leaders. On the contrary, the initiative for capitalist investment comes from the new countries themselves.

2. Soviet loans cannot fully meet the needs of the new countries for capital, and the latter will have to rely, at least in part, on Western capital if they are to advance.

3. The growth of the state sector of the economy in the new countries increases rather than decreases the size of the private sector.

4. Native capital can only be accumulated at the expense of the local population, whose well-being is thereby decreased.

5. In many cases the national bourgeoisie is regressive rather than progressive.

6. The forced development of heavy industry is not necessarily the best policy. More emphasis might be placed on increasing labor productivity, which in underdeveloped countries means more attention to light industry.

7. The so-called socialism of the national bourgeoisie is a sham, and more harmful than helpful.

Let us examine these criticisms of present-day Soviet policy in some detail before proceeding to an examination of alternative policies.

Many Soviet writers have noted that state capitalism in underdeveloped countries has been characterized by an increase in foreign investment. One pair of writers on state capitalism in Asia reveal that they had expected the leaders of new countries to have got rid of foreign firms, but found they had not done so.[4] Another writer gave details on the same tendency in India, the size and importance of which have made it the most thoroughly analyzed of the underdeveloped countries. Between 1948 and 1959, foreign capital in India increased from 2,558 million rupees to 6,107 million, that is, 2.3 times. Such a sharp increase in foreign investment, wrote the Soviet analyst, "accelerates the tempo of the development of capitalism" and increases the exploitation of the workers.[5]

Soviet writers have devoted a good deal of attention to the recent phenomenon of mixed companies. Their opinions on how far such companies are truly independent vary somewhat, but the author of the most ambitious monograph on the subject has concluded that only in a minority of cases do the underdeveloped countries play a dominant role in mixed companies.[6]

Only a minority of Soviet writers emphasize the growth of foreign investment in the underdeveloped countries, as in the passages just cited. The prevailing tendency is to dwell on the expansion of the state sector without mentioning the concomitant increase in foreign investment. This selectivity conveys the impression that events are moving in the direction desired by the Soviet Union.

Although the direct statement that foreign investment is increasing is made only occasionally, the fact is often implied by the treatment commonly accorded to the American aid policy of recent years. Soviet writers have given their country credit for much of the American aid by arguing that the favorable terms offered by the Soviet Union have forced the United States to follow the Soviet example of giving aid to state-owned enterprises. Thus far, the Soviet writers have argued that American aid to the state sector of the underdeveloped economies will hasten the advent of socialism in those countries. If this were true, it would mean that the Soviet example had forced the more economically powerful capitalist countries to act against their own long-range interests in the effort to maintain a foothold in the new countries. It is equally possible, of course, that the Soviet Union is acting against its long-range interests in expending resources to maintain its newly won position in countries that may become capitalist and even friendly to the West. It is also possible that the competitive Soviet-American effort is not giving either side a significant political advantage, but is effective primarily in bringing benefits to the emergent nations. If this is true, and remains so, then Soviet policy will have failed because its goal is the ultimate extension of Communism rather than the development of viable non-Communist national states.

The second in our list of Soviet arguments against current Soviet

policy reflects a realization of the obvious: Soviet aid and loans cannot begin to meet the needs of the new countries. One set of writers presents the argument quite unequivocally:

> The creation of a developed modern economy demands great capital
> investments and not a single underdeveloped country can manage
> with its own means alone. There are only two foreign sources [of
> capital]: cooperating with the socialist camp or inviting private and
> state capital from the countries of the capitalist system. And al-
> though it is conceivable that some countries can establish a program
> of economic reconstruction almost exclusively on the basis of in-
> ternal resources and Soviet aid, in a majority of cases the countries
> that have entered the path of liquidating backwardness still require
> foreign capital (in one form or another and in greater or lesser
> measure).[7]

As a consequence of this analysis, the authors feared that the newly
won independence of many African states would be threatened,
and that the new middle classes would become the prey of foreign
monopolies.[8]

Some Soviet writers have also revised the classic Marxist view
that capitalist nations force their investments on industrially weaker
nations because the returns are larger. As a matter of fact, they
now point out, American investment in underdeveloped countries
has lagged far behind investments in Europe where the rate of
return is much lower. The uncertainty of conditions in the new
countries and the possibility of expropriation by the state has dis-
couraged the investment of foreign capital.[9]

Here, then, is a gloomy prospect for the orthodox Soviet intellectual. The new countries need foreign capital to enter upon the
path of political development, but the capitalists, far from aiding
in their own ultimate defeat out of short-sighted greed, refuse to
invest unless returns and risks are brought into balance.

A third disappointment voiced by some Soviet writers concerns
the relationship between public and private enterprise in the emergent countries. The general expectation had been that the development of state capitalism would reduce the sphere of activity and
the amount of private capital invested in the new countries. Presumably this would help in the transition to socialism because there
would be no capitalist *class* opposed to socialization, but rather a
state bureaucratic machinery that would suffer no loss in the transition. Yet even in the more "progressive" states, the growth of state

capitalism is accompanied by the development of privately invested capital.[10]

A fourth complaint against economic policies in the underdeveloped countries is that capital is accumulated at the expense of the masses. This complaint reflects a more general disillusionment. It was Marx who emphasized that the bourgeoisie accumulated capital by exploiting labor; yet the Soviet Union has followed their example. It is embarrassing to recognize this truth. But Soviet writers have found fault with the corresponding policies in underdeveloped countries. Here are some examples: "The general character of the goal cannot hide the fact that the methods for the development of the economy are chosen by the governments of the non-socialist countries above all in the interests of the bourgeoisie and at the expense of the toiling masses."[11] One article is quite explicit on the subject:

> *However, this mobilization of resources* [for state capitalism] *is accomplished basically at the expense of the toiling classes whose standard of living has hardly risen since the winning of political independence. . . .* In the sphere of agriculture, as was noted above, radical agrarian reforms have not been undertaken, and to this day the landowner and usurer are masters in the villages of India, Iraq, Morocco, and other liberated countries, not to speak of the Philippines, Pakistan, or Turkey.[12]

Even in Indonesia, where the Communist Party is important, the leading Communist detects the same tendency, although he phrases his thought more tactfully:

> The basic condition for avoiding the capitalist path of development is the struggle of the working class, the mass of people and the general democratic movement. In addition the national bourgeoisie, in the interests of the whole nation, should also "make sacrifices" but these will be modest "sacrifices" in comparison with those borne by the toilers.[13]

A fifth apprehension expressed by some Soviet writers concerns the basic character of the bourgeoisie in the underdeveloped countries. Just as many in the West fear that state ownership of a sector of the economy will lead to socialism, so many in the Soviet Union fear that private ownership of part of the economy may lead to capitalism. One writer warns that "the national bourgeoisie in the last analysis pursues its own class goals which are radically different from the goals of the toilers."[14]

Other analysts have noted that the Indian bourgeois groups in the Congress Party promote the interests of the rich, and that within the bourgeoisie the conservative landholding classes are more powerful than the presumably more progressive industrial bourgeoisie.[15]

Another source of Soviet dissatisfaction with the national bourgeoisie in the new countries is the rough treatment accorded to local Communists. Soviet complaints on this score have often been muted, because Moscow's policy gives priority to the anti-imperialist role of the national bourgeoisie in the new countries and relegates the support and protection of local Communists to second place. "Even now," writes a Soviet authority, "in a majority of the liberated countries, the Communist parties are in the underground. Is that right? No, certainly not."[16] But the same writer, following current Soviet policy, does not suggest that toleration of local Communists be made a condition for Soviet diplomatic, military, or economic aid.

The sixth topic of debate is the priority hitherto accorded to the development of heavy industry. The classical Marxian idea was that colonies provided raw materials for the metropolis which converted them into manufactured goods and thereby profited greatly. Even when the colony achieved political independence, a single-crop economy would make it totally dependent on the world market price and thus prolong its economic servitude. The only escape from this disadvantageous position was the development of native industry. Soviet theorists have stressed not light industry, which is best suited to the processing of the natural products available in most underdeveloped countries, but heavy industry, partly one suspects, because the latter has been the basis of Soviet development and partly because many leaders in new countries prefer it to light industry.

As one Soviet writer points out, this policy creates inefficiency. Underdeveloped countries that import machinery at high prices and at the same time spend 30 per cent of their import budgets on food and textiles (Ghana and the former Belgian Congo), or 25 per cent for textiles while exporting cotton (Uganda), or 17 per cent for the import of food (Egypt) could do better if they improved the productivity of labor in agriculture and light industry. The whole economy would advance faster if the emphasis were on improving the productivity of labor in general, rather than on heavy industry per se.[17]

Since peasant proprietorship is so popular as an objective of agrarian reform and so widespread in the newly independent countries, investment in agriculture in most countries would mean narrowing the state sector rather than widening it. The Soviet debaters are aware that the differences in their views have important practical consequences. The argument about heavy industry produced the following rare instance of open disagreement with an article in the official journal of the Communist Party:

> Comrade G. Shmidt, of the Moscow State University, spoke against the interpretation of the question of economic independence given by Comrade Ul'ianovskii in the magazine *Kommunist* for January, 1962. He considers it incorrect to put forth economic independence as the most immediate economic task and as the basic political slogan of the progressive elements in a number of underdeveloped countries. The basic slogan that mobilizes the masses in the struggle with imperialism in his opinion should be the democratic solution of the agrarian question.[18]

Shmidt's view is quite opposed to Ul'ianovskii's. If the immediate objective of the newly liberated countries is economic independence, then the national bourgeoisie should be encouraged to build the state sector and heavy industry. But if the most immediate task is the solution of the agrarian question, land reform is the order of the day, and in most countries this means conflict with the bourgeoisie.

Another striking instance of divergent views on this subject was furnished by a symposium in the September issue of *Kommunist*, the chief organ of the Communist Party of the Soviet Union. One contribution to the symposium was entitled: "The Peoples Are Against the Capitalist Path." The one immediately following was called: "The Progressive Role of the State Sector."[19] The former article argued that the newly independent countries "would require centuries to close the gap in . . . industrial development" even if the present rate of development were slightly increased. It followed that it was "impossible to move forward without going [directly] toward socialism." The author of the second contribution, while admitting that the state sector of the economy played a progressive role in some newly independent countries and a regressive role in others, generally approved of the state sector because it was anti-imperialist and because it was an intermediate step on the path to socialism.

The seventh objection to orthodox policy toward underdeveloped countries, unlike the first six, has now become the official line, more or less. At one time, Soviet commentators were pleased when the leaders of new countries stated that their goal was socialism, even though it was realized that something quite different from Soviet socialism was meant. The following is a sample:

> The leading figures of many of the liberated countries speak of social-ism. Naturally, socialism in the conception of the bourgeois and petty bourgeois leaders of the liberated countries is not identical, and is often opposed, to the Marxist-Leninist concept of socialism. But it is characteristic that already today a leader wishing to win popular sympathy cannot but come out with a recognition of socialism as the path ensuring the development of the country to national inde-pendence. . . . This is the banner of the times.[20]

Today, however, the general Soviet view is that these socialist slogans are harmful, because socialism cannot be built until the national democratic revolution is completed. To pretend that so-cialism has arrived, says the head of the Indonesian Communist Party, "discredits socialism in the eyes of the people."[21] One pair of writers complains that many of the national bourgeoisie who call their programs socialist are really interested in a more rapid develop-ment of capitalism. They want to stifle the growth of the class con-sciousness of the toilers.[22]

If national bourgeois "socialism" is unacceptable, what are the alternatives? Soviet analysts offer two. The first is to skip the capi-talist stage in countries where the bourgeoisie is largely unformed; the second is the policy of national democracy, of which Cuba is the prime example.

Soviet writers like to point to the examples of Mongolia and the Central Asian republics to demonstrate that it is possible to skip a historical stage in the development of a society from pre-capitalism to socialism. But the analogy is imperfect because in the Soviet Union, and to a lesser extent in Mongolia, Soviet control over eco-nomic and political life was complete, while in new countries dis-tant from the Soviet Union control is far from complete.

The most frequently mentioned candidates for a rapid transition are Ghana, Guinea, and Mali. What little foreign investment exists in these countries is under strict control; local capitalism is poorly developed; in Guinea and Mali there is no private property in land. Hence state capitalism can change to socialism with a minimum of difficulty, provided comprehensive Soviet aid is sent.

Soviet writers have noted that in some of the new African states "hundreds of thousands of people build roads, bridges, dams, schools, etc., without pay." The new states use this method because they are short of funds, explain the Soviet commentators. Presumably, since this use of labor is devoted to the transition to socialism, it cannot be compared to the exploitation of the masses of which the bourgeois circles in less "progressive" developing states are accused.[23]

The attraction for the Soviets of paying attention to the smallest and least developed countries is understandable. Even comprehensive aid could be relatively inexpensive, and the political pay-off could be a new socialist state. At the same time, investment in countries with well-developed middle classes seems to promise only modest gains and may even lead to the consolidation of capitalism. The small countries seem to offer the possibility of spectacular success at cut prices.

Small states without a middle class are put in the same category as national democratic states, but interestingly enough the concept of national democracy arises as a result of experience in Cuba, a country that had until recently an important middle class. We have the word of a Soviet authority that this was so. "The idea of national state democracy advanced by the Communists and the workers' parties is not the fruit of ratiocination in offices; life itself gave it birth."[24] The inactivity of the Cuban Communist Party in the early stages of the Castro revolt is strong evidence that the Soviet leaders misjudged the potential strength of the 26th of July movement. In other words, the success of the Castro movement was a windfall on which the Communists did not count, but which they have been glad enough to accept. The acceptance was cautious for a long time, because it was feared that Castro might betray the true revolution. As an important Soviet writer on the new countries has put it:

> The experience of the development of the Cuban revolution has shown that the representatives of the radical petty bourgeoisie, in the course of the development of the real national revolution, [may] come over to the positions of the working class and socialism, and enter the ranks of the active fighters for the socialist reconstruction of society, but it is also possible that there will be cases of the betrayal of the interests of the toilers, temporary retreats and withdrawal from the further development of the revolution.[25]

This statement and others have made clear that the Soviet Union is pursuing the policy of promoting national democracy with a full knowledge of the risks involved. The magazine *Kommunist,* the major organ of the Communist Party, published some sobering comments on the Cuban affair. The head of the Uruguayan Communist Party insisted that the Cuban revolution was not a model for Latin America. "It would be a mistake to think that the clocks all over the continent are sounding the same hour." "We do not want to force the leading body of a whole continent, the inhabitants of which number more than 200 million, and sometimes speak in different languages, into the Procrustean bed of a prepared pattern."[26]

One can readily understand why a Latin American Communist leader should not want as the model for Latin America a revolution in which the local Communist Party played a far from glorious role. Although Soviet leaders worried for a time that Castro might betray them, they gradually increased their confidence in him and at one point even tried to convert Cuba into a strategic military base. Soviet leaders also hoped that the Castro movement might become a genuine Communist movement—even if Cuban Communism was not completely subservient to Moscow's dictates.

If this should happen, it would be a turning point in the history of Communism. Many middle-class individuals all over the world have become Communists; in fact it appears that an important part of the leadership of Communist parties comes from this class. But no non-Communist political party has ever before transformed itself into a Communist Party. Professor Vernon Aspaturian has suggested that the new middle classes in the underdeveloped countries furnish the Communists better opportunities for this kind of conversion than traditional middle classes, since the former often possess little or no property.[27] The intelligentsia of the new countries are largely persons with skills to offer rather than property to protect. (Nasser, the professional soldier, Castro, the lawyer, are prototypes of this class.) If and when their countries become Communist, neither they nor their associates need suffer much materially, and they may hope to consolidate and extend their political position. Thus other local nationalists besides Castro may find it in their interest to turn Communist, especially if their countries are far distant from the centers of Communist control, but Soviet acceptance of this new breed of Communists is not so simple a matter.

Every movement that aspires to universality faces the problem of the dilution of faith. When the early Christian church consented to absorb various elements of paganism it spread rapidly, because converts, at least in the first generation, had to make few important accommodations. Are the Soviet leaders prepared to accept as Communist a large number of local parties with policies that diverge in important aspects from those of traditional Communism or conflict with current Soviet aims? If Communism is diluted, it may be easier to swallow, but are Soviet leaders prepared to spread the faith at the cost of political control?

Perhaps the Soviet leaders have not faced the problem in these bare terms, but the trend of events now forces them to do so. Recent Soviet discussions indicate that the Soviet leaders will try to get on good terms with any nationalist leaders who might become candidates for conversion. Soviet writers now point to the opportunities missed in 1952 in Egypt and in 1953 in Iran. In Iran, the Tudeh Party fought against imperialism and against Mossadegh, and as a result Mossadegh failed. In Egypt, too, an incorrect analysis was made. The general Soviet opinion was that Nasser would not go any farther than Mustapha Kemal in Turkey.[28] In Iran, the opportunity missed was that of detaching a state from the Western alliance system; in Egypt, that of influencing Nasser's domestic policy.

Transition to the Soviet brand of socialism is difficult when the local Communist Party is proscribed and when the national leader maintains that he is already a socialist. The lesson that the Soviets seem to have learned is to cooperate with any revolutionary movement in underdeveloped countries until it shows hostility to Moscow. There is always enough time for the Soviet Union to abandon a nationalist leader, but the right moment for joining him may slip by unnoticed and beyond the possibility of recovery.

The conclusions to be drawn from the Soviet writings quoted above are necessarily tentative. It seems unlikely that the Soviet Union will undertake any large new commitments to extend economic aid to underdeveloped countries that have not so far received such help. It may reduce its commitment to Egypt after completing the much publicized Aswan High Dam. If Moscow heeds the questioning voices now being raised in the U.S.S.R., its tendency may well be to concentrate its assistance on rather small and backward countries where modest investments can produce political changes favorable to the extension of Soviet power.

Some Factors in the Communist View of Neutrality

—MASAO ONOE

The metamorphosis under Khrushchev of the Soviet approach to neutrality and the "neutralist" world has produced a seeming paradox. On the one hand, the Soviet leader praises and actively courts the neutralists in the expanding "third world" between the capitalist West and the socialist bloc. On the other, he restates the basic premise of Communist ideology that "there can be no neutrals" in the struggle between capitalism and Communism. The paradox is deceptive. Khrushchev is accommodating to the realities of the "neutralism" that for the developing nations of Asia and Africa has emerged as the answer to the problem of survival in a world dominated by the hostile confrontation of the Western and Communist blocs. It is an accommodation that in no way disavows a world view premised on a struggle between capitalism and Communism in which Communism will inevitably triumph. And Khrushchev has been at pains to restate his dedication to this premise in the face of Chinese Communist charges that his trafficking with bourgeois elements in the neutralist states, like his coexistence with the West, dilutes the Communist struggle and betrays the cause of revolution.

Neutrality, Coexistence, and Communist Theory

Soviet recognition of the neutralist world as a major force to be reckoned with in the formulation of Communist strategy and tactics is broadly related to Khrushchev's view of coexistence between Communism and capitalism as a more or less long-term proposition. China's Mao, in objecting to what Khrushchev advances as a "creative" adaptation of Marxism-Leninism to the contemporary era, finds ready-made arguments in the scriptures of Lenin and Stalin. These scriptures were written at a time when neutralism was not a significant political force; and the Lenin-Stalin view of co-existence as no more than a brief pause in a no-quarter struggle between capitalism and Communism made the notion of an emergent third world between the two hardly credible.

A brief look at what Lenin, Stalin, Mao, and Khrushchev have said on the matter of coexistence and neutrality will shed some light on the differences—and will bring out, at the same time, the underlying continuity in their thinking.

LENIN'S VIEW

Lenin expressed his contempt for the notions of coexistence and neutralism with a baldness that has been intentionally disguised in recent Soviet propaganda aimed at the non-aligned world. Animated by the expectancy that world revolution was close at hand, Lenin's thinking gave short shrift to both coexistence and the problem of neutralism in the "era of imperialism." After the Bolshevik revolution, Lenin clung to Marx's theory of simultaneous world revolution and regarded it as unthinkable that the Soviet regime, born of the revolution and completely isolated, could exist in harmony with the capitalist powers. He expounded his views on this point repeatedly in the aftermath of the Bolshevik victory. At the Seventh Congress of the Russian Communist Party in March, 1918, the first congress after the Revolution, Lenin said:

> We are living not only in a state, but in a system of states, and the existence of the Soviet Republic side by side with imperialist states for a long time is unthinkable. One or the other must triumph in the end. And before that end comes, a series of frightful clashes between the Soviet Republic and the bourgeois states is inevitable.[1]

And in the autumn of 1920, when the Soviet regime was successfully emerging from civil war and intervention by Western powers at home:

> Now we have moved from war to peace. But it should not be forgotten that war will visit us frequently. As long as capitalism and socialism remain, we cannot live in peace. In the end, one or the other will triumph—a funeral dirge will be sung either over the Soviet Republic or over world capitalism.[2]

Lenin's views on this score were shared by Trotsky, Bukharin, and all the other leaders of the Russian Revolution. The notion of a third path, a path midway between Communism and capitalism and committed to neither, was inconceivable in a world on the brink of revolution. The outlook of the revolutionists stemmed less from an assessment of the realities of the world situation immediately after the Russian Revolution than from basic assumptions about revolution and class struggle. Lenin flatly asserted that there could be no neutrality at any stage of class struggle: "Any kind of propaganda of neutralism is either a hypocritical cover for counterrevolution or an appearance of complete unconsciousness. . . . The idea of neutralism is nothing but a mistaken and contemptible pretext."[3]

STALIN'S VIEW

Stalin's writings were no less adamant on the subject of neutrality. They did, however, contain the first real formulations of a Communist doctrine of "peaceful coexistence" vis-à-vis the non-Communist world. Stalin introduced the concept of peaceful coexistence between Communism and capitalism as a temporary truce—a measure of expediency at a time when the long-awaited revolutions had failed to materialize in Western Europe. He recognized the realities of the situation in his concepts of "socialism in one country" and "capitalist encirclement." And it was in this period that his first use of the term "peaceful coexistence" occurred. In his report to the Eleventh Party Congress, in December, 1925, Stalin announced that "a temporary balance of power" between Communism and capitalism had emerged. "This," he said, "put an end to the war against socialism and gave rise to a period of 'peaceful coexistence.'" His emphasis was clearly on the "temporary."

It was evident from the outset that Stalin's concept of coexistence in no way implied indulgence of neutralism. At the Eighteenth Party Congress, in March, 1939, Stalin lashed out at neutralism as an attitude that "connives at aggression and unleashes war." It represented an impermissible passiveness that set out "not to prevent the aggressors from doing evil things." The Great Soviet Encyclopedia published on March 3, 1939, expanded on the theme:

> Neutrality, in the epoch of imperialism, in the practice of mutual relations of capitalist states, has been transformed into a form of special, unarmed participation in war. . . . The position of neutrality in the contemporary imperialist system is, under all conditions, not only a dangerous illusion that does not to any extent really prevent the neutral state from being drawn into war, but is, indeed, a

connivance with aggression and a factor stimulating the unleashing of war.

MAO'S VIEW

Mao Tse-tung's outlook closely parallels Stalin's. In his *Lun Jen-Min Min-Chu Chuan-Cheng (On the People's Democratic Dictatorship)*, issued in July, 1947, Mao categorically rejected "the illusion of the third path":

> You lean to one side. Exactly. To lean to one side is the lesson taught us by the forty years of experience of Sun Yat-sen and the twenty-eight years of experience of the Communist Party. We firmly believe that, in order to attain and consolidate victory, we must lean to one side. In the light of the forty years and the twenty-eight years of experience, the Chinese people either lean to the side of imperialism or to the side of socialism. There is no exception to this rule. To sit on the fence is impossible, and there is no third path. We oppose the Chiang Kai-shek reactionary clique, which leans to the side of imperialism. We also oppose the illusion of the third path. Not only in China, but in the whole world, one leans without exception to the side of imperialism or to the side of socialism. Neutrality is a hoax. The third path does not exist.

Mao's view is rooted in the theory of a world-wide class struggle that by its nature precludes non-alignment except as a transient and illusory phenomenon. As early as 1926, Mao wrote in his *Chung-Kuo She-Hui Ko Chieh-Chi Ti Fen-Hsi (An Analysis of the Various Classes of Chinese Society)* of the inevitable eventual line-up of all the "classes in between" with either the oppressed or the oppressors. There was no middle ground:

> The present world situation is a situation where the two forces, the revolutionary and the antirevolutionary, are engaged in their final struggle. These two forces unfold two big banners: On one side is the big red revolutionary banner raised high by the Third International and signaling all the oppressed classes of the world to assemble thereunder; on the other side is the big white antirevolutionary banner raised high by the League of Nations and signaling all the antirevolutionary elements of the world to assemble thereunder. Those classes in between must undergo rapid disintegration, scampering perhaps to the left to join the revolutionary faction or perhaps to the right to join the antirevolutionary faction. There is no spare "independent" ground for them.[4]

The Chinese Party's view has remained essentially unaltered. It was reiterated in characteristic form in an article by Mao originally published in the Chinese Party theoretical journal *Red Flag* and reprinted in *Pravda* on April 2, 1959:

> All political forces must decide the question: either to break their ties with imperialism, rely upon the forces of the popular masses and mobilize them, enter into alliance with socialist countries and all anti-imperialist forces of the world in order to make possible the achievement of the final victory in the struggle against imperialists, or to fear or suppress the forces of the popular masses, to have a hostile attitude toward the socialist countries and all anti-imperialist forces, and by such a course to become inevitably criminals, traitors to the national interests.[5]

The Soviet Party under Khrushchev has no quarrel with this formulation in principle. Its misgivings relate to heavy-handed application of the theory in practical policy. And it should be kept in mind that Mao's own uncompromising statement of the issue in doctrinal terms is not always exactly reflected in Communist China's practice in its relations with the non-aligned countries. The rulers in Peking exercise discretion when it serves their interests. They have provided economic aid to some of the non-aligned countries, insofar as they have been able, and have sought assiduously to match and outdo the Soviets in posing as champions of the anti-colonialism of the new nations. The inflexible, doctrinaire nature of their approach, compared to Moscow's, manifests itself primarily in a tendency to put greater emphasis on proselytizing radical groups within these countries rather than on cultivating good relations with their governments. It is perhaps to Khrushchev's willingness to court the "bourgeois" regimes in the new nations that the Chinese take the strongest exception.

KHRUSHCHEV'S VIEW

Molotov and the Chinese Communists stand on firm ground in charging Khrushchev with fraudulently attributing his peaceful coexistence line to Lenin, whose writings in fact offer virtually no support for it. Current Soviet expositions of the coexistence concept make this painfully evident in the paucity of actual quotations from Lenin on the subject. Similarly, Lenin's writings contain little that could be mustered in support of Khrushchev's approach to the "bourgeois" regimes of neutralist states.

Khrushchev treats coexistence as something more than a series of brief interludes in a succession of major Communist-capitalist wars leading to final Communist victory. The nuclear facts of life, the new vitality of the West since World War II, a vitality unforeseen in Lenin's day, and the general failure of Communist revolutions in the former colonial regions after the war appear to be among the principal factors that have underlain the evolution of the concept of coexistence. Under Khrushchev it has become a concept of long-term accommodation in a more or less permanent nuclear stalemate. Despite the bitter Chinese Communist complaints, however, Khrushchev's approach in no way dispenses with the Marxist-Leninist view of a final Communist-capitalist death struggle: for Khrushchev, peaceful coexistence boils down to class war conducted by means short of unleashing a nuclear holocaust in the camps of *both* antagonists. Answering Chinese charges that he has renounced the class struggle, Khrushchev stated his case succinctly—to cite one good example—in his speech to the Supreme Soviet on December 12, 1962: "It does not pay us, the people who are building Communism and our brothers who are creating socialism, to die either with or without music. We must bring the cause of Communism to the final victory."

On the score of neutralism, Khrushchev's proffer of aid and support to the neutralist states no more implies support of the *doctrine* of neutralism than it implies acceptance of the "third world" as a *permanent* feature of the world scene. Mao's real complaint is that Khrushchev's policies go too far in backing potentially or actually hostile non-Communist regimes. Khrushchev, viewing the exploitation of the neutralist regimes as eminently useful in the struggle against the West, regards a frontal attack on any of them as, in most cases, both foolhardy and unproductive or positively harmful at the present stage. The considerations involved in his approach are tactical. In no sense do they imply a repudiation of Lenin's basic conviction that neutralism can have no permanent future. In the final analysis Lenin, Stalin, Mao, and Khrushchev are in agreement in the fundamental belief that neutralism, like coexistence, is a phenomenon that will pass away in a Communized world.

Neutrality, Neutralization, and Communist Tactics

Rejecting the concept of neutrality, the Communists manifest a remarkably clear-sighted appreciation of the practical value of neutralization as a tactic under appropriate circumstances. Indeed, it was Lenin who firmly established the tactic of "neutralizing" middle-of-the-road forces in order to facilitate the liquidation of the main enemy. Lenin theorized that "after the victory of the proletariat in the towns," "the bourgeois strata which are the direct and determined enemy of the revolutionary proletariat" would engage in "all the sorts of manifestations of resistance and sabotage as well as direct armed actions of a counter-revolutionary character." Thus he prescribed the following tactics to be used toward the small and middle peasants in the struggle against the "kulaks," or "big" peasants:

> The revolutionary proletariat cannot set itself the task—at least not in the immediate future and in the initial period of the dictatorship of the proletariat—of winning over this stratum, but must confine itself to the task of neutralizing it, i.e., making it neutral in the struggle between the proletariat and the bourgeoisie. Vacillations of this stratum between these two forces are inevitable; and in the beginning of the new epoch, in developed capitalist countries, its main trend will be toward the bourgeoisie. . . . The victorious proletariat will directly improve the position of this stratum by abolishing rent and mortgage. In the majority of capitalist countries the proletarian state should not immediately abolish private property completely; at all events, it guarantees both the small and the middle peasantry not only the preservation of their plots of land, but also the enlargement of the latter by the addition of the total area they usually rented (abolition of rent). The combination of measures of this kind with a ruthless struggle against the bourgeoisie fully guarantees the success of the policy of neutralization.[6]

It goes without saying that after the elimination of the "big peasants" the small and medium peasantry, also members of the enemy bourgeois class, would be the next target of the agrarian revolution.

Neutralization as a tactic in class struggle has been extended repeatedly by the Soviet Union into the foreign policy sphere. It has been employed more often as a tactic for defense of the Soviet Union's own security than as a means of attack on its enemies. But Khrushchev in effect has also transferred the Leninist technique of neutralizing potentially hostile class elements to the international plane. Certainly a major objective of his policies toward the non-aligned world is to keep it neutralized while he presses the struggle against the main enemy, the capitalist West.

In its primarily defensive application in the period prior to World War II, when Soviet diplomacy was preoccupied with protecting the Kremlin's weak international position, the tactic of neutralization was well illustrated by the Soviet policy toward the Baltic states. On September 28, 1926, the Soviet Union concluded a treaty of friendship and neutrality with Lithuania. The treaty, the first pact of neutrality ever signed by the Soviet Union, provided that in the event one of the contracting parties was attacked by a third power, the other contracting party would remain neutral. It further provided that neither party would join in any alliance of third powers designed to impose economic or financial sanctions against the other.

The Soviet Union then signed similar treaties with other small neighboring countries, including a pact with Latvia on March 9, 1927. What happened to these treaties? The pacts of "neutrality" later developed into treaties of "non-aggression." But when the German attack on Poland in September, 1939, precipitated the war in Europe, the Soviet Union took advantage of the German preoccupation with Western Europe and, after invoking the secret protocol of the Nazi-Soviet non-aggression pact signed on August 23, 1939, annexed the three Baltic states by the summer of 1940.

Post-war Soviet documents justify the annexation of the Baltic states on the basis of the need at the time to build Soviet defense lines against anticipated German attacks. The Soviet explanation is evidently partly genuine. But abandoning the policy embodied in the Soviet pacts with these small powers was purely an exercise in *Realpolitik*. The Kremlin redefined its defensive needs in accord with its expanding military power. It signed the pacts when its military posture was weak and all it could hope to attain was assurance that the Baltic states would remain neutral in case of an attack on the Soviet Union. When its military power reached the necessary level, it showed no compunctions about liquidating the independent existence of these small powers, and by so doing eliminating the danger that they might succumb to the pressure of third powers hostile to the U.S.S.R. The original neutralization of the Baltic states had served its tactical, temporal objectives, and neutralization gave way to Communization.

The remarks of French Academician Professor Pierre Cot, published in *Pravda* on October 3, 1951, are illuminating in this connection:

In the struggle between war and peace and between freedom and slavery, there is absolutely no room for a neutral stand. But in the

struggle for peace, the practical value of neutralism cannot be ignored, for if Western countries should adopt neutralism as their policy, they will drop out of the North Atlantic Treaty Organization,
which in the Soviet view is a system for a new world war.

THE IMPLICATIONS FOR JAPAN

The persistent pressure put on Japan to adopt a neutral policy
at the time of the revision of the Japan–U.S. security treaty in the
autumn of 1960 is a good example of Moscow's tactic of neutralization. The Soviet efforts to neutralize Japan were blatantly calculated to alienate Japan from the Western alliance. But the majority of the Japanese knew that the Soviet Union could scarcely be
expected to respect the neutrality it proposed for Japan once she
had turned away from the United States and adopted a neutral
course. They knew that they could expect the Soviet Union and
Communist China to exert even greater efforts and greater pressure
on Japan to force her into their orbit. They could look both to the
history of Soviet behavior and the immutable essence of Communist doctrine. Neutrality, in the Communist view, can only be a
steppingstone.

The Japanese, of course, recall that Japan and the Soviet Union
signed a treaty of neutrality on April 13, 1941. And the Soviet declaration of war on Japan on August 8, 1945, while the treaty was
still in force, is fresh in their memories. For Japan, courted in the
post-war world by the Soviets on the one side and the Chinese
Communists on the other, this lesson in history can hardly be over-
emphasized. While the Soviet Communists recognize the existence
of the "third world" between the Communist and capitalist camps,
they do so only because they see in that world a means of tipping
the balance of power against the West. In the final analysis, the
Communists will not and cannot recognize the neutral path in any
genuine sense of the word. The "destruction of capitalism" and the
final world-wide victory of Communism remain their overriding
objectives, enshrined in the new Soviet Communist Party program
—Moscow's Communist Manifesto for the contemporary era—and
held today with no less vigor than in the days of Lenin and Stalin.

TWO

NEW NATIONS IN TRANSITION

Notes on Democracy and Leadership in the New Afro-Asian States

I

The contemporary world is afflicted by a sense of crisis. While societies undergoing major changes have experienced the same feeling in the past, seldom has it spread so far and wide among diverse cultures and political communities. It colors political thought and practice in today's world both on the domestic and international planes. However defined, it is generally thought to transcend any single community.[1]

The awareness of crisis involves general recognition that at the very moment modern technology and organization make the vision of "One World" seem viable, the most formidable forces make it seem illusory. We are confronted with a world rent by ideological conflict and endangered by nuclear-armed superpowers facing one another in hostile array. The risk of war and civil war is ever-present. At the moment Western rational thought had expected nationalism to fade away, an exuberant new nationalism has burst forth in the non-Western world. And, finally, when the idea of democratic self-government appears to have won the high ground in the new countries, partisan conflict and ideological combat have put the very meaning and assumptions of democracy to a new test. Where the model of Western democracy had been unchallenged as the way to political emancipation, now the rival Soviet model is fervently promoted as the answer to the developing nation's problems at home and abroad.

The Soviets not only claim that the U.S.S.R. provides the model for the new country in transition to modernity but assert that their ideology both explains the contemporary world crisis and provides its ultimate solution. In this connection, they offer a series of familiar propositions that have been elaborated since the Twentieth Congress of the CPSU in 1956.[2]

First of all, "the principal result of the progressive development of our epoch" is declared to be the formation of the bloc of Communist states—"the world socialist system." According to the Soviets, this "system's" feats of industrialization and collectivization exert a powerful influence on the rest of the world and provide it with the model of the future.

Secondly, the rise of this "socialist system" as a world force is represented as a key factor in the collapse of the colonial system. The post-colonial states of Afro-Asia—saddled with a "colonialist" legacy of poverty and distress—have embarked upon a continuing revolutionary process. This process is carried forward by "national liberation" movements that at the present stage are passing through "national bourgeois" revolutions.

Thirdly, the camp of "capitalism-imperialism"—the seat of the contemporary crisis—is suffering a general decline under the impact of "the socialist and national liberation revolutions, the growth of a world socialist system and the disintegration of the colonial system." According to the Soviet argument, the "capitalist camp" led by the United States struggles vainly against these trends, which constitute an overreaching revolutionary process and confirm Lenin's prognosis of imperialism's decay. Altogether, this signifies that the world's balance of forces is tipping in favor of the "camp of socialism" and against the forces of imperialism. Stalin's concepts of "capitalist encirclement" and the inevitability of imperialist wars are now superseded by ringing affirmations of "peaceful coexistence." In the present Soviet outlook, peaceful coexistence is depicted as the best method of conducting the world-wide class struggle toward its current goal, which is to channel the "national liberation movements" toward the next stage of the revolutionary process. By a ruthless inner logic, Soviet doctrine excludes any conception of a more stable world or any solution of the contemporary crisis that is not linked to the continuous extension of its own hegemony. "Meanwhile," to use the apt comment of François Bondy, "the relation to states which still hold themselves aloof from this hegemony and thus from the true order, is called 'co-existence.'" In addition, the manifestly provisional nature of co-existence is underscored by Soviet support for "little" wars of national liberation as a part of the general pattern of revolutionary transition—a line that at present corresponds with the insistence of some Afro-Asian leaders that the goals of the new nationalisms must not be sacrificed for the sake of a "static peace."[3]

Finally, the Soviets have propounded the concept of the "national democratic state" as an appropriate transitional regime for the new states. Essentially, a "national democracy" must be non-aligned and free from Western ties; it resists Western "neo-colonialism" and severs or reduces remaining links with the West; it must not use "dictatorial and despotic methods" against any group (i.e., particularly Communists), and secures its economic and political independence through industrialization and agrarian reform under state auspices. The concept is clearly a compromise formula envisaging Communist cooperation with nationalist regimes and enabling Communists to pursue their revolutionary aims openly in the new states.[4]

Obviously, certain elements of the Soviet diagnosis have a core of truth—though the theme of internal disintegration in the West is the least plausible. Despite the serious internal strains and divisions in the Soviet bloc, the massive growth of Soviet power and influence, Soviet feats of technological and military prowess, and Soviet industrial growth have enhanced the appeals of Communism and of the Soviet pattern of economic development in Afro-Asia. These appeals appear to be particularly influential among those Afro-Asians who, in the name of anti-colonialism, welcome any diminution of the stature and prestige of the Western powers. In addition, the "dynamic" concept of the "national democracy" with its stress on a continuing revolutionary process neatly ties in with the wide demand for rapid change in Afro-Asia. However, the concept's implicit demand that nationalist leaderships eventually share power with the local Communists already appears somewhat unrealistic—a point the Chinese Communists have raised in their dispute with the Soviets.

The national leaderships of most Afro-Asian countries are unlikely wittingly to help in the preparation of their own downfall by entering into the fateful associations explicitly assigned to them. Most Afro-Asian leaders can be expected to share Kwame Nkrumah's sentiment expressed a decade ago. He then said that he and his party would not allow "Russian masters" to replace the "British masters" or permit the substitution of "one imperialism for another" in his country.[5]

No less than the Soviets, the West also has become generally aware of the crucial import of the post-colonial emergence of Afro-

Asia in this period of world crisis. Despite real disagreements between those Western powers that have ruled significant colonial empires and those that have not, all recognize that the colonial revolution and its aftermath will profoundly affect the political and social environment of the West itself. In addition, the Western powers have generally demonstrated their determination to give real assistance to the new states in the solution of their pressing problems of transition.

In contrast to the Soviet approach, Western spokesmen of the open society are reluctant to present the new states with prefabricated political models for their adoption. The closest approach to such a model is perhaps embodied in a report made to the U.S. Senate in 1960 by a group of American scholars.[6] The report cautiously asserts that "a gradual consensus" about the American interest in the future of the transitional societies is emerging. The report defines this interest as seeing that the new states:

1. Maintain effective independence, especially of powers hostile or potentially hostile to the United States.

2. Do not resort to violence in their relations with other states. The development of modern weapons has made the outbreak of violence anywhere in the world exceedingly dangerous for all nations, especially because of the opportunities it opens for intervention by Communist or other extremist powers.

3. Maintain effective and orderly government internally without resort to totalitarian controls. The effort to impose rigid controls is likely to produce tensions within a society which cannot indefinitely be contained. Our interest therefore lies in the emergence of institutions for the wielding and transfer of power by consent of major groups; this is essentially what we mean by the creation of 'democratic' forms of government.

4. Are capable of progressively meeting the aspirations of all major classes of their people. This is a condition which must be met if the first three objectives are to have much chance of realization.

5. Are willing to cooperate in those measures of international economic, political, and social control necessary to the functioning of an interdependent world community.

6. Accept the principles of an open society whose members are encouraged to exchange ideas, goods, values, and experience with the rest of the world.

We believe that nothing in this set of American interests need be in any way inconsistent with the legitimate interests of the people of any independent nation, and that these shared interests can be advanced only by mutual understanding and effort.[7]

These propositions, in a sense the obverse of the Soviets' "national democracy,"[8] clearly rest on Western concern with a peaceful international order, and on the assumption that the give and take of a responsive and responsible democratic system can prevent the eruption of conflict within and without. And it sees a partial answer to the contemporary crisis in the creation of "open societies" by the young nations—societies likely to contribute to the formation of an open, freely communicating world order. Needless to say, the actual characteristics of the emergent nations' initial political institutions were more the result of a special set of historical circumstances than of a careful weighing of political alternatives.

II

As Asian and African societies emerged from colonial dependency, they tended to accept the general validity of representative democracy, typically in the parliamentary form. The first generation of intellectual leaders of the new nationalist movements were primarily under the influence of a liberal form of nationalism. The next generation was, however, increasingly under the spell of Marxian socialism, although without necessarily feeling compelled to relinquish the liberal heritage. Altogether, two factors seemed to count most heavily in determining the character of the post-colonial constitutions. There was the actual "availability" of parliamentary systems including, especially in the case of former British possessions, practical though limited preparation for instituting such systems. Coupled with this, the indigenous intellectuals often possessed a fairly intimate if bookish familiarity with the record of parliamentary government.[9] In addition, there was the well-nigh universal acceptance of the idea of democracy as the basis of legitimate government. Raymond Aron was deeply impressed by this when he wrote after a meeting with representatives of the Afro-Asian states:

Apparently almost everybody wants to have representative government and public liberty, everybody wants elections and parliaments. (Even the Russians, as the Afro-Asians shrewdly noted, profess these same values.) Is this only, as in hypocrisy, the tribute paid by illiberal vice to liberal virtue? But . . . what other principle of legitimacy does there exist? Ours is a world in which the grand principle of self-determination has somehow become absolute. The other possible principles of legitimacy seem all to be dead and obsolete. . . . Military regimes nowadays present themselves in terms of temporary expediency . . . we were all brought back to the awareness that even when our elections and parties and parliaments (old as well as new) were not working too well, a fiction had still desperately to be upheld. Existing power needs to be justified. To be elected democratically would seem to be the greatest justification. I suspect that there is some fundamental link between the dynamism of modern society and the principle of self-determination.[10]

Since the attainment of independence by many former colonies, a new element has entered the developing situation. After the first years of experience with democratic institutions, disillusionment has become widespread in a great many of the newly independent Afro-Asian countries. Rupert Emerson wrote some years ago, in a study of representative government in Southeast Asia:

The record of representative institutions and of large-scale sustained economic and social advance among non-European peoples is a surprisingly meager and barren one, lending little encouragement to the naïve belief that all that is needed to bring democracy and prosperity is to put an end to colonialism.

And he went on to suggest that in apparently comparable areas of Asia, the Middle East and Latin America, "the adoption of democratic constitutions has not prevented the actual drift of governments in the direction of dictatorship or oligarchy."[11]

Both the Western governments and the Soviet Government have, each in their particular fashion, been impressed by the international implications of the drift away from democracy and of domestic instability in the new societies. In the West, the hope was raised that the support of economic development would help create the social environment essential to a viable democratic system. Needless to say the trend of events also roused emotional responses. Thus some observers contended in effect that the old colonial authoritarians were quite right in maintaining that democracy or fully representative government was clearly unworkable under Asian or African conditions. It also led to a considerable amount of soul-searching on the part of those responsible for Western policy as to what really constituted the relationship between economic aid, economic growth, and political development in various societies—and hence to a greater realization that not only the problems of economic, but also those of political development in the Afro-Asian world required far more careful study than they had hitherto received.

In response to the widely acknowledged need for a more refined understanding of the problems of democracy in non-Western environments, Western scholars in the social sciences have in recent years devoted increasing attention to the phenomena of political change in societies undergoing transition in a period of international crisis and uncertainty.

In the last few years, this reappraisal has coincided with the breathtakingly rapid addition of a large number of new African states to the international community. At the same time, the emergence of certain African political leaders, keenly aware of the relevance of the Asian experience and of the complexity of the problem before them, has both extended our range of vision and emphasized the need for further study. For example, Sir Abubakar Tafawa Balewa of Nigeria has expressed a theme often raised by the African leaders in this way:

> With the failure of parliamentary democracy in many newly independent countries, it has become fashionable for a school of political philosophers to assert, sometimes with an air of superiority, and often with that of finality, that democracy cannot be exported. . . . Some . . . even assert that the African or the Asiatic [sic] is basically authoritarian and dictatorial. It would seem that these philosophers do not appreciate the difference between the failure of parliamentary democracy on the one hand and the failure of democracy on the other; the Westminster brand of democracy, or what has been referred to as "cricket" democracy, is one method of ensuring democracy as a form of government. If that method fails, another might succeed. . . . The failure of parliamentary democracy in a newly independent country should therefore be regarded as a temporary aberration rather than as a permanent deviation from the democratic ideal.[12]

The question of the meaning of democracy is again with us. The controversy over the concept of democracy is an old one, but today it is complicated by the fact that democracy is universally conceived to be a virtue in itself. This is clearly demonstrated by the way in which it is praised on both sides of the Iron Curtain. In this case, such verbal agreement clearly spells basic disagreement about meaning.[13]

However, for the purpose of this paper, it is important to recall that, in the eighteenth and nineteenth centuries in the West, the achievement of constitutional democracy involved revolutionary processes by which power was transferred from older oligarchies to wider social groups, primarily in the middle classes; while political leadership shifted to new men, acting in behalf of those groups. Fundamentally, the process involved broadening the base of power and, in varying degrees, surrounding its exercise with suitable restraints. It aspired to a shared sense of community and a certain agreement on ultimate values and goals, much of which nationalism would provide or facilitate. It resulted in a pattern of settled, formalized procedures. These included the freely competitive participation of citizens and groups in the political process, the legitimizing of decisions by the majority vote, and the operation of regularized restraints upon authority.

One approach to the problems involved in the transfer of democratic institutions to non-Western societies is to argue that democracy in the accepted sense is so deeply rooted in the long social, economic, and cultural tradition of Western communities that it can hardly be dissociated from that matrix. And there are some obvious European national experiences—such as those of Germany, Italy, Spain, or even France—to suggest that much in the failures or misadventures of democracy is attributable to cultural variations. It is not tenable, however, to presuppose that some societies may be culturally incompatible with democracy, especially if we bear in mind the distinction between the functions and aspirations of democracy on the one hand and its armory of evolved practices, such as the "Westminster model," on the other. Tacitly assuming such a distinction, it has been suggested that considerable significance may be attached to the character and duration of the tutelary relationship between the former imperial authorities and the former colony; that, "although democracy is antithetical to imperialism, the short-term prolongation of an enlightened and liberal imperial rule may sometimes increase the long-term prospects for democracy."[14]

Granting all this, it is well to remember that some of the very assumptions, practices and devices of "classical" democratic politics have been subjected to increasing criticism by certain Western students who are mainly concerned with the Western experience. They find all the more reason, when turning to the problems of the new Afro-Asian countries, to stress that it is the broad purposes and functions of democracy, rather than any particular set of techniques, that are fundamental. One such writer even claimed recently that "the constitutional techniques, traditions, and standards of the Old World are largely irrelevant to the novel problems of the New Africa. Sovereignty, the concentration of force, the delineation of territorial boundaries, the streamlining of jurisdictions, and all the other paraphernalia of the nation-state are already hampering the healthy evolution of the very political systems with and around which they grew up. This is true even of some of the most cherished of Western institutions, like the parliamentary opposition as an instrument for enforcing a government's accountability and protecting the rights of minorities . . ."[15] It may be objected that the writer rather overstates his case here; in dealing with Africa, he is perhaps too much influenced by the special conditions following upon independence. Even now, we may assume that such matters as "sovereignty" (which is closely related to certain manifestations of national self-esteem), or boundaries, let alone the much more immediately relevant question of the presence of an opposition of some kind, cannot be so easily passed off as culture-bound phenomena. His call for constitutional experimentation and innovation is unexceptionable, and clearly many African and Asian leaders are in agreement with it.

One of them, President Ayub Khan of Pakistan, set forth some time ago certain pragmatic criteria for what he expected would be a truly indigenous adaptation of democracy to the special circumstances of Pakistan. His view of the prerequisites for the success of any democratic system in his country was as follows:

1. It should be simple to understand, easy to work with and cheap to sustain.

2. It should put to the voter only such questions as he can answer in the light of his own personal knowledge and understanding without external prompting.

3. It should ensure the effective participation of all citizens in the affairs of the country up to the level of their individual horizon and intellectual calibre.

4. It should be able to produce reasonably strong and stable governments.[16]

Whether the recently proclaimed Pakistan constitution will in practice comply with these rational criteria remains to be seen.

One modern analytic approach to the problem seeks to demonstrate a calculable relationship between certain non-political prerequisites and democratic patterns.[17] Seymour Lipset set out to determine whether he could establish, on quantitative grounds, correlations between certain socio-economic factors and selected aspects of a democratic system. He used selected indices of economic development as a basis for comparing Western European and Latin American democracies and dictatorships. His efforts were carried further by James Coleman[18] who gathered appropriate data on African and Asian countries. Thus, he employed such criteria as wealth, urbanization, education and industrialization "to examine the relationship between economic development . . . [and] political competitiveness—an essential attribute of democracy." Broadly speaking, he concluded that if countries are grouped according to "major differentiating categories of competitiveness," using "mean scores of economic development," a major correlation between economic development and political competition was evident. If, however, one tried to establish such a correlation for individual countries as such, the findings became rather unpredictable. Such findings suggest that economic modernization can be regarded as only one of the factors that condition political institutions and conduct. Of course, the whole question of the underlying relationship between these two spheres remains a key problem for students of politics and economics.[19]

From Coleman's findings we are, however, led to the view that the adoption and adaptation of democracy form one aspect of the complex problems of modernization in a traditional society. It is a fact of fundamental importance (which modern social scientists have learned from the work of social anthropologists and sociologists) that all societies, however tradition-bound they may appear, are at all times undergoing change. The rate and type of change, of course, varies according to the society, the time, and the particular aspect of its culture under consideration. Just how deliberate political change affects and is affected by a given social system poses crucial questions. In this connection, David Apter recently presented in a highly suggestive essay interpretations of certain pertinent findings from his studies of the political systems of the Ashanti in Ghana and the Buganda in Uganda.[20] He distinguishes between two kinds of traditionalism, one described as "instrumental," the other, somewhat infelicitously, as "consummatory." He designates as instrumental systems those, like that of the Buganda, that "can innovate easily by spreading the blanket of tradition upon change itself. . . . Such systems can innovate without appearing to alter their social institutions fundamentally." They are hierarchic—those in authority are the established interpreters of the tradition. Hence the system is as adaptable as they will allow, except for its basic structure. The ruling authority cannot be challenged without grave consequences. In a "consummatory" system, such as that of the Ashanti, society, state, and authority are all part of "an elaborately sustained high-solidarity system in which religion as a cognitive guide is persuasive. Such systems have been hostile to innovation . . ." Since, in a society of the latter type, one finds great resistance to change, political change produces new social groupings, outside and beyond the old ones, which gradually decline. Clearly, a society of this type will respond to innovations caused by democratic practices with deep social dislocations and tensions. As traditional groupings are impaired, the loyalties of their members decline. New social organizations are needed to which they may turn. This need may be satisfied by some of the new functional groupings, such as unions or parties, that come in the wake of change. As Apter puts it, the effect of innovation in Ashanti society in Ghana was actually "cultural withdrawal which prepared the ground for mass nationalism in Ghana after the Second World War." Adherence to the emerging new national party, the Convention People's Party, was one response: it brought "a new coherence to Ghana as a national society." Yet, insofar as this traditional society refused to adapt to innovations, the rising mass party became the most obvious manifestation of modernization. The party became a direct challenge to the traditional society and to its continued ability to present itself as *the* authority. The resultant enmity between the modernizing and the traditional groups allowed little room for compromise. This deep-seated enmity also blocked the possibility of any fundamental consensus between these groups. Hence, the continued existence of the traditional society in a coherent form appears as a real threat to the national integration of the community, and consequently to the chances of establishing a national consensus and of creating a democracy.

We may conclude that, when the values and practices of the innovating democracy confront a society of the "consummatory" type, an aggressive political organization is likely to appear that will for some time continue to regard the traditional forces as the enemy—and will in turn derive a growing sense of unity and of mission from this confrontation. Some students of the politics of Southeast Asia[21] have stressed the fact that, in certain areas at least, the Communist Party's strongest appeal has been its provision of new loyalties and a sense of community for men who have become alienated from their traditional attachments. Doubtless, it is especially this aspect of social and cultural transition that makes the characteristics of available political alternatives a matter of crucial importance.

In the case of the Buganda, the traditional autocracy of their society has shown an impressive capacity to absorb innovation of all kinds—except the crucial political one that involves questioning or jeopardizing authority itself. Here, the type of political modernization that looks to the establishment of a democratic system would appear to have no chance, except, one may assume, after total destruction of the traditional order. (In the actual political situation, the integrity of the system has for the present been salvaged; while retaining its hierarchic structure, it has become part of the federal system of Uganda.)

To be sure, Apter's construction has been somewhat over-simplified here. Whatever its specific validity or broader applicability, however, his analysis illuminates the importance of a more sophisticated understanding of the changing social structures of diverse cultures by those concerned with political development in Afro-Asian societies.

III

As one views the experience of the newer Asian and African states, it is clear that only a very few of them have thus far evolved political systems substantially in accord with the Western democratic models to which so many had turned. Nor is this surprising, when one considers the magnitude of the task of nation-building in traditional societies that are experiencing grave dislocations, intensified by the so-called "revolution of rising expectations" and the high priority assigned to accelerated economic development. The most crucial problems for the early stage of these young nations have quite characteristically been those of national consolidation, internal order, and security, and the promotion of welfare on an expanding economic foundation, all of which are interdependent and interacting.

Some political scientists, interested in an orderly classification of contemporary governmental patterns, propose to describe the majority of the new nations as either "tutelary democracies" or "modernizing oligarchies," terms the aptness of which may be questioned by others.[22] In the former type of state, which is commonly equipped with the formal paraphernalia of Western democracy (from broad suffrage to representative legislature), the executive wields effective power, typically supported by a dominant nationalist party (with considerable variations in the relationship between the government bureaucracy and the party). Their ruling elite is normally imbued with democratic values and a strong zeal for modernization.

In the "modernizing oligarchy," parties are relegated to an inferior role (and may even be eliminated, as was until recently the case in Pakistan). The substance of authority rests in the executive or the military, or both. The ruling elite, which may or may not be animated by democratic values, regards modernization as the principal goal; this naturally leads to an overriding concern with governmental efficiency and economic development, and strong reactions against such practices as corruption and nepotism.

Such tentative categories are useful, even though their application must depend greatly on the appraisal of the available evidence. Characteristically, they are based upon an analysis more concerned with political forces than legal forms, and seek to link political relationships with the process of change. They also affirm that the rise of pre-eminent nationalist parties, often with autocratic tendencies, is a key phenomenon in the political development of a large number of new Afro-Asian states. As one student of African affairs has put it: "the nationalist party and the national hero" emerge from the struggle for independence as "two major instruments of integration."[23]

The new leaders, whatever their differences of personal style, power, or social background may be, are, in many cases, the same men who, as inspiring and successful agitators, led their nationalist revolutionary movements to victory. But the consolidation of the new societies demands considerably more than the agitator. A few of the new leaders may assume the manner and function of the calmly deliberate national leader who rises above partisanship, an image of stable authority in an unstable community. It is perhaps no accident that this particular style is especially well embodied in Sir Abubakar Tafawa Balewa of Nigeria, a leader who was never himself the leader of a national mass party. A recent newspaper comment described him as one who, although of humble birth

> . . . is the image of an aristocratic leader in a demagogic age. He is more of a statesman. . . . [He] rules, or tries to rule, a people already trained by colonialists to achieve objectives by agitation. Sir Abubakar rules this bunch by sheer aristocratic personality. The sad truth . . . is that the people have been used to the worship of agitators. . . . We aren't yet as 'tamed' and are more hooliganistic than Sir Abubakar would have wished.[24]

The outstanding figures who were the leaders of mass movements in the process of liberation have often become "sources rather than . . . executors of power and policy."[25] As a consequence, their leadership in many instances retains an intensely personal, charismatic character that defies the careful differentiation of governmental roles and jurisdictions regarded as normal in contemporary Western constitutional systems. This may have both objective and subjective implications. Thus, it was critically observed, a few years ago, that Kwame Nkrumah's role as Prime Minister had "not been sufficiently depersonalized," that the Prime Minister still carried

> a mystique of public morality, not only in the eyes of his followers but also in his own eyes as well. He personally is indeed the symbol of Ghana, of anti-imperialism, of self-government, of freedom, and, in certain respects, he regards the state of Ghana as his own creation and an extension of his own personality and life.

Whatever their self-image may turn out to be, such leaders are national symbols, and it is questionable whether the outside critic is in a position to urge such a "depersonalization" of their institutional functions.

These leaders are promoters and engineers of national unity and hence frequently and characteristically masters of the spoken word. It means that they are builders of a national unity that as yet exists only as an aspiration on the part of those of the population who are fully capable of envisaging it. This has been part of the special role of the Westernized intelligentsia to which Asian leaders like Nehru and a majority of today's African leaders belong. They have become guardians of an often still precarious national independence. Can they themselves be necessarily immune to the very crisis of modernization that they seek to control and direct? Some of them may well be afflicted with the psychological insecurities that are part of a social system in transition, and hence hampered in the task they have assumed.[26] As a defense against the insecurities of the world crisis, a policy of non-alignment has characteristically been adopted by the popular leaders of new states. To range themselves on the side of the West, that is, on the side of former colonialist countries, can readily appear to imperil independence and, in some cases, to be a politically unwise challenge to the sensibilities of rising non-Westernized elites in some of their own communities. On the other hand, it is most relevant to their domestic policies that some form of socialism has been a normal part of the outlook of the Westernized intelligentsia to which they belong. Marxian socialism provided them during their formative years with a sharply defined interpretation and condemnation of the colonial system; it also opened up generous vistas for the remodeling of societies from which they themselves had often become estranged.

The nationalist leaders are the principal advocates and managers of modernization. They lend the prestige of their names to the continuing attempt to provide improved welfare and economic development. Thereby, they frequently become involved in head-on encounters with the traditionalist forces in their societies. Depending on their outlook and disposition, they may at the same time be cast in the essential role of mediators between the forces of modernization and those of tradition. Here their own "embedded ambivalence,"[27] symptomatic of a state of transition among the Westernized intellectuals, may become an asset or handicap as it reflects an acceptance (and in some respects a rejection) of Western culture, coupled with a rejection (and an acceptance, in other respects) of their own traditional way of life. As politicians, they may find it necessary to make concessions or to retreat, which, in turn, is likely to antagonize those intellectuals who are politically most advanced and the radical political forces. Conceptions such as Pan-Africanism, the African personality, and *negritude*, which have played such a role in Africa for a number of years, may in this connection provide a symbolism by which some of these leaders can more readily justify modernization as a process. Modernization thus acquires a higher dignity if it can be claimed that what is essentially African and uniquely valuable in their cultures will be preserved and indeed will be raised to a higher plane of fulfillment beyond and above accidental national boundaries, in the name of some supranational solidarity.

This role of mediation may be crucially important in helping to bridge the gap between the more highly educated and urbanized social groups and the mass of the rural, predominantly agricultural population, who tend to retain their attachment to traditional ways of life and to the traditional bonds of tribe, caste, and extended kinship. The availability of such a paternal intermediary often helps to ease the strains of accelerating change. Hence, the national leader must speak, persuade, exhort, chide, and console those whom modern mass media increasingly permits him to reach "in person."

The influence and prestige of the national leaders are so highly prized that, perhaps in proportion to the regime's sense of insecurity, criticism of the leader's person or policy, subversion, or potential antagonism may all be regarded as varieties of disloyalty that justify the use of formally lawful or even unlawful acts of coercion, at times requiring legislative, administrative or judicial manipulation. It is not only African states that have such devices as preventive detention and deportation, which serve as effective weapons in the hands of the leadership and its supporting cast. The necessity for such measures was recently elaborated in a vigorous and colorful statement by Ghana's Minister of Information, Mr. Tawia Adamafio:

> Now and again we have been accused of taking strong measures against certain persons, and some of our critics have been so personally bitter as to call us all sorts of names . . . and been so naïve as to suggest that we trump up cases. . . . We have always answered . . . that the conditions obtaining in our country and our own circumstances oblige us to take these strong measures, and therefore we have a duty to ignore their ignorant criticism. We have stated that we are a young nation and we must maintain vigilance all the while in order to frustrate the plots of our enemies and detractors and defeat their machinations against us . . . [there is] abundant evidence . . . that there is subversion, intrigue and conspiracy by imperialists, colonialists and neo-colonialists and their agents to break Ghana . . . put out the flames of nationalism lit by Dr. Kwame Nkrumah, our outstanding leader, and defeat his efforts to liberate the whole of the African continent. . . . We often wonder why some of these critics are so daft as to imagine that . . . liberation suddenly . . . makes a newly independent country an exact social and political image of their own countries in spite of the differences in the conditions and circumstances of life [in such a newly independent country].[28]

Such a statement, regardless of its belligerence or use of certain ambiguous slogans, reflects important concerns of the leadership. It expresses preoccupation with the security of a new and unsettled state, makes stereotyped use of the personality cult, and shows determination not to be hampered by Western opinion.

The problems of "modernizing oligarchies" cannot be considered in this paper, except to note the symptomatic importance of military leaders in such systems. Characteristically, these men belong to a Westernized intelligentsia that until recently had appeared as a group only in the lagging societies of such non-Western and non-colonial countries as Turkey and Egypt. Unlike old-fashioned military strong men, such leaders, in seizing and retaining power, have proceeded to harness military strength and loyalties to serve ideological and political goals. They have become spearheads of nationalist and revolutionary undertakings, often bringing energy and experience in organizing to the process of modernization and social reform in their countries.

The interdependence of the roles of pre-eminent national leaders and the phenomenon of the dominant or single party has been assumed by much of the foregoing discussion. A few aspects of such party regimes may be recalled for our purpose. For Africa alone, even rudimentary statistics are eloquent. In 1961, out of twenty-five African states (excluding South Africa, Ethiopia, Libya, and Morocco) seven had only one political party with no rivals in existence; in another six, although an opposition existed, power was in the hands of a single dominant party that held all, or virtually all, seats in the representative assembly.[29] Thus in a substantial majority of new African states, one national party dominates the political system, a condition not unknown in a number of Asian countries. The Indian National Congress, the national party, is fast becoming an example; after many years of life, it is displaying symptoms of declining cohesion and vitality, although no opposition party has emerged as a genuine alternative. The dominant parties were generally founded upon the national movement that enlisted a substantial cross-section of the community in support of its struggle for national independence. Parties of this type from which the Ghanaian Convention People's Party and the Indian National Congress are notable variations, partly because of their respective ages and the character of their leadership, claim to represent their evolving national communities as a whole.

One argument in behalf of the dominant or monopolistic party has been that, in some instances, there was no genuine alternative. It is a view that at least implies the existence of emergencies. According to this concept, the states of post-colonial Africa have either tended toward one-party systems and, consequently, enjoyed stability or have experienced a "breakdown" of the party system. The breakdown leads to instability and possible military ascendency,[30] or, more importantly, to an incapacity to sustain vigorous modernization policies where political coalitions with traditional forces impede rapid progress and reforms. A supporting argument, valid only in certain circumstances, holds in effect that the dominant mass party satisfactorily fulfills the needs of a forum of opinion since it allows full and free discussion prior to the adoption of a policy by the leadership. It is remarkable, however, to hear Nkrumah and Sékou Touré spell out, by way of demonstrating their democratic preferences, the principle of "democratic centralism"[31] that has for many years been regarded as one of the universally discredited fictions of Communist Party organization. Other leaders have apparently placed a much more realistic emphasis upon the need to provide full opportunity for dissent within the framework of the dominant party, which they are inclined to envisage as a natural provisional arrangement during the first years after independence if (in the words of Sylvanus Olympio) "nearly everyone is agreed on the essentials."

What are the primary political functions of these parties? They serve as community builders, even in the most basic sense of becoming "a community for all the uprooted," in which "the sense of ritual, the art of direct discourse, the passion for solidarity" may become rekindled,[32] once again giving the people experiences of which the weakening of traditional bonds had deprived them. Parties function as catalysts to rally mass support for the process of modernization initiated by the leadership, and they serve as forums and channels of communication through which groups and individuals, local and regional bodies, may express their responses upon learning the wishes of the great leader. One might add that the advocates of such parties tend to invoke some equivalent of Rousseau's theory of the general will, reinforced by a Rousseauan faith in public rituals.

Of course, this is not to suggest that the various national mass parties display identical characteristics wherever they prevail. The extent to which their functioning allows the realization of certain basic democratic values varies from place to place. It is, however, necessary to bear in mind the priority given at this stage to the building of an effective consensus and to the reduction of entrenched traditional hierarchies in the new nations. Thus, one recent careful examination of single-party systems in West Africa[33] reached the conclusion that these mass-party systems were becoming democratic, although in varying degrees, in the sense that decisions involved general consent, respect for established procedures, and were made "in harmony with such values as social equality . . . under conditions in which opposition can be expressed." According to this writer, the parties were broadly representative; issues were publicized, and discussion stimulated. In the light of these findings, the single party may be considered a suitable political system for some multi-lingual communities, characterized by tribal-ethnic divisions and a great social distance separating the elite from the masses.

Thus the existence of separate opposition parties is regarded by some as superfluous, while others, such as Chief H. O. Davies, Léopold Senghor or Dr. Azikiwe of Nigeria, have expressed their belief in its indispensability. It may also be significant that, in certain non-Western societies, the very concept of a political opposition, which is not simply an enemy, appears to encounter serious language barriers.[34] In the Ibo language (Eastern Nigeria), we are told, it can only be rendered as the equivalent of "those who mean no good" or "those who always disagree." An election victory becomes the defeat of the smaller by the larger army, which then proceeds to impose its will upon the prostrate enemy, a conception that precludes any concern for the rights of minorities. Whether under such circumstances it is still most appropriate for a Western political scientist to urge the indispensability of an effectively formalized opposition is surely debatable.[35] Thus at a conference in Nigeria Apter insisted on its functional utility even for political systems that were operating in an atmosphere of continuing struggle and were bedeviled by the fear of factionalism, corruption, and separatism. It is likely that only those who no longer needed to be convinced were sufficiently impressed by the well-tested "classical" argument that an adequate representation of interests, truly effective information, and constructive criticism and control of the government ultimately depended on an organized opposition. Responsible and realistic African critics like Chief Davies have urged that, in the name of political and constitutional rectitude, a deliberate "extermination" of the opposition party should not proceed without an explicit popular mandate.[36]

IV

Clearly, the current is running strongly in the direction of "democracy with strong leadership," "guided democracy," or "tutelary democracy" (call it what you will) in the developing new states of the Afro-Asian world. This trend does not in itself demonstrate any special affinity with one or other of the contending political-ideological formations into which the world is divided. Julius Nyerere was recently reported to have declared:

> The people who anxiously watch to see whether we will become 'Communist' or 'Western democrats' will both be disconcerted. We do not have to be either . . . but we have the lessons of the East and the West before us, and we have our own traditions to contribute to mankind's pool of knowledge.[37]

It is a statement that not only bespeaks the self-confidence of the new national leader, it also brings out a point that has perhaps been insufficiently stressed in the current discussions.

As far as technology and economy are concerned, lagging societies today enjoy the advantages of the availability of advanced and tested knowledge and working models. Similarly, the new emergent Afro-Asian states can doubtless derive some parallel political benefits from models supplied by other countries, even though all concerned have become increasingly impressed with the problems of adapting social and political institutions.

The problem of finding suitable political forms that occurs in the new countries poses another challenge to the West. From the Afro-Asian point of view there are certain appealing aspects of Marxism-Leninism, and these are significant among the modernizing elite. Marxism-Leninism offers both an interpretation and a forecast of political development, in which politics and economics are closely connected; it is a sworn enemy of entrenched traditionalism; it justifies all means that advance the revolutionary cause; its road to salvation lies in the creation of a rational and modern industrial order; the revolutionary transformation requires a disciplined struggle under the tight direction of an elite; and it holds the image of a good society, a society worth fighting for. It is true that an increasing number of the new leaders have recognized the terrible cost exacted from a society that proposes to apply this solution. The ideological appeal of Marxism-Leninism retains importance, quite apart from any negative realities of the example of the Soviet Union or Communist China and even, as experience suggests, apart from the activities of local Communist parties. Yet the suggestion that the ideological differences between Communism and Afro-Asian revolutionary nationalism are tending to disappear, is not tenable.[38]

Clearly, if constitutional and democratic practice, buttressed by an adequate theory, is to become sufficiently workable outside the Western sphere, we can hardly afford to be satisfied with all its time-tested features. In recent years, we have begun to raise disconcertingly critical questions about certain nineteenth-century assumptions concerning Western political man. The time has come to make constitutional-democratic doctrine less culture-bound than before.[39] Challenged by the new Afro-Asian realities, we should respond with a modern democratic theory of political development and a meaningful revaluation of the requirements of a just order.

The Social and Political Role of the Intelligentsia in the New Countries

—KLAUS MEHNERT

During the last three decades, in his travels through many countries outside the industrialized areas of the world, the writer has been impressed by the fact that one element of the population exercises an influence far beyond its numerical strength. This element is the intelligentsia. The experiences accumulated in the course of these years of travel, coupled with the writer's feeling of affinity for his fellow intellectuals, have produced the following study.[1]

DEFINITION

The term "intelligentsia" is used here to denote specifically those intellectuals who are experiencing internal conflict between allegiance to traditional cultures and the influence of the modern West. Within these terms of reference it is not the amount of knowledge or education that determines membership in the intelligentsia. For the purpose of this essay, no man, no matter how learned, is classified as a member of the intelligentsia if he has retained his identity with his national background—if, for example, he is a theologian of the traditional religion, a performer in the traditional theater, a teacher of the traditional wisdom, or an artist, poet, or musician of the traditional style. As long as he remains integrated in his society and accepts the values of that society as his own, he is likely to remain essentially a conservative without that revolutionary spark which, under this definition, would class him as a member of the intelligentsia.

If, on the other hand, he is an intellectual who has felt the impact of Western civilization and has been drawn into the vortex of conflicting ideas, he enters the ranks of the intelligentsia. There have, of course, been rebels among the traditional intellectuals, but these people have usually rebelled as individuals rather than as a group. Within the intelligentsia, however, rebelliousness is a common characteristic. Beset with doubts about traditional cultural values, its members have felt a driving need to search for something new. This is what has united them and this is what has kept them united, at least as long as they have remained within the ranks of the opposition.

THE IMPACT OF THE WEST

Contact with or conquest by the West did not immediately and automatically turn the intellectuals of a country into an intelligentsia. The transformation occurred only when a conflict between the old and the new developed in their thinking. In Africa and Asia, the Western powers came as conquerors: they overwhelmed the conquered people not only with their guns, but also with their civilization. In many Asian and African nations, the majority of the population, including the intellectuals, tended at the outset to accept the rule of the West. Japan assimilated Western civilization to an extent that enabled her after a few decades to win a victory over Czarist Russia, one of the strongest military powers at the time. Other countries, such as China, tried to take from the West only the guns and the ships while preserving their age-old ways of life intact, an undertaking that proved impossible and led to national humiliation. On the whole, it appeared that the faster a nation became Westernized and the greater its success in achieving a respected position in world affairs, the less it was affected by the problem of the intelligentsia. Conversely, when conflict between the old traditions and the new values introduced from the West became prolonged and intense, an intelligentsia inevitably emerged and gained in influence.

THE "RETURNED STUDENT"

An understanding of the intelligentsia can perhaps most readily be gained by examining the case of the "returned student." In China particularly, this term has been used to denote the many thousands of young people who produced a powerful ferment within their country after their return from studies abroad. The same pattern occurred in many other countries. It did not matter whether a student had actually studied in a Western country; many took on the characteristics of the "returned student" simply after exposure to Western culture in missionary schools in their own countries. It is a fact, in any event, that the vast majority of Africans and Asians who qualify as members of the intelligentsia have been exposed in some way to Western education.

In Africa, the great majority of the present political leaders who entered politics from the ranks of the intelligentsia experienced the clash between their own traditions and those of the modern West. Some had studied in Western schools and colleges on African soil. For example, Félix Houphouet-Boigny of the Ivory Coast studied medicine at Dakar, and Julius Nyerere of Tanganyika prepared himself for the teaching profession at Makerere College in Uganda. Others had similar experiences after spending years of their student life in the West: in Paris, Léopold Sédar Senghor of Senegal and Habib Bourguiba of Tunisia; in London, Sylvanus Olympio of Togo and Sir Abubakar Tafawa Balewa and Obafemi Awolowo of Nigeria; in the United States, Hastings Kamuzu Banda of Nyasaland, Francis Nwia Kofie Kwame Nkrumah of Ghana, and Benjamin Nnamdi Azikiwe of Nigeria. In most cases, the attitude of these men toward the West has been marked by a mixture of fascination and repulsion, the negative sentiments having frequently been induced and fed by personal humiliations suffered at the hands of the white man.

These characteristics of the intelligentsia of Africa apply also to that of Asia, and even to the intellectuals of nineteenth-century Russia. When Russia was—compared with Western Europe—an underdeveloped country, her intellectuals, too, were torn between pro- and anti-Western feelings; Russia was, in fact, the country in which the phenomenon of the intelligentsia first appeared, and it was in Russia that the term "intelligentsia," in the special meaning used in this essay, had its origins.

EARLY PROBLEMS OF ADJUSTMENT

Having come to know the West, the members of the intelligentsia found it impossible to merge again completely with their original environments. The individualism and liberty of the West were all too different from the tight rules of *family, clan,* and *tribe* that they had once accepted unquestioningly. Nor could they, on the other hand, live the life of Occidentals, for the simple reason that most of them did not earn enough money to do so, and because the Occidentals usually kept aloof from them. They appeared as Westernized foreigners to their compatriots who had stayed at home and as "natives" to the Westerners. Those who married daughters of the Western country in which they had studied (the same country, in most cases, that dominated their homeland) were exposed to additional conflicts. The young wives faced serious problems of adjustment in a new environment that seemed strange and often repulsive to them and that, in turn, often rejected them. For many intellectuals the net result was disorientation, even confusion—a loss of the old values without a compensating ability to accept the new ones.

Although some intellectuals remained loyal to their *religion* (particularly if it was Islamic), many became estranged from it after joining a Christian denomination—frequently in their early years, in a mission school—or as a result of exposure to agnostic, if not atheistic, ideas in the West. Whichever way they went, some of their spiritual heritage, superstitious if not always religious, lived on in many of them, preventing them from feeling fully at home in their new belief (or disbelief). The writer recalls the troubles of a German college in China where he once taught: a building newly acquired for use as a dormitory was shunned by the students because it had been built on the site of a former cemetery and was believed to be inhabited by ghosts. Fritz Schatten tells of African students in a modern Western school using magic fountain pens to assure success in their examinations.[2]

Economic adjustment was also a problem for the members of the new intelligentsia. Ordinarily, their country was not sufficiently developed to have much use for the skills and knowledge they had acquired in the West. Unwilling to accept positions that they felt beneath the dignity of an intellectual, reluctant to go into the villages where their work was urgently needed (as teachers, for example, or agricultural advisers), they tried to eke out an existence in the cities under conditions far removed from those they had dreamed of during their student days. Their resentment against those above them grew, especially against the Westerners who occupied so many of the attractive positions in the country's economy. They were angered at the notion that foreigners, whose qualifications seemed no better than their own, should be paid more than they were.

Nor did they find it easy to accommodate to the *political* system of their country. The colonial rule of the foreign power made them feel oppressed and downtrodden, particularly after they had tasted the freedom of Western countries; and they usually regarded the native political system, on which foreign rule had been superimposed, as feudalist, reactionary, and oppressive. Those among them who had political ambitions were unhappy because of the scarcity of positions open to them in the civil service, where the best jobs were held by members of the local aristocracy, if not by foreigners.

THE TURN OF THE TIDE

Many members of the new intelligentsia thus faced, sooner or later, a profound personal crisis and a serious, often insoluble problem of adjustment. Of course, there were always some who succeeded in overcoming these difficulties. Some writers, artists, and scientists acquired reputations at home as well as abroad that saved them from the indignities endured by so many of their less successful compatriots. Others managed to reach the higher ranks of the civil service, secured honored positions, and thus developed a certain allegiance to the colonizing power. Among these people there were some who cast their lot with the foreigners, adopting the foreign manners, mannerisms, and language.

The first generations of returned students and of people who had come into contact with the West were the most likely to accept the West and its domination unquestioningly, because they were still overawed by its power, its wealth, and its intellectuality; they were impressed by a West that was still supremely confident of its superiority, its divine right to rule the world and to carry "the white man's burden." Later generations began to discover flaws and to find grounds for disillusionment. After the fratricidal disaster of World War I, the West was less sure of itself, and was rent increasingly by doubts and internal conflicts. People who had resigned themselves to being ruled by an overwhelmingly strong West began to have second thoughts after seeing the Western countries slaughter and starve each other for four long years. The outbreak of the "May Fourth Movement" of Chinese students in 1919 was an example of this reaction. The same young people who had once looked for guidance and inspiration to England, France, and—especially—America now suddenly turned against their erstwhile mentors and denounced them as evil and predatory.

Such a turn of the tide occurred, in one way or another, among the intelligentsia of most African and Asian countries. Having rebelled against the once admired West, the members of the intelligentsia could no longer return to the way of life they had rejected. Again the "May Fourth Movement" in China was symptomatic:

its young proponents were opposed in equal measure to domination by the West and to a return to the old China of Confucius. But where were these people to go if they closed the door to the West as well as to the past? This, indeed, was the big question for the new intellectuals.

THE NEW NATIONALISM

The answer was soon evident. With remarkable unanimity, the intelligentsia of Africa and Asia found its new inspiration in nationalism, a force which until then had scarcely been known in their countries. If they could not be Englishmen, Frenchmen, or Americans, they wanted to be as Chinese, as Indian, as Egyptian, or as Cuban as possible. Probably few of them realized that this nationalism, too, had its origins in the West—that it was in fact foreign to their countries, which with few exceptions were not nations in the Western sense of the word but rather conglomerations of tribes with different customs and different languages, brought together by the fortunes of colonial wars.

Nationalism, whether logically applicable or not, became the rallying cry of the intelligentsia, the mainspring of its life and thought, the most important and sometimes the sole substitute for the older values rejected or lost. Nationalism was least potent in the intelligentsia of those countries that, like Thailand, did not have to go through a violent struggle against colonial powers. Interestingly, the strongest outburst of Thai nationalism in recent years was directed not against the West but against neighboring Cambodia, with whom a quarrel arose over possession of an ancient temple situated on the Thai-Cambodian border.

POLITICAL NATIONALISM

There were many facets of the new nationalism that thus took hold of the intelligentsia and filled its need for a clear-cut aim in life. In the first place this nationalism was, of course, political. It was permeated with desire for independence and hence directed against the colonial power. But it was aimed also, in many if not most cases, against the traditional native rulers—the Maharajas, the Bao Dais, the "chefs" or chieftains—because so many of them had collaborated with the colonial power and because they obstructed the intelligentsia's rise to power. Political nationalism, coupled with the impulse toward independence, became the passion and often the profession of the intelligentsia. In countless cases, its members moved straight from school or college into the ranks of the fighters for freedom, into the open or secret independence movements and, frequently, into the prisons of the colonial power, prisons that for many of them turned out to be seats of advanced study in the field of revolutionary nationalism.

Anti-colonialism was, and often remains, the core of political nationalism. This can be observed even in countries that freed themselves from colonial rule more than a decade ago. Nationalism by definition needs a foreign opponent; and where such an opponent no longer exists in fact, he survives in the mind of the nationalist. It must be added that quite a number of the leading nationalists in the new countries have been able to rise above such feelings of enmity toward the former foreign ruler. One might well measure the stature of a political leader in a new country by his ability to be realistic and unemotional in his attitude toward the colonial power that he once fought and at whose hand he once suffered.

One peculiar form of political nationalism is that expressed in the "pan-" movements (pan-Africanism, pan-Asianism, if not pan-Afro-Asianism) among the intelligentsia in a number of countries. This is a sort of supra-nationalism, a desire not only to merge one-self into one's nation but to merge one's nation into an entire continent, and thus to multiply that nation's strength and glory by the strength and glory of neighboring countries. So far these "pan-isms" have not been too successful, even in such a relatively homogeneous area as the Arab world. More often than not, the cry for unification calls forth resentment rather than support from the neighboring states. But the sentiments of "pan-ism" exist and will undoubtedly play a considerable role in the years to come.

Despite recent setbacks, the surprising success of pan-Europeanism as reflected in the Common Market may be explained by the fact that the peoples of Europe, after two devastating world wars, have begun to outgrow their intense nationalism and are willing to relinquish some of their sovereignty in the common interest. Western Europe, recently divided by age-old antagonisms, is today in its post-nationalist era; national independence is for these countries no longer a newly acquired and therefore priceless treasure. The new Afro-Asian countries, on the other hand, are still in their age of nationalism, having only recently obtained independence after generations of struggle. In Europe, nationalism of the traditional type is to be found now only where national independence is lacking and where the presence of a foreign power is felt every day—in Poland, for example, or in Hungary.

CULTURAL NATIONALISM

There is also cultural nationalism, the desire to prove to oneself and to the West the grandeur, age, and depth of one's own civilization. In all these countries, not only in those that possessed well-known ancient treasures, part of the intelligentsia concerned itself at the outset with the rediscovery and glorification of the cultural past. Even among the most modern-minded intellectuals, whose eyes were turned toward the future, there were many who felt reassured by the thought that their country, too, had a history of its own. Treasures of the past, long of interest only to Western archaeologists, became symbols of the new nation's special personality.

In a number of countries, particularly Moslem ones, cultural nationalism also included a kind of religious nationalism, and led to a revival and intensification of religious sentiments that, many thought, symbolized part of the nation's spirit.

SOCIAL NATIONALISM

Finally, there is what might be called social nationalism. It grows out of a newly discovered feeling of closeness to "the masses." Nationalism, if strongly and sincerely felt, cannot be a matter for the intelligentsia alone; it must expand to encompass the entire nation. Those who wish to bring this state of affairs into being feel a need to know more about the masses; and once they do, they are appalled by the misery in which the people live. Hence arises the desire to change social conditions in the country.

To be sure, interest in "the masses" is for some nationalist intellectuals rather academic and sometimes no more than a pose, the masses appearing as tools to be manipulated in the game of politics. But for many others it is something very real. Writers especially play frequently on the social theme. The leading novels and essays in the China of the nineteen twenties and thirties, for example, notably those by Lu Hsun, Pa Chin, Lao She, and Mao Tun, were filled with compassion for the downtrodden. This, of course, was before these writers became Communist literary functionaries in a country where compassion toward downtrodden compatriots is no longer permissible.

SOCIALISM

The social aspect of nationalism leads us to the second strongest motive force among the intelligentsia in the new countries: socialism. As in the case of nationalism, few intellectuals give much thought to the Western origins of socialism. They have found that socialism, like nationalism, provides an explosive revolutionary force to be used against the existing order. That they should themselves feel little sympathy for capitalism is not surprising; they have experienced some of its worst features—in the slums of the big Western cities where they lived as penniless students, in the miserable *bedonvilles* that had sprung up around plantations or factories in their own countries, in the exploitation of their countrymen. Capitalism in colonial territories for a long time possessed many of those unpleasant features of early Western capitalism that impelled Marx and Engels to write *The Communist Manifesto* in 1848.

Anti-capitalist sentiments were heightened when the capital was in the hands of foreigners—not necessarily citizens of the colonial powers, sometimes even foreigners of Asian or African origin. Exploitation by the capitalist who was also a foreigner was doubly resented. This resentment was transferred also to those who, like the compradores in China, collaborated closely with Western firms. Socialist tendencies were strengthened because many young intellectuals spent their student years in the West at a time when socialism was much in vogue among their Western fellow students, particularly in the twenties and thirties of this century.

The intellectual, having little talent for a successful business career, was inclined to look upon the business class with contempt if not hostility. The one way in which it was easiest for him to envisage himself in a position in the economic life of his country was as an official in a socialized—that is, state-run—economy. There he would not feel out of place, because his would be not a business job but a governmental one. To take China once more as an example: by the second half of the nineteenth century, Chinese intellectuals who went into business were doing so in the manner of Sheng Hsuan-huai, one of the first Chinese to press for industrialization; these entrepreneurs worked in close cooperation with the government, in a relationship that the American scholar Albert Feuerwerker has aptly termed "mandarin enterprise."[3]

Finally, socialism appeared to be the only sure method for the quick industrialization of countries poor in capital and modern skills; so it seemed, at least, to many intellectuals before they realized the large problems and drawbacks of state-run—which means bureaucratic—economies.

Thus, nationalism and socialism were the two outstanding dynamic forces at work within the intelligentsia of the new countries. These forces answered the need for a "cause" and gave the intellectuals the group feeling that they craved after breaking away from the traditional groups of their youth. It is in periods of crisis that individuals wish to submerge themselves in a group in order to find fellowship and security. The nation (politically and culturally) and the people (socially) were the two super-collectives from which the new intellectuals drew the longed-for feeling of warmth and community.

The greater an individual's awareness—and an acute awareness of life is characteristic of the intelligentsia—the greater is his need to find an ultimate meaning in existence, particularly in a period when values cannot be taken for granted but must be rationalized. It is in such times as these that the thought of being superfluous is particularly painful; here one might be reminded of nineteenth-century Russia, where the ranks of the intelligentsia were swelled by people who wished precisely to escape the guilty feeling of superfluousness.

Of course, the process in countries affected by the impact of the West and by modernization was by no means uniform. There were many variations and deviations from the pattern outlined here. This brief essay seeks only to identify the main lines of development, which were more or less similar in the great majority of cases. It will suffice to single out one important exception, Japan, which modernized itself with almost unbelievable speed.

FROM OPPOSITION TO POWER

Independence once achieved, the position of the intelligentsia customarily changes completely—from an intelligentsia in opposition to an intelligentsia in power. Contrary to the contemptuous belief of many politicians that intellectuals are by nature unfit for political leadership, it is precisely from among the intelligentsia that the new political leadership has come. This happened partly because, during the struggle for independence, the intellectuals came to be regarded as genuine representatives of the people's aspirations and as the group least compromised by association with the former colonial masters. It happened also because the intellectuals had built up the political organizations—frequently clandestine—which now became the backbone of the new political structure.

The intelligentsia has been most successful in those countries where it has produced outstanding leaders who command the respect and loyalty of a majority of the people. Nehru is the best-known Asian statesman of intellectual background who has managed to retain the loyalty of the majority of the nation's intelligentsia. Mao Tse-tung, too, could be classified as a former member of the intelligentsia; but he lost the following of the intelligentsia when its members realized that his was a dictatorial regime, not a democracy.

Intellectuals are by nature liberals, if not anarchists. Having fought against oppression by the state, they did not change their attitude overnight after independence was won. It is only during national emergencies that they are willing to forego the advantages of liberty and submit to dictatorial rule. Thus, the Chinese intelligentsia accepted Mao's dictatorship during the war against Japan and during the exciting first years after the establishment of the new regime. It withdrew its support and sympathy for the Communist Party when it saw that the dictatorship was there to stay and that the intellectuals, year by year, were as a matter of principle denied even the most limited freedom of thought and expression. The Chinese intelligentsia also discovered what it might have known before, had it studied the course of the Russian Revolution and the "liquidation" of the Old Bolshevik intelligentsia by Stalin: a totalitarian regime requires not people with independent minds, but obedient functionaries, *apparatchiki* or cadres—the very opposite of intellectuals.

Just as the Chinese intellectuals failed to anticipate what was in store for them under Communism, so some intellectuals in Asian and African countries today do not realize the fundamentally anti-liberal character of this system. They toy with the idea that the establishment of a Communist regime in their country might be the proper short cut to industrialization, unaware of the price that would have to be paid in intellectual liberty. In general, however, people who think this way are exceptions. Most intellectuals in the new countries are averse to Communism, mainly because they understand that by joining the Communist camp their country would lose a good deal of its hard-won independence and stature in world affairs. Here, incidentally, lies one of the attractions of Titoism for the intelligentsia in some new countries: It seems to combine Communism with national independence.

In distinguishing between totalitarian regimes (such as in China) and authoritarian regimes (such as in Burma or Pakistan), one finds, of course, that the latter display a considerably greater tolerance toward the intelligentsia. In some countries of Africa and Asia, the intelligentsia, having enjoyed freedom for a number of years after independence, did accept authoritarian rule, often exercised by military men, once it became convinced that democracy, due to the diffusion of purpose and effort, did not work as well as had been hoped. Such acceptance of an authoritarian regime or a "guided democracy" was not always wholly voluntary; depending on the degree of force employed by the regime on the one hand, and the strength of the liberal tendencies and traditions among the intelligentsia on the other, more or less serious conflicts arose between the regime and the intelligentsia. But usually the exhilaration of independence was still strong enough to convince at least part of the country's intelligentsia of a need to cooperate with an authoritarian regime, at any rate as long as it believed the regime was bringing more advantages than disadvantages to the country. When a regime proves to be efficient in the development and strengthening of the nation, the intellectuals may be willing for a time to forego some of the freedoms of thought and speech on which they normally insist. If, on the other hand, authoritarianism seems to be solidifying into a permanent institution, the major part of the true intelligentsia will wind up in the ranks of the opposition, and perhaps even return to the underground tactics it employed in the period of its struggle for independence. In the latter case, however, it may well find that a native authoritarian regime can be even tougher and more dangerous to fight than the colonial regime ever was.

NEUTRALISM

In addition to nationalism and socialism, a third passionately held idea has arisen among the new intelligentsia. This is the concept of neutralism. The writer does not wish here to attach either positive or negative connotations to the terms "neutrality" and "neutralism." Neutrality is defined as the attitude of a country which adheres, in the manner of Sweden or Switzerland, to a policy of strict non-involvement in world power politics and concentration on its own affairs. Neutralism is defined as participation in world politics by a country or group of countries under the slogan of "active neutrality," combined with a tendency to gather other countries of similar persuasion into a "third" camp outside and between the two great power blocs. The Bandung Conference of 1955 included delegations from countries allied with one or the other of the two power blocs; the Belgrade Conference of 1961 was the first really neutralist conference: only those countries unattached to either bloc were represented.

Neutralist tendencies among the intelligentsia of the new countries are easy enough to understand. These people, overwhelmed by the magnitude of the task of modernizing their countries, do not wish to be sidetracked from this task by involvement in world power struggles, and still less by involvement in a third world war. They want to do their share in relaxing world tensions, which, in their view, stem mainly from the evils of old-style power politics; and they believe these evils must be exorcized by a superior morality. They realize also that by closing ranks they will become, if not a third force, at least more powerful than when they stood alone and that a country attached to neither bloc is likely to be wooed by both. Finally, a "third" position in the face of power conflicts is the one most congenial to many intellectuals. What intellectual has not felt the lure of "standing above" the conflicts of the world, and of feeling superior as a result?

In the West, the term intelligentsia is rarely encountered today, and in the Soviet Union it is misused by being used to classify all those who work with their minds. In the new countries, too, the word will lose its special meaning after a few more decades. By then, the intellectuals of today will have been drawn into the professions, into the day-to-day work of their country's reconstruction. They will thus have become increasingly specialized and differentiated and will thereby have given up the close fellowship of a free-floating, fighting community that has little to lose and a new nation to gain. By then, even politics will have become a career instead of a passion.

But in most new countries this is still far off. In the meantime the intelligentsia will remain the most important political group in the countries of the non-aligned world.

The Role of a Constitution in Developing Political Systems: The Nigerian Example

—KALU EZERA

"All constitutions," writes Sir Ivor Jennings, "are the heirs of the past as well as the testators of the future."[1] This statement is as true of the Asian Commonwealth countries amongst which Sir Ivor's experience mostly lay as it is of most other developing countries that have recently attained independent nationhood through constitutional means; it is particularly applicable to the states of West Africa.

One of the most spectacular developments of the twentieth century has been the constitutional transfer of political power to diverse colonial peoples—a process that has involved an unprecedented series of constitution-making experiments. Shortly after World War II, India, Pakistan, Ceylon, and Burma won their independence through constitutional means. More recently, the same process took place in Ghana, Malaya, Sudan, Nigeria, Sierra Leone, and in about a score of French-speaking African states. Most of these countries have adopted written constitutions and the main reasons for this are evident. Firstly, most of the Asian and African states were dependencies of European colonial powers such as Britain, France and Belgium. Before relinquishing power, most of the colonial powers deliberately pursued policies designed to create conditions for establishing the ultimate independence of their respective territories. Written constitutions, modeled more often than not on that of the "mother country," were promulgated. The belief in the desirability of a written constitution can, of course, be traced to the ideals and sentiments of the French Revolution, as well as to the writings of the founding fathers of the United States. The motive of the constitution makers is aptly expressed in Thomas Paine's dictum that "a government without a constitution is like power without right." Secondly, the dissolution of the Asian and African empires of Great Britain and France in many areas posed the problem of sustaining the cohesion of heterogeneous social and cultural entities formerly held together by imperial rule. In such cases, a federal constitution was adopted as a solution. Here Professor Max Beloff's shrewd observation applies: "Whereas in Asia and Africa, federalism has been thought of as a solution to the political problems of countries which had previously been held together by external imperial rule, in Europe it has been a question of bringing within a federal framework units of government hitherto separate and sovereign."[2] Thirdly, as Professor McIlwain has said: "The existing law was no sufficient guarantee of the liberty of the subject without additional constitutional sanctions . . . which conform with growth in the thinking of mankind that has made governors responsible to the law, and politically, to the governed."[3]

Of course, it must be kept in mind that constitutions with liberal and democratic content have sometimes been unscrupulously used as props of tyrannical rule. Indeed, most dictatorial and totalitarian regimes advertise some form of written constitution. However, while a constitution per se is not a guarantee of democratic government, no representative government can succeed without one, whether written or unwritten.

Governmental instability in most Latin American countries and failures of parliamentary government in most countries of Asia and Africa are not necessarily due to the inherent incapacity of their peoples for constitutional government, but to the absence in those countries of what Walter Bagehot, over a century ago, called the "prerequisites" of successful parliamentary government.

In most developing countries, the minimal economic and social basis for stable constitutional democratic government is still lacking. Professor Charles Issawi, discussing the future of democracy in the Middle East, specifies some of the factors that are generally recognized as essential before constitutional democracy becomes viable; they include an advanced level of economic development, broad distribution of wealth, industrialization, homogeneity of language and religion, general education, and the habit of cooperative association.[4] In face of the fact that annual per capita income is far less than $300 in most developing countries, it is not surprising that parliamentary democracy, the child of prosperity, does not thrive in the developing regions of the world. Yet this argument cannot be pressed too far; for a low economic level alone is

not sufficient to make parliamentary democracy impossible, otherwise, India's experiment would long ago have crumbled, instead of
being relatively successful.

THE CASE OF NIGERIA

With the foregoing considerations in mind, a look at a specific
constitutional experiment along federal lines may throw light on the
general question of the prospects for constitutionalism in the developing areas. Despite a recent setback that mars the record, Nigeria provides a "positive" example of a working constitutional system that may be useful in the investigation of the factors favoring
successful development of such a system in an emerging country.
The Nigerian example is particularly noteworthy for the following
reasons: Firstly, Nigeria is the largest African country, both in size
and population, that has joined the family of independent states as
a member of the Commonwealth. Secondly, the peaceful way in
which it reached this status and has since maintained parliamentary
government inevitably provides a model for other emergent states.
Lastly, while the country's constitutional evolution may not be
wholly unique, it stands in a class by itself in many ways; it is an
example par excellence of an African country where a federal constitution has been successfully instituted, and has provided (at least
up to the present) a solution to the political and governmental
problems of its heterogeneous society.[5]

Historically, the geographical entity now consolidated as the Nigerian state is an artificial creation of the British. Its existence was
made possible only a half century ago, when Britain conquered the
Moslem emirates of what is today Northern Nigeria and sought to
forge a single political unit out of a region inhabited by a welter of
tribes and peoples. But not until 1914, with the amalgamation of
Northern and Southern Nigeria, did the present Nigerian territory
come into existence.

The historical evolution of the country has been marked by a
succession of constitutional experiments. First, the Clifford constitution of 1922 was officially imposed and remained in effect for
nearly a quarter of a century. Second, came the Richards constitution of 1946 which first introduced the concept of "regionalism"
into a country that formerly had been ruled as a unit. Third, the
Macpherson constitution of 1951 introduced the ministerial system of government and began the evolution of a party system, at
least in the regions. Fourth, the Lyttelton constitution of 1954 es-

tablished for the first time a "true" federal system by increasing the powers of the regional governments and the legislatures relative to the central government. Lastly, two further constitutional conferences in 1957 and 1958 brought internal self-government to the regional units, and in turn led to final independence for the whole of Nigeria on October 1, 1960.

While Nigeria's initial political forms were more or less arbitrarily introduced, the emergence of Nigeria was not imposed from the outside. On the contrary, it evolved in stages as a direct result of the deliberations of the Nigerian leaders themselves at a series of constitutional conferences held both in London and Nigeria. It should, however, be noted that in these conferences, the British administration played a significant role in the examination of the types of constitution considered for Nigeria. This "godmother" role of Britain in regard to her dependencies does great credit to a country that has no firsthand familiarity with the mechanics of a federal constitution because of her unwritten constitution and her unitary and parliamentary form of government. It might be said that British policy accorded well with John Stuart Mill's plea that: "When the conditions exist for the formation of efficient and durable federal unions, the multiplication of them is always a benefit to the world."[6] There can be no doubt that British policy regarding the transfer of power, particularly in Ghana and Nigeria, was a "creative abdication of power" in which nationalism and colonialism, to a large degree, worked together in genuine partnership in the constitutional development of these countries. This, however, is not to say that no external influences or forces helped change the outlook in British colonial policy. Certainly, the Atlantic Charter, the growth of the Labour Party as a force in British politics, the emergence of dynamic nationalism in the dependent territories, the impact of the local press, and the growth of trade unionism were influential. All these and more played a part in accelerating constitutional reforms through the stimulus they gave to the demands for self-government and independence.

Since independence, Nigeria has striven to show that she abides by the letter and spirit of constitutional democracy and, indeed, she has become a showcase of parliamentary democracy in West Africa if not in the whole African continent. The reasons for this are not hard to find. Firstly, Nigerian leaders seemed determined to make a success of the experiment in parliamentary democracy and the concepts of law and justice—legacies that they as well as their counterparts in other Commonwealth countries have in the main inherited from Great Britain. Nigerian leaders have apparently developed a strong faith in the system and are dedicated to its continuance. Secondly, checks and balances built into the federal constitution make it difficult, at least for the present, for a dictator to emerge, quite apart from the fact that the deep-rooted tribal traditions of the peoples of Nigeria are inimical to tyranny. Lastly, Nigerian unity, once precarious, has been fairly stable since independence, and centripetal forces have generally been stronger than centrifugal ones. Two of Nigeria's three major political leaders (Dr. Azikiwe and Chief Awolowo) voluntarily gave up their regional domains on the eve of independence to stake their political future in the central parliament—actions that immediately removed one of the peculiar weaknesses of federalism in Nigeria. The third, the Sardauna of Sokoto Sir Ahmadu Bello, has, however, remained in his regional capital as Premier of Northern Nigeria and leader of the Northern People's Congress (NPC). His action has somewhat deflected the pull of political gravity away from Lagos, the federal capital, toward Kaduna, the Northern regional capital.

In order to appreciate the intricate problems that have arisen in the relationship between the regions and the federal government and the role of the courts in the Nigerian constitutional set-up, an understanding of the main provisions of the federal constitution is essential. Perhaps the most prominent aspect of the Nigerian constitution is its legal supremacy. The constitution's supremacy arises partly from its status as a written statement of the fundamental laws of the land and partly from the fact that the legislatures derive their powers from it. In addition, the courts are empowered to judge the constitutionality of any laws enacted by the legislatures and declare void any enactment that is deemed inconsistent with the provisions of the constitution's provisions.

As in the United States and most other federal states, the Nigerian constitution leaves a significant share of legislative authority in the hands of the regional governments. As in the Tenth Amendment of the U.S. Constitution, all powers not specifically enumerated as reserved to the central government belong to the regional governments. Also, both the federal government and the regions have "concurrent" powers to make laws pertaining to numerous subjects. This is by no means to suggest that the enumerated and concurrent powers delegated to the federal government are meager. Despite powers residing with the regions, the part played by the central government in the sphere of concurrent powers has been assuming increasingly extensive proportions, now that the central authorities are becoming bolder in exerting firm leadership. In this regard, it is important to note that the Nigerian constitution stipulates that "if any provision of the law of the federal legislature of a region is inconsistent with any provision of a law of the federal legislature which the federal legislature was competent to enact (whether federal or concurrent) . . . the federal law will prevail and the regional law will to the extent of the inconsistency be void."[7]

The constitution's catalogue of concurrent legislative powers covers no fewer than twenty-eight different fields, including such subjects as labor, higher education, industrial development, industrial and scientific research, electricity, gas and water power, insurance, and statistics. There is hardly any aspect of national industrial life on which the central government may not legislate. It should be mentioned, however, that one school of thought in Nigeria seeks to place a restrictive interpretation on concurrent federal power. The proponents of this approach contend that unless a federal law is drawn in such a way as to have "covered the field" and consequently to have rendered any regional law on that subject void, federal law cannot take precedence, as only a constitutional amendment can deprive a regional legislature of its powers to make laws.[8]

Until recently, the federal-regional relationship ran smoothly and no open friction between the central and local governments was discernible. Of late, however, a political conflict has emerged in the Western Region that poses serious constitutional issues for the Nigerian political system as a whole. Though the conflict began as an internal affair of the Western Region, it soon led to the intervention of the federal government in an effort to settle the matter. The federal government declared a state of emergency in the Western Region, and assumed full authority over the territory.

The events that led to the crisis originated within the Action Group Party, the ruling political party in the Western Region. The regional Governor removed the Premier of the Western Government, Chief Samuel Ladoke Akintola, from office following his ouster as a deputy leader by his party. Akintola refused to abide by the Governor's order, alleging that his removal was invalid since he was not allowed to verify his leadership on the floor of the regional legislature, where, he claimed, he would have obtained a vote of confidence. Accordingly, he filed a court action challenging his removal from office. In the meantime, the ruling Action Group Party successfully prevented the summoning of the regional legislature, and chose a new candidate, Alhaji D. S. Adegbenro, for Premier; he was quickly appointed by the regional governor.

The legislature, which the deposed Premier had been consistently denied the right to convoke, was then summoned to determine whether the new Premier would obtain a vote of confidence. When the regional legislature assembled on May 24, 1962, disorder and utter confusion erupted. Chairs were tossed right and left and the Speaker was pursued by supporters of the deposed Premier wielding the mace. The police had to resort to tear gas to clear the Chamber. A second attempt was made to reconvene the assembly under police guard. But this second meeting did not even begin. Pandemonium again reigned. Police again cleared the legislative Chamber with tear gas and, this time, on orders from Sir Abubakar Tafawa Balewa, Prime Minister of the Nigerian Federation, they sealed it. During these developments the deposed Premier had appealed directly to Queen Elizabeth to remove the Governor.[9]

These events led the Prime Minister of the Federation to call an emergency session of Parliament on May 29, 1962, to declare a state of emergency in Western Nigeria, and to institute emergency powers in the region including authority for the detention of persons, "restriction orders," and imposition of curfew.

The Prime Minister argued that a properly constituted government was lacking in Western Nigeria—with its two "Premiers," a governor whose authority was under challenge and a legislature in disarray. He argued therefore, that the federal government was in duty bound to restore peace, order and tranquillity in the region. Chief Awolowo, the opposition leader, argued that a state of public emergency could not be justified in Western Nigeria and warned that the federal government's action would be "a gross misuse of power" involving a violent assault on democratic institutions in Nigeria.

The emergency regulations were, however, enacted and a caretaker regional government, headed by Senator Dr. Majekodunmi, the federal Minister of Health, as Administrator, was appointed by the federal government. Restrictions were placed upon the movements of all the leading figures in the dispute, including the two rival premiers, the Action Group Party leader, the leader of the opposition in the federal Parliament and also the leader in the Western legislature of the National Council for Nigeria and the Cameroons (NCNC), which was the opposition party in the Western Region.

This unfortunate episode was the most serious test so far of Nigeria's parliamentary system. It also raised complex constitutional questions that put the constitutional functions of the court system to test.

At the time of writing, the emergency regulations have been observed without incident. The federal Supreme Court has, however, dismissed two interlocutory motions filed by the Action Group Party legal adviser and the newly appointed Premier. The court was asked to enjoin the federal government and the Administrator of Western Nigeria from restricting their activities. But judgment has been reserved indefinitely on an original motion filed by the Action Group Party challenging the constitutionality of the federal government's declaration of a state of emergency in Western Nigeria.[10] Whether the courts can significantly contribute to a resolution to the crisis in the Western Region remains to be seen.

Clearly the courts bear an important responsibility in Nigeria's political system because of their role in interpreting the constitution, as is the case in most democratic countries with federal constitutions. Indeed, the federal Supreme Court of Nigeria has already exercised its prerogative in declaring some acts of Parliament invalid.

CONSTITUTIONS AND CONSTITUENCIES

It is fair to say that the leaders of most new states have generally attempted to keep in mind the point of Balfour's statement that "Constitutions are easily copied, temperaments not; and if it should happen that the borrowed constitution and the native temperament fail to correspond, the misfit may have serious results." While the constitutional model provided by the "mother country" has, for example, been deeply influential among West African states, mechanical imitation has been more or less avoided. This has been particularly true of Nigeria and of its close neighbor, Ghana. Thus Ghana's constitutional scheme departs substantially from that of Great Britain, although retaining the unitary form. Its constitution is written—unlike Britain's—and has a presidential rather than a parliamentary executive. The president also wields wide powers combining full executive authority with titular headship of the state. The Parliament of Ghana has also discarded much of the traditional protocol characteristic of that of Great Britain. A uniquely African element of Ghana's constitution is its provision for the "surrender of sovereignty, in the interest of African unity." In the former French colonies in West Africa, as in Ghana, engagement in the movement toward African unity—expressed in the philosophy of *negritude*—is influencing the constitutional pattern. Compared to Nigeria and Ghana, however, these states were initially more deeply involved in the political system of the mother country. France had regarded them as "Overseas France" and their representatives held seats in the French National Assembly and even occupied parliamentary and ministerial posts. However, the former French colonies have not adopted the French multi-party parliamentary system, but have substituted one-party systems and the kind of strong presidential system adopted by De Gaulle in France—a solution that seeks to answer a developing country's need for clear and stable lines of political authority.

If the political systems of the West African states have on the whole shown a fair degree of viability, the glaring example of constitutional failure in Africa is of course the former Belgian Congo. It is likely to become the classic demonstration of what happens when the principles so aptly stated by Balfour are flouted. Here, in a territory of diverse cultures, tribes, and traditions, a federal solution would have seemed compelling. Yet a unitary and highly centralized governmental structure was installed with its seat in Leopoldville. That unhappy land's tragic plague of strife and civil war can in large part be traced to the original deficiencies of its constitution.

The examples of the Nigerian and Indian brands of federalism suggest the way to correct the error typified by the Congolese experience by their attempt to strike a balance between centrifugal and centripetal forces. Their concept of federalism has utilized constitutional measures to emphasize, promote, and guarantee national unity, while at the same time preserving the varied traditions, cultures and heritages of the different peoples of their countries.

But some may argue that the existence of national identity and purpose is far more critical for developing political systems than any constitutional framework or scheme as such. The experience of India and Ghana can be cited to make this point.

For a long time India was a huge and heterogeneous collection of princely states. British colonial administration attempted to weld the various peoples of India into a single entity, without much success. It was not, therefore, surprising that on the eve of Indian independence, this massive territory split in two along Moslem-Hindu lines, giving birth to the state of Pakistan. National consciousness was then woefully lacking in India, in spite of the vigorous efforts of the Indian National Congress to instil a spirit of unity among the people.

On the other hand, Ghana—a small country with peoples varying in language, cultures and traditions—was able to animate its peoples with a spirit of nationalism. Through the preachings of its leaders, like Danquah and Nkrumah, Ghanaians were made to see the need of presenting a common front against the colonial power that was the common foe. The fire of nationalism, spread by the country-wide nationalist movement led by Kwame Nkrumah, eventually forged the diverse peoples of Ghana into one nation.

Without doubt, the sense of national identity and purpose is necessary in the successful formation of a state. If this is recognized in the formation of new states, part of the foundation for a workable constitution can be laid. However, it seems apparent from the Nigerian experience that these factors can be exaggerated and the role of a sound constitution in developing a national identity underestimated.

The example of the makers of the American Constitution can be cited here. As Leland Goodrich has pointed out, the framers of the American Constitution, while creating much that was new, drew heavily on institutions and principles already present in the colonial and English backgrounds of the Americans. American experience shows how a federal constitution can be used creatively to identify and define a national sense and purpose—not from the whole cloth but from existing materials. While the builder of a state must be inspired by a vision of the future and be adept at applying new political ideas and methods, the acid test of leadership lies in his ability to build on the solid ground of the past and present.

FEDERAL CONSTITUTIONS AND NEW STATES

Where the federal solution has been employed in developing countries to cope with cultural diversity, the constitutional experts have usually relied on a fairly explicit written document including a catalogue of fundamental human rights. Their intention has been to strike a balance between the principles of liberty and authority in the structure of the state; and to keep that balance from being easily upset. Their hope has been to produce a constitution rigid enough to protect individual and minority rights and sustain the integrity of the state's components, and flexible enough to be responsive to duly constituted majorities. The constitution makers seek to establish exact and concrete provisions that provide a test and standard for official conduct and legal action. They normally design its provisions to reduce the risks and limit the application of the discretionary powers allotted governmental authorities. Often directly inspired by the American courts and their power of judicial review, they seek to create an independent judiciary that will be a jealous guardian of the constitution and of the political and civil rights defined therein.

Of course, no one argues that a written constitution—whether federal or unitary—is a sufficient guarantee of all these things. We have too many examples of constitutions that are not observed. Mussolini had no difficulty whatever in warping the written constitution of Italy to conform to his whims and caprices. In the Soviet Union today, the written constitution is completely subordinated to the Communist Party. The Presidium of the Party, mentioned nowhere in the constitution, is the most powerful ruling body in the country. Indeed, it is a law unto itself, above and beyond the constitution. Closer to home, the President of Ghana repeatedly avows fidelity to the fundamental liberties guaranteed by Ghana's constitution. But many are asking whether such avowals bear any meaning in practice. It is generally known that Ghana, despite its democratic professions, is unfortunately manifesting distinctly totalitarian tendencies and threatens to become a one-party police state.

Clearly, the restraints and inhibitions which a constitution imposes are properly observed only where the leadership of a state is dedicated to both the letter and the spirit of the constitution. Nevertheless, a tradition of observance of fundamental rights is unlikely to emerge in a country—especially one of the new countries —where they are not given some kind of constitutional expression. Expressions of good intentions alone are no safeguard. The safeguarding of the people's rights and liberties from reckless politicians and high-handed officials is likely to be a real possibility *only* when there is a constitution that defines those rights and liberties and a judiciary that courageously defends them.

CONCLUSION

It cannot be gainsaid that a constitution plays a most vital role in a developing political system. It sets legal limits to power. It defines the political responsibility of the governors to the governed. It often can act as a stimulus to national unity and stability. In times of internal crisis, the constitution has always formed a rallying point for the progressive forces of law and order. In such crises, it can be a symbol that helps restore the people's confidence and pride in the destiny and future of their country. But military coups d'état can and often have swept away the entire constitution of a country at a stroke. In ex-colonial countries, however, military juntas easily gain power only when the political leadership becomes corrupt and loses the incentive to rule with justice, honesty, and efficiency. Unfortunately, constitutions of many developing countries have been cast aside in favor of a military rule. Among these are the United Arab Republic, Sudan, Iraq, Pakistan, Burma, and Thailand. However, there are signs that the wheel may be approaching full circle. More and more military juntas have been instituting one form of constitution or another to build legal props under their governments. Thus the prospects for constitutionalism in the developing countries may be good over the long run, and it may become more and more generally recognized as essential in a modern state.

The Idea of African "Neutralism" and "Non-Alignment": An Exploratory Survey

–EDWARD W. BLYDEN, III

The espousal of "neutralism" or "non-alignment" by the African states can be traced to the Bandung Conference of Afro-Asian states in 1955. Afro-Asian neutralism or non-alignment in its barest essentials is commonly thought of as a diplomacy of non-commitment with respect to the "Great Powers," or more specifically, to the Soviet Union and the United States. Partly a response to the cold war, Bandung reflected the striving of the *nonwhite*, non-Western, nations of Asia and Africa for a common program of action in a world divided by the East-West conflict. The common purpose of the participants of the Bandung Conference was to safeguard the newly won or soon-to-be-won independence of their respective nations. Their common concern was what they conceived to be the danger of "neo-colonialism" and "neo-imperialism" from East and West.

However, if we say that the terms "neutralism" and "non-alignment" have been borrowed from Bandung it is also necessary to say that they have become "Africanized" in the course of their usage on the African continent. They have become overlaid with connotations drawn from African political thought and experience. Thus, a look at some of the key ideas and events that have formed African political thinking provides a good starting point in any effort to comprehend the meaning of neutralism and non-alignment in their African context.

AFRICAN THOUGHT AND NEUTRALISM

While Afro-Asian neutralism or non-alignment can be represented as a reaction to the cold war, the sentiments that Afro-Asians commonly attach to these concepts derive from the common experience of the former colonial peoples in their struggles for self-government and independence. For Africans, these sentiments are expressed in the goal of a politically independent and united continent completely freed from alien rule and domination and asserting itself in world affairs. Herein lies one of the main driving forces behind much of the thinking, writing, dreaming and planning of African nationalists for over a century.[1] Indeed, African use of the term neutralism or non-alignment has become closely bound up with the idea of "Africanism" or "negritude," or, more broadly, "Pan-Africanism" and with its ancillary or related themes of "African personality," "total liberation," "independence and unity" or "doctrine of Africa," and the rest. As Colin Legum aptly expresses it: "Pan-Africanism has produced a language of its own which conditions the thinking and the politics of the entire continent. . . . Emotions have been converted into ideas, and ideas into slogans."[2]

Thus, with this background of modern African political and nationalist thought, the ideas of neutralism and non-alignment in African diplomacy should not be treated simply as a reaction against the cold war, or merely as a profitable, short-term Machiavellian strategy calculated to take advantage of both East and West.

From the standpoint of current African nationalist and political thought, the motto of the *African Morning Post*—"Independent in all things, and neutral in nothing affecting the destiny of Africa"— was a prototype expression of the ideas now involved in the African concepts of "neutralism" and "non-alignment." The motto of the newspaper, which was published in Accra from 1934 to 1955, embodied what is meant by these concepts in current diplomatic usage—that is, *the avoidance of ideological, military, economic or other political entanglements with the great powers.*

The slogan was popularized throughout West Africa during the period in the nineteen thirties when the position of editor of the *Post* was held by Nnamdi Azikiwe. Then a young, unknown Nigerian journalist recently returned from study in the United States, Azikiwe was destined to emerge as the "Father of the African 'Renaissance' "[3] and, eventually, as the first African Governor General in the Commonwealth of Nations. But even at that early stage of his career when he was editor of the *African Morning Post* he had already made some scholarly contributions to American and British learned journals and periodicals on African, colonial, and related international questions. He had also published an important and ably documented treatise on Liberian politics and diplomacy.[4]

Thus, when he became editor of the *Post*—a position held only for a brief period (1935–38) before his enforced departure from what was then the Gold Coast[5]—he was highly conversant with both colonial issues in general and African political affairs in particular. He was well prepared to embark upon his crusading mission to bring about the African renaissance. Azikiwe declared at that time that: "The philosophy of The New Africa hinges itself on five bases—indispensable to its realization: 1. Spiritual Balance; 2. Social Regeneration; 3. Economic Determinism; 4. Mental Emancipation; 5. National Risorgimento";[6] Azikiwe felt it was necessary to "revolutionize African thought towards the glorification of African institutions" through a "gradual educative process" rather than by "a rigid change."[7] The scholar turned crusader, however, soon found himself pegged an "agitator" by his critics. He proudly accepted the label, saying,

> An agitator, in Colonial parlance, is equivalent to a demagogue in Western domestic politics. But both terms do not necessarily denote the same thing. . . . If there were no agitators, everything would be at a standstill. . . . Society would be stagnant. . . . Someone must challenge social injustice. Someone must rouse society from its lethargy. . . . That is why "agitators" are born. . . . If you could stir up your generation into activity in *the right direction* you should be proud to be an agitator. . . .[8]

For the next two decades and more, Azikiwe—later joined in proselytizing his nationalist, Africanist doctrine by one of his earliest disciples, Francis Kwame Nkrumah—was to wage a relentless campaign, both literary and political, to free Africa from foreign rule and promote the cause of an independent and neutral Africa in world affairs. His well-known book, *Renascent Africa*, a testament of "Africanism" and Pan-African nationalism, published by the author himself in Lagos, in 1937, contains many of the characteristic elements of contemporary African neutralism and non-alignment. In a poignant but exuberant passage discussing "Our Raison D'Etre," he exclaims:

> *"No true son or daughter of God likes to exist in a man's or a woman's shadow. . . ."* and "How can the African exist side by side with the European, the American, the Asiatic, the Australian, without thinking in terms of liberty—the right to live and to enjoy life as abundantly as do his colleagues of other continents, *"with or without their cooperation?"* he asks.[9]

It should be noted here that Azikiwe's Africanist ideas took wing in the Gold Coast, now Ghana. For nearly a century, this territory had been gradually emerging as the focal point of the African renaissance—the force at once centrifugal and centripetal that was to generate (in the mild phrase of the British Prime Minister Harold Macmillan) the "wind of change" now felt all over the continent and throughout the world.[10] Azikiwe's *Renascent Africa*, appropriately enough, was written at the Trocadero Hotel, Accra, Gold Coast, in January, 1937, though published in Lagos. Indeed, much of the book's thought and content, including its five-point "philosophy," are drawn from contemporary Gold Coast life and thought. It is no accident then, that, in crystallizing and restating the century-old Africanist theme, Ghana should have taken the lead rather than Azikiwe's own Nigeria or, for that matter, Sierra Leone or Liberia, the two oldest "democracies" in Africa. In this connection, it is relevant to take note of two leading Gold Coast figures of an earlier generation, Aggrey and Hayford, whose visions of the future contributed greatly to the emergence of the nation of Ghana. James Eman Kwegyir Aggrey (1875–1927),[11] popularly known as "Aggrey of Africa" was a scholar, a teacher, a minister of religion, and an educational reformer. He envisioned the emergence of a "Youth Movement coming in Africa that would one day startle the world."[12]

Aggrey's contemporary and, undoubtedly, one of the greatest and most prolific contributors to modern African political thought, Joseph Ephraim Casely-Hayford (1866–1930), was similarly a man of diverse talents—scholar, lawyer, nationalist politician, statesman, legislator, and journalist.[13] He expounded the idea of a Pan–West African Union and had, some two decades or so earlier than Azikiwe, given expression in even more precise terms to the idea of an African national risorgimento originating in Ghana.[14]

As early as 1903, Hayford had written: ". . . the Gold Coast and Ashanti [i.e., what is now Ghana] will lead the way in what will prove the grandest conception of the twentieth century—grandest because Ethiopia will have at length raised up her hand unto God . . ." and

> The thing will be done with the free will and consent of all the peoples of West Africa upon native lines; and in all this the Gold Coast and Ashanti will lead the way, not by coercion in any shape or form but by free choice, as becomes a free people. . . . You may call it a picture of Utopia. I call it a picture of the new civilization that is to

be. . . . It is bound to come . . . the country must move with the times, and we do not intend to stand still.[15]

Yet, neither Aggrey nor Hayford could, by any definition of the term, be described as a "neutralist"; least of all, as an advocate of "non-alignment." On the contrary, they both were cooperationists of the first order; and in the case of Hayford, both a cooperationist and an integrationist.[16] Both men were, in fact, avowedly and un-ashamedly pro-Western African nationalists. But, if they were not neutralists according to current Afro-Asian usage, their arguments for Africa's liberation and eventual greatness in world affairs were the precursors of the political thinking that now comes under the heading of African neutralism and non-alignment.

Azikiwe's "renaissance" theme, Nkrumah's "African Personality" idea, Senghor's *"negritude"* and Sékou Touré's "doctrine of Africa,"[17] all share a common ancestry in Aggrey's and Hayford's concepts of Africa's special, distinctive, even unique, role in world affairs.

BANDUNG AND "WHAT IS NEUTRALISM?"

Thus, when the representatives of the new African nations went on their pilgrimage to Bandung, they carried their own distinctively African political outlook with them. Of course, they found much common ground with the other conferees at Bandung and they were in general agreement with them that this common ground should be expressed in a joint pursuit of a policy of neutralism in world affairs. But it soon became evident that the general agreement concealed ambiguities when it came to a matter of precise definitions and actual practice. The Africans, like so many of their Bandung colleagues, soon discovered that they had to attempt their own working definitions and that such definitions were naturally colored by their own political outlook and experience. How the Africans have handled the problem can perhaps best be illustrated by a review of what was said at Bandung and a look at how the concept of neutralism and non-alignment has evolved in African thinking since then.

Despite all protestations to the contrary and despite expressions of continued good will towards the West and the former "mother countries," Bandung aimed at the creation of a unified front of the emergent peoples of Asia and Africa. The common enterprise of the participating states was to win recognition in the international community as the equals of the older states of Europe and North

America. While obviously motivated by considerations of their separate racial identities from the white peoples of the world, as well as of their common historical experience as colonial or ex-colonial peoples, the conference participants in general strove to avoid any show of racialism and chauvinism in their approach to the problems facing them.

President Sukarno of Indonesia, who acted as host to the conference, set its tone in his opening address. He said:

> Let us not be bitter about the past . . . let us remember that the stature of all mankind is diminished so long as nations or parts of nations are still unfree. Let us remember that the highest purpose of man is the liberation of man from his bonds of fear, his bonds of poverty, the liberation of man from the physical, spiritual and intellectual bonds which have long stunted the development of humanity's majority. And let us remember, sisters and brothers, that for the sake of all that, we Asians and Africans must be united.[18]

Despite its aura of a high-level international convention of state leaders and dignitaries, it also was a sentimental gathering of "brothers and sisters" of the colored races of the world, of Asians and Africans, who saw themselves primarily as representatives of peoples, not as diplomatic plenipotentiaries. They gathered to exchange views and consider solutions to common problems that impinged on their freedom and equality in world society: problems of dependency or colonial status; human rights and self-determination; racial segregation and discrimination; war and the threat it posed to the peaceful development of the new nations. Jawaharlal Nehru, Prime Minister of India, expressed the consensus of the conference in his closing speech:

> Our primary consideration is peace. All of us are passionately eager to advance our countries peacefully. We have been backward. We have been left behind in the race. . . . We have to make good rapidly because of the compulsion of events. . . . We are determined not to fail. . . . We are determined not to be dominated in any way by any other country or continent. . . . We are determined . . . to discard the age-old shackles that have tied us not only politically but economically . . . the shackles of colonialism and other shackles of our own making. . . .[19]

From such sentiments the concepts of neutralism and non-involvement in the conflicts between the older nations arose.

Despite all the speeches, resolutions, declarations and other pro-

nouncements, however, no clear and precise definition of the term
neutrality (or of its later variant "neutralism") emerged at Bandung.[20] None has, so far, been evolved. Yet the leaders of every
Asian and African state represented at the conference, as well as
those of African states established since then, repeatedly speak as
if the Bandung idea of "positive neutrality" or, as it was later
styled, "positive neutralism," provides a clear-cut guide for state
policy. That there is no agreement as to the precise meaning and
usage of the concept, even among some of its more enthusiastic
advocates, is borne out in some of the statements emanating from
Asian and African sources.

Nehru, for example, complained to the Asian Legal Consultative
Committee in New Delhi, in April, 1957, that there was great need
for "an eminent body of scholars and jurists [to] throw light on the
term 'neutrality' as currently used in international relations, so that
at least our thinking may become straight." Protesting the way the
term had been used since Bandung, Nehru said:

> Delegates here must know how vaguely the word "neutrality" or
> "neutralism," as it is sometimes called, is used now . . . sometimes
> as a term of abuse, sometimes in a different way, but mostly in a
> manner which does not describe what is meant exactly. . . . If a
> country is supposed to be neutral today, then, presumably, some
> other country which is not neutral should be described as belligerent.
> And yet that would be a wrong description because the other coun-
> try is not engaged in regular or recognized warfare. I do not quite
> know how international law or jurists of repute would define what
> is called "cold war," which is, presumably, some kind of suspended
> belligerency.[21]

Despite the complaints the term retains its ambiguity up to the
present day when it is used by Afro-Asians.

There appears to be increasing recognition, however, that "neutralism" was somewhat of a misnomer from the start and that the
terms "non-alignment" and "independence" better express the motive behind the policies of many Afro-Asian states. Thus, Nigeria's
Dr. Azikiwe asserted in August, 1961, that neutralism should be
defined as "non-alignment" and an "independent policy." According to Azikiwe,

> such a policy . . . should not oblige [its] members . . . either to
> inherit the prejudices of other nations or to join forces directly or
> indirectly with any bloc of nations against any other bloc in any war,

or to act in such a way and manner as to give the impression that any particular bloc or group of nations is right or wrong in its approach to the solution of international problems.[22]

As early as 1957, President Nkrumah of Ghana had indicated his discontent with the term neutralism. He had declared that "the Government of Ghana does not intend to follow a neutralist policy but it intends to preserve its independence and to act as seems best [to it] at any particular time."[23] And Nkrumah soon began to resort to such terminology as "positive neutralism" and "non-alignment" to describe his policies, terminology that he, perhaps more than any other leader, has popularized in Africa.

If the terms neutralism and neutrality lacked clarity and precision, their variant "non-alignment" has caused less confusion. As is seen from Azikiwe's definition, the meanings commonly attached to the latter have come to include those earlier embraced by the former. Indeed, non-alignment has now generally superseded neutralism in the vocabulary of Asian and African states. Nkrumah, Africa's most persistent exponent of non-alignment, asserts that non-alignment presupposes and enjoins independence and freedom of action, and claims the prerogative of sovereign African states to judge global political issues impartially. In his own words, "We must be free to judge issues on their merits and [to] look for solutions that are just and peaceful, irrespective of the issues involved. . . ." Non-alignment, he and other African statesmen insist, is not indifference. On the contrary, they assert that it is a policy of commitment to "positive action" in international affairs, particularly with regard to world peace and cooperation. Nkrumah takes pains to emphasize that non-alignment is not meant to imply indifference to such crucial issues as peace or war and declares that "powers which pursue policies of goodwill, cooperation and constructive international action will always find us at their side. . . ."[24] Both in word and deed a genuinely African policy of non-alignment proclaims both an "Africa first" orientation and an "open door" to all nations fostering peaceful coexistence in international affairs.[25] Though a newcomer among Africa's non-aligned statesmen Julius Nyerere, first Prime Minister and later President of Tanganyika, ably expressed the spirit of African non-alignment in his first policy statement in December, 1961. He emphasized his government's unwillingness to have "a friendly country choosing enemies for us." And as if to demonstrate the point in one of its first acts as a state, the Government of Tanganyika simultaneously announced the establishment of diplomatic relations with the U.S.A., the U.S.S.R. and the People's Republic of China. No other African Commonwealth country had acted with such speed and evident deliberateness in asserting its newly acquired sovereignty.

But the African state whose statement of policy perhaps is most representative of the general point of view of African non-alignment is the Sudan. The Sudan set out the following guideposts of its policies at the conference of Independent African States in Accra, in April, 1958:

> 1. NEUTRALITY, with respect to the two Eastern and Western blocs, and cooperation with either of them if such cooperation is in the interests of the Sudan;
>
> 2. NON-ALIGNMENT toward any of the Arab blocs and endeavours to bring them closer together and reconcile their differences;
>
> 3. COOPERATION in all fields with independent African Nations and encouragement of liberation movements in the dependent territories of the African continent and elsewhere;
>
> 4. AVOIDANCE OF MILITARY PACTS except for the defense of the Sudan against overt aggression;
>
> 5. ACCEPTANCE OF FOREIGN ECONOMIC ASSISTANCE and loans which do not detract from the independence and sovereignty of the Sudan; and refusal of offers of conditional aid or loans which might warrant any foreign intervention in the domestic affairs of the country.[26]

By slogans, mottos, challenging hints to the great powers, and the like, the non-aligned try to leave no room for doubt as to their meaning when they declare their neutralism and non-alignment. Something of the mood and temper of the political leaderships of the non-aligned African states is conveyed in various statements of their chief figures. Thus Nkrumah declares: "As we would not have British masters, so we would not have Russian masters." His colleague within the Casablanca group of African states, President Nasser of the United Arab Republic, asserts: "I will not become the stooge or satellite of anybody." Or, again, "We say what we believe, whether this pleases or displeases." Sékou Touré of Guinea tells the U.N. General Assembly: "The question is not for us whether we are going Communist or going the democratic way; the question is rather for you of East and West—'Are you for freedom or are you for colonialism?' "[27] Azikiwe of Nigeria, a long-time champion of the doctrine of independence for Africans in all things, declares that: "The gravamen of any policy endorsed by us should be based upon an independent and not a neutral attitude, especially with reference to issues which affect the destiny of Africa or the people of African descent no matter where they may live."[28]

Such statements as the foregoing, whether made in government declarations or in political propaganda speeches, are all animated by a fierce zeal for independence. Thus the participants at the Cairo meeting of non-aligned states in June, 1961, which prepared the way for the Belgrade Conference, were united on the point that the policy of African non-alignment means a policy of independence. All the conferees agreed that such a policy involves non-participation in "multilateral military alliances" (e.g., NATO, SEATO, CENTO, or the Warsaw Pact), "support of liberation and independence movements," non-participation in bilateral military alliances (such as the former Anglo-Nigeria Defense Pact or the mutual defense arrangement between Liberia and the United States), as well as the denial to the great powers of facilities for the establishment of military bases on African soil.

UNITY AND DIVERSITY

It is, of course, apparent that, since Bandung, African states espousing neutralism and non-alignment have pursued policies notable for their diversity and individual variations. Observers of the African scene have become accustomed to simplifying matters by dividing African states into more or less distinct categories according to whether their policies are deemed radical, moderate, or conservative. The picture conveyed is of an Africa divided, and the ideal of African unity is seen as a figment of an impassioned African imagination. Most familiar are the labels "Casablanca" and "Monrovia," which have often been invoked to depict a polarization of African states into two camps. The division has been based on differences of approach in policies both groupings represent as neutralist or non-aligned. Most African participants at the Belgrade Conference of non-aligned states in September, 1961, themselves tended to regard the community of new African states as now sharply split into categories of "non-aligned" and "aligned." But like most generalizations about the African states, such a view is misleading. While the principles of non-alignment enunciated at Belgrade provide a more meaningful criterion for identifying the policies of individual African states than the Casablanca-Monrovia classification, those African states that did not send representatives to Belgrade should not *ipso facto* be considered outside the pale of the non-aligned. Most of the non-participants are in fact clearly not aligned. At most, some may be described as not unequivocally committed to either alternative—Tanganyika, Somalia, and the Congo (Leopoldville) would be cases in point. In actuality, the areas of disagreement separating the several groupings are much narrower and less significant than the pronouncements and attitudes of their respective representatives or sensational newspaper headlines (both African and foreign) would suggest.

Beneath the differences among the new African states a consensus regarding the basic policy goals for Africa is clearly discernible. Differences in styles of leadership and differences in policy methods and implementation among the various groupings of the new African states disguise broad agreement on the principles of African unity and independence, the necessity of removing alien rule from the continent, the elimination of racial discrimination and segregation against the black man throughout the whole of Africa, and the promotion of peaceful relationships among the states of the world community. It is not assuming too much to assert that the preamble of the Declaration of the First Conference of Independent African States of April, 1958, fairly represents the over-all outlook of the entire community of African states, even though only the eight new African states existing at the time signed it. The signatories agreed to strive for

> . . . unity among ourselves . . . solidarity with the dependent peoples of Africa . . . friendship with all nations . . . unity of purpose and action in international affairs . . . fundamental unity of outlook on foreign policy so that a distinctive African personality will play its part in cooperation with other peace-loving nations to further the cause of peace . . . to avoid being committed to any action which might entangle our countries . . . to recognize the right of the African peoples to independence and self-determination and . . . to hasten the realization of this right . . . to uproot forever the evil of racial discrimination in all its forms wherever it may be found . . . to raise the living standards of our peoples . . . to coordinate our economic planning through a joint economic effort . . . to increase trade among our countries [by] improving communications between our respective countries . . . to encourage investment of foreign capital and skills, provided they do not compromise the independence, sovereignty and territorial integrity of our States.

Hardly a single one of the dozen or more conferences, declarations, protocols, charters or statements that have issued from the continent since the above Declaration has failed to subscribe in broad terms to its principles and purposes. Students of African politics generally agree that the new African states are dedicated to these purposes whether they are expressed cautiously and diffidently by the Monrovia group, boldly and assertively by the Casablanca powers, or moderately and discreetly by the Brazzaville grouping. This is true of the Brazzaville states despite their continuing ties with France.

Also despite wide variation in their policies, whether those of Casablanca or Monrovia, non-aligned, not-so-aligned, or on-the-fence, there has been a notable similarity in the behavior of African states toward Washington and Moscow. African leaders of all shades of political outlook—from Haile Selassie to Sékou Touré—have sooner or later sought to demonstrate their impartiality toward the cold war antagonists by visiting both Washington and Moscow. Thus, the intent behind the visits to both cold-warring capitals is pointedly expressed in Nkrumah's borrowing of Jefferson's diplomatic dictum: "Peace, commerce and honest friendship with all nations, entangling alliances with none." Whatever specific political or material advantages in trade and aid individual African leaders may hope to gain through such visits, and no matter from which particular grouping of African states the visitors may come, it can be confidently asserted that all the states in question regard themselves as pursuing genuinely independent policies, whether or not the policy in a particular case bears the "non-aligned" label.

Similarly in the field of trade and aid agreements with the U.S.A., the U.S.S.R., and other countries of the Eastern and Western blocs, the African states consciously strive to strike a balance in such arrangements that is consistent with the concept of non-alignment. Clearly, most of the African states want to avoid putting all their eggs in one basket. A random sampling of the headlines filling the pages of the African press in the past few years makes this evident. For example:

GHANA SIGNS AGREEMENT WITH U.S. AND U.S.S.R.

U.S., GUINEA SIGN JOINT AGREEMENTS

NIGER AND CZECHOSLOVAKIA SIGN TRADE AGREEMENTS

U.S.S.R. AIDS GHANA ($40,000,000 LONG-TERM CREDIT)

CANADIANS TO TRAIN GHANA'S ARMED FORCES

KHRUSHCHEV OFFERS AID, FRIENDSHIP TO ETHIOPIA ($100,000,000 LONG-TERM CREDIT)

U.S. FIRM ACQUIRES SHARES IN SENEGAL PHOSPHORATE FIRM

VOLTA GETS $84,000,000 FROM WORLD BANK, U.S., U.K.
U.S. TO CONSTRUCT MAJOR HARBOR IN SOMALIA

THE INSPIRATION OF THE FOUNDING FATHERS OF THE UNITED STATES

It is no accident then that the teachings of America's founding fathers on the diplomacy of a new nation have inspired not a few present-day African statesmen. Many African statesmen—some of them founding fathers in their own right—have consciously drawn upon the political writings of the founders of the United States for reasoned justifications of non-alignment in foreign policy, particularly regarding the great powers. The view now being widely circulated by certain historians in the United States that there is no recognizable parallel between the nationalism of the Thirteen Colonies that produced the Adamses and the Jeffersons, the Franklins and the Madisons, and the nationalism that now produces Nkrumah, Azikiwe and Touré, is certainly not borne out by the record of that period in American history.[29] Any doubt on this point can be removed, for example, by reading the excellent two-volume documentary history of the period entitled *The Spirit of '76*;[30] as well as the scholarly study of the press of the day by the senior Schlesinger.[31] Thus, to write, as has one such historian, that the leaders of the American revolution and of the young republic, would look like moderates alongside Kenyatta, Nkrumah, Makarios, and other colonial nationalists of our day, is to distort the record.[32]

It is sufficient to note that in nearly every one of the pronouncements that have issued from the new African states, whether jointly or separately, the same themes that ran through the declarations and other pronouncements of America's eighteenth-century nationalist statesmen recur. They include the desire to avoid entanglement or involvement in the quarrels and differences of the existing great powers—then, in the rivalry between Britain and France, today, in the cold war between the U.S.A. and U.S.S.R.; recognition of the dangers of interference or intervention and the advantages of abstention; resistance to commercial and trade restrictions and the espousal of rapid economic development of their countries; a demand for full and free exercise of the prerogatives of sovereignty, including the right to recognize *de facto* governments; the withdrawal of foreign governments, agencies and influences from their respective continents; and, finally, the promotion of the idea of an association of states.[33] Thus, the so-called twin doctrines of nonintervention and neutrality, the principle of *de facto* recognition of governments, the Monroe Doctrine or variants of it, and the idea of a continent-wide association of sovereign states are all recognizable features of the current ideas underlying African policies of neutralism and non-alignment.[34] "The United States," said Nkrumah, "should be the first to appreciate the realistic reasons (behind our policy) why we as a small country should endeavor to preserve normal relations with the two other great powers of the world today —the Soviet Union and China."

THE SOVIET MODEL

If the attitudes of the African states have been heavily influenced by the American colonial experience, it is also true that in the area of economic development and industrialization the African states incline toward the socialist system exemplified by the Soviet Union. Like their Asian counterparts in the Afro-Asian community of neutralist and non-aligned states, the African states naturally lean to the West in the realm of spiritual and cultural heritage after some two centuries or more of historical, sentimental, and even emotional ties with the West. However, in matters affecting the material well-being of their peoples and the enhancement of the prestige of their countries, they are clearly attracted to the Soviet model. Socialism or the socialist type of economy is seen as the most efficient means of achieving that massive scale of development and progress that has become an imperative for the backward and underdeveloped countries.

Yet, true to their professions of a non-alignment in all questions in which one or other of the cold war powers serves as an example, the neutralist non-aligned states insist that they are inspired by the example, *not* the specific practices and techniques of the systems employed by any of these powers. Expressing the view of most Asian and African statesmen that socialism is the most suitable economic system for the development of their countries, Nehru asserted:

We say . . . that we want a socialistic pattern of society. That is a phrase which means, in one word, socialism. . . . We have not approached this question in any doctrinaire way. . . . If our friends the Communists rely on Marx . . . they rely on something that is out of date. I think Marx was a very great man and all of us can learn from Marx. But the point is that it is grossly unfair to ask Marx, who belonged to the middle of the nineteenth century, to tell you what to do in the middle of the twentieth century. . . .

The same views in different phraseology have been repeatedly advanced in recent years by a number of African leaders. Mamadou Dia of Senegal, a recognized economist in his own right, after a recent (1961) visit to Sweden, Denmark and Yugoslavia concluded that "the kind of socialism practiced in Scandinavia—pragmatic and non-doctrinaire—was a more useful model for Senegal than the doctrinaire Marxist approach of Yugoslavia"; and intimated, in passing, that his visit to Scandinavia "had confirmed his view that it will be possible for Senegal to establish a socialist society without nationalizing industry."[35]

A point that may be obvious but can hardly be overstated in any assessment of African policies of non-alignment is that African political leaderships do not conceive of their policies as Eastern or Western, but as African. Africanism is the touchstone of the policy-maker in the new African states. It is noteworthy in this regard that serious writers on Africa have been struck by the pervasiveness of the pan-African impulse in contemporary African politics. Leading students like Padmore, Shepperson, Fyfe, Hargreaves, and Dike have been unanimous in pointing to an intimate interconnection between the ideas of pan-Africanism and African neutralism and non-alignment.

The quest for an African identity preoccupies the leaders of the new Africa and is shaping the emerging political consciousness of the continent. Nkrumah expresses it when he declares his hope that Ghana's policies "will become a center for the discussion of African problems as a whole . . . our aim is to work with others to achieve an African personality in international affairs." Sékou Touré expresses it in his repeated invocations of "African personality" in all areas of life—economic, political, social, and cultural—in the new African states; what he calls the "doctrine of Africa," for Africa, in world affairs. And Senghor expresses it in his theme of *"negritude."* They all share the vision of a unique mission for the new African states both in African and international affairs; unique because of their belief in a separate and distinct African personality.

THREE

COMMUNIST POLICIES IN NON-ALIGNED COUNTRIES

The Soviet Union Seeks a Policy for Afro-Asia

—DAVID T. CATTELL

Traditionally, both the United States and the Soviet Union have looked upon Africa as an appendage of Europe with few indigenous political forces. What Communist movements existed in Africa were the minor agents of the relevant European parties. Soviet analysts lumped Asia and Africa together, while observing that Africa was at an earlier stage in its anti-colonial struggle. Few, if any, Soviet scholars even traveled to the area. Now, the sudden appearance of a series of new and untried independent governments in Africa has made the whole continent appear in a new light.

It might be assumed that the Soviet Union, with its claim to a monopoly of truth, would have been the first to come up with a definite and consistent strategy. Lenin's theory of imperialism appears to be a ready-made vehicle on which to load a policy, and Leninism has the further advantage of being popular among a large part of the intellectuals in the underdeveloped world. Superficially, such a prediction seems borne out by Soviet writings, but a more careful and extended reading of Soviet and Communist works on Asia and Africa, together with an analysis of Communist actions, suggests that this first impression merely covers a hesitant and uncertain position which, at most, indicates only a general direction. Even on basic issues the Soviet authors seem unsure of themselves, and the actions and statements of their leaders are no better.[1] This uncertainty is in direct contrast to Soviet pretensions, but it is, nevertheless, typical of Soviet foreign relations.

On domestic issues the Soviet leadership generally adopts a position pointing to a precise pattern of action. Although circumstances and unforeseen results may later force a shift, there is a definite program at any given time. But in respect of foreign relations a consistent policy has been rare. Ignorance of foreign areas, divergence of goals from means and ideology from reality may in part explain the lack of a dynamic strategy, but similar differences of myth and reality in domestic politics have never kept the regime from coming up with a positive, if often inaccurate, course. In the domestic field, the leadership is confident that it can command the environment and remold society.[2] International relations, on the other hand, present a very different setting, over which the Soviet leadership has little control. A widespread lack of knowledge about the motivation of the outside world and the remnants of a traditional inferiority complex vis-à-vis the West amplify the insecurity. Thus the Soviets conclude that the West is forever hatching plots of the most subtle kind.[3] The very innocence and stupidity of some Western actions only seem to confirm their analysis. Stalin dealt with his suspicions and fears of Western plots by closely limiting his objectives and acting only when the odds were heavily weighted in his favor. When he did take risks, as in the Spanish Civil War and the alliance with Hitler, things turned out badly, and not as predicted. It is against this background that the emerging policy of the Soviet Union toward the underdeveloped areas after World War II must be analyzed.

It is not surprising that Stalin, with his attention and his troops in Eastern Europe, avoided a positive policy in Asia and Africa, at least until 1948. The relatively few references to these areas in Soviet writings were propagandist in nature, designed as part of the campaign to undermine Western Europe and the United States. By 1948, Stalin's limited aims in Eastern Europe had been for the most part achieved and a year later Russia had been given an ally in Communist China. Furthermore, the withdrawal of Western European powers from parts of Asia seemed an opportunity too good to miss. Copying the successful strategy employed by the Chinese, and the Communist guerrillas in the Philippines, Malaya, and Indochina, international Communism, directed from Moscow, tried to recreate the conditions of war in the underdeveloped countries by encouraging outbreaks of violence and exploiting peasant discontent. The results were disappointing. Even the weakest of the new Asian states succeeded with Western help in putting down the Communist outbreaks, and the Korean War consolidated Western defenses.

It was against this background that Khrushchev, from about

1955, began to test out new policies in dealing with the under-developed countries of Asia and Africa.

While keeping Lenin's theory of imperialism for propaganda purposes, Khrushchev decided in practice to reverse the tenets of Lenin's theses. Not only did he deny the inevitability of wars between the Communist and capitalist camps; his doctrine of peaceful coexistence repudiated Lenin's argument that imperialist wars between capitalist states served as the midwife of the socialist revolution. The socialist revolution, according to Khrushchev, can be achieved by limited forms of violence, including those wars termed in Communist parlance "wars of national liberation."[4] In practice, Khrushchev has avoided engaging the Communist world even in a limited war. His repudiation of violence in the revolutionary struggle went even further in the suggestion that in some situations the transition to socialism may be peaceful. The explanation given is that the position as a great power achieved by the Soviet Union, and the horrors of global war, have altered the world situation.[5] But while reducing the violence of the socialist revolution, Khrushchev has been careful not to change its direction, or the intensity of the competition on the economic and political levels. In effect, he is gambling on divorcing the use of military force (except in limited areas) from political competition. Up to now, this divorce has been achieved only in a few stable societies with a highly developed sense of the rule of law. Khrushchev, however, hopes to bring it about not by respect for law, but by fear of war. Neither history nor his Russian and Communist suspicions of the West will permit him to rely on disarmament and the rule of law. In this new situation, political and economic issues assume major importance, and because in practice, Communists consistently treat economics as another form of politics, the two issues become one.

In spite of the greatly altered world situation, the Communist strategy and tactics in Asia and Africa that emerged after 1955 were in large part a renewal and reformulation of earlier lines. The apparent newness of the approach was largely due both to the newly powerful position of the U.S.S.R. in projecting it, and the flexibility of its application in contrast to Stalin's rigidity. The concept of the united and popular fronts formulated in the nineteen thirties and early nineteen forties was rehabilitated. The Communists again sought to persuade the socialists into an alliance, and as before the socialists for the most part rejected the offer. In fact, Communist influence in Western Europe was reduced with the resurgence of Western prosperity in the nineteen fifties, and Communism in the capitalist world fell to a new low ebb. This made it all the more essential to exploit the crises of the underdeveloped areas. Here, the popular front could assume a broader base by supporting national independence and become a national front of all anti-colonial groups (resurrecting a Communist line of the nineteen twenties). The struggle against the bourgeoisie could be abandoned or concealed behind the cloak of an alliance. Such an alliance was necessary if the Soviet Government hoped directly to influence the new states, for the open contests of 1948–49 had proved that, by themselves, the local Communists were extremely vulnerable.

In the past, Communists had discriminated between the different sections of the national bourgeoisie, singling out the petty bourgeoisie as the most reliable allies. But after 1955 such distinctions were dropped. While still ideologically claiming leadership for the proletariat in the national liberation struggle, in practice and in much of its propaganda the Soviet Union acknowledged and acclaimed the leadership of the national bourgeoisie. This was most marked in regard to Africa, where the Communist groups were forced to give up independent active struggle and to cooperate with the native leadership, seemingly almost to the point of their own elimination. The Communists further refrained from creating parties where they did not previously exist in Africa, except in Angola, where Portugal was trying to perpetuate the traditional colonial pattern.[6] In dealing with Africa, the Soviet Government dealt exclusively with the native elite, whatever its political hue, from the Emperor of Ethiopia and President Tubman to Marxists like Sékou Touré; and it was in Africa, too, that the Soviet Union went the furthest in denying the class struggle and suggesting that, in alliance with the Soviet Union, the national bourgeoisie could lead the country into the socialist revolution.[7] Khrushchev, like Stalin before him, apparently decided that in most cases the native Communist parties had very little chance of assuming power, were a source of embarrassment, and were expendable. He appears to have hoped that the resentment of the new leaders against their former rulers and frustration would lead them into the Soviet sphere.

Support for the native bourgeois elite put an end to the simple Stalinist dichotomy of the Communist camp versus the rest of the world, and introduced, between the two camps, a number of primarily neutralist states that, in Communist theory, together with the Communist bloc, made up the "zone of peace" as against the war-mongering capitalist states. The term proved to be very successful among the underdeveloped countries because it seemed to recognize the concept of a neutralist bloc at a time when the United States was still trying to push them into military alliances. It was, however, another case of words having a different and more favorable connotation to unsuspecting Asians and Africans than that intended by the Soviet leadership. The former tended to assume that the U.S.S.R. was thinking in terms of a genuinely three-camp world based on long-term coexistence and non-interference by the Communist camp in the neutralist camp. But such a proposition—that development can be in two or more directions—is contrary to Communist ideology and ambitions.[8] Thus in place of the "either-or" world of Stalin, Khrushchev introduced a linear, but not a multidimensional, world. It was conceived primarily as a device to enable the Soviet Union to support and deal with the various underdeveloped countries. As long as an underdeveloped state was not closely allied with the West, the Soviet Union concluded there was an opportunity to extend its influence. Therefore, Soviet propaganda refrained from criticism and extended offers of political support and limited economic assistance. Since few of the underdeveloped states were considered hopeless, any change of government was treated carefully and all criticism withheld, even in the case of military and right wing governments, until the direction of the country's foreign policy was shown to be clearly pro-Western.[9] It is possible to assume from the evidence that Khrushchev's position resolves itself into the formula that as long as states or leaders were moving toward a more pro-Communist attitude on the scale extending from capitalism to Soviet socialism, they were considered friends and highly praised. If they were standing still on the scale there was still no criticism, although less praise. Only if the state or leader reversed direction and moved toward capitalism did criticism begin. Even then, the criticism tended to be mild, in order not to arouse too much hostility in the hope of in time "saving" the country.[10] Only when an underdeveloped country directly allied itself with the West did the criticism become a tirade.

The primary function of Soviet propaganda, however, was not to guide the new states but to present a favorable image of Communism as the wave of the future and an unfavorable one of capitalism as in a rapid decline. The methods and arguments used were the same for internal and external consumption. The example of "the great Soviet successes" was intended to show how Communism could bring quick solutions to industrialization for underdeveloped countries. The old Stalinist line that it was the October Revolution and the victory of Russia in World War II alone that accounted for the successes of the anti-colonial struggle was recognized as unpopular, and Communist propaganda stressed rather the power of the Soviet Union as a restraining force on the capitalists, and the willingness of the U.S.S.R. to aid the struggle for national freedom. At the same time, the internal struggle of the anti-colonial forces was given equal stress. These themes were initially quite effective and accounted for much of the growth of Communist prestige, particularly after the retreat of the British and French in Egypt in 1956. The whole character of the approach was opportunist, expanding Soviet influence by those means requiring a minimum of Soviet commitments and with only a superficial covering of Marxian ideology. But the chief change from Stalinism was an end of Soviet uninterest and the development of flexibility in respect to both time and space.

What did the Soviet Union hope to accomplish by its new and vigorous interest in Asia and, particularly, Africa? The inclination in the West was to assume that the Soviet leaders sought immediate Communist control under Russian leadership to replace the influence of the West in the underdeveloped areas. But can it be assumed that the Kremlin was so unaware, or so dedicated to expanding the Soviet bloc, that it was willing to take on the liabilities and risks of hegemony regardless of cost? Certainly the problems that faced it in Eastern Europe, and the shock and pressure of the Chinese struggle for industrialization, made the leadership wary of assuming control of and responsibility for the industrialization of the underdeveloped areas. The prospect of large new drains on the Soviet economy was not likely to appeal to the leadership, still less so as, despite Communist wishful thinking, the Western economies continued to grow, and showed no signs of imminent collapse. There was also the problem of defending and assuring military control over satellites. Thus it is doubtful that the immediate ambitions of the Soviet Union were so all-encompassing for the underdeveloped areas; instead the traditional aim of weakening the capitalist West was still primary.

Lenin had concluded that colonies were the lifeblood of capitalism. The apparent struggle of the French and British to recapture and maintain their oil holdings in the Middle East in the nineteen fifties seemed to confirm that the collapse of colonialism was leading to a crisis in Western Europe. The West could not get along without the vital profits of colonialism. Furthermore, the increasing U.S. investments and aid abroad were, in Communist terms, nothing more than the expansion of American colonialism and the basis of the post-war prosperity of the United States. Western economists even agreed to the latter interpretation, stressing the importance of foreign trade and investment to the American economy. Thus, it is reasonable to assume that Khrushchev planned no more than his propaganda claimed: by eliminating Western political influence and economic ties with Asia and Africa, the decline of capitalism would be hastened.

Khrushchev may also have decided that the support of the underdeveloped countries would be useful in the game of international politics. The Soviet leaders seem aware that the United States and Western Europe are sensitive and responsive, at least in part, to the opinion of the leaders of the underdeveloped countries. Thus, mobilizing votes in the United Nations against the West is not a fruitless game but an important political instrument. Although this is contrary to the propaganda image of the Western leaders as inhuman, Machiavellian types the Soviet leaders are aware of the practical results that public opinion has achieved. Furthermore, the Soviet Union itself, following its revolutionary tradition and belief in propaganda, is also sensitive to world opinion; although it never permits itself to be openly subject to its influence, it makes every effort to achieve general acceptance of the Soviet view.

Finally, Khrushchev has shown no desire to run serious risks for the glory of acquiring an empire. His so-called aggressiveness can be better explained as the traditional Communist, if not Russian, defensive policy of assuming the attitude of offense but at the same time minimizing risks. Although Khrushchev's policy toward the underdeveloped countries has been bolder than Stalin's, it falls far short of that of a would-be conqueror. Hesitation and caution has been the pattern. The defensive posture of the Soviet Union has been even clearer in its often confessed fear of hostile military bases and its use of the anti-colonial struggle to eliminate them.

From the Soviet experience in trying to influence the underdeveloped parts of the world in the period from 1955 to 1960, it is possible to make some estimate of its success and its own conclusions and doubts about its achievements. Typically, the Soviet policy makers were caught in their own theory of imperialism. This does not mean that, as a propaganda line, the theory did not succeed, especially since the Soviet Union no longer claimed for itself an exclusive role. In fact Soviet propaganda, overstressing the popular role in achieving colonial independence, was exactly what the new elite wanted to hear and believe. But as a basis for policy this exaggeration of the importance of either the role of the Soviet Union or of the native struggle introduces some serious errors and overlooks other important factors.[11] Without deviating from a Marxian interpretation, it is possible to see the decline of imperialism in a very different light. Granted that an important aim in launching the imperialist era at the end of the nineteenth century was to acquire new areas of capitalist exploitation, in practice the colonies have not in general paid off: The devastation of two world wars, the growing cost of policing and defending the empires, and the need for large investments in the colonies, especially after World War II, was a drain on the countries of Western Europe that they could not afford. Thus, when they recognized that the outgo was increasingly more than the income, and that the cost of maintaining control over a discontented population was going up, they granted, one by one, independence to their colonies, often without regard to the consequences.[12] The raw materials, including oil, that the colonies have to offer were by the nineteen fifties in overabundance on the world market and it was cheaper to deal with independent countries than to assume political responsibility for the areas. Furthermore, modern technology had created a vast number of synthetics which eliminated absolute dependence on many items. Even the strategic possession of these raw materials and areas in time of war became of doubtful value. Such an interpretation would seem to be more realistic than the Soviet explanation as to why the West was willing to give up its colonies and why their loss has not brought an economic decline. In fact, the Western European countries freed of colonial burdens and competition are in a period of regeneration.[13]

It is this renewed economic and political dynamism in Western Europe, coupled with the Soviet bloc's failure to experience a similar self-generating boom, that is doing most to undermine Communist policies toward the underdeveloped areas and in international relations in general. It is difficult to convince elites in underdeveloped countries that Communism is the wave of the future when the Common Market appears to be succeeding while the Soviet

Union struggles unsuccessfully with a chronic agricultural crisis, the "Great Leap Forward" in China has been reversed by starvation, and a wall through Berlin is built to keep the population of East Germany from escaping. For the concrete problems faced by the underdeveloped countries in their search for viability these facts are more impressive than missiles, atomic weapons, and sputniks which for them are in a world beyond. In the area of missiles and weapons, the leaders of Africa and Asia are concerned only that the competition does not lead to war. The Soviet themes on the zone of peace against the West and the growing crisis of capitalism have thus far not won many adherents.

For the real needs of the underdeveloped countries, the U.S.S.R. has little to offer, and certainly no more than the West. Their primary needs are four: (a) capital, (b) trade and markets, (c) technicians, and (d) organizational techniques. With respect to both trade and capital, Soviet sources have thus far proven limited and erratic, and there is no indication that the situation is likely to change. The demands within the Soviet bloc are still too great. The Soviet supply of technicians is perhaps its most useful contribution, and in most cases can be provided at less cost than a supply from the West. Organizationally, Communist agricultural planning experiences have little to offer and, together with the capitalist examples, are not well received in most underdeveloped countries. The solution will undoubtedly have to be uniquely African and Asian. Industrially, the Soviet experience, as is becoming increasingly evident, is not outstanding, and the underdeveloped countries are finding the West here has as much, if not more, to offer. The Soviet claim that

> the support given to Cuba by the Soviet Union and the other socialist countries has enriched the Cuban people to come through with flying colors in their fight against the economic blockade imposed by the United States and other imperialist states and has helped them to develop their national economy successfully

is as yet a fiction.[14]

The more sophisticated leaders of Asia and Africa also refuse to accept the Soviet line that only two choices exist: the capitalist and the Communist roads.[15] In most cases, they envisage a mixed economy. Although Soviet propaganda has tried to convince these countries that the West is trying to force them into capitalism, in fact, Western leaders, including officials of the U.S. Government, recognize the need in these new states for a large amount of social-ism, but warn against its becoming top-heavy and arbitrary.[16]

In general, Soviet policies have had to compete with an increas-ingly effective policy on the part of the West. The Egyptian crisis was the last effort of Western governments to employ old-style colonial methods. They found they would no longer work, and dis-covered that they were also unnecessary. The loss of control over the Suez Canal was not crucial. Thus, in the Congo crisis the West-ern governments have refrained from making or supporting any attempts to reassert imperialist control.[17] Although at first the African and Asian states tended to go along with the Communist propaganda that the governments of Western Europe were behind the groups trying to restore European hegemony in the Congo, gradually they recognized that these groups had limited support and that even the Belgian Government was being forced into a hands-off position. Thus, the Soviet Union was unable to turn the Congo into another affair that would play into its hands as the Egyptian crisis had done. In fact, it can be argued that the stub-born support of the Soviet Union for Gizenga and against the United Nations and Dag Hammarskjöld became unpopular.[18]

In the end, the African and Asian leadership did not appear to be particularly susceptible to Soviet enticements. The leaders are intensely nationalistic and suspicious of outside influence of all kinds. Having just gained power, they are being careful not to lose it. This does not mean that they are not pleased and even flattered (some more than others) by Soviet offers and attentions, but they see the Soviet Union only as a counterbalance against the over-whelming influence of the West, against which they still harbor strong resentment. Furthermore, their needs are so great they cannot afford to reject the offers of either side.[19] Thus in the strong tide of African nationalism, Soviet Communism is suspect as an international European movement, Soviet propaganda on the non-exportation of revolution and peaceful coexistence not-withstanding.[20]

Thus, the course of events and the lack of any clear-cut success have been forcing the Soviet Union to re-evaluate its policies. In fact, it is possible to ask: has the Kremlin's position come almost full circle back to Stalin? Certainly the resurgence of Western Eu-rope has turned the primary focus and attention of Soviet foreign policy back to Western Europe. The road to London and Paris is not via the Orient or Africa. As it was under Stalin, Soviet propaganda about Africa is again pervaded by fears of the United States and Europe. The continued presence of Western military bases and the imperialism of the Common Market are the dominant themes.[21] It is also clear that competition with the West is still a political and military conflict, not an ideological or economic one, as Khrushchev has tried to make it. Neither "Communism as the wave of the future," nor the economic superiority of the Communist system is currently winning many supporters. Thus the Kremlin must again resort to political maneuvers and to military authority and action, as in Cuba. Like Stalin, Khrushchev is finding it difficult to influence those he does not militarily control. The only difference is that Stalin never expected to influence what he did not possess, while Khrushchev continues to try, but thus far the results have not been encouraging. In those cases where by the fortune of events it has been possible to possess a distant land, as Khrushchev has been able to penetrate Cuba, the dangers of over-commitment and the embarrassments of possible failure tend to be undermining factors. There is also the danger of independent Communist movements going off on their own adventures against the interest and wishes of the Soviet Union because they are in a hurry to assume power. Today the danger is even greater, although the indigenous Communist movements may not on the whole be any stronger. As part of his anti-Stalin program, Khrushchev has given them more autonomy. To withdraw this grant and return to the disciplined control of Stalin would be impossible, because the parties would need only to appeal for support to the more adventurist leadership of Peking. Although Stalin had Trotsky and Tito as revolutionary rivals, one was without a country and had only a few followers, in spite of Stalin's paranoiac fears, and the other possessed only a weak and backward country heavily dependent on the United States for its existence. Khrushchev has a more serious rival in China, which more and more openly challenges his leadership of the revolutionary left. Even though, for a moment, China seemed stunned by internal weakness, it has nevertheless recently asserted its leadership and hegemony over Asia by invading India.[22]

Militarily, too, the situation today is not much different from that in Stalin's time. The stalemate of the nineteen forties between the atomic weapons of the United States and the conventional armaments of Russia has changed in form but not in substance. The scientific feats of Russia in space and a slightly greater economic surplus remain Khrushchev's main advantage over Stalin in playing the game of international politics.

But even if the position of Khrushchev has not greatly changed, he does not appear to want to return to Stalin's passive policies vis-à-vis the underdeveloped areas. Beginning in 1961 (some authorities have argued that it was earlier),[23] Soviet analysts began a re-evaluation of the Communist position, and three alternative policies with regard to the underdeveloped countries are apparently under consideration: (1) to rely for influence on the Communist parties composed largely of malcontents and operating primarily as a small fifth column, waiting for a favorable moment and another Castro; (2) to initiate civil wars or wars of national liberation as a means of molding a formidable military force capable of assuming control; or (3) to adopt some modification of the present policy of appealing to the national bourgeois elite. The first policy seems to offer little more than the continued political isolation of the Communist movements, waiting for Soviet military forces to put them into power, which at the moment seems unlikely. The local Communist parties, however, seem to prefer this to subordinating themselves to the leadership of the national bourgeoisie. Evidence of support for the second alternative of promoting civil war can be seen in Khrushchev's sanctioning of wars of liberation. It is this formula that has accounted for the most outstanding Communist successes of the past. It was the civil wars of Russia, China, Yugoslavia, and Vietnam that permitted the Communists in those countries to create a disciplined, military organization capable of establishing totalitarian Communist control. Today, however, the difficulties of such a strategy are numerous. First of all, it is the policy being urged and pursued by the Soviet Union's revolutionary rival, Communist China. More serious is the fact that the military movements so created are self-made and, therefore, quite independent of Moscow's influence, as the Chinese example so clearly indicates. Furthermore, a popular, Communist-inspired civil war based on anti-imperialism is becoming less and less feasible as the underdeveloped countries achieve their independence from European domination. Probably the most serious drawback to this strategy is the danger of another Korea, and the possibility of a local war expanding into a major war. The lesson of Korea and the closeness of a general war in 1950 has not been entirely forgotten. Nevertheless, under strong Chinese pressure Russia may again be experimenting with this alternative in Laos and Vietnam. It is difficult to say. Superficially, it would appear that the Soviet Union is acting as a restraining influence on North Vietnam and China.

Khrushchev's ultimate policy choice will depend on his immediate goals. If he can no longer hope to use the underdeveloped countries to undermine the capitalist economy, and does not want a world empire, what more limited objectives can he be seeking? Does he want, as China apparently does in Southeast Asia, hegemony in limited areas, or is he only looking for enough influence in the underdeveloped areas to use as a political weapon against the West? To what extent does he work for constant chaos in the area as a means of manipulating the situation to his own purposes? The problem of continuous political upheaval is that, although it may momentarily benefit local Communist parties, it either creates a political vacuum that invites outside military intervention (currently by United Nations forces) or an anti-Communist military dictatorship takes over. In neither case has the U.S.S.R. or the local Communist Party been able to benefit. Under military dictators, in spite of mass discontent, the Communist parties have never fared well. As discussed above, hegemony, even limited hegemony, is both expensive and dangerous for the U.S.S.R. Any moves by the U.S.S.R. to assume control are likely to bring both a political and a military reaction from the West and most likely also from the underdeveloped countries themselves. Thus, a reasonable estimate of current Soviet goals in Asia and Africa is that they are looking for a loose political alliance with the underdeveloped countries against the West and the opening up of eventual markets for Soviet goods, markets that will thus be denied to the West.[24] Oil is one commodity the Soviet Union already has in surplus and for which it is seeking world outlets. At the same time, the Soviet Union cannot abandon its position as the leader of revolutionary tradition in the underdeveloped world, if for no other reason than the fear that Communist China might take over. The tactics of the Soviet Union as they have emerged within the last couple of years seem to bear out the above conclusions.

The Soviet program of action can still be characterized as hesitant and opportunistic. In each country, it attempts to keep open as many roads as possible. The Soviet press still refrains from criticism[25] and seeks an alliance and identification with any movement or leader that is popular (ranging from Peronism to the King of Morocco) and that has not openly declared for the Western camp.[26] This does not mean, however, that the U.S.S.R. treats all leaders alike. They and their programs form a hierarchy, and the warmth of the treatment they receive depends on six factors: (1) their degree of friendship with the Soviet Union, (2) their acceptance of Soviet aid, trade and technicians, (3) their hostility to the West, (4) the speed at which they are breaking up colonial and pre-colonial economic and social relations, (5) the amount of agricultural reform and nationalization of production, and (6) their discouragement of private capital, particularly foreign capital.

While the Soviet Government plays along with the national bourgeoisie, Communist writings are more and more laying the basis for an attack on certain sections of it by stressing that only parts of the national bourgeoisie and intelligentsia can be relied on. Their dependability varies, depending on the level of development toward the socialist revolution and the particular circumstances at the time. "The antagonistic character of contradictions between the national bourgeoisie and working class is concealed by the unity of interests in the struggle against imperialism."[27] The earlier line, that it is possible for the national bourgeoisie to lead the socialist revolution in alliance with the U.S.S.R. has been dropped,[28] and recently there has also been an increased stress on the role of the Communist parties.[29] Leadership of the national and socialist revolutions must be taken by the proletariat in alliance with the peasantry headed by the vanguard of the Communist Party. In Asia, this permits the Communist parties to serve as the focus of opposition to the current bourgeois leadership, both loyally, if permitted, and as an underground movement. But there still has been no move by the Soviet Union, itself, to strengthen the parties except perhaps in the military situation of Laos and Vietnam. Thus the Communist parties in India, Iraq, Egypt, Algeria, and the Sudan have to fend for themselves and the Soviet Union refuses to use its friendship or loans to bargain for better treatment of the Communists.

In Africa, the Soviet Union apparently still hopes that it can exercise a direct influence on governmental elites. In the newly independent states of tropical Africa, the Communists are still cautious about creating parties. "In those countries where the capitalist forms have not taken a firm root, non-capitalist development could ensure a more rapid growth of productive forces. This type of development is possible within the framework of a national democratic state which can build on a political foundation."[30] The Communist analysis concludes that the national bourgeoisie in tropical Africa is too small and weak to be the leader, and that the real force of the anti-colonial revolution is and has been the proletariat, which in the struggle has grown strong.[31] The proletarian-type origins of the Soviet friends in Africa are continually being stressed. So in effect the Soviet analysis implies (but with reservations) that the proletariat is already in control in many African states and that these countries are in a transitional stage on the road to a socialist society.[32]

The Soviet objective of bringing about a complete evacuation of Western European and American influence in Africa is also still being pursued by various tactics, such as perpetuating unrest, playing the United States and West Germany off against the former colonial countries, and convincing Western investors that Africa is going socialist. The Soviet Union still makes a great deal of propaganda out of its aid, trade and, especially, cultural contacts with the underdeveloped countries.[33] But while there was a hint earlier that support from the U.S.S.R. could be demanded by underdeveloped countries almost as a right, no such implication appears any longer in Soviet propaganda. "Where will the underdeveloped countries find the means needed for economic development? The experience of the socialist countries shows that *the principal source is internal accumulation,* primarily the national income."[34]

Recognizing that the loyalty of the leaders of the underdeveloped world to the U.S.S.R. cannot be bought or depended on, and that the city rabble is fickle, the Communists have in the last couple of years emphasized the need to develop disciplined non-Communist groups within the new countries of Africa. Primarily, the Communists have put their organizational efforts into three areas:

Firstly, they have pushed nationalization of industry and agricultural reform as the means to eliminate foreign and native capitalists and large landowners. They seem especially fearful of the growing middle class of peasants who have some training in agricultural techniques and the use of machinery, and try to turn the poor peasants against them. Soviet literature is full of material on the agricultural situation in Asia and Africa.[35] The Soviet leaders recognize the popularity of land redistribution and undoubtedly remember what their land reform programs in Eastern Europe accomplished on their behalf in the period immediately after World

War II. At the same time, the Communists seek to organize the peasantry into centrally controlled unions and cooperatives and, of course, with Communist personnel in key positions.

Secondly, the Soviet Union seeks to build up a group of skilled bureaucrats, engineers, scientists, and managers who are trained in the Soviet bloc and sympathetic to Communism (in some cases they may be turned into outright agents). Special efforts are made to attract impressionable young African students to Eastern Europe. Once they are enrolled in the institutions of higher learning the Komsomols give them special attention.[36]

The third and most important organizational effort has been made in the area of trade union activities. The Communists have always opposed the apolitical attitude, especially in the use of strikes, of most Western European trade unionists and are, therefore, much encouraged by the growing political role of the African trade union movements.[37] It is clear from Soviet materials that within the last couple of years the Soviet leaders have come to see their best chance of a mass-disciplined following is among the trade unions, and are giving them special consideration and attention. They have given full endorsement to the African Trade Union Conference, strongly supported by the U.S.S.R.'s closest friends in Africa, and are pleased by its anti-colonial political orientation and by its insistence that affiliates cannot be a member of a world body as well. Although this restriction also includes the Soviet dominated World Federation of Trade Unions (WFTU), the Communists are trying to make up for this minor shortcoming by establishing unofficial relations between the two bodies.[38] But it is really at the local trade union level that Communists hope to build the core of their strength. Various centers for training trade unionists have been set up in the Soviet bloc and include among their participants labor leaders from Africa. Control over the trade unions would give them an organization with few rivals in Africa. The difficulty is that African leaders, particularly those with a leftist, Marxist leaning such as Nkrumah and Sékou Touré, also look to the trade unions for a political following. This may lead to competition in which the Communists are likely to be at a serious disadvantage.

In conclusion, it is interesting to note that in meeting the tactical problem of creating an organized following in Africa there appears to be one faction at least that would like to relax the ban on Communist parties, insisting that a hard core Communist nucleus is essential in any organizational activity.[39] Politically-oriented trade unions are not enough, because of their divided economic and political interest. The rank and file of Communist trade unions may be easily manipulated under normal circumstances, but in times of crisis they tend to fall apart.[40] But whether there are to be Communist parties or not, it is clear that the first flush of optimism about sweeping the new African leaders off their feet is passing, and that the Soviet Union is turning to more traditional methods of agitation and organization as the basis for any long-standing influence in Africa.

Thus, the present outlook for a rapid extension of its hegemony in Africa is not encouraging for the U.S.S.R. The current flush of Western prosperity, particularly in Western Europe, and Western moderation and sensitivity in dealing with the underdeveloped world present formidable obstacles. Nevertheless the increasing dichotomy between rich and poor nations and the overwhelming problems of the new countries are factors favoring the Communists. The Soviet Union may merely be waiting for the disgruntlement of the outcasts of the Common Market and the reluctance of the West to aid underdeveloped areas over a long period to play into its hands. But even then it is doubtful whether the U.S.S.R. would automatically step into the breach. It would first carefully consider the costs.

The U.S.S.R. and Ethiopia: A Case of Traditional Behavior

—SERGIUS YAKOBSON

The present *modus operandi* of the Soviets in Ethiopia seems to be in many ways a refined and ideologically refurbished version of the Russian policy of pre-Revolutionary days.

Russia's interest in Ethiopia is centuries old. An offer to join forces with Ethiopia and the Protestant West in the struggle against the Moslem Turks reached Moscow before Peter the Great. Hiob Ludolf's pioneer work, *Historia Aethiopica,* was translated into Russian in the seventeenth century, and the teaching of the Amharic language became a part of the Khar'kov University curriculum nearly 150 years ago.

It is true that a permanent Russian diplomatic mission was established in Addis Ababa only in 1902. But long before that date, Russia gave close attention to Ethiopian affairs. In the nineteenth century, relations between the two countries were already developing along manifold lines—political, military, religious, cultural, and technical—and various political and social forces of the old regime were at work to orient Ethiopia toward Russia. To the farsighted Russians of pre-Soviet days, peaceful penetration of Ethiopia meant not only a means of influencing and controlling the fate of the country, but also a promising means by which to enter the interior of Africa, to exert influence on Egypt and the whole Nile area, to get a foothold on the Red Sea, and, last but not least, to keep check on the British. Ethiopia thus seemed to be a most suitable postern gate into the African continent.

The pre-Revolutionary political leadership of Russia tried, however, not to show its hand. It wanted to avoid open involvement in colonizing plans for East Africa, as well as any entanglement in Ethiopia's resistance against the pressures and encroachments of her neighbors and of the colonial powers. But advice was given freely, and large assignments of arms—rifles, rounds of ammunition, cannons—along with musical instruments to equip a military band, were clandestinely shipped to Ethiopia. Old Russia's aid was gratefully received by Ethiopian rulers; only the gift of a phonograph aroused Negus Menelik's indignation. He said he was "no child who wanted musical boxes."[1]

Of lasting importance in fostering Ethiopian good will toward Czarist Russia was the dispatch by the Russian Red Cross Society of a first aid unit to Ethiopia during the Italo-Ethiopian war at the end of the nineteenth century and the medical aid rendered by the hospital established at a later date in Addis Ababa by Russian doctors. Memories of this type of assistance continue to linger in Ethiopia.

The pages that Russia and Ethiopia shared in history's annals were skillfully glorified in a contemporary setting by Emperor Haile Selassie during his mid-1959 visit to the Soviet Union, when he declared:

> Ethiopia may be proud of the fact that one of its citizens fought on the side of Peter the Great and of the fact that, thanks to this, it became bound up with your greatest poet, Alexander Pushkin. Our country remembers with eternal gratitude the speedy help in the form of arms, which the people of this great country gave to us at the time of our decisive struggle with imperialism in the last years of the last century. But this aid was expressed in the furnishing not only of arms but also of medical aid which was so greatly needed, particularly at the time of the battle at Adowa. The furnishing of this aid demonstrated in the decisive hours of our history that the people of this great country over the course of many years, have always stood on guard for the cause of freedom and the independence of nations.
>
> However, your great country furnished aid not only during times of danger; its magnanimity extended also to periods of peace and progress. Thus, our Menelik II Hospital, set up at the beginning of the present century was, before World War I, staffed by Russian doctors. Therefore we note with a feeling of great satisfaction that this great humane tradition is being carried on even now in the great work which Soviet doctors and nurses are now carrying on in the hospital named for Dejadzmatch Blacha in our capital.[2]

The Emperor might have mentioned three further points in recapitulating the record of relations between pre-Revolutionary

Russia and Ethiopia. Technical aid given Ethiopia by Russia—for instance, in gold mining operations and geological surveys in the Wollega Province; the training of Ethiopian students in Russian educational establishments—for instance, Mr. Teclé Hawariat, who pleaded the cause of Ethiopia before the League of Nations, had been one such student; and the striking contribution to the promotion of Russian aspirations in Ethiopia made by the Russian Orthodox Church. In Ethiopia, the activities of the Church far exceeded normal missionary efforts and trespassed on political ground. In promoting the idea of a union between the Russian Orthodox Church and the Ethiopian Orthodox Church, which was part of the Coptic Church, it openly advocated a political course of action: establishment of Russian spiritual leadership in the affairs of the Abyssinian Church was evidently to lead to political ascendancy as well.

The Emperor's account, meant of course for Soviet consumption, was incomplete in another respect: it glossed over a more recent historical event—the material support given to Italy by Soviet Russia during the Italo-Ethiopian conflict of the nineteen thirties.

It took about thirty years from the downfall of the Russian monarchy before the Soviets were in a position to continue in Ethiopia where Czarist Russia had left off.

In the early years after the Russian Revolution, Ethiopia served as a sanctuary for some of the White Russian emigrés who, incidentally, became staunch admirers of the Negus, and not merely because he was their savior and protector. For more than four months, for example, the Grand Duke Alexander Mikhailovich was a guest of the Negus. Each night he dined with him, and "the more the Negus talked about the mistakes committed by my relatives," the Grand Duke related in his memoirs, "the clearer it dawned on me that we should have put an Abyssinian at the head of our Imperial Council. . . . He liked to hear my stories of the reign of my relatives because they helped him to decide what he should not do."[3]

Afterward, during the Italo-Ethiopian conflict of the nineteen thirties, Moscow chose to show its contempt not only for the observance of moral standards in the conduct of foreign affairs, but even for its own theory of just and unjust wars. While vociferously denouncing Fascist Italy before the international forum in Geneva for its unprovoked and predatory attempt to subdue the people of Ethiopia, Soviet Russia at the same time pumped vast supplies of raw materials into Mussolini's war machine—oil from Batumi, coal from Feodosiya and Nikolayev, and wheat from Sevastopol. And this at prices higher than those prevailing on the world market.

It was World War II that heralded the return to the more or less traditional pattern of Russo-Ethiopian relations. In the spring of 1943, exactly two years after the liberation of Ethiopia by the British, the U.S.S.R. and Ethiopia exchanged notes concerning the establishment of diplomatic relations. This policy decision was indicative of the intention of the Soviets to regain their predecessors' influence; in order to secure a foothold in East Africa the Soviet legation was provided with a sizable staff.

However, it is only within the last few years that a large-scale effort has been made by Moscow to overcome Ethiopian animosity toward the Soviet system, to detach Ethiopia from the West, and, if at all possible, ultimately to win its exclusive friendship. This intensive Soviet drive was symbolized by the elevation of the respective Soviet and Ethiopian diplomatic missions to embassies in June, 1956, and, three years later, by the state visit of the King of Kings to the "homeland of socialism."

Up to the middle of the nineteen fifties, the Emperor was a staunch supporter of the West. He dispatched detachments of the imperial bodyguard to the fighting front in Korea. They fought valiantly—not a single Ethiopian soldier is known to have been taken prisoner by the Communists. Ethiopia's voting record in the United Nations was similar to that of the other nations of the free world.

Then a new series of developments set in. After its participation in the Bandung Conference of 1955, Ethiopia came out strongly in support of the pan-African movement at the conferences of independent African states held in 1958 at Accra and two years later at Addis Ababa. Simultaneously, it began to play an active role in the consultations, decisions, and actions of the uncommitted nations—whether at the gathering of the heads of neutral states in Belgrade shortly after the Soviet renewal of nuclear testing or at the latest disarmament conference at Geneva. In fact, at the time of his stay in the Soviet capital in 1959, Haile Selassie was awarded the honorary degree of doctor of law by Moscow University explicitly for "high achievements in the cause of strengthening peace and strengthening of the Bandung principles of peaceful coexistence of states with different social and economic orders."[4]

Nevertheless, all this does not necessarily add up to a change of heart on the part of the Emperor, but rather to a modification of the mode of political behavior. At heart, Haile Selassie remains as before—a convinced anti-Communist.

One can only guess at the reasons for the metamorphosis of the former stalwart of collective security into a backer of the made-in-Moscow concept of peaceful coexistence. A variety of factors must have contributed to the Emperor's decision to seek a new approach in safeguarding the independence and further advancement of his country. On the whole, his decision must have been reached within a framework of uncertainty and uneasiness about the way the world's history was moving, and a need to trim his sails to the "wind of change" sweeping not only Africa but other parts of the world as well.

The cold war seemed to be dragging on without changing markedly the balance of power in favor of the free world. On the contrary, the political, military, and economic posture of the Soviet Union seemed to have been enhanced by the latest developments. It was perhaps too early to assess the effect the de-Stalinization process, initiated by Chairman Khrushchev in his anti-Stalin speech of 1956, would have on the might of the Communist camp. But the launching of Sputnik in September, 1957, was eloquent proof of Soviet technological progress, and the impressive annual growth rate of the Soviet economy admittedly outstripped that of other more advanced industrial societies. The Emperor must, of course, have been aware of the dangers implicit in the new Soviet ruble diplomacy, but he must have pondered whether he could afford to ignore the material and technical aid liberally distributed by Moscow and readily accepted by other Afro-Asian nations. The continuous deterioration of relations between Ethiopia and Britain, the economic recession in Ethiopia, as well as in the United States, and the huge funds and technical resources required for the five-year plan of economic development adopted by the Ethiopians in 1957 must have carried particular weight in shaping his decision.

In addition, there were political considerations. Relations with Egypt under Nasser, whose pan-Arab ambitions the Emperor dreaded, left much to be desired. Fears of the creation of a "greater Somalia," the establishment of which was allegedly being encouraged by Great Britain and Egypt, and of Moslem encirclement haunted Haile Selassie. A roadblock had to be established to prevent the Somalis from seeking support in the Communist camp. The sensitivity of a small nation's leader and his anxiety lest his country lose its identity in a struggle between the great powers must particularly have prompted Haile Selassie to adopt a neutral position. In his Moscow speech, quoted previously, he had already commented pointedly on the non-participation of small nations in the negotiations concerning the settlement of the Berlin question, and again during the short sojourn in Belgrade on his homeward journey he specifically warned the great powers not to repeat the mistakes of the Berlin Congress of 1878 and of the conference at Yalta. Finally, the collapse of the colonial system in Africa confronted Ethiopia with a challenge—that of establishing herself as a major component of a radically changed African continent and of becoming at last the spokesman for the new and independent Africa. In an official publication of the Ethiopian Ministry of Information issued in 1960 the following explanation for the omissions of the past occurs: "Ethiopia's role in the struggle of African freedom had been limited, but the limitation had been due not to lack of enthusiasm but rather to the limitations imposed on a nation that had much of her own problems to solve, and the fast-moving wheel of time to race against."[5]

On the other hand, if any single event was primarily responsible for deciding the Emperor upon reappraisal of his formal alignments and conduct of foreign affairs, it was presumably the poor showing the Western powers made in their handling of the Suez crisis; their actions on that occasion resulted in their moral and political defeat, and in the massive Soviet penetration of Egypt. The latter situation was dangerous for Ethiopia, traditionally a favorite target of Egyptian intrigues and attempts to stir up trouble.

In the old days, Haile Selassie was referred to by *Pravda* "not as the Lion of Judah but as the jackal of American imperialism."[6] Now, in the summer of 1959, the Emperor's journey to the Soviet Union was designed to become a landmark in the latest phase of Russo-Ethiopian relations. The Soviet leaders knew how to please and impress Haile Selassie. In a Leningrad exhibition opened for the occasion at the Museum of Anthropology and Ethnology, the Ethiopian Bible was placed next to the photographs of the gifts to be given to the Soviet hospital in Ethiopia established there in 1946. The Emperor was honored not only by the award of an academic degree, but also of the Suvorov military order, one of the two highest Soviet military decorations. As a token of Soviet technical prowess, he was presented with an IL-14 twin engine plane for his private use. And a two-week tour of the country, which included inspection of industrial sites and irrigation projects, provided specific evidence of the economic and technical might and progress of the Soviet Union, and of its ability to help the industrial and agricultural development of Ethiopia.

The effort was not lost upon the Emperor. Afterward, he extolled the "industry and diligence of the people"[7] and praised Soviet Russia as "the world's greatest power" not forgetting, however, in his eulogy to give due credit to Peter the Great as well. The journey also "elicited his admiration for certain state-socialist development methods which he described as 'very useful.' " In return, the Emperor and his party ". . . were hailed as the representatives not only of Ethiopia, but of the whole African liberation movement," and Haile Selassie did not mind "accepting this identification."[8]

The high point of the Emperor's visit was, however, the granting to Ethiopia of a long-term credit of $100 million at a low rate of interest, a credit that was to enable the Soviet Union to render economic and technical aid "in the form of survey work, the supply of equipment and materials, and other forms of economic assistance."[9] This was the second largest credit ever granted by the Soviet Union to an African nation and was obtained by the Emperor, according to his own words, "without asking."[10] The goal of the Soviet action was, among other things, to open the gates of Africa to a large number of Soviet technicians and to strengthen Ethiopia's state ownership in industrial undertakings at the expense of private enterprise and investment.

The exchange of letters regarding the credit arrangements was, moreover, backed up by the signing on July 11, 1959, of a special Soviet-Ethiopian trade agreement. It was concluded for a period of three years, but was to remain automatically in force thereafter unless explicitly terminated by either of the parties. Each party received most favored nation treatment. The U.S.S.R. was to export to Ethiopia "machinery and equipment, tractors and agricultural machinery, light and heavy motor vehicles, bicycles and motorcycles, road building machinery, rolled metal products, oil and oil products, cameras and film, medical supplies, household goods, chemicals, textiles, window glass, canned fish products, etc." In return Ethiopia was to "export coffee, raw hides, oil seeds, sheep and goat skins, and other traditional produce. Payment was to be made in freely convertible currency."[11]

Little is known about the upshot of the private talks which took place in Moscow between Chairman Khrushchev and his illustrious guest, but Paul Wohl, a veteran observer of the Soviet scene, must have been on the right track in assuming that relations with Egypt were the crucial point in these *pourparlers*. "Moscow apparently expects," he wrote, "to use its newly gained position in Ethiopia as a means of pressure against President Nasser should the latter turn against the U.S.S.R. By building up Emperor Haile Selassie as the champion of the African liberation movement, the Soviets also have cast a shadow on President Nasser's claim to leadership in Africa."[12]

On October 12, 1959, three months after the end of the Emperor's conversations in the Soviet capital, the former head of the African Department of the Soviet Foreign Ministry, A. V. Budakov, was appointed ambassador to Ethiopia, which, according to Soviet plans, was now to become a showplace of the Soviet policy of co-existence in Africa.

It is an ungrateful task to speculate today on even the immediate political future of the world, particularly since a rejuvenation of leadership in a number of countries is bound to create a new political climate before long: Konrad Adenauer is eighty-six years old, Chiang Kai-shek seventy-four, Charles de Gaulle seventy-one, and Harold Macmillan and the two major Communist figures, Khrushchev and Mao Tse-tung are all sixty-eight. In Ethiopia, Haile Selassie, who is seventy, still continues to keep a firm grip on the whole life of his country, and as long as he remains at the helm of state, Moscow has little chance, even if it wants to, to change the order of his Empire. No Communist Party exists there; nor is there a powerful Communist controlled union movement, nor any youth or women's front organizations. But when nature takes its course and a new, less experienced, national leader takes over in Ethiopia, the rather antiquated political and social order of the country may have severe difficulty in warding off reform pressures bound to develop from within and from without.

For the time being, in their effort to penetrate the country politically and establish their influence on a broader basis, the Soviets use three traditional media—medical aid, education, and the Russian Orthodox Church.

In a country whose population is 22 million and where the total number of native and foreign physicians can still be counted in the hundreds, a hospital is today as significant in "selling Russia" to the Ethiopians as it was half a century ago. Medically and politically trained, the personnel of the Soviet Red Cross Hospital in

Ethiopia attend to both body and soul of the local population. According to a recent Soviet source, about 600,000 Ethiopians received treatment from the Russians between 1947 and 1957.[13] Additional medical aid, also meant to influence public opinion, was rendered through the Soviet Red Cross and Red Crescent Society shipments of medicine for Ethiopian flood victims. A new Soviet trade agency, "Medexport," handles the transfer of pharmaceutical goods to Ethiopia.

The Soviet cultural offensive in Ethiopia has proceeded so far without striking innovations along the lines chartered by the Soviets for other foreign countries, mixing cultural objectives with politics. A standard agreement on cultural cooperation was signed by the Soviets in Addis Ababa on January 13, 1961, providing for exchange of scientists, teachers, students, cultural and sports delegations, theatrical companies, and tourists. Specifically, under the terms of this arrangement, the Soviet Union was to delegate scholars to lecture at the University College at Addis Ababa and to study Amharic there, while Ethiopia was to send students to Russia for the study of agriculture and education and to be trained as radio announcers in Amharic. No Soviet cultural exchange is complete, however, without the participation of the Bolshoi Ballet, a part of which came to Ethiopia in January, 1962. The Emperor himself attended the performance and presented gold medals to the group.

Where 95 per cent of the population is illiterate, audio-visual media are particularly appropriate for attracting wide attention and for unobtrusive dissemination of propaganda. In the capital and the more remote provinces of Ethiopia, Soviet films dealing with such conspicuous topics as the Emperor's visit to the U.S.S.R., the Soviet people's war effort, and developments in the Congo have been shown. A photographic exhibition organized by the Soviet authorities in Addis Ababa seems, according to an account by a Soviet witness, to have appealed particularly to the elite—students, teachers, priests, government workers, and journalists, some of whom were already studying Russian.[14] What, however, can more favorably impress a foreign audience than the world of children's dreams, gay, rich in color, and free of the drab reality all around? In November, 1961, a display of Soviet children's paintings and books was opened to the public in the Ethiopian capital.

Lectures extolling the economic progress and beauty of the Soviet Union, the virtues of economic, technical, and cultural cooperation between the U.S.S.R., Ethiopia, and other African countries, and the merits of Soviet youth organizations and education were offered by Soviet speakers within the framework of the Festival of Soviet-African Friendship, celebrated in Addis Ababa in 1961. Another platform for indoctrination was the World Youth Forum in Moscow to which was invited the president of the student council of the Addis Ababa University College, the only higher educational establishment in Ethiopia.

As to the education of Ethiopians in the Soviet Union, two government officials of the Ethiopian Ministry of Information were awarded five-year Soviet government scholarships, beginning in 1961, for the study of cinematography and related subjects. Other Ethiopian students devoted themselves, also on Soviet government grants, to the pursuit of veterinary medicine and engineering.

For the training of Ethiopian youth at home, the Soviet government undertook to build a special technical school for 1,000 boys and girls as a gift to the government of Ethiopia.

Cultural exchange programs, as a rule, are not a one-way street. In the fall of 1961, after having visited Red China, an Ethiopian theater company came to the Soviet Union. Finally, a show of Ethiopian *objets d'art* in Moscow was made a part of the political-cultural rapprochement.

As it once did under the Czars, the Orthodox Church today again plays a significant role in Russo-Ethiopian cooperation.

After the seizure of power by the Bolsheviks in 1917, the old ties between the Russian and the Ethiopian churches ceased to exist. The Russian Church, violently persecuted by the Communist government, for obvious reasons could hardly serve as a bridge between the two countries.

Only when the Great Patriotic War made the Soviet government realize the potential value of the support it could derive from the Church, domestically as well as internationally, did the situation change. The reopening of the Ecclesiastic Mission of the Moscow Patriarchate in Jerusalem in 1948 led, ten years later, to the resumption of formal contacts between the churches in Russia and Ethiopia. With the blessing of the Russian Patriarchate and the Soviet government, the head of the Jerusalem Mission and an inspector of the Leningrad Theological Seminary came to Ethiopia for three weeks in January, 1959. They were warmly received by the Emperor and the populace—an exultant student of theology even hailed them "as a delegation not simply of the Moscow church, but as though from Christ himself."[15] Six months later, the Emperor during his stay in Moscow paid a personal visit to the Patriarch Alexis who decorated him with the religious order of Vladimir the Holy, first class. And finally, in the same summer of 1959, the Metropolitan of Harar, as a representative of the first Patriarch of Ethiopia, repaid the visit of the Russian church dignitaries. The elevation of the Ethiopian Church to the rank of a Patriarchate and its emancipation from the Coptic Patriarchate in June, 1959, seem further to have stimulated the interest of the two churches in each other.

The chains fastened by the Communist leadership on the Church in the Soviet Union having never been removed, Moscow knew how to collect its due, even for the little freedom it granted the Church in the conduct of its foreign relations. An article in the issue of the official organ of the Moscow Patriarchate for May, 1961, summarized the new relationship between the churches of Russia and Ethiopia in the following revealing words:

> Of course, it is understood that mutual knowledge on a closer and more detailed level between the Church of Ethiopia and Orthodoxy is extremely useful for both sides. On the one hand, it should aid in testing and strengthening the consciousness of the unity of the Church, and, on the other, make its contribution to the movement of peace supporters and to the cause of the struggle for the national liberation of the peoples of Africa.[16]

The offers by the Russian Church to aid the Ethiopian Church in its opposition to the Vatican, to the preachers of the Koran, and to the Protestant groups, the "avant garde of American imperialism," served Moscow's grand strategy. Church officials of both countries were sophisticated enough to understand the political climate in which they were operating. The Russian Church representative did not fail to take note of the close ties existing in Ethiopia between church and state. On the other hand, the assistant director of the Ecclesiastical College of Addis Ababa, upon his return from the Soviet Union in 1961, stressed the important role played by the Russian Orthodox Church in the struggle for peace.

Resumed within the framework of an old pattern, the relations between Moscow and Addis Ababa seem to have moved on an even keel after 1959. However, neither side appeared to be particularly tempted to enlarge the base of existing relations or to force the tempo of development. Potential mutual advantages must have been carefully weighed against other considerations and especially suspicions of ulterior motives.

Those who expected spectacular results from the "gigantic" Soviet offer of a $100 million umbrella credit must, by now, be disappointed. Neither Khrushchev nor the President of the Soviet Union has so far visited Ethiopia, in spite of the promises publicly given to the Emperor during his sojourn in Moscow. At the time of writing, in June, 1962, only a fraction of the 1959 credit has actually been used by Ethiopia—$2 million in convertible currency for the Emperor's land reform program. In addition, with much delay, a contract was signed in 1961 for the construction by the Soviets of an oil refinery costing $12 million at the port of Assab, the first refinery to be built in Ethiopia. It has been calculated that its output will be 500,000 tons a year, enough to ensure the supply of high-grade gasoline and fuel oils for Ethiopia. And only in January, 1962, in the town of Bahar Dar, did the Emperor lay the foundation stone of the technical school offered by the Soviets two years earlier.

Some U.S. government experts are inclined to interpret the "failure to implement with dispatch [Soviet] bloc-supported projects" as being "probably due in large part to increasing Ethiopian wariness that bloc aid might promote Communist subversion." No one can doubt the validity of this assumption, but it has to be recognized that the Ethiopian situation is not unique, but rather a typical one. By the end of 1961, the heavy Soviet propaganda barrage notwithstanding, the U.S.S.R. had extended to the whole of Africa only one-tenth of the loans that the Communist leadership claimed to have granted. And in the case of Ethiopia, there seems to have been a special, weighty reason for this state of affairs—the desire of the Emperor to avoid, in all circumstances, dependence upon or identification with any of the groups opposing each other in the divided world of today. The Ethiopians' "dexterity in balancing opposing influences," has been referred to in the *New Republic* of April 13, 1959. An article by Jeanne Contini in the *Reporter* of May 25, 1961, goes a step farther in the same direction by pointing out the Emperor's efforts to reduce interference of foreign powers in Ethiopian domestic affairs by "dividing up the control of even individual projects." A rather entangled pattern of foreign aid thus evolves:

The Ethiopian air force is being trained by the United States, Sweden, and Great Britain. The army has been trained and equipped by the United States, while Norway is training the navy. West Germany is participating with the United States in the Blue Nile power dam project; Italy built the Koka Dam; Yugoslavia is working on the Scebeli; the major burden for essential highway construction is being borne by the United States, but contracts for roads have also been awarded to Israel and Italy. Technical training centers have been or are being built by the United States, Sweden, and the Soviet Union. There is a Russian-staffed hospital in the capital, and Czechoslovakia has recently contributed a $20-million credit for the purchase of hospital equipment.

However, perhaps the most important element in the present record of Soviet failure to dislodge the West in Ethiopia is the fact that Haile Selassie's pattern of behavior in handling the Soviet angling for total partnership is as personal as it is national in character. In the words of an astute student of Ethiopian developments: "Ethiopia is no country which wants to be hurried even in the most advantageous economic circumstances. Caution, diffidence, secrecy are national characteristics."[17]

Soviet Economic Policies Toward Afro-Asian Countries

–G. WARREN NUTTER

Among the notable changes in Soviet foreign policy since the death of Stalin has been the promotion of commercial relations with non-Communist countries undergoing economic development. This program has involved deviation from at least two important policies: economic isolation from the non-Communist world and active hostility toward "bourgeois" governments. This deviation is motivated by the belief that the advent of Communism in emerging nations will be hastened by stimulating the state's role in economic development.

There is a twofold basis for this belief. Firstly, the Soviet Government believes that economic development—and hence Communism—enters its initial phase when a colony becomes independent; any help extended by other countries at this stage is considered a boost along the inevitable path to Communism, even though the government prevailing in the new country at the moment may be "bourgeois nationalist." The local Communist Party is counted upon to agitate for revolution, to achieve a place in coalition governments, and, ultimately, to seize power. Meanwhile, Soviet bloc countries can guide industrialization into socialist channels by giving assistance only to economic undertakings of the state.

Secondly, it is recognized that economic growth, if made rapidly enough, can undermine traditional ways of life and bases of social order, leading to political instability and, eventually, chaos. The stage will then be set for the rise to power of the disciplined Communist Party. Hence, if economic growth does not lead to Communism through its good effects, it must do so through its bad ones. By this interpretation, Communism cannot lose.

THE DEVELOPMENTAL LOAN PROGRAM

The primary instrument chosen for aiding economic growth has been the extension of loans to the governments of underdeveloped countries. A few outright gifts and grants have been made, mainly by Communist China, but they are exceptions. Normally, each loan is connected with a specific project that the receiving country wishes to undertake; the lending country in the Soviet bloc restricts its decision as to whether to lend or not, and offers little advice on the advisability of projects unless asked to do so. Most of the loans have been made for the development of industry, but they cover a wide variety of other activities as well—the more important are multi-purpose installations (for reclamation, irrigation, and hydro-electric power projects, and so forth), the provision of transportation facilities, and exploration for minerals.

The formal terms of loans are generous. Interest rates are low, seldom higher than 2.5 per cent, and often lower. The normal period of repayment is 12 years, sometimes less and frequently more. The first payment is usually due no sooner than a year after the project is completed, though in some cases repayment must begin the year following each specific drawing on a line of credit. The form of repayment is often left vague in the contracts, the lending country indicating a willingness to accept local currency or bartered goods, but retaining the right to require convertibility into gold or other currencies. The specifics being subject to negotiation, the Soviet-bloc country making the loan remains in a position to exercise an important degree of discretionary control over terms.

In almost all cases, a loan is merely the financial counterpart of a specific list of goods and services that the Soviet country agrees to supply under the designated terms. That is to say, the agreement is in fact for a loan in kind to be repaid in kind or in financial equivalents. Each loan therefore represents exports of particular goods and services from the Soviet bloc country to the borrowing nation, goods and services that will later be replaced by a flow of goods in the opposite direction. The borrowing government is not free to shop around for goods and services in other countries or, for that matter, in the lending country itself. Acceptance of the loan involves simultaneous acceptance of the material form it will take.

The value of goods and services being provided is derived from prices set through negotiation. The prices chosen seem generally to be those prevailing in international markets at the time agreement is reached on the loan, though Soviet bloc products do not always measure up in quality to those more widely traded. Instances have been known where prices both higher and lower than the international level have been charged, depending on the country being dealt with. A similar process of negotiation is involved in determining prices for goods to be delivered in repayment of loans.

It becomes clear that Soviet bloc loans in this program are essentially barter agreements providing immediate delivery of Soviet bloc goods in exchange for deferred delivery of goods by the recipient country, terms of exchange being determined bilaterally through negotiations. The arrangements therefore partake of the general disadvantages of bilateral barter, in addition to the unique disadvantages of dealing with a state trading monopoly. The flexibility of terms and the role played by negotiation and re-negotiation mean that any Soviet bloc country that extends a loan retains wide power to determine the benefits for the recipient country.

It is often claimed that there are no strings attached to Soviet bloc loans, but from what has already been said, one may doubt that this is true in any meaningful sense. It is a fact that Soviet bloc countries, by contrast with Western countries and international agencies, do not set down in advance the explicit conditions required of projects and programs for which loans are to be extended. Nor do they offer advice unless requested. But conditions are implicit in the very decision to support or not to support a project. Moreover, each loan involves an agreement on the specific basket of goods to be provided by the lending country, whereas loans and grants from Western countries and international agencies seldom tie the recipient down to a particular list of goods or source of purchase. The recipient country is generally free to shop around. Moreover, the use of loans from the Soviet bloc is strictly limited to government enterprises in the recipient country, a limitation that ensures that their effect is to expand the socialized sector of the economy. Finally, the Soviet Union has not hesitated to modify or cancel its obligations by unilateral action when the recipient country has incurred its displeasure. The outstanding case has been the credit of $353 million extended to Yugoslavia in 1956 but effectively revoked two years later in reprisal for Yugoslavia's behavior with regard to the Hungarian revolution.

The current program of aid to underdeveloped countries was initiated in 1954, when the Soviet Union and Czechoslovakia made three small loans to Afghanistan to finance two grain elevators, a

TABLE 1

SINO-SOVIET BLOC DEVELOPMENTAL LOANS AND GRANTS* EXTENDED TO UNDERDEVELOPED COUNTRIES OUTSIDE THE BLOC, 1954–61

(in millions of U.S. dollars)

	New Commitments by Two-Year Periods				Cumulative Total	
	1954–55	1956–57	1958–59	1960–61	1954–60	1954–61
All Countries	125	1,119	1,210	1,928	3,609	4,382
Africa, Asia, Middle East	125	650	1,456	1,568	3,171	3,799
Latin America and Europe		469	−247	360	438	583
Africa						
Ethiopia			153	447	278	601
Ghana			112	2	114	114
Guinea				182	50	182
Mali			41	69	107	110
Somali Republic				65		65
Sudan				62		62
Tunisia				22	8	46
Asia	125	459	775	764	1,826	2,122
Afghanistan	10	111	92	2	215	215
Burma		42	−30	81	12	93
Cambodia		22	12	31	55	65
Ceylon		16	42		58	58
India	115	146	512	190	933	963
Indonesia		109	139	393	509	641
Nepal		13	7	35	41	55
Pakistan				33	3	33

Middle East	191	528	358	1,066	1,076
Cyprus		6	1	6	1
Iran					6
Iraq		138	78	216	216
Turkey	10	7		17	17
Syria	181	−4	1	179	178
Egypt		338	278	604	615
Yemen		43	1	44	44
Latin America		106	360	322	466
Argentina		104		104	104
Bolivia			2		2
Brazil		2	2	4	4
Cuba			357	215	357
Europe	469	−353		116	116
Iceland	5			5	5
Yugoslavia	464	−353		111	111

Source—Data compiled by U.S. Department of State. Derived from *The Sino-Soviet Economic Offensive in the Less Developed Countries* (U.S. Department of State [Washington, D.C.: May, 1958]); *The Communist Economic Offensive Through 1960* (U.S. Department of Defense [Washington, D.C., November, 1961]); *Background for Mutual Security, Fiscal Year 1961* (U.S. Department of State [Washington, D.C., 1962]).

Note: Sums and detail may not agree because of rounding.

* Grants amount to about $221 million, mainly given by Communist China. The remaining figures apply to credits. Excludes loans and grants for military purposes.

flour mill, a bakery, a gasoline pipeline, three cement plants, a cotton textile mill, a leather processing plant, and to provide road-building and agricultural machinery. From this modest credit of around $10 million to be utilized over a period of years, the program has expanded steadily and substantially, at least through 1961. Since none of the Soviet bloc countries has provided a comprehensive account of the loan program, the volume of credit extended can only be estimated.

According to recent official statements, the Soviet Union made commitments of loans totaling more than 2 billion foreign exchange rubles, or $2.25 billion, over the years 1955–60 to some fourteen Asian and African countries outside the Soviet bloc.[1] This figure seems to agree with tabulations by the U.S. State Department of Soviet bloc developmental loans that show a total commitment of $2.9 billion by all members of the bloc to those fourteen countries over the same period (see Table 1). The volume of commitments to all countries outside the bloc is recorded by the State Department as having reached $4.4 billion by the end of 1961, of which $3.8 applies to Africa, Asia, and the Middle East. Since there is little evidence of additional commitments during 1962, the figures probably hold for the present as well.

These commitments apply over relatively long periods of time, and only a portion of them has so far been put to use by recipient countries. As in the case of commitments, there are no definitive accounts of utilized credits, although some data have begun to appear in Soviet sources. For example, a recent article appearing in the Soviet Union presented statistics on the value of equipment shipped from the Soviet Union in fulfillment of credits extended for construction of enterprises in underdeveloped countries outside the Soviet bloc (see Table 2). These shipments amounted to around $250 million over the three-year period 1958–60. Since credits were used to purchase items in addition to equipment, total utilization of credit was certainly larger than this amount, but it is difficult to say how much larger.

Estimates made by the U.S. State Department indicate that by the end of 1961 recipient countries outside the bloc had utilized $1 billion, or less than a quarter, of the commitments made by all Soviet bloc countries, the rate of utilization rising from about $190 million during 1955–56 to about $490 million in 1960–61 (see Table 3). According to these estimates, the volume of credit utilized by the end of 1961 had reached the level of total commitments made by some point in 1958, account being taken of the cancellation in that year of most of the credits to Yugoslavia. Hence there is an average lag of about three years in the utilization of credits. It is impossible to predict the course to be followed in future years by the rate of utilization of credits. Although new commitments showed a substantial rise between 1958 and 1961, the effect of this on future utilization may be offset as repayments increase. If new commitments do not continue to rise—and there is every indication that they fell sharply in 1962—the net rate of utilization will inevitably decline and ultimately become negative, when repayments overbalance drawings on remaining credits.

TABLE 2

VALUE OF EQUIPMENT DELIVERED BY THE SOVIET UNION TO
UNDERDEVELOPED COUNTRIES OUTSIDE THE BLOC UNDER
TERMS OF DEVELOPMENTAL LOANS
(*in millions of U.S. dollars*)

	1955	1958	1959	1960
Total	1.1	111.2	68.6	67.9
Afghanistan	1.0	9.7	14.5	17.3
Ceylon		0.4	0.3	
Guinea				0.1
India	0.1	97.2	33.9	17.9
Indonesia				5.0
Iraq			0.2	4.2
Turkey		0.2	1.2	3.6
United Arab Republic		3.1	16.5	17.7
Yemen		0.5	2.0	2.1

Source—I. Kapranov, "The U.S.S.R.'s Technical Assistance to Foreign Countries," *Problems of Economics*, April, 1962, p. 50 (translated from *Vneshniaia Torgovlia*, 1961, No. 6). Rubles converted into dollars at exchange rate of 1.1 dollars per ruble.

Note: Sums and detail may not agree because of rounding.

The Soviet program of developmental loans may be put into perspective by comparing it with aid programs of the more advanced economies outside the bloc (see Table 4). Over the five-year period 1956–60, underdeveloped countries have utilized for developmental purposes about $36 billion in grants and credits extended governmentally and privately by the member and associated countries of OECD together with Japan. About half the flow of aid came from the United States; two-fifths was in the form of grants requiring no repayment. Within this period the flow of aid from the West was fifty times that from the Soviet bloc—from the United States, twenty-five times; from France, nine times; from the United Kingdom, six times, and from West Germany, four times. Japan, Italy, and the Netherlands each supplied more aid than the entire Soviet bloc.

TABLE 3

SINO-SOVIET BLOC DEVELOPMENTAL LOANS AND GRANTS UTILIZED[a] BY RECIPIENT UNDERDEVELOPED COUNTRIES OUTSIDE THE BLOC, 1954–61
(*in millions of U.S. dollars*)

1954		0
1955		3
1956		107
1957		80
1958		205
1959		162
1960		185
1961		306
	Total	1,048

Source—Estimates by U.S. Department of State. Derived from *Hearings, Foreign Assistance Act of 1962* (Committee on Foreign Affairs, U.S. House of Representatives [Washington, D.C., 1962]), Part II, p. 334.

[a] Excludes loans and grants utilized for military purposes.

A breakdown of Western aid by receiving area is not currently available, but it may be useful to indicate the distribution of governmental aid for development from the United States. Over the period 1956–60, the U.S. Government provided bilateral grants and loans to underdeveloped countries that were utilized to the extent of $11.2 billion. Of that sum, $4.3 billion went to the Middle East (including Greece) and Southeast Asia, $4.5 billion to East Asia, $1.5 billion to Latin America, $0.6 billion to the rest of Africa, and $0.3 billion to Europe (excluding Greece).[2] It is doubtful whether any of the countries outside the Soviet bloc except Cuba and Guinea has received and utilized more developmental aid from the Soviet bloc than it has from the U.S.A. alone. Iraq, Syria, Egypt, Yemen, Ghana, and Indonesia are likely to be additional exceptions in the near future, as they continue utilizing existing bloc commitments.

TABLE 4

DEVELOPMENTAL LOANS AND GRANTS FROM OECD MEMBER AND ASSOCIATED COUNTRIES AND JAPAN UTILIZED[a] BY RECIPIENT UNDERDEVELOPED COUNTRIES, 1950–60

(in billions of U.S. dollars)

	1956	1957	1958	1959	1960	1950–55[b]	1956–60
Governmental	3.3	3.9	4.5	4.5	4.9	11.4	21.0
Loans	1.0	1.1	1.4	1.7	1.5	3.6	6.7
Grants	2.2	2.7	3.1	2.9	3.4	7.8	14.3
Private loans & investments	2.8	3.5	2.8	2.7	3.1	9.6	14.9
Total	6.1	7.4	7.3	7.2	8.0	21.0	35.9
France	1.1	1.1	1.3	1.3	1.3		6.1
West Germany	0.4	0.5	0.5	0.8	0.6		2.9
Italy	0.1	0.2	0.1	0.2	0.3		0.9
Japan	0.1	0.1	0.2	0.1	0.3		0.8
Netherlands	0.3	0.1	0.2	0.2	0.2		1.1
United Kingdom	0.6	0.9	0.9	0.8	0.9		4.0
United States	3.2	4.1	3.7	3.0	3.8		17.8
Other countries[c]	0.3	0.3	0.4	0.5	0.6		2.2

Source—The Flow of Financial Resources to Countries in Course of Economic Development 1956–1959 (OECD, April, 1961); *ibid., in 1960,* Feb., 1962.

Note: Sums and detail may not agree because of rounding.

[a] Excludes loans and grants utilized for military purposes.

[b] Annual average multiplied by six.

[c] Austria, Belgium, Canada, Denmark, Ireland, Luxembourg, Norway, Portugal, Sweden, and Switzerland.

OTHER FORMS OF ECONOMIC ASSISTANCE

The Soviet bloc has supplied large numbers of engineers and technicians to underdeveloped countries, but almost all have been provided on a strictly cash basis. In this respect, the program of the Soviet bloc bears no resemblance to Point Four and other technical aid programs of the West. According to the count made by the U.S. State Department, there were some 8,500 technicians from the Soviet bloc employed in underdeveloped countries outside the bloc during the last half of 1961, about two-thirds of them in the Middle East and virtually all the rest in other parts of Africa and Asia.[3]

Members of the bloc have also extended credits to finance purchase of military equipment by underdeveloped countries outside the bloc. By the end of 1961, the volume of those credits had accumulated to around $2 billion plus a large loan, the amount of which is unknown, to Cuba.[4] Of the known credits of $1.2 billion extended up to the end of 1960, 95 per cent were accounted for by Iraq, Egypt, Syria, and Indonesia (see Table 5). The last-named country alone accounted for 42 per cent. There is no doubt that the Soviet bloc has undertaken a major role in arming three countries in the Middle East (Iraq, Egypt, and Syria), one in Southeast Asia (Indonesia), and one in the Western Hemisphere (Cuba).

On the other hand, the magnitude of Soviet military aid looks very small when put beside the U.S. military assistance over the same period (see Table 5). And it must be recalled that the U.S. aid is in the form of grants, while the Soviet aid is in the form of loans that must be repaid. In comparing the two programs, however, it must be kept in mind that much of the U.S. program, par-

TABLE 5

LOANS BY SINO-SOVIET BLOC AND GRANTS BY UNITED STATES TO COUNTRIES OUTSIDE THE BLOC FOR MILITARY PURPOSES, 1954–60
(*in millions of U.S. dollars*)

	Sino-Soviet Bloc	United States
All countries	1,200[a]	16,975[b]
Africa	6	44
Middle East and Asia	1,194	8,082[c]
Middle East and South Asia	1,194	2,951
East Asia and Pacific	—	5,131
Latin America	[a]	397
Europe	—	8,282[c]

Sources—The Communist Economic Offensive Through 1960 (U.S. Department of Defense [Washington, D.C., November, 1961]); *Statistical Abstract of the United States,* 1961 (U.S. Bureau of the Census [Washington, D.C., 1961]), p. 872.

[a] Excludes Cuba, which has received large loans, the amount of which is unknown.

[b] Includes grants of $170 million to unspecified areas.

[c] Greece included in Middle East, not in Europe.

ticularly in Europe and the Far East, has no counterpart in the data shown for the Soviet bloc. The proper counterpart would be data on the extent to which the Soviet Union subsidizes the military effort of Communist China and the European satellites. In any event, the program of military assistance of the Soviet bloc is directed to one set of countries, in and out of the bloc, and the U.S. program to another.

SOME EFFECTS OF SOVIET POLICY

The Soviet policy of developmental and military credits should have its proximate effect on the structure and balance of the foreign trade of the Soviet bloc, since the economic counterpart of the loans is a net flow of goods and services out of the bloc to underdeveloped countries initially, and a reversed net flow later on. It is interesting to note that the Soviet Union had an export surplus in commodity trade of about $1 billion over the seven years 1954-60[5] which might be interpreted as the real counterpart of net credits to underdeveloped countries. But this does not seem to be the case, since trade between the entire Soviet bloc and all underdeveloped countries was roughly in balance over the five years 1955-59, the latest period for which such data appear to be available (see Table 6). There may, of course, have been some underdeveloped countries importing more from the bloc than they were exporting to it and vice versa, but in the aggregate the commodity flow seems to have been roughly equal in both directions. In a regime of multilateral trading, this balance could be consistent with net lending by the bloc: through triangular exchanges, the underdeveloped countries could run an import surplus, and the bloc an export surplus, against

TABLE 6

SINO-SOVIET BLOC TRADE WITH UNDERDEVELOPED COUNTRIES
OUTSIDE THE BLOC, 1955-59
(*in millions of U.S. dollars*)

	Exports	Imports
1955	535	628
1956	686	635
1957-59, annual average	819	821

Sources—Joseph Berliner, *Soviet Economic Aid* (New York: Frederick A. Praeger, 1958), p. 85; *Economic Survey of Europe*, 1960 (Geneva: Economic Commission for Europe, 1960), p. V-10.

third parties. But this cannot happen in a regime of bilateral exchanges such as the one enforced by the bloc. Hence we are led to conclude that the underdeveloped countries as a group have accumulated ruble balances in their bilateral clearing accounts with countries of the Soviet bloc, and that these balances are large enough to offset utilized credits from the bloc. That is to say, the underdeveloped countries seem to have been lending enough on short term to the bloc to cancel out their borrowing on long term from the bloc.[6]

In the aggregate, trade with Soviet bloc countries accounts for only a very small fraction of the total foreign trade of underdeveloped countries, running around 3 per cent in recent years.[7] Considered in relation to aggregate production, it is even less important: annual imports from the Soviet bloc apparently accounted for less than 1 per cent of aggregate national income of the underdeveloped countries around 1958.[8] Cumulated utilized credits from the bloc, both developmental and military, would amount to less than 2 per cent of aggregate national income for a recent year; cumulated committed credits, to less than 6 per cent.

At the same time, the trade and aid program of the bloc has been of considerable significance for some individual countries. In recent years, trade turnover (imports plus exports) with the bloc has amounted to more than 20 per cent of total turnover in the case of Afghanistan, Egypt, Syria, Iceland, and Yugoslavia; it has run between 10 and 20 per cent in the case of Turkey, Greece, Guinea, and Uruguay.[9] Cumulated credits committed to date amount to more than 25 per cent of national income for a recent year in the case of Egypt, to more than 40 per cent in the case of Syria and Afghanistan, and to more than 20 per cent in the case of Burma and Yemen.[10] In most other cases they have been under 10 per cent and generally less than 2 or 3 per cent.

It is clear that the Soviet bloc program of economic aid to underdeveloped countries outside the bloc has had its main impact in a few strategic countries. In the aggregate, the volume of resources expended has been small, and evidence available to date even indicates that there has been no net flow of resources out of the bloc into these areas. For maximum effectiveness, this small volume of resources has been concentrated in a few countries where, presumably, the payoff for the bloc is expected to be greatest. Whether the program has been or will be a success or failure depends on the vantage point from which it is viewed.

Soviet Economic Aid to Non-Aligned Countries and the Soviet Program in South and Southeast Asia

—TETSUJI YASUHIRA

I

Although foreign aid is only one of the many aspects of the Soviet Union's foreign policy, it is, perhaps, the one that has best mirrored the changes since Stalin's day in Soviet strategy and tactics toward the former colonial and semi-colonial areas of the world. Soviet aid to the underdeveloped countries does not, of course, denote a new-found interest. The Soviet Union has from its foundation evinced a strong interest in those areas, since it regards their "liberation" as a crucial step toward the ultimate objective of a Communized world. Through the Comintern and later the Cominform, Moscow gave its support to the struggles for power of foreign Communist parties, relying primarily on propaganda and the promotion of "class struggle." Before the adoption of economic aid as an instrument of penetration, however, the economic and social development of an underdeveloped country was treated by the Soviets as an internal issue that the local Communist Party should simply exploit as best it could.

After World War II, a series of Communist attempts to win power in countries around the world through insurgent outbreaks generally ended in failure. The cases of China and North Vietnam were notable exceptions. Most of the revolts in Europe and Asia led only to the suppression of Communist parties and the spread of public hostility to Communist aims. As a result, insurgency was gradually abandoned as a major strategic line of the world movement. Signs of the changing attitude of the Communist bloc toward the nationalist governments of the new countries began to appear as early as 1951. In 1952, a Moscow economic conference issued a call for international cooperation to promote the rapid industrialization of such countries, and it was soon after this that the first Soviet offers of economic and technical aid were made. Khrushchev further modified the Soviet approach to the former colonial areas after Stalin's death. Under the banner of "peaceful coexistence" and "economic competition," the soft sell replaced the hard. The old theories of imperialism and colonialism, ill-adapted to the situation of the new independent states, were refurbished under the labels of "neo-imperialism" and "neo-colonialism." Armed with these new epithets, the Soviet Union turned its efforts toward dissuading the new states from accepting economic aid from the United States or Western Europe, warning that it would lead to subjugation and loss of their newly won independence. While trying to keep out Western influence, the Soviet Union at the same time seized every opportunity to declare its readiness to aid the new states and to convey the notion that the Soviet Union wielded economic and political resources that could match those of any Western country.

Today, the Soviet Union's obvious lag behind the United States in economic power is brushed off as transitory. Repeatedly, Khrushchev has asserted that the Soviet economy, with its high growth rate, will surpass that of the United States in twenty years under conditions of "peaceful coexistence." The Soviet Union has magnified its economic prowess and heavily publicized its economic assistance abroad in a patent effort to boost its prestige and build a good name in the developing countries. Despite the sacrifices it imposes on the hard-pressed Soviet economy, the economic aid program is regarded by the Kremlin as an effective long-term investment for expanding Soviet influence in the new countries and undermining that of the West. The aim, at least for the moment, is to lead newly developing countries toward pro-Soviet neutrality and to enhance the U.S.S.R.'s prestige and power in world politics. For this purpose, rather than encouraging revolutionary "class struggle" through the Communist parties in such countries, Moscow now prefers to help their indigenous nationalist leaderships (the "national bourgeoisie") and thus win their favor and draw them into a unified "national front" under the slogans of anti-imperialism and anti-colonialism. Just how far the Soviet Union is now relying on the approach through economic aid to win support for its foreign policy goals may be seen clearly in India and Egypt. These countries, despite the severity of the measures they have enacted against local Communists, receive more economic aid from the Soviet bloc than any other newly developing countries.

The Soviet appeal to the former colonies centers on a contrast between Western economic aid, pictured as a neo-imperialist effort to retain the old imperialist rule, and aid from the Communist bloc, stemming only from friendly and selfless motives. The effort to dramatize this contrast is manifest in the Soviet aid formula, which is distinguished by some features not commonly found in Western ones:

1. Economic aid from the Communist bloc is largely in the form of loans and includes few gifts. Free grants from the bloc, when they are made at all, are often little more than extravagant diplomatic courtesies. Thus, when Bulganin and Khrushchev visited South and Southeast Asia in 1955, they presented, among other things, 15 buses and some hospital equipment to Afghanistan, farm machinery worth $1 million to India, and one transport plane each to Burma and India. Western economic aid, by contrast, consists largely of grants: between 1954 and 1957, the United States provided economic aid totalling $2,560 million, of which $1,780 million, or 70 per cent, was in the form of grants.[1]

2. Communist loans usually are offered on easier terms than private Western credits. Interest, which is 3 to 6 per cent in the case of Western loans, averages only 2 to 2.5 per cent for Soviet loans. Moreover, Soviet loans are extended over longer periods than Western loans, normally for ten to twelve years.

3. From the signing of an agreement to its implementation, the aid procedure of the Communist bloc is flexible and unencumbered, enabling the donor to capitalize on every opportunity to achieve propaganda effect. Western aid, by contrast, is extended under relatively strict conditions: the signing of an agreement is followed by a series of steps such as fund allotment, contract signing, and goods delivery, and the execution of the program continues to be supervised after the funds are granted.

4. Communist bloc loans are often repayable with local money or local products, saving the borrower the trouble of raising foreign currency funds to repay the debts. This is an important attraction to newly independent nations, which suffer from chronic shortages of foreign exchange. Western loans, to keep the borrower from defaulting on payments, provide for new contracts to replace the old ones or allow extensions of the term for repayment. The Communist bloc, with its general shortage of material resources, can find uses for most kinds of products supplied by the developing countries and can accept them regularly. The Western powers, on the

other hand, can obtain the necessary commodities through free market channels and do not always wish to import them from the recipients of their aid loans. The Communists have also fostered the idea that the bloc countries, with their controlled or planned economies, are free from business fluctuations and therefore more reliable as markets for the surplus products of developing countries. Hence the new countries often believe it easier to repay Communist loans.

5. Aid from the Communist bloc, especially from the Soviet Union, concentrates to a large extent on showy construction items having manifest propaganda value, such as power plants, heavy industrial plants, oil development, iron works, and other key industrial projects. India's Bhilai steel works and Egypt's Aswan High Dam are among the best-known examples. Western aid, by contrast, often takes the form of farm products, foodstuffs, educational and health projects, and assistance in light industrial development —items not directly contributory to major industrialization. Although Western farm surpluses have eased food shortages—for example, in India and Pakistan—and their counterpart funds have been used for internal development, this sort of aid alone does not satisfy most new nations, which tend to be preoccupied with the idea of industrialization. The Western attitude, however, has shifted considerably of late. India's second five-year plan, for instance, involved aid projects in which the Soviet Union, West Germany, and Great Britain each constructed government-owned steel plants capable of producing over a million tons of ingots a year. In addition, private steel manufacturers carried out expansion programs with aid from the World Bank. For the country's third five-year plan (1961–66), the United States contemplates such aid items as steel mills and chemical fertilizer plants.[2]

6. Communist aid concentrates largely on government-owned undertakings (the public sector), whereas Western aid generally favors free enterprise (the private sector). In a country such as India, where native private capital is deep-rooted or where foreign private capital plays a part, friction may occur between the government's policy of expanding the public sector of the economy and U.S. partiality for free enterprise. In the case of India's second five-year plan, the United States was at first disinclined to offer aid because it looked with disfavor on India's approving attitude toward the Soviet Union's line of priority for the public sector. On this issue, however, the U.S. and Indian viewpoints appear to be

reconcilable so long as the basic principles of a mixed economy are sustained in India.

Soviet propaganda seeks to derive maximum capital from all these features. Moscow is aware that an aid program with emphasis on heavy industry is highly attractive to most developing nations, with their eagerness for full-fledged political and economic independence, quick industrial development, and improved public welfare. In the eyes of young nations eager for industrialization, the Soviet Union is an attractive model. These nations are impressed by the Soviet Union's transformation from a backward agricultural nation into the world's second industrial power within the span of thirty-five years. They tend to link this achievement with the "socialist" system and the "heavy industry first" policy. Of course, the Soviet Union quite openly employs its aid to lure the new states toward socialization on the Soviet pattern.[3] The Kremlin evidently also hopes that facilitating the industrialization of a new country will result in reducing its dependence on Western industrial products and that, over the longer run, a Western overproduction crisis can be induced.

Exploiting the fact that Soviet aid consists primarily of low-interest loans rather than free grants, Moscow's propagandists claim that the free aid provided by the West is in fact tied to political conditions, and camouflages the actual economic relationship between the Western powers and the newly developing peoples. The "actual relationship," according to the Soviets, is that the Western capitalist powers, through their monopoly systems, import raw materials from the underdeveloped countries at low, unstable prices, while selling the new countries consumer goods at monopoly prices to make exorbitant profits; a meager portion of these profits are returned to the exploited countries in the form of free development aid. By contrast, the fact that Soviet aid is provided on a loan basis, in connection with normal trade, is advanced as proof that it is free from ulterior motives and intended only to promote economic interchange with the developing nations.

The Soviet Union also profits from the fact that the proud young nations are usually better prepared psychologically to accept low-interest loans than free grants. Moreover, with no record of colonial rule in the developing areas, the Soviet Union has the advantage of appearing innocent in the eyes of the new nations. The fact that Soviet trade is on a governmental basis underscores the impression that the Soviet Union can act without regard to commercial considerations—although political rather than economic factors have motivated this practice at times. As a result, Soviet aid may initially be welcomed by a new nation, but second thoughts tend to arise sooner or later. Moscow's own propaganda betrays the Soviet Union's real motives: while hurling charges of "imperialism" and "colonialism" at the West, Soviet writings clearly anticipate that the economies of the developing countries will gradually become more and more tied to the Communist bloc. Soviet aid is seen as part of the spadework of preparing for eventual Communist take-overs in such countries through the nationalization of industries and the concentration of economic power in the hands of the state.

In keeping with these objectives, the Soviet Union places great emphasis on technical assistance in the form of training of skilled workers, technicians, and technical leaders. In India, for example, an educational agreement was concluded in connection with the establishment of the Bhilai steel works. The U.S.S.R. trained cadres of unskilled Indian workers for a period of 2 to 9 months, provided 300 skilled Indian workers with the technical training needed for operating the steel works, and gave on-the-spot training to an additional 500 engineers and technicians. Finally, some 300 skilled workers and 135 engineers were invited to study Soviet technology in the Soviet Union.[4]

Outside the framework of such training agreements, increasing numbers of students, technicians, economists, scholars, and officials from developing countries are invited to the Soviet bloc countries. For obvious reasons, the Soviets make every effort to draw as many candidates as possible for this training from among the leaders of "progressive" youth movements.

Since World War II, the U.S.S.R. has been systematically training experts for assignment in foreign countries. Initially, most of them were sent to the Eastern European satellite countries and later to Communist China. Since 1953, Soviet experts have been travelling to developing countries: In this period about 80 per cent of those working outside the U.S.S.R. have gone to Egypt, Syria, India, Indonesia, and Afghanistan. The technicians double as propagandists and political recruiters. A Soviet comment on the technical aid program during 1960 provides an idea of its scale:

> The enterprises and projects built with the U.S.S.R.'s technical assistance are mass schools for training local personnel—builders, erectors, and operators. In accordance with the agreements concluded,

several thousand Soviet specialists were sent in 1960 to twenty-seven countries, including fifteen economically underdeveloped countries.[5]

It has been estimated that in projects of equal dollar value, the number of Soviet experts employed on project sites is about five times the number of American experts. In Egypt, for example, where Soviet aid roughly equals that given by the United States, some 1,500 Soviet technicians are permanently employed, as against 200 Americans. In India, the steel plant financed by Moscow engages 1,000 Soviet technicians, while 200 British technicians suffice to run a steel plant of the same size financed by Great Britain.[6]

II

Between 1954 and 1961, according to available statistics, the Communist bloc as a whole extended to the developing countries economic credits totalling about $4,680 million, of which $1,150 million was actually used. Of the latter, the Soviet Union provided about 75 per cent, Communist China and Czechoslovakia each supplied approximately 0.8 per cent, and East Germany, Rumania, Poland, and Hungary made minor contributions.

Military aid from the Communist bloc between September, 1955, and mid-1961 totalled $1,800 million, distributed among ten countries (not including Algeria's FLN). During 1960 alone, Communist economic and military aid amounted to $1,500 million.[7]

Unlike Western aid, which is distributed among developing countries without particular favoritism, Communist aid tends to be concentrated in specific areas, reflecting the Soviet bloc's effort to derive maximum political effectiveness from its limited resources. So far the great bulk of Soviet assistance has been extended to a handful of South Asian and Arab nations, primarily India, the United Arab Republic, Indonesia, Iraq, and Afghanistan. The Soviet aid offensive has even extended to CENTO and SEATO members such as Pakistan and Thailand and, more recently, to a number of African and Latin American countries. Communist credit is distributed among recipient areas roughly as follows: Southeast Asia, 45 per cent; the Middle East, 25 per cent; Latin America, 15 per cent; and Africa, 0.1 per cent.

Statistical comparisons of Soviet and Western aid totals are, of course, misleading in that Soviet aid is inseparable from trade. Moreover, the Soviets include military assistance in reporting their official aid totals, inflating the total figures. Finally, statistics on the magnitude of Soviet assistance are misleading unless the fact that most of it is stretched over long periods is kept in mind.[8]

Moscow expects that the introduction of Communist facilities and goods into the new countries will make them dependent on Soviet-made parts and involve them in new consumption habits, and eventually lead them into reciprocal barter trade relations with the Communist bloc. To repay what they owe the Soviet Union, the recipient countries will thus ship their products to the Communist bloc instead of selling them on the Western market as in the past, and will soon find themselves regularly depending on the Communist market.

A look at the content of Soviet economic assistance to key countries of South and Southeast Asia will give a more precise idea of this pattern.

INDIA

India today may be called the focal point of East-West competition in foreign aid. U.S. aid, unrivalled in amount and applied to a wide variety of fields—agriculture, manufacturing, mining, transportation, communications, education, and public health—on the whole consists of items less pretentious and less propaganda-oriented than Soviet aid. The latter, though much smaller in amount, concentrates on heavy industries and is given on easy credit terms as follows:

1. Interest—2.5 per cent on all types of credit.
2. Term of repayment—12 years except for medical supplies, for which the term is 7 years.
3. Currency for repayment—Indian rupees; repaid funds will be used by the Soviet Union for purchasing Indian goods.

The psychological advantage of these loans over free grants is their apparent respect for Indian pride; moreover, Moscow's claims that they are free of political strings fall on receptive ears among the Indians.

By the end of 1961, according to its announced statistics, the Soviet Union had promised India credits totalling $775.4 million (for 32 construction projects), a figure that equals 20 per cent of the total foreign aid accepted by India. However, the part of this credit that had actually been used at that time was $240.8 million.

Although the United States attaches importance to development of the private sector while the Soviet Union gives priority to the public sector, there are signs that the aid competition has led to some alteration in the approach of both rivals. Thus, each side is now trying to invade the other's favorite territory: the United States shows interest in helping in the construction of the Bocaro steel mill, the fourth biggest item among India's public sector projects, and the Soviet Union and Czechoslovakia threaten to make their first advances into India's private sector.

Heavy industry and oil development remain, however, the principal fields for Soviet aid. Among heavy industry projects, the most successful has been the construction of the Bhilai steel mill. In February, 1955, the Soviet Union provided $131.4 million in aid for the Bhilai steel plant, which, when completed on March 3, 1961, had an annual steel ingot capacity of 1 million tons. In June, 1960, the U.S.S.R. made further aid available for an additional steel capacity of 2.5 million tons a year. After the completion of this expansion program, Bhilai will account for a quarter of India's total steel production. The Soviet Union also sent 1,000 engineers to Bhilai and supervised the entire operation, from the preparation of blueprints for the mill to the training of personnel for its operation.

In the field of oil development, Soviet survey teams have discovered oil in Cambay, Assam and Ancleshwar. They are also constructing the Neiveli thermal power station, Barauni oil refinery, heavy machine-building and mining equipment plants, and other facilities.

In November, 1957, the Soviet Union granted $124 million for heavy machinery and coal-mining machinery plants, a precision optical instrument plant, a thermal power plant, and other construction projects in the second five-year plan; and in May, 1959, $20 million was made available for the construction of pharmaceutical, surgical instrument and other plants.

In September, 1959, India received a $375 million Soviet credit as economic assistance for the third five-year plan—specifically for developing the Bhilai metallurgical plant, as described above; for expanding a heavy machine-building plant in Ranchi to an annual production capacity of 80,000 tons; for increasing the annual capacity of a mining equipment plant in Dourgapore to 45,000 tons; for enlarging the Neiveli thermal power station to a capacity of 400,000 kilowatts, and increasing that of the Corba thermal power station by 200,000 kilowatts; for constructing the Singhrauli thermal power station in Uttar Pradesh State with a 250,000 kilowatt capacity; for completing the oil refinery in Barauni; and for constructing a heavy-duty electric equipment plant and a precision instrument factory.

Developed with this Soviet aid, India's first heavy machine-building and mining equipment plants are "public sector" industries and will have the capacity to produce 1 million tons of steel and 8 million tons of coal a year. As the Soviets put it, "Soviet assistance to India in organizing oil extraction and in building oil refineries will materially reinforce the state-owned sector in the oil industry and thus will strengthen India's economic independence."[9]

On February 21, 1961, a $125 million long-term credit agreement was concluded for building a 480,000 kilowatt hydroelectric power station on the right bank of the Bhakra River and an oil refinery with a crude oil processing capacity of 2 million tons a year in the state of Gujarat; for constructing a coal dressing plant in Kathara with an annual capacity of 3 million tons and building a fire-brick plant; and for exploration and development of oil and gas deposits.

The investment involved in India's third five-year plan is higher than in the second one. It appears to total between 105 and 110 billion rupees in the public and private sectors combined, the former accounting for 75 to 80 billion (as against the public-private investment total of 67.5 billion rupees in the second five-year plan). The investment total for the current plan includes an estimated foreign exchange requirement of some 35.5 to 36 billion rupees (approximately $7.5 billion) for the entire period of the third five-year plan. Of this total, the public sector portion, amounting to 26 billion rupees, accounts for 41 per cent of the net investment in the public sector of 63 billion rupees (75 billion rupees of public investment minus 10.5 billion rupees of expenses), as against 21 per cent in the second five-year plan—indicating how heavily the third plan is dependent on foreign capital.

Of the foreign exchange requirement of some $7.5 billion, $2,225 million was secured as aid from the free world by the end of 1961; the Communist bloc promised assistance totalling $618 million (including $500 million of Soviet aid).

Thus, foreign aid to India has so far been provided for the most part by the free world, with the United States taking the lead. The present question is whether India will be able to obtain the remaining billions of dollars required for its third five-year plan. Indeed, the success of the plan appears to hinge on this unknown factor. The fierce competition between East and West in aiding India could help, at least, to assure the acquisition of the balance.[10]

INDONESIA

Communist bloc assistance to Indonesia has become increasingly active since its inception in 1955. When civil conflict erupted in the country in February, 1958, the Communist aid effort was given a boost when the West showed its sympathy for the revolutionary regime while the Communist bloc unequivocally backed the central government. As a result, closer relations quickly developed between the bloc and the Indonesian Government. These ties were further strengthened by subsequent military and economic assistance from the Communist bloc, which became more and more active after Khrushchev's visit to Indonesia in 1960 and the inauguration in 1961 of Indonesia's eight-year plan for national development, backed by Communist aid.

Under the first economic and technical assistance agreement signed on September 15, 1961, the Soviet Union extended a $100 million credit to Indonesia, with a 12-year term of repayment and an interest rate of 2.5 per cent. The aid items included construction of a metallurgical plant with an annual steel capacity of 100,000 tons, motor roads, a technological school in Ambon, two rice farms, a stadium in Djakarta, and other similar projects. The metallurgical plant, the first state-owned installation of the sort to be built in the country, is expected to supply a third of the nation's ferrous metal needs. The two rice-growing farms on Kalimantan island are expected to play a vital part in the government's program for boosting production to achieve national self-sufficiency in this basic food crop. The 700-kilometer motor roads planned for Kalimantan are to provide access to its natural resources and open the way for people from Java to settle on the island.

In February, 1960, during Khrushchev's visit to Indonesia, the signing of the second economic assistance agreement made Soviet credit available for the construction of an aluminum plant, an Askhan hydroelectric power station in Northern Sumatra, and a metallurgical plant with an annual steel capacity of 250,000 tons. Further Soviet credit totalling $2 million was granted on January 1, 1961, to build nuclear reactors for peaceful uses of atomic energy. These credit agreements also call for technical assistance. Some 2,000 Soviet engineers are now in Indonesia, providing construction assistance and technical guidance.

An arms purchase credit agreement was signed on June 10, 1961, following preliminary discussions in Moscow in January between

Kremlin officials and an Indonesian Government delegation headed by Nastion, Minister of National Security. Although the details are not known, it appears that Indonesia will obtain fighters, bombers, jets, warships, submarines, torpedo-boats and tanks. Indonesia has similar arms purchase agreements with Poland and Czechoslovakia, from which it is receiving fighters, bombers, and transport planes.

With its economy under fairly severe strain, Indonesia naturally finds it difficult to obtain foreign assistance on a commercial basis. Soviet aid to Indonesia manifestly is motivated by political rather than economic considerations.

BURMA

Burma has not made much headway in economic construction since it achieved independence in 1948. The country professes neutrality in foreign policy and development along socialistic lines in domestic policy. Until recently foreign aid to Burma has been meager, among other things because of the political instability that has dogged much of the country's brief history. Having now launched its second four-year plan, however, Burma is eagerly seeking outside financial assistance.

As early as December, 1955, a Soviet-Burmese assistance agreement was signed as the upshot of the visit of Khrushchev and Bulganin to that country. The Soviet Union agreed to supply materials and technical services for industrial projects, irrigation projects, and farm development, and, in addition, to build a technological research center in Rangoon. This aid agreement was represented as an exchange of "gifts." In return for the Soviet "gift," Burma gave the Soviet Union a "gift" of rice. The relatively small-scale Soviet assistance totalled some $16.6 million. The technological research center is scheduled for completion in 1963. A hospital, hotel, theater, stadium, information center, and exhibition hall for farm and industrial displays were also thrown in among the promised gifts; of the total construction costs, 40 per cent or $10.08 million, was to be repaid with Burmese rice over a 20-year period. But owing to various complications, these latter projects were later cancelled with the exception of the plans for the hotel, hospital, and research center.

Up to 1960, foreign aid to Burma had reached a total of some $180 million. Communist bloc aid accounted for only a negligible portion of this total, partly because Burma was not eager to accept it. But the Communist bloc watchfully waited for opportunities to capitalize on Burma's economic difficulties and stepped in with trade offers at the right moment. Thus, in 1955–56, when Burma was having difficulty finding markets for its key export, the Communist bloc purchased large quantities of Burmese rice. This action paid dividends in terms of Burma's reaction, but still did not assume the form of long-term assistance.

Burma's need for economic aid became pressing in 1960–61. Having worked out an ambitious economic development program based on its second four-year plan, Burma now began to look actively for foreign assistance for its implementation. In January, 1961, Communist China entered the picture and granted Burma about $80 million in credits on easy terms. This represented the largest amount of aid ever given by Peking to a non-Communist country, and provides a measure of Peking's interest in expanding its influence in Burma. Thus, full-scale Communist assistance to Burma appears to be beginning, and here again there is a prospect of increasing competition between Eastern and Western aid.

AFGHANISTAN

Afghanistan has been the scene of a singular competition between the U.S.S.R. and the United States in the field of foreign aid. By December, 1961, foreign aid to the country amounted to more than $300 million, of which Soviet aid accounted for some $180 million and U.S. aid $140 million—one of the few cases in which Soviet aid topped that given by the United States. The Soviet Union, moreover, granted longer periods for repayment and lower interest rates than the United States.

Afghanistan, in fact, was the first non-Communist country to receive Soviet credit. In 1954, the Soviets extended credit for construction of a flour mill and a bakery ($3 million) and for street paving in Kabul ($2 million). Moscow was credited at the time with using imagination by entering the field with projects designed for maximum propaganda impact at minimal cost. But it was not until 1956 that the Soviets mounted a serious aid drive in the country. In that year, Afghanistan received a credit of $100 million for a wide range of projects: three hydroelectric power stations (total capacity, 80,000 kilowatts), a fairly large automobile repair factory, 850 kilometers of highways, an irrigation canal in Gerarabad, improvement of Kabul Airport, and preliminary surveys for oil and gas were included in the aid program. In July, 1957, Afghanistan received an additional Soviet credit of $15 million. All told,

Soviet credits accounted for a third of total investments in the country's first five-year plan, ending in 1962.

Since 1955, Afghanistan has become increasingly dependent on the Soviet Union for its economic development needs and is now seeking more foreign assistance than ever before for its third five-year plan. The Soviets obviously regard Afghanistan as a prime target of their economic aid offensive, and their aid efforts there are likely to increase in the future.

PAKISTAN

A member of SEATO and CENTO, and a recipient of U.S. military aid since 1954, Pakistan has from the outset made clear its commitment to the Western camp—a commitment that has survived the strain imposed on it by Western military aid to India in the Sino-Indian border conflict. Nevertheless, the Soviet Union has courted the Pakistanis.

Until 1960, Pakistan had received no Communist aid at all. In 1960–61 the Ayub administration, in launching the country's second five-year plan, expressed its willingness to accept economic assistance regardless of ideological considerations, and in March, 1961, Pakistan signed its first aid agreement (for oil development) with the Soviet Union. Under this agreement, Soviet credits totalling $30 million were promised to a country that had formerly been an exclusively Western preserve. Pakistan is to repay the debt over a period of 12 years at the low interest rate of 2.5 per cent. Payment will be in Pakistani rupees. The rupee counterpart fund deposited by Pakistan will be used by the Soviets to purchase Pakistani products. The assistance focuses on oil prospecting and research and includes provision for prospecting equipment, machinery, materials, etc., to be imported from the Soviet Union.

As a result of its acceptance of this Soviet aid, Pakistan received strong protests from American, British, and Dutch companies. Though rich in oil, the country has found it extremely difficult to undertake oil development on a commercial basis under existing conditions. The fact that the Soviet Union offered assistance in the face of these difficulties is a measure of its eagerness to win a foothold in Pakistan.

At about the time of its oil settlement with the Soviet Union, the Pakistani Government asked for Soviet assistance in carrying out a 10-year program to protect farmland from salt-water damage (a total investment of 5.9 billion rupees). In July, 1961, the Soviet

Union agreed to send experts to cooperate in this program. Pakistan is also willing to accept Soviet aid for its second five-year plan.

CAMBODIA

Neutral Cambodia skillfully exploits the rivalry between East and West to obtain aid and favorable trade agreements from both. The country receives most of its assistance from the West—88.5 per cent of the total. Of the U.S. aid funds, 70 per cent goes to military assistance, whereas the Communist bloc devotes its limited funds to eye-catching projects calculated to produce maximum propaganda effect. Communist assistance to Cambodia has been coming from the Soviet Union, China, Czechoslovakia, and Poland, with China in this instance taking the lead.

Soviet assistance has so far consisted of the following projects: The Soviet Union built a Red Cross hospital as a "gift" under a cultural and scientific agreement signed in Pnompenh on May 31, 1957; on December 3, 1960, Sihanouk and Khrushchev issued a joint communiqué in which Soviet credits for power plant construction and related technical assistance were promised; in addition, Cambodia sought and obtained Soviet agreement on assistance for a survey of natural resources; and on June 24, 1961, an agreement was signed in Pnompenh for the establishment with Soviet funds of a technological school for 1,000 students.

CEYLON

The foreign policy of the Bandaranaike administration has favored closer ties with the Communist bloc. Soviet assistance to Ceylon began about 1956, and in February, 1958, the two countries signed an economic and technical aid agreement involving low-interest, long-term Soviet credits of $30 million repayable in Ceylonese goods or sterling (or other appropriate foreign currency).

The aid program includes the following items from an ambitious list of projects: construction of an iron mill, construction of a tire and tube manufacturing plant, multiple development of the Malwata Oya valley, construction of a fruit refrigeration plant, a survey of peat deposits north of Colombo, construction of a flour mill, aid to cotton growing in Hambantata, and sugar cane growing in Kantalai.

Ceylon seems satisfied with the progress made on these projects. Dias Bandaranaike, Ceylon's Finance Minister, visited Moscow in March, 1962, for talks to consolidate the aid relationship between the two countries still further. Evidently these talks resulted in Soviet agreement to help with domestic costs as well as with foreign exchange in the construction projects; to treat the Soviet credit of $30 million not as an upper limit but as a base for possible future increases in aid; to consider construction of a second cement plant, a sugar refinery, and a textile plant; and to provide assistance in training between 200 and 300 Ceylonese engineers each year. Thus it is apparent that the Soviet aid program for Ceylon is now in high gear.

III

From the above rough outline of the pattern of Soviet assistance to countries in South and Southeast Asia, it is apparent that this region is indeed a crucial one in Soviet foreign aid strategy toward the newly developing areas. It is true that Soviet assistance, though considerable in the specific fields where it is concentrated, is of much smaller total magnitude than the Western economic aid programs. But it can be argued that the Soviets are receiving proportionately greater returns than the West in political and propaganda terms. The anti-Western legacy in many developing countries prepares the way for acceptance of the Soviet claim that Western aid carries political strings and that Soviet assistance will help bring true political independence and economic well-being to the recipients. Concentrated on basic industry and public sector expansion projects, Soviet aid appeals to the nationalism and eagerness for rapid economic growth that are strong in the developing countries. Especially when a conflict of interests between a Western power and a developing country arises, the Soviets are quick to move in with offers of aid and support.

An important question in the aid competition between East and West is, of course, that of the extent to which the Soviet Union can step up its economic assistance in the future. Though this question is not easily answered, some of the key factors relevant to it can at least be cited here.

1. The first such factor is the increasing economic power of the Soviet Union itself. How much more economic assistance will it be able to afford? In Khrushchev's "peaceful coexistence" theory, what matters most if U.S.–Soviet economic competition in terms of growth rates in national income. So far, the Soviet economic growth rate has been higher than that of the United States, but recently the Soviet economy has encountered many difficulties and is showing

signs of a slowing down in its rate of growth. At a time when investment in internal construction and defense costs are rising, will the U.S.S.R. be able to increase its foreign aid rapidly without seriously affecting its domestic economic goals? This question may be critical in view of the plans to sustain the high growth rate envisaged in the new Soviet party program.

2. The Communist bloc today, including the Soviet Union, is short of foreign exchange. Thus, increased economic assistance will have to be accompanied by more and more reciprocal barter agreements, which can become a major hindrance to trade expansion.

3. Although Soviet economic aid has some aspects that are attractive to the uncommitted countries, it has others that tend to make them wary. For instance, the counterpart fund deposited in the recipient country for aid received could be utilized for financing the propaganda activities of the local Communist Party. Another fear is that exchanges of engineers and workers under aid agreements might facilitate Communist infiltration and subversion.

In the final analysis, the outcome of the economic aid competition between East and West will be determined less by high-flown propaganda than by which side actually contributes most to the economic and political independence and material welfare of the recipient countries.

Leadership Cohesion in Communist China and Underdeveloped Asian Countries

—RODERICK MacFARQUHAR

Analyses of official Chinese Communist doctrine and policy concerning the "third world" of Asia, Africa, and Latin America are vitally important; but equally relevant to this topic are various aspects of the Chinese internal scene and various domestic policies of the Chinese leaders, which, while not adopted with the "third world" immediately in view, may nevertheless have a considerable effect on non-aligned countries by force of example. Indeed, there have been a number of occasions when the Chinese themselves have made it clear that they feel they can provide instruction for the rest of Asia.[1]

The importance of Communist China as a model has certainly not been neglected. Non-Chinese commentators have suggested that major successes in China could well prompt other countries to copy her. This dictum has been applied particularly to the economic sphere, for obvious reasons. China, like almost all other underdeveloped countries, aims at the rapid creation of a highly industrialized economy that will permit the fullest assertion of national power and the general raising of living standards. The Soviet precedent, while a somewhat dubious one with respect to the speed with which the people at large get higher living standards, showed that the Communist system was one which could be brutally effective for this purpose. The victory of Mao Tse-tung in 1949 and the subsequent erection of a Communist model in an Asian context immediately made that model even more clearly relevant in the eyes of China's Asian neighbors.[2]

While Chinese economic policies, achievements, and failures have received the greatest attention in the outside world, it is in fact the motive power behind these policies that should be the most interesting aspect of the Chinese model. This motive power consists of leadership and organization. These elements are in varying degrees common to all societies, but they are particularly vital in underdeveloped countries, where tremendous efforts have to be called forth from the people if the national goal is to be achieved. To be more specific, underdeveloped countries seem to require: (1) a national leader who commands the respect and loyalty of his countrymen and is able to convince them of the rightness of his policies and inspire them to put every effort into their fulfillment; and (2) an efficient body of trained and honest administrators to put the program of the leader into action and to help arouse the people.[3]

It has been truly said that with respect to organization, non-Communist Asians have shown themselves "far weaker and less adept" than the Communists.[4] The application of Leninist principles of organization in the totalitarian society of China helps to explain those long lines of Chinese peasants working tirelessly at dams and other construction projects. Without the wholesale adoption of the same system, it is doubtful whether non-Communists can ever hope to rival the Chinese in this sphere. To this extent, Communist organization is not an adaptable *portion* of the Communist model in the sense in which, say, collective farms are. Non-Communists can perhaps take comfort from the fact that while the system may get results more quickly, it also leads more quickly to mistakes, and to mistakes of far greater magnitude, as for example, the failure of the "Great Leap Forward."

Chinese leadership, or rather the cohesion of the Chinese leadership, the topic of this essay, is also largely inimitable, but, it will be argued, for quite different reasons. Before examining the degree of cohesion within the Chinese Communist leadership and analyzing its causes, three points must first be briefly clarified.

1. It seems rational to assume that whereas the peoples of probably all underdeveloped countries require a single leader, perhaps a charismatic personality,[5] if they are to be inspired to perform the numerous heavy tasks ahead of them, the actual government of the country should rest in the hands of a group of men rather than solely in the hands of a leader who completely dominates his colleagues. Clearly no leader, however able and conscientious, can efficiently cope single-handed with all major problems; and the conscientiousness of a single all-powerful leader is likely to degenerate. Without making any high estimate of Stalin's conscientiousness,

this seems to be one of the lessons we can draw from the reports of how he operated.

2. It seems even clearer that the cohesion of ruling groups is vital. One has only to look at what took place in Algeria just after independence or to remember the Indonesian rebellion of 1958. One obvious danger, other than the disruption of the normal life of the country that ensued in those two cases, is that the army may take over from the civilians, as it did in Burma in 1958. Cohesion is, of course, even more vital in a non-Communist than in a Communist country; there has as yet been no instance of a change in the nature of the regime stemming from a split in the leadership in a Communist country. The reason lies in the strength of Communist organization.

3. With respect to cohesion of leadership, the organizational system of democratic centralism would appear to have brought no special advantage to the Communists. It might be argued that such cohesion can be secured in Communist states because a dissident leader cannot resign from the Communist Party and set up an opposition party in the manner in which the former Indian Governor General and Congress Party leader Dr. Rajagopalacharia set up the Swatantra Party. While there are some grounds for such an argument, the attempt by Malenkov, Molotov, and Kaganovich to unseat Khrushchev in 1957 is proof that the Communist system does not in itself guarantee cohesion of the leadership. (Actually, it could be argued that the possibility for opposition to develop in a non-Communist state, while it may lead to defections from the leadership, also increases its stability, since those who remain together will think much alike; on the other hand, Communist dissidents who remain within the ruling group, though disagreeing with the majority, merely set up tensions within the group.)

If these points are accepted, it is obvious that the degree of success achieved by an underdeveloped country will depend in large measure on the quality of the men at the top and the way in which they work together. It is virtually impossible to attempt to measure the abilities of the Chinese leaders against those of their contemporaries in other underdeveloped countries. But it is possible to attempt to compare the degree of cohesion they have achieved with that achieved elsewhere and to suggest reasons for it.

Since the advent of the Communist regime in China, the top leadership—the Politburo—exhibited a high degree of cohesion until fairly recently. Until 1958–59, only Kao Kang in 1953–54 had broken with his colleagues. Since then, there have been Ch'en Yun, P'eng Teh-huai, Lin Po-ch'ü and Chang Wen-t'ien. Of these five, Kao and Ch'en could be said to have belonged to the very core of the leadership.[6] If one goes back over the whole period of Mao's leadership, a span of almost thirty years, there is only one more name to be added—that of Chang Kuo-t'ao, who never reconciled himself to his defeat by Mao in the final contest for supreme leadership and simply defected to the Kuomintang. If one compares this record with the roughly thirty years of Stalin's control over the Soviet Party, during which fourteen Politburo members were expelled—and killed—including such leading Old Bolsheviks as Trotsky, Zinoviev, Kamenev, and Bukharin, the Chinese experience appears somewhat exceptional. Nor has the Soviet pattern changed since the death of Stalin, although the fate of dissidents seems to be less final under Khrushchev. In the past nine years or so, twenty-two members of the Soviet Politburo have lost office, including such top men as Molotov, Malenkov, Kaganovich, Bulganin, Voroshilov, and Beria. Of the full members of the Politburo confirmed on March 6, 1953, after Stalin's death, only two—Khrushchev and Mikoyan—have not lost their positions. Of the four candidate members, only one retains his.[7]

The record of the Chinese is also good when compared with that of those of their Asian neighbors with as lengthy an experience of governing. The splitting up of the men who led Indonesia to independence—symbolized finally by the end of the duumvirate of Sukarno and Hatta—has already been mentioned. In Burma, too, the split was at the highest level, between U Nu on the one hand and U Kyaw Nyein and U Ba Swe on the other. As in Pakistan, the quarrels within the leadership led eventually to a military take over.

In Thailand, Pibul Songgram and Pridi Panomyong, who led the coup that ended monarchical autocracy in 1932, were never able to cooperate for very long; more recently, in 1957, the triumvirate of Field Marshal Pibul, Police General P'ao Sriyanonda, and Field Marshal Sarit Dhanarajata was disrupted when the latter staged a coup and his two associates went into exile. India has been the more fortunate, with only Dr. Rajagopalacharia breaking away from the top leadership four years after independence.[8]

What, then, are the reasons for the success of the Chinese in maintaining the cohesion of their leadership until so recently?

First and foremost, this cohesion depends upon the unchallengeable position of Mao himself. In most states, one problem that must concern the supreme leader is the possibility that he will be ousted by one of his senior colleagues. In a relatively stable society, such as the United States, the constitutional guarantee of a fixed term for the President eliminates this problem. In a similar society, such as Britain, which does not have this constitutional provision, the problem can arise from time to time despite the commanding nature of the position of Prime Minister.

Underdeveloped countries committed to rapid modernization are relatively unstable societies by virtue of the magnitude of the tasks they have set themselves. Indeed, the key problem of leadership in such countries is how to maintain a substratum of stability which will ensure that change is orderly but not held up.[9]

This permanent state of relative instability must affect the men at the top. What, in more developed countries, might be routine decisions become matters of great importance, complexity, and urgency; the possibilities and consequences of error become much greater. The leadership is in a sense living in a permanent state of crisis,[10] and disagreement within its ranks becomes much more serious. This is particularly the case in totalitarian states, where policy disagreements can be treated as political disagreements to be dealt with by "organizational" measures including even execution, and where there is no orderly process that provides for the succession to the supreme leadership.

In the case of China, the supreme leader—Mao—occupies an almost impregnable position. He does so by virtue of his generally correct analysis of the way in which to conduct the Communist revolution and his successful leadership of that revolution to victory. It must be remembered that the conduct of the Chinese revolution was a matter of considerable dispute within the Soviet and Chinese Communist parties until Mao took over in 1935. A number of leaders and methods were tried and found wanting until Mao finally triumphed. It is worth noting, too, that Mao's election to the chairmanship of the Party was the first major change in the Party leadership to be initiated by the Chinese themselves, unprompted by Moscow. This doubtless lent a greater "legitimacy" to his occupancy of the post.[11]

Mao's successful leadership of the Chinese revolution meant that he became the Chinese Lenin, the symbol as well as the architect of revolutionary victory and the forward march of history. This symbolic importance of Mao, together with a general extolling of his virtues and abilities, have become part of an extensive "cult of personality" centering around the Chinese leader.[12] But even without the cult, the symbolic importance of Mao makes him virtually indestructible. Khrushchev could destroy the myth of Stalin, the man who built Russia into a great industrial power, because there was always a greater myth to fall back on; even if he had wanted to, he could not have destroyed the myth of Lenin, the architect of the revolution, without sapping the very foundations of Communist rule in Russia. Mao is both Lenin and Stalin; and if the failures of the "Great Leap Forward" have considerably diminished the capital accruing from his role as China's Stalin, as China's Lenin he has an inexhaustible credit balance upon which to draw. The only comparable figures in the Communist movement today are Tito and Ho Chi Minh.

There is another aspect of Mao's successful leadership of the revolution to be taken into account. His colleagues at the top are all of the same generation as himself. Nearly all of them joined the Communist movement in the first half-dozen years after its inception in China.[13] All of them had an equal chance to rise to the top, and in fact the Communist Party today contains a number of people who were once senior to Mao.[14] That Mao eventually outpaced them all and justified his success by leading them to victory must have given them a healthy respect for his abilities. Psychologically, there must be a tremendous tendency to react to a mistake on Mao's part with the words "He's been much more right than wrong in the past, this is merely one slip," rather than with "This mistake proves Chairman Mao is finished."

If Mao's achievements make his ascendancy unquestioned, his unquestioned ascendancy means he has no need to rid himself of any of his colleagues because of their power aspirations. On the other hand, Stalin, after the death of Lenin, was faced with the fact that although he was Secretary General there were other men in the Party, notably Trotsky, who had played a role as great or greater than his own during the revolution and the early years of the regime. Since he was aiming above all simply for supreme power for himself, and since it was not going to come his way by right of achievement, he used his control of the Party apparatus to purge his colleagues. Even Khrushchev, despite his rout of the "anti-Party group" and the dismissal of Marshal Zhukov in 1957, has felt compelled in recent years to dismiss as scapegoats a number of Politburo colleagues whom he had originally brought into the top leadership as his own men. This is surely because he feels that his position, though strong, is not unchallengeable.[15]

In short, historical factors make it extremely unlikely that any of Mao's colleagues will want to get rid of him, or that he will want to get rid of them to safeguard his personal position. This is the basic explanation of the cohesion of the present Chinese Communist leadership.

The situation is clearly different in a large number of the Asian countries that have achieved independence since World War II. In Indonesia, Sukarno has long played a leading role in the nationalist movement; and by virtue of his superb oratory he has been able to command a great deal of popular support. But he seems never to have gained a personal ascendancy over his colleagues like that of Mao—an ascendancy based on a clear superiority in planning for victory. This may have been because he was not able to work closely enough with his colleagues during vital years of the independence struggle; the fact remains that he never became so much a symbol of the new Indonesia that those who disagreed with him hesitated to oppose because opposition would inevitably have failed or would have undermined the new state.

Burma and Pakistan had the misfortune to lose their outstanding leaders, Aung San (by assassination) and Jinnah, in the hour of independence. In Burma, U Nu who took over after Aung San's death was able to build up a remarkable degree of personal prestige in the country at large. But he could never become the symbol of the Burmese independence struggle and he clearly never established an unquestioned ascendancy over his senior colleagues. In Pakistan, Liaquet Ali Khan, Jinnah's lieutenant and premier of the new state, though not a charismatic personality, could doubtless have held the leadership together. But his assassination in 1951 left no one with the prestige to perform this vital role, and the Pakistani leadership disintegrated into power-seeking factions.

In India, the situation was complicated by the odd role of Gandhi within the independence movement, a role that was clearly the dominant one but which did not prevent men like Nehru from achieving great standing in the country. Consequently, when Gandhi was assassinated less than six months after the achievement of independence, Nehru was potentially in a position to play the vital symbolic role of leader of the independence struggle. But he had never gained a personal ascendancy over his more right wing colleagues in the Congress Party; in particular, he might have been overthrown by Patel if the latter had not suffered a serious heart attack shortly after the death of Gandhi. Subsequently, Patel was content to work in joint harness with Nehru, and with the former's death in 1950, Nehru emerged clearly as the dominant figure in the Indian leadership. It was only by virtue of that ascendancy that the Indian leadership was able to accommodate such radically opposed figures as Krishna Menon and Morarji Desai for so long. In all the countries of Asia, Nehru is the only man who has established the kind of dominance that has enabled him to maintain cohesion in the top leadership similar to that achieved by Mao.[16] It was not until the national crisis brought on by the Chinese invasion and the accompanying revelation of Menon's administrative incompetence that Nehru was forced to dismiss the man whose political views he had so often defended. The gravity of the crisis, coupled with Nehru's confession of error in his estimates of the Chinese, has sapped even his standing. That he has not yet had to resign as Prime Minister is striking evidence of his continuing ascendancy.

There are other important factors accounting for leadership cohesion in China. One is the shared vision of what China's goals should be. In 1949, all the Chinese leaders knew that their final objective was to restore the ancient supremacy of China and wipe out the memory of the national humiliations of the previous hundred years. They knew, too, that, as was natural, they would from then on roughly copy the Soviet model for the organization of the state and the engineering of a rapid industrialization program. Since the Chinese Communists came to power after two decades of civil war, the lines had long since been drawn between those who supported their goals and methods and those who did not.

In other underdeveloped countries, particularly in former colonial territories, such unity of purpose is far less common. As already mentioned, the ultimate goals will normally be rapid industrialization, higher living standards, and the assertion of national power. But whereas individual leaders may have firm ideas on how to attain them, the exigencies of the anti-colonial struggle have usually meant that these ideas have never been thrashed out with colleagues prior to the attainment of independence. If they are raised, any disagreements are papered over in the interests of unity in the common fight against the foreigner. The Congress Party, for instance, accommodated the most diverse views. Even Gandhi and Nehru held very different opinions as to the kind of society they wanted in post-independence India. One major exception to this general rule of papering over disputes was, of course, the split in the Indian independence movement on religious grounds that led to the partition of the Indian sub-continent.

Another factor making for cohesion in China is the long period during which the present leaders worked together, fought together, and even governed together before coming to power. Although the need to fight guerrilla warfare against Nationalists and Japanese meant that the top men were working apart from time to time, Mao made sure that this did not disrupt the unity of the Party.[17] The military struggle to the death must also have emphasized the importance of unity at the top far more than could any events in countries where the risks for the individual were less final, and where it was perhaps possible to lead a moderately normal life outside "office hours." Then again, the many years' experience of administration acquired by the Communist leaders meant that they were able to avoid the kind of bickering that can occur when a group of men unaccustomed to holding powerful governmental posts is suddenly faced with the immense problems they entail.

Few other leaderships in non-Communist underdeveloped countries have been so fortunate. Consider the Indonesian leadership, for instance. Men like Sukarno, Hatta, and Sjahrir were imprisoned during the nineteen thirties. During the Japanese occupation, the Indonesian nationalists decided to split their forces, with some leaders working with the Japanese, others leading the underground resistance. Whatever the effectiveness of this tactic, one of its long-term consequences was that the Indonesian leaders never had the same chance of working intimately together over a long period of years as did the Chinese. As a result, to take one example, a disagreement over whether or not to make an immediate proclamation of independence in 1944 could lead to the kidnapping of Sukarno and Hatta by Sjahrir.[18]

The Indian leadership was somewhat more fortunate in its captivity in that during World War II, men like Nehru, Patel, Pant, and Azad were imprisoned together. The fact that Nehru and Patel were never fundamentally reconciled to each other only goes to show that discussion divorced from action is of limited value in solving problems of practical politics.[19]

Other factors that make for cohesion in the Chinese leadership are more difficult to assess. Provincial loyalties are quite strong, and an examination of the membership of the Politburo reveals that seven of its twenty-six members (prior to Lin Po-ch'ü's death) come from Hunan (the province of Mao and Liu Shao-ch'i), five from Szechwan (the province of Chu Teh and Teng Hsiao-p'ing, the Party's Secretary General) and four from Kiangsu (the province of Chou En-lai and Ch'en Yun).[20] Three of the remaining twenty-two provinces[21] are represented by two members apiece, four others by one member each. It is true that Szechwan, Hunan, and Kiangsu are among the seven most populous provinces of China; but of the other four, only one—Shantung—is represented, and that by only one member. The clear implication is that, at the very least, the importance of provincial loyalties has not been overlooked by Mao and his closest comrades-in-arms in picking their colleagues. But the uncertain value of this factor is evidenced by the fact that of the top-level dissidents of the past thirteen years, two were Kiangsu men (Ch'en Yun and Chang Wen-t'ien) and two were from Hunan (P'eng Teh-huai and Lin Po-ch'ü). Clearly, provincial loyalties may be a contributory factor toward cohesion but not a decisive one.[22]

Another factor, only superficially contradictory to the last one, is the firm conviction of the leaders, over and above their provincial loyalties and despite linguistic differences, of their "Chineseness" based on their common cultural background. All members of the Politburo except one are ethnically Chinese—what the Chinese call "Han"; the exception, Ulanfu, a Mongol, is highly sinicized. There are divisive forces among the Han, and it is difficult to state how formidable they might become if totalitarian controls were removed. But it is hard to believe that they would be as powerful as the kind of divisions that exist between, say, Javans and Sumatrans in Indonesia, or the ethnic-linguistic-regional differences that divide Dravidians from Aryans in India.

Given all these factors favoring cohesion among the Chinese leaders—the symbolic importance of Mao and his personal ascendancy over his colleagues, unity of purpose, the long years of comradeship, selection of leaders to take advantage of provincial loyalties, and their overriding ethnic-cultural unity—one has to examine why this unity has been partially disrupted, particularly recently.

The case of Kao Kang is relatively simple to understand in terms of the factors listed above. Kao was an independent Communist leader in northwestern China when Mao arrived there with his weary followers at the end of the "Long March." After years of political infighting, Mao had recently become Party chairman. A newcomer to Kao Kang's territory, he appears to have treated him with the deference due to a man who knew the local lay of the land. Presumably, he wanted to enroll Kao under his banner without any further trouble. At any rate, the result was that Kao Kang came into the main body of the movement fairly near the top; while he accepted Mao's leadership, he had never been in the position of having vied with him and lost. Nor had he shared with Mao and his other senior colleagues the experiences of the northern expedition, the Shanghai massacre, the Nanchang uprising, the Canton commune, the Kiangsi Soviet, and the "Long March."[23] Nor were there any provincial ties between him and his senior colleagues. To give such a man the overlordship of such an important region as the industrial northeast (Manchuria) under the new regime was probably a mistake on Mao's part,[24] but from his public utterances it would appear that Mao trusted Kao implicitly.

This is not to suggest that Kao's rebellion against the center can be explained simply in terms of a desire for personal power. There were key issues of economic policy at the heart of the dispute. But it would appear that a major element in making Kao decide to attempt to win his point by "organizational" means was that he was far less conditioned by background to the concept of group solidarity under Mao. Even so, the evidence suggests that he never dreamed of being able to supplant Mao himself, but was attempting to oust Liu Shao-ch'i and Chou En-lai from their positions as Mao's principal lieutenants; possibly he felt that if he could carry sufficient votes in the Politburo, Mao would throw his support to him.[25]

There are no similar factors of background to explain the cases of Ch'en Yun, P'eng Teh-huai, Lin Po-ch'ü, and Chang Wen-t'ien: all were old revolutionary comrades—although it perhaps has some bearing that Chang was once a leading member of a faction that opposed Mao, and that there is some evidence to suggest Mao and P'eng did not get on too well in the early nineteen thirties.

To this day, the precise role played by Ch'en Yun in the opposition to the "Great Leap Forward" is not known, although it seems he did not associate himself with P'eng and was probably more restrained in his criticism. Now apparently something of a back number (although still, like the other dissidents, formally a member of the Politburo), he has nevertheless appeared more often in public than the others. P'eng and Chang suffered more, probably because they were more intemperate in their criticism and because they took what the Chinese must have considered the virtually treasonable course of communicating their views to the Soviet Party. Of the P'eng group, Lin Po-ch'ü, who died within a year and was accorded a national funeral, was apparently treated the most lightly, presumably because his was a supporting role and because of his status as one of the Party's "grand old men."[26]

There can be only one explanation of this disruption of the cohesion of the Chinese leadership, and that is the depth of the crisis brought about by the "Great Leap Forward." One has only to remember the humiliating admission of statistical exaggeration, the back-yard steel fiasco, the triumphant creation of the communes followed by the gradual retreat from them, the appallingly long hours the population was compelled to work during the height of the Leap, to understand the vehemence of the opposition.

Unity of purpose was listed as above as one of the important reasons for the cohesion of the Chinese leadership, and a common determination to follow the Soviet pattern was cited as one element in this. But the "Great Leap Forward" represented a radical departure from the Soviet pattern; it was an attempt to chart a completely new, Chinese (and perhaps Asian) road to Communism. If the Leap and the communes had been successful, there can be little doubt that Mao would have been able to carry his colleagues with him in rejecting the Soviet pattern. Not only were they unsuccessful, but the claims made for them were so extravagant that they became not just new means to the same end but ends in themselves, to the extent that some cadres felt that the establishment of the communes was equivalent to the establishment of Communism itself. This, coupled with the fact that some leaders had opposed the new course from the start, must have effectively shattered the whole sense of direction of the Chinese leadership, at any rate temporarily.

What is more, the error was on so vast a scale that it appears that P'eng and his group may have gone so far as to throw doubts on the most important factor in the cohesion of the leadership— the hitherto unquestioned supremacy of Mao himself.[27]

Yet, while it is clear that the Leap episode shook the Chinese leadership literally to the core, its subsequent cohesion has been impressive. The Leap has been abandoned, but the change of line has not shattered the regime's top leadership; only one member of the supreme Politburo Standing Committee wavered. While the dissidents have been punished, and P'eng and Chang Wen-t'ien have been denounced in Party circles, their names have not been publicized and they have not formally been dismissed from their Party posts. Ch'en Yun has apparently not been denounced even within Party circles.

If one compares this with what happened to Kao Kang, certain conclusions emerge. The Kao Kang case was publicized, and it was announced that Kao had committed suicide. Yet there was no reason why the Party should not have said that Kao had been executed if he had been, or if he had died under interrogation; it could have said he was executed even if he had committed suicide. Such a course would have served as a warning *pour encourager les autres*. It is this writer's belief that he probably did commit suicide, that this was why the case had to be publicized, and that his suicide was officially described as a final act of defiance because it meant that Kao refused his colleagues the chance to reform him.

The Kao and P'eng episodes seem to show that the Chinese leadership does not like to publicize its internal feuds—partly because Mao, being personally secure, unlike Stalin and Khrushchev, does not feel compelled to warn off future dissidents; partly because he believes that such old comrades as P'eng and Ch'en should not simply be thrown into the dustbin of history, and that they are reformable;[28] and partly, and most importantly, because he believes very strongly in the value of cohesion at the top for its own sake.

Lenin was quite ready to split the Communist movement to ensure the acceptance of his ideas; Mao is prepared to face a split only in the last resort when his hand is forced (as in the case of Kao) or when he feels (as in the case of his dispute with Khrushchev over the policy of the Communist bloc) that the consequences of a policy with which he disagrees will be even more disastrous than the consequences of disunity.[29] This emphasis on unity is basic to Mao's political thinking and has presumably been absorbed by his colleagues; and it doubtless explains why an opponent of the Leap like Chou En-lai survives unharmed to lead the retreat to saner policies while other opponents are punished.[30] Chou must have been prepared to accept the fact that however disastrous the Leap had been, it would only add to the confusion if recriminations were bitter and led to a disruption of unity at the top. This emphasis on unity is the one non-historical factor underlying the cohesion of the Chinese leadership and, therefore, the one factor that can be imitated elsewhere.

What can be learned from this analysis by other developing countries that seek to study the Chinese model? Primarily, that cohesion of top leadership is a major asset in an underdeveloped country; that in China this cohesion has undoubtably been strong, and has therefore been a leading factor in enabling the Communist regime to accomplish what it has; that in China cohesion is not a function of the Communist system but principally of certain unique historical factors; and that therefore in this respect (with the one exception made in the last paragraph) China cannot act as a model for anyone. Top leaderships in other countries have either been shaped by similarly propitious circumstances, in which case cohesion will be good, or they have not, in which case it will be bad. A final lesson to be drawn is that the course of events can undermine even a high degree of cohesion and that presumably, also, a low degree of cohesion can be improved over a period of time, especially if there is a will to unity.

Communist China and the Non-Committed Countries: Motives and Purposes of Communist China's Foreign Policy

—FRANZ MICHAEL

The writer regards Communist policy not as a collection of policies of individual Communist countries, all with differing motives and *raisons d'état*, but as a *Gesamtpolitik* of the Communist bloc and movement. Its goal is, as the Communists themselves forever proclaim, the conquest of the world for the Communist system, a goal to be reached by the exploitation of all conflict situations in the non-Communist world through a variety of strategies, all sanctified by the doctrine. The conflict within the bloc has not changed this over-all purpose of Communist policy.

GOALS AND STRATEGIES OF COMMUNIST CHINESE FOREIGN POLICY

There can be no doubt that the Communist Chinese leaders regard "their revolution as part of the world socialist revolution," and that this world revolution is the major goal of their foreign policy. The stress on China's role in the "ascendancy of the world socialist system" and the battle against "imperialism," a term that in Communist terminology characterizes the whole stand of the West, have been constant themes of Chinese Communist declarations. Within this framework the policy toward the "oppressed nations" is to help them in their "struggle for national liberation, people's democracy and a socialist future" and thus to support their role in the general fight against the evils of capitalism and imperialism, a fight that will end, in the Communist view, with the victory of "socialism."[1]

In order to interpret the relation of individual political moves of the Chinese Communists to this over-all purpose, it is useful to differentiate between the long-range objective of Communist policy and the more immediate goals of Communist Chinese strategy and tactics, a distinction made by the Communists themselves. In a report on the Chinese Communist use of cultural propaganda, Herbert Passin has defined the three levels of Communist Chinese foreign policy objectives. The long-range objective "is certainly revolutionary subversion, the overthrow of existing governments, and the establishment of Communist governments linked to the Communist Bloc." The intermediate and short-range objectives are to gain recognition as a powerful state and a model for revolution in underdeveloped countries, and the exploitation of day-to-day events for this over-all purpose. Only by relating Communist Chinese strategy and tactics in this way to over-all Communist objectives can we, in the writer's view, understand Communist policy.

In the non-committed countries, the strategy to accomplish this goal of revolutionary subversion and Communist seizure of power follows in general two main lines of attack. The first line is the sponsorship and support of Communist parties, which, where feasible, foment revolutions to bring about a direct accession to power, alone or in alliance with whatever discontented elements can be exploited. The second line of policy, justified by Lenin's theory of imperialism as a capitalist phenomenon, is the alliance with national revolutions in the dependent colonial and so-called semi-colonial countries in their fight for national emancipation and independence. It is the second line on which the Communists mainly rely today.

Lenin's theory of imperialism as the final stage of monopoly capitalism was used as the theoretical justification for shifting the emphasis of revolutionary action to Asia after the Soviet hope for a revolution in Germany, the heavily industrialized center of Europe, had been given up. A new policy was then initiated by Lenin to sponsor revolution in what today are known as the underdeveloped countries of Asia, not only by the establishment of Communist parties but also by the support of nationalist movements. This shift of policy was dramatically underlined by the sending to China of Joffe, the same Comintern agent who had smuggled arms to the German Communists. It was Joffe who in 1923 negotiated the agreement with the Chinese Nationalist leader, Sun Yat-sen, that initiated the period of Communist–Chinese Nationalist cooperation. The purpose of the Communists in this cooperation was to support a nationalist revolution in China that would deal a blow to the imperialist powers and secure an advantage to the Soviet Union, which could collect its reward by exploiting the revolution for

Communist infiltration. The theory was that China, still in the "feudal" or "semi-feudal" stage, was not ready for a Communist take-over, but that a Communist alliance with a "progressive" element of the bourgeois nationalist revolution could lead to a pre-socialist stage from which a socialist revolution might later emerge. This was the basis of the cooperation with the Kuomintang, which brought disaster for the Communists in 1927 but was renewed more successfully in the united front policy of 1935. Even the Communist victory in 1949 was, in doctrinal terms, a pre-socialist revolution that maintained the fiction of a united front with other groups and established a People's Republic.

This Leninist concept, as applied in China, has now become the main Communist policy towards the non-committed countries. It allows the Communists to cooperate with nationalist movements, exploit their grievances, and extend Communist influence in any form that opportunity permits.

The two Communist strategies—the support of the leadership of nationalist movements and direct action by Communist or Communist-inclined leftist parties—can supplement each other or they can collide. As long as the strategies are directed against a colonial government, the two can operate side by side. But once national independence is secured, a choice between the two strategies becomes necessary, unless the two can be manipulated skillfully and under cover. Both these lines of strategy have been applied interchangeably by the Soviets as well as by the Chinese Communists towards the non-committed nations of Asia, Africa, and Latin America.

To what degree, however, these Soviet and Chinese policies are coordinated or in conflict and competition with each other depends obviously on the relation of these two Communist parties and their leaders.

The Conflict Within the Communist Bloc

If we are faced with a Communist movement that has one framework of policy centered in a Communist bloc that has one doctrinal system from which it derives its strategies of attack, how then can one explain the conflicts within that movement and that bloc—the arguments and counter-arguments as to policies to be taken, the mutual accusations and disagreements on this or that political action? How do we explain the conflict between Khrushchev and Mao Tse-tung? The dispute has, in the writer's view, to be seen as a factional power struggle inherent in the system of "democratic centralism," similar to the intra-party factional strife so characteristic of Communist parties, but now transferred to another plane by the growth of the Communist camp since World War II. This to the writer is the key to the Sino-Soviet conflict. A number of different explanations have, however, been put forward.

The conflict has been seen by some as a clash between different lines of development of Communist ideology, an ideological schism that will rend apart the unity of the Communist doctrinal pseudo-religion. Those who have tried to give a deeper meaning to the present verbal cold war between Moscow and Peking have attempted to select and isolate the ideological issues on which Soviet and Communist leaders seem to be divided. In my opinion, however, there is no issue on which truly basic ideological differences can be shown.

The main points usually advanced by those who believe in the possibility of an ideological split concern the strategy of "peaceful coexistence" with the West and, sometimes, the strategy toward the non-committed nations. There is also the question of Chinese Communist doctrine related to the policy of the communes and the "Great Leap Forward." Of these alleged conflicts of principle, the most important is the question of war or peace and coexistence.

It is a common popular misunderstanding of the Sino-Soviet conflict that Khrushchev has propagated "peaceful coexistence," while Mao has been for war. Yet, as has been pointed out by Zagoria and other students of the conflict, the Chinese Communists have not advocated war with the West as a means of world conquest any more than have the Soviet leaders. Nor has Mao or any other Communist Chinese leader declared war to be inevitable. Khrushchev, on the other hand, has never excluded the possibility of war. The disagreement, as far as there has been one in the verbal battle between the Soviets and the Chinese Communists, has not really touched on the matter of principle, even though it has been fought in part with quotations from Lenin. The argument comes down to a Chinese Communist demand for a tougher line in the political debate with the West—hardly a matter of principle.

It must also be remembered that so far as the over-all political line of the bloc is concerned, Mao Tse-tung has assumed the role of the opposition to the dominant Soviet leadership and therefore has been freer to strike an aggressive note in his propaganda statements than has Khrushchev, who has the final responsibility for Communist policy (though Khrushchev, by the way, has often talked aggressively enough). For Mao, it is nothing new to be in a position of opposition without responsibility and to use it for propaganda statements on foreign policy. We have only to remember the statements of the Communist Chinese before their take-over in China, when they could afford to be more patriotic than the Nationalist Government, and at one time went so far as to declare war on Japan from the safety of their territorial base in southern China. Anyone who has read Mao's strategic writings and has followed Chinese Communist military policy knows how cautious the Chinese Communists have been in principle and practice. And as to their willingness to negotiate with the imperialist devil America, we have only to remember Chou En-lai's statement at the Bandung Conference and on other occasions. Shifting between a hard and a soft policy has been as much a Chinese Communist as a Soviet tactic. If doctrinal schism is a matter of principle and conviction, there is little of that in Communist Chinese strategy. Luther's statement *Hier stehe ich, ich kann nicht anders* ("Here I stand, I can do no other"), might be modified for Mao to "Here I stand, but I could do other."

As to policy toward the non-committed nations, neither of the Communist contenders differs on the Leninist doctrine and Communist practice of anti-imperialism—doctrine and practice that are elastic enough to cover many strategies. It has sometimes been held that China, having become Communist at a different stage of social and economic development from the Soviet Union, is the appropriate model for the underdeveloped countries of Asia, Africa, and South America. And it is very true that Communist China has played this role of the model for revolution for Asian and African nations to the hilt. But there is no doctrinal conflict over the fact that different stages exist in the development towards socialism and Communism, and the special role that Communist China can play.

The Chinese experiment with communes presented a challenge to Soviet leadership when the Chinese Communists claimed that they had even by-passed the Soviet Union on the way to Communism. But the conflict was not over the way itself but over the stage that had been reached and the possibilities in China at that time. When the communes proved to be a vast failure, and the Communist Chinese leaders were forced to retreat from almost all aspects of the experiment, they did so without ever admitting a doctrinal error. Doctrinal errors, so it seems, can be committed only by those who are losing the battle for power, not by those who remain in control. The doctrine itself is elastic enough to cover many advances and retreats.

But if the schism is not ideological, is it, as some believe, a conflict of national interests, a rivalry of big powers? This argument brings us to the question of whether we are dealing in essence with China and Russia as state entities. In speaking of Communist Chinese foreign policy, we too often ignore the fact that this policy represents not the determination of a government, but that of a Communist Party. When we too easily generalize that China does this or China wants that, we disregard the role of the Party in a Communist state, where government does not represent the will of the people at large, but is, according to Communist doctrine itself, the tool with which the Communist Party carries through its policy and maintains its dictatorship. The policy objectives with which we have to deal are therefore those of the Chinese Communist Party, which controls the Chinese state but which is also a member of the world Communist movement carrying through the Communist revolution at home and abroad.

To what degree are these parties linked to the states which they control? What gives the Chinese Party its "Chineseness" or the Soviet Party its Russian characteristics? In the writer's view, only two things: Firstly, the parties are made up of Chinese and Russians respectively, which means that the cadres of each have whatever characteristics they have retained from the environment in which they grew up. But it has to be said immediately that the training of a Communist cadre is meant to eradicate as much as possible these traditional inheritances, and to create a different type whose only loyalty is to the party. The second characteristic that differentiates one "national" party from another is the assigned area of action that imposes upon the party and its members a preoccupation with the local problems, which, however, have to be handled within the framework of the over-all policy.

Those who hold that there is a "national" aspect of Chinese policy that forms the second ingredient in the over-all policy motivations of the Chinese Communists usually name security and big power status as the main goals of this "national" policy. But are these goals peculiar to the national state? Any state, Communist or national, will protect itself and may want to enlarge its power. The state structure, which is the tool of whatever policy is to be carried out, must be secure; and the more power the state has, the better it can accomplish its goals. The power and security of the state are therefore the means, not the content, of policy and do not by themselves indicate the purposes that this policy is to serve.

What, then, is the content of this state policy in Communist China? Does it differ from the over-all Communist purpose? There can be no argument that the Communist goal is to transform Chinese society into a Communist system. Communism does not represent the Chinese cultural tradition; it is at war with it. It attempts to break all the loyalties and beliefs of the past and to replace them with loyalty to the Party and its purposes and belief in Communist doctrine.

But the Chinese state is larger in territory than the area of Chinese society, and it has been claimed that Communist China's territorial aspirations are a continuation of the old imperial tradition. The Communists do indeed operate within the old imperial borders and even try to push them to the limit; but theirs is a different operation. The imperial dynastic control did not attempt to impose its administrative structure, system, social order, and Confucian beliefs on the imperial domain outside China proper. Nor did the Nationalist Government; it tried to hold on to the territory of the empire, but did not attempt to maintain more than a —mostly shadowy—Chinese control over other ethnic groups.

The Communist purpose has been entirely different. The prime example is the Communist conquest of Tibet. What was at stake there was not Chinese control over the Tibetan nation, but destruction of Tibetan cultural and national traditions and the establishment of a Communist system in the "Chinese Region of Tibet." This goal is much more far-reaching than that of imperial China. It also includes much more than the political and economic control of which traditional imperialism has been accused.

The Communist goal was not understood at first by many of the non-committed nations that have fallen victim to Chinese propaganda. The unwillingness to see the Communist purpose in what he believed to be an Asian brother-nation, caused Nehru to trust the Chinese promises of cultural autonomy for the Dalai Lama's government and led him to what he thought to be a workable agreement at the sacrifice of Tibet's political freedom. It is precisely this kind of confusion arising from mistaking Communist for nationalist purposes that has delayed the formulation of counter-policies by the West and the non-committed nations.

The same danger of misunderstanding the Communist motives

exists with regard to Communist foreign policy. If Communization is the goal within the territory controlled by the Chinese Communist Government, Communization is also the goal of the Chinese Communist foreign policy. The purpose is not to expand the territorial control of the Chinese state, but rather to extend the Communist system. There has been no attempt—and the writer does not think there will be one—to take over North Vietnam or other countries of Southeast Asia. The political goal is to promote, directly or indirectly, a Communist revolution in these countries and to assist the take-over of power by local Communists, who will then form governments that will join the fraternity of the Communist world organization.

In this sense, it is misleading if the Communist build-up of power in non-committed countries by the use of force and by outside Communist pressure, and the enforced alignment of the conquered countries with the Communist system is referred to as "Communist imperialism." If the word imperialism is to be given the meaning that the Communists have used, to interpret—in their own rather colored way—the various Western political and economic systems of control established mainly in the nineteenth century and mostly gone today, then "imperialism" does not adequately describe what the Communists, Chinese or Russians, are trying to do. The pluralist tradition of Western imperialism left a great deal of cultural autonomy to dependent peoples and presented in itself a multiplicity of systems. The Communist system is the spreading by force over the world of Communist monism. Communist China's foreign policy has this long-range goal, and in the writer's opinion no political objective can be discerned that is in conflict with it. The fact that Communist policies cannot be explained in terms of interests of states remains, even if it is recognized that Communist states now are totalitarian states, different in kind and in purpose from the states of the non-Communist world.

We do not do justice to the Communist system if we apply to it the traditional categories and definitions of the state of Western political or legal science. The reality of the Communist movement and the inter-relationship between Communist parties and Communist states cannot be explained with nineteenth-century concepts of the state even if they are extended to include totalitarian state power. It is therefore not enough to interpret the conflict within the Communist bloc as a clash between totalitarian states.[2] The emphasis on the state rather than the Party omits the prime motive of the ideological motivation which differentiates these powers from those of the non-Communist world. These totalitarian states are controlled by their parties, and while each state is an individual application of the Communist system, the parties are part of the world movement, which represents more than the sum of individual states, and which has as its basic political purpose world conquest for Communism. In the Communist belief and reality, the state is the structure the Party uses to apply its dictatorship. A Party that controls a state is of course more powerful than a Party that does not, and it is the conquest of power by parties in other states than the Soviet Union that has complicated the matter. If there is conflict, it is not between states, but between parties that control states.

These parties do not represent national interests, and whatever their differences on strategy and tactics as they affect their own particular situation, their overriding concern is Communist revolution. The struggle between parties and leaders is for influence and power in determining the strategy of the movement that serves this Communist aim. Since there is no ideological break in the movement, no schism in the church, no Protestant rebellion, no basic disagreement on the tenets, all arguments on strategy remain within the framework of Communist doctrine accepted by all. That this doctrine maintains that there is one line of all human development in the past, the present, and the future, only one historical truth and one correct policy at each given moment that can be scientifically determined—the major unilinear aspect of Communist policy has not been challenged by the contesting parties and leaders. The problem is that this unilinear doctrine requires a final authority to determine the Communist "truth."

The decision on what was the right line of the moment was in the past made by the leader of the Soviet Party and transmitted by the Comintern. The fact that only the Soviet Party had the territorial base to carry the movement made it possible for Lenin to establish Soviet control over the international movement at the time of the establishment of the Comintern. Under Stalin, this system was strengthened and vulgarized. But there is in the last analysis no theoretical base for the Soviets' leading role. The doctrine only maintains that the Communist vanguard, as the most advanced historical force, is to express the historical line and its application to any given situation. It has never been made clear who in this vanguard is to express it. The Soviet control of the Comintern was not a matter of theory. It was a matter of Soviet state power. Since today there are other parties in control of the wherewithal of government, this monopoly of decision-making by the Soviets has been challenged. Soviet Russia is no longer the only fatherland of the Communist movement, and no organizational form has been found to determine how the representatives of the parties possessing fatherlands of Communism are to settle their conflicting views on strategy and take their part in decision-making.

There is no politburo for the bloc. The original suggestion that all countries conquered by Communist parties should join the Soviet Union has not been carried out, for whatever reasons. The only organization that exists for joint decisions of the Communist movement are the inter-party conferences, which are entirely unsuited for the purpose. They are unwieldy, and make no distinction even between those parties that are in control of states and those that are not. They also do not possess a method of procedure that could lend itself to real decision-making. The necessity for unanimity in the acceptance of resolutions in these conferences can only lead to compromise formulas at best, not to true political decisions. But even if the conferences had a parliamentary procedure, this would hardly be the form of decision-making that could be used in the Communist bloc. Communist "truth" cannot be revealed by free vote. These conferences are not therefore a suitable tool for the system of "democratic centralism" inherent in the Communist movement.

There has been an obvious search for new methods of control. Since the Soviet Union is no longer the "fatherland of socialism" and the sole country where Communists are in power, the authority of the Soviet leaders over the Communist movement can no longer be based on this distinction. The problem became acute after the death of Stalin, whose personal prestige still carried weight even after the end of the Soviet Party's monopoly of control of a state. To maintain Soviet authority, to make the Soviets "more equal" among theoretically equal fraternal parties, a new stress has been placed on the concept of the stage of development. Only the Soviet Union has already reached the socialist stage and is on the way to Communism. The other Communist states remain people's republics and lag behind in several degrees. Thus, there has been an attempt to build a pyramid of authority among the Communist states of the bloc;[3] it was this concept of Soviet authority by virtue of greatest advancement that Khrushchev used to introduce the new blueprint for the Communist millennium, not to a meeting of

Communist parties, but to the Twenty-second Congress of the Communist Party of the Soviet Union, with the implication that its acceptance by that Congress would give it the sanction of a blueprint for all Communist development.

The Chinese Communist leadership has opposed this Soviet monopoly of authority for Communist strategy. The conflict, which has come to a head since 1958, has been partly a personal one between Khrushchev and Mao Tse-tung. It is, as the writer has tried to state elsewhere, a personal power struggle in which the whole position of Mao Tse-tung has been at stake. It is an unsolved conflict for leadership no longer within one party, but now within the Communist bloc and the Communist movement. In many ways, this power conflict resembles an intra-party conflict, such as that between Khrushchev and Malenkov. In such conflicts, each contender will have to claim to have the right interpretation of history, to be the true prophet of the party line. It is the necessity for calling on the sanction of the doctrine and the Church fathers by the rivals that gives such conflicts their so-called ideological aspect, even if no real ideological principle is at stake and if positions can easily be shifted by either of the contestants.

What Khrushchev and Mao Tse-tung fight over is the power to decide the strategy for the camp. There is no challenge of the principle of monism and of the principle of unilinear development. What the Chinese Communist opposition has attempted is to attack Khrushchev's leadership, to flatten his pyramid, and in this way to strengthen the role of the Chinese leader in the movement. The strategy has been to gain allies within other parties and to attack the authority of the Soviet leader.

The principle of "democratic centralism," on which each Communist Party is based, always leads back to assumption of authority by a leading figure. There is a grouping in each Party around that figure; and opposition, cleavages, and conflict revolve around him in a power struggle unique to the Communist system. The power struggle in each group is related to struggles in other groups in the movement as a whole, so that there is an inter-relationship between the conflicts within each of the "national" parties.

The problem of the Communist bloc is then to provide a political arena and define a political procedure through which the democratic centralism of the bloc can find its expression. It is this procedure, or the absence of it, with which we are concerned. The conflict between Khrushchev and Mao Tse-tung, or between the

Soviet and Chinese Communist parties, is only an expression of this structural problem. It is an example of the problem of inter-party relationship within the bloc. The conflict results from the absence of a clearly defined theoretical basis for resolving problems of authority and decision-making in the changing structure of the expanded bloc. The situation is not "polycentric," but amorphous. The concept of the center is there, but it remains uncrystallized.

There is still the authority of Moscow, though it has been challenged. The control of the movement is still in the hands of the leader of the Soviet Party, and he has the unofficial, non-theoretical tools of control: the tanks, the secret police, and the financial and economic weapons most of all, and also the political connections with factions and cliques within the bloc. Rewards and punishments for right or wrong behavior are, however, no longer entirely in his hands. He also has had to admit the equality of the fraternal parties, and is theoretically reduced to the pious fiction that all member parties of the movement, as the vanguard of the historical force, will come to a unity of purpose through a sort of osmosis. In practice, it does not work that way.

COMMUNIST CHINESE FOREIGN POLICY

If the Communist purpose of China's foreign policy, and the Chinese Communist position in the bloc is understood in this way, the conclusion follows that Chinese Communist policy serves two purposes, which are, however, not equal in importance. The major purpose is the over-all goal of Communist revolution. The secondary purpose is the strengthening of the position of the Chinese Communist leaders within the bloc and increasing participation in the determination of over-all Communist policy. The two purposes will not conflict—at least not from the Communist Chinese point of view, but the second purpose may well give its special slant to Chinese Communist foreign policy, and will always be a stimulus to add some special, Chinese dimension to the over-all Communist attack.

In carrying out their Communist policy, the Chinese Communists have had the special advantage of being able to point to their country as a model of the successful application of socialist theory to underdeveloped countries. China was mainly agricultural, had little industry, and was called by the Communists a "semi-colony." Being Orientals, the Chinese Communists could exploit the anti-white, nationalist emotions of the formerly colonial countries of Asia and Africa. All this, and in addition China's location in Asia and her historical link with her neighbors, gave the Chinese Communists their special advantages in carrying out over-all Communist policy in the underdeveloped countries.

Actually, it was the Communist Chinese who reintroduced Leninist strategy into the Communist policy towards the non-committed nations of Asia and Africa after World War II. The policy of the united front, which Soviet Russia used so successfully in Eastern Europe after the war, was not applied by her in Asia, Africa, or South America in the same period. There the line laid down at the Calcutta Conference of 1947 called for direct Communist takeovers, as were attempted in Burma, Indonesia, and Malaya. These attempts failed. The shift in policy from subversion back to the more cautious support of nationalist governments came really as a result of Chinese initiative taken at the Bandung Conference in 1955.

The Bandung Conference has been perhaps the greatest success of Chinese Communist foreign policy so far. It initiated the policy of support for African and Asian national "anti-imperialist" aspirations and led to the organization of so-called Afro-Asian solidarity—one of the main instruments of Communist policy in the non-committed countries of Asia and Africa, and later of the New World. It was the renewed application of Lenin's formula for Communist policy in what today are called the underdeveloped or developing countries. The Chinese policy at Bandung was based on the "Five Principles of Peaceful Coexistence," the Chinese version of a formula that Stalin's policy had reapplied two years before.

Soviet Russia was not represented at Bandung, and the political success of the Bandung Conference was indeed a Chinese triumph. If there had been a division of roles within the over-all Communist strategy, China would obviously have been assigned the role of propagating Afro-Asian solidarity as a tool of Communist policy. This strategy certainly did not represent any "leftist-adventurism," or a drive for leftist Communist military action. On the surface, the Chinese Communist policy was to support the "national liberation" movements without any hint at Communist subversion, which indeed seemed expressly excluded by the promise of non-interference in internal affairs contained in the "Five Principles." The Afro-Asian governments represented at Bandung were anything but Communist, and if the anti-imperialism of Lenin's formula included their nationalist struggle in the Communist doctrinal interpretation of historical development, there seemed to them no cause for alarm in a cooperation with China, which, though Communist, stressed its willingness to work for mutual goals that were vaguely described under the terms nationalist aspiration, economic progress, and peace.

If Communist China was the logical Communist power to initiate and present this policy, the Chinese Communist initiative not only affected Communist world policy but also strengthened the Communist Chinese position in the bloc. Though at the time of Bandung the Soviet-Chinese conflict had not yet taken shape, the Soviet leaders obviously could not permit the Chinese Communists to monopolize this important aspect of Communist policy. They hurried to enter the field.

In the Afro-Asian solidarity conferences in Africa and Asia that followed the Bandung Conference, the Soviets participated—attempting to be as Asian as possible by sending some Islamic representatives from Soviet Asia who were ethnically Oriental and could therefore modify the picture of the Soviet Union as a white, European power. When a secretariat was set up at the Afro-Asian Solidarity Conference in Cairo in 1957, both Soviet and Chinese representatives played a major role in the staff that determined the program.

Soon the Soviets undertook the primary role in this program, since it was they rather than the Chinese Communists who had the means to provide the support that would give reality to the solidarity expressed at the conferences and in the agreements of the Afro-Asian group. The goal of this policy was more than the political emancipation of the countries of Asia and Africa from Western control. True independence, according to the Communist interpretation, could only be gained if the economic links with the West were cut, since all Western economic aid was, in Communist terms, Western economic imperialism. To win this battle for the support of the non-committed countries, the Communists had to offer their own support, which, of course, was claimed to be of a very different nature from that of the West—it was an unselfish gesture to assist these countries to gain true independence.

Communist China was not in a position to provide much of this kind of aid. In the years after Bandung the Communist Chinese were concerned with their own program of industrialization, carried through largely with Soviet aid, and had little to spare. And since the catastrophic failure of the "Great Leap Forward" and the commune policy, Communist China has experienced an economic collapse that has created a crisis at home and made it impossible to carry on any substantial program of economic aid to the non-committed nations. The Soviets took the lead in this field at the 1957 Conference in Cairo, when their delegate offered far-reaching economic support to underdeveloped countries.

The Chinese Communist role in this over-all policy was most effective in the field of propaganda. The image of a fraternal Asian country that, thanks to Communist leadership, had through its own strength started a course of rapid industrialization and would in the near future overtake not only Japan but England in industrial development, was presented through all means of propaganda—books, pamphlets, the radio and newspapers, the speeches of Chinese Communist leaders, well-organized exhibits, cultural missions sent abroad by the Communist Chinese, and tours given in China to a growing number of foreign visitors. This Chinese Communist propaganda offensive was extremely successful and comparatively inexpensive. In promoting it, the Chinese made good use of their highly developed mass organizations. The mass demonstrations in the major cities of China in support of the national aspirations of this or that country, usually timed to coincide with the visits of important political leaders, were easily organized. They meant practically nothing, but helped to create the image of the Chinese people as the defenders and allies of the causes of the African and Asian countries, most of whom were as yet new in representing their interests in the complex field of international diplomacy.

The image of themselves that the Chinese Communists created by propaganda was at first highly successful. Its impact on the non-committed world served the cause of Communism all the better, the more the recipients of the propaganda mistook the Communist purpose and were fascinated by what they thought was a nationalist example that they might follow. The propaganda impact has been lessened, however, by the economic failure in China and by the inherent discrepancy of the Communist policy, whose Communist purpose eventually reveals itself.

There was little substance in the way of actual aid behind this propaganda. So far China has made only a few well-announced gestures of financial and economic aid, mostly given to small countries where a small amount of aid could be blown up into a big propaganda story. Guinea and Ghana in Africa, Cambodia, Ceylon, Nepal, Indonesia, and Burma in Asia[4] have been typical recipients of such Chinese aid, given as loans at low interest or as outright gifts or deliveries of grain. Such aid was also given to India before the conflict, when in the Indian famine of 1951 the Chinese immediately offered to send 100,000 tons of rice. Aid was also given to Egypt, beginning with a gift of $5 million in 1956, the year after the Bandung Conference.

This aid, which is almost negligible in comparison with that given to the underdeveloped countries by the Soviet Union, let alone the United States and other Western powers, is still an astonishingly large amount for a country in China's economic plight. It was of course fully exploited in propaganda, and may well have been the minimum necessary to give the Chinese Communist propaganda offensive some credence.

The special role of the Chinese Communist Party in the over-all Communist offensive is not limited however to supplying the propaganda image of an Asian brother-nation. The Chinese claim that their experience with guerrilla warfare can be most usefully applied in the battles of the non-committed nations. Such military action serves a double purpose. It straddles the line between the help given to national emancipation movements in their battle with colonial rule and the direct support of a Communist take-over in the country. As the colonial system disappears, this support of guerrilla warfare can less easily be camouflaged as part of the national "anti-imperialist" struggle. A policy of military support has, therefore, only limited use because it can come into conflict with and discredit the policy of supporting national leadership.

The Communist Chinese clamor for military action by national movements has in fact in many cases been more propagandistic than real. The offer at the Suez crisis to send 280,000 Chinese volunteers was, in view of the problem of transporting such an army and of other practical impossibilities, a mere gesture, certainly of less value than the Soviet threat of full-scale nuclear war. The vociferous propaganda support of the Algerian FLN had little practical application except for the Chinese grant of credits of $10 million for the purchase of arms by an Algerian Government that was recognized by Communist China long before its official existence. Chinese Communist spokesmen used the final establishment of independence in Algeria as a proof of the "truth of our epoch— that colonial peoples can win liberation only through struggle" and that the struggle had to be "armed struggle" with the sacrifice of "the lives and blood" of "the heroic sons and daughters of the country."

Beyond this doctrinal support of armed conflict, few practical measures have been taken by the Chinese Communists in areas not close to the borders of their country, except perhaps for the support given to left wing military groups in the Congo, Somaliland, and Cameroon, and whatever support Chinese military missions in several parts of Africa and Asia may have provided secretly.

In Africa and Asia, Communist Chinese policy continues to be implemented along the lines of traditional diplomatic relations with the existing governments of the non-committed nations. Through the policy, initiated at Bandung, of cooperation with national governments regardless of their political color, the Chinese Communists attempted to maintain their influence over the non-committed countries and to prepare the ground for eventual Communist infiltration. In the sphere of the policy with which we are concerned, this has been the most important aspect of Communist strategy and the one particularly suited to the Chinese situation. Its impact, however, has been weakened by the growing realization among the neutrals of the other form of Communist policy—aggression and subversion, exemplified by the border fights and threats in the Himalayas and in Southeast Asia; in the lessons of the Communization of countries like Tibet, and in the support given by the Chinese to Communist infiltration and guerrilla warfare in Laos and Vietnam.

The more aggressive aspect of Communist Chinese policy has never been entirely neglected, even at the height of the era of the Bandung spirit. A new emphasis on it started, however, with the final military subjugation of Tibet and the destruction of its cultural tradition, which was followed by the Chinese Communist invasion of the Himalayan borderlands. The threat to the Indian borderlands in particular not only undid the friendly relations with India that the Chinese had carefully developed, but created a hostility that destroyed the whole basis of Chinese political relations with the largest of the neutral nations. The question remains whether the gain in the expansion of the Communist system in Tibet, the strategic strengthening of the Chinese position in the borderland, and the element of intimidation that this aggressive policy produced have been worth the price. The Chinese Communists may well calculate that such long-range gains are worth a loss of good will. Indian hostility did not even necessarily interfere with the continuation of the second strategic line—the "anti-imperialist" policy of supporting national governments in other countries of Asia and Africa.

Much the same considerations hold true for the Chinese Communist support of the guerrilla warfare of the Viet Cong and Pathet Lao in Vietnam and Laos. It is believed that Chinese advisers and technicians helped in the training and organization of North Vietnamese forces and that these in turn have been instrumental in the build-up of the left wing units in Laos, to which they have also given direct military support. The success in Laos has in turn made possible the Communist acceleration of guerrilla warfare in South Vietnam. In contrast to the military moves against India in the Himalayas, which were undertaken by the Chinese Communists without any recognizable Soviet support or even approval, the guerrilla warfare operations in Laos and Vietnam have by no means been a Chinese monopoly. Much of the equipment and support of these forces has come directly from the Soviet Union, and it seems that this has been an area of close cooperation between the Soviets and the Chinese Communists.

Whatever the internal relations between Soviet and Communist strategies in any of these ventures may have been, it is evident that both policies, that of direct aggression and subversion and that of diplomatic support and aid to neutral governments, have been used by both the Soviets and the Chinese Communists. It would be impossible, in principle, to distinguish between the basis of Soviet or Chinese Communist policy, describing one as more conciliatory and the other as more aggressive. Their respective stance depends entirely on the time and the place.

But since Chinese Communist policy is motivated by the goal of strengthening the Chinese leaders' position in the policy-making councils of the Communist bloc, as well as by the over-all Communist purpose, some moves by the Chinese Communists have not only a general Communist purpose but also the specific purpose of expressing an approach different from that of the Soviet Union at the time. The double motivation of Chinese Communist policy— to promote Communism and to strengthen the Chinese position within the bloc—does not weaken the effectiveness of the over-all Communist effort. In fact, it may well make it more dangerous. If on certain major issues the Chinese choose a line different from that of the Soviet Union, the result is a double-pronged attack which becomes all the more dangerous because it originates from different sources within the Communist bloc. At the time when Soviet Russia was discredited because of the bloody suppression of the Hungarian revolution, when it would have been very difficult for the Soviet Union to play the role of a promoter of peaceful coexistence, Chou En-lai visited not only the European satellites but Southeast Asia and South Asia in the spirit of Bandung. When Communist China became unpopular because of Tibet and the Indian frontier violations, the Soviet leaders, as the protagonists of peaceful coexistence, were highly successful in their propaganda journey through South and Southeast Asia. If ever the Indians were deceived by the propaganda of the Asian brother-nation, and thought that they understood Communist China better than the West, they were rudely awakened by the events in Tibet and the threat to their own border. However, as they still do not see the over-all Communist purpose behind Chinese or Soviet moves, they are now inclined to believe that they can deal on friendly terms with Soviet Russia and might gain its help to balance the Communist Chinese threat. While the Indians try to gain support from the Soviet Union, the Chinese Communists are negotiating a settlement of the Kashmir border issue with Pakistan. The bloc as a whole can therefore exploit the India-Pakistan conflict, and have it both ways—to the advantage of over-all Communist policy. These and other cases of a double-pronged attack tempt one to speak of a policy of divided roles. The fact that these divided roles represent at the same time an intra-bloc fight and are not based on common agreement, does not make the double policy any less dangerous. The Communist *Gesamtpolitik* is as formidable as a result of internal struggle as if it were the result of common planning and may even be worked by the Communists in a way that takes advantage of their internal struggle for position to gain advantages for the common cause.

In my view, we face not conflicting policies of rival totalitarian states, but a much more complex situation of different strategies of attack, all taken from the same book of Communist warfare. If the Communist attack is to become more sweeping, our defense must be equally broad. It is futile, in the writer's view, to count on exploiting an imaginary break between the Communist states by playing up to one or the other. We would only strengthen the parties in control. What we can do is assume a multiple policy of our own by giving our support to those national aspirations that Communism tries to distort for its purposes and by fighting Communist infiltration and organization with direct counter-moves. It is most important to establish a military line of defense and to answer guerrilla warfare in its own terms. It is more important, perhaps, to provide the economic aid and support the economic and social reforms and transformations that are necessary for the strengthening of a free development in the non-committed nations. It is even more necessary to attack the fictions of the Communist doctrine and expose their use in a propaganda effort that has been effective largely because the true purposes of Communism have not been believed any more than the revelations once openly expressed in Hitler's *Mein Kampf.*

Communist Tactics in Non-Aligned Countries and the Ideological Quarrel Between Moscow and Peking

—ERNST KUX

The significance of the ideological controversy between the Soviet and the Chinese Communists lies not so much in the latent conflicts within the Communist camp, or in the possibility of a break between Moscow and Peking, as in its clarification of Communist aims and the related strategies and tactics of the Communist parties. The central point of the quarrel is how the Communist Party line is to be adapted to the modern world situation: the second industrial revolution, the colonial peoples' achievement of independence, the conquest of outer space, the development of new weapons, the establishment of global communications, the total character of world policy, the new political constellations and the cultural, social, and economic consequences arising from them.

The Soviet Union and China, the Communist bloc and the international Communist movement must adapt to these changes and learn how to influence and exploit them if they do not wish to dissipate their power, lag behind the general development, and relinquish all hope of achieving the "triumph of Communism on a world scale." But such adaptation is not easy for the Communists, and not only because of the absolutist character of their dogma and their utter dependence on ideological, political, and economic patterns. They are beset with permanent power struggles and unresolved national differences in their own camp. Their ideological and programmatic comments on current events fall far short of grasping present-day developments, even when they try to allow for practical politics, technical and economic developments, social changes, and cultural trends. The character of their totalitarian system limits practical action. What they call "modernization of Communism" is usually no more than a return to the old Communist arsenals (for instance, the renaissance of Leninism) or the application of theoretical and practical principles to unrelated areas and situations. The modern world's increasing complexity does not help to solve the basic contradiction between Marxist theory and practice—to unite the "specific conditions" with the "general law," the prognosis of the future with the absolutism of Communist aims.

The Communists could not afford to ignore the tremendous significance of the colonial peoples' achievement of independence, the political changes in Asia, Africa, and Latin America, and the creation of a "third world." They claim, of course, that Marx and Lenin enabled them to foresee these developments and influence them. But the actual commitment of Moscow and Peking to the emerging nations dates back only to Stalin's death, Chinese participation in the Bandung Conference, and Soviet military aid to Nasser in 1955.[1] Both the Soviet and the Chinese Communists in this period adopted a more flexible policy toward the newly independent states: Peking proclaimed the "Five Principles" as a means of wooing the Asian peoples; Khrushchev, at the Twentieth Congress of the Communist Party of the Soviet Union in 1956, acknowledged "the emergence in the world arena of a group of peace-loving European and Asian states that have proclaimed non-participation in blocs as a principle of their foreign policy"—a group he tried to bring to his side within the framework of a "vast peace zone" extending beyond the rigid confines of Stalin's empire.

In 1958 and 1959, as increasing differences arose between Moscow and Peking over the form Communist strategy was to take, opinion became more and more divided over the correct policy to be adopted toward the national liberation movements.[2] The question of Communist tactics in non-aligned countries has since become a major subject of ideological controversy, tied in with such issues as "peaceful coexistence," the "building of Communism," and the organization of the international Communist movement. In the process, the question of Communism in the "third world" has been thoroughly aired and all the possible tactics have been designated. And it has become evident that no change of course or adjustment of policy could do away with the existing problems.

THE COMMUNIST VIEW OF OUR EPOCH AND OF "NATIONAL LIBERATION"

Khrushchev has made it clear that the "general strategy and tactics of world Communism" are inseparably linked with the "question of the character of our epoch."[3] Although the new program of the international Communist movement, the Moscow statement of 1960, tried to give a "scientific Marxist-Leninist definition of the epoch," its vague compromise formula failed to resolve the deep-rooted differences in the world outlook of Moscow and Peking.[4] These variations in the interpretation of the "characteristics of our epoch" also express a difference in approach toward the "third world." Khrushchev holds that

> the main thing now is to achieve, by steadily developing the economy of each and every socialist country, the preponderance of the world socialist system as regards the absolute volume of output. . . . Our success in Communist construction will be of exceptional significance for the destinies of the peoples of Asia, Africa, and Latin America.[5]

Mao Tse-tung counters that "the balance of forces is not simply a contest of economic power, but also one of manpower and the morale of man."[6] For the Chinese "the world situation today is one in which 'the strong winds foretell the coming storm,' " and they define our epoch as "an age in which the oppressed nations of Asia, Africa, Latin America, and all over the world are striving for complete liberation, and when imperialism and colonialism are heading for utter defeat."[7]

Consequently, for the Chinese Communists the "decisive factor" is not "economic construction," but the "militant will of the world's people" and the "just struggle of the peoples against imperialism."

In keeping with their evaluation of the present world situation, the Soviet Communists favor a policy of "peaceful coexistence" in order to safeguard their "full-scale Communist construction" and thus smooth the way for "class struggle on a world scale" and the "struggle of the colonies and dependencies for liberation from the imperialist yoke," and to achieve the victory of world revolution without a third world war. Peking argues that coexistence numbs the fighting spirit of the peoples, thereby helping the "imperialists."[8] In the opinion of the Chinese, imperialism will never leave the stage of history of its own accord. As Mao put it: "As a rule, where the broom does not reach, the dust will not disappear by itself."[9] National independence can only be achieved by "determined struggles."

Of great importance in this connection is the issue of whether the colonial system can be abolished permanently by means short

of a third world war. On this point, Liu Chang-sheng has stated
that a false theory of war and peace "can keep the oppressed peoples forever in the state of enslavement."[10] The only thesis the
Chinese will accept without qualification is that of Mao Tse-tung:
"In the end the bomb will not destroy the people; the people will
destroy the bomb"; in a third world war "several hundred million
more will turn to socialism," and the "victorious peoples" after an
all-out nuclear war "will build a beautiful future for themselves on
the debris of dead imperialism."[11] The Soviets are convinced that a
destructive war would only make difficult the process of constructing this society. They argue against "madmen" who wish for such
a catastrophe, warning that a world war with thermonuclear weapons would lead to "the complete destruction of the main centers
of civilization and the wiping out of whole nations, and would
bring immeasurable disaster to the whole of humanity."[12]

The Chinese, of course, are not all-out for full scale war, but they
hold that all peoples must be prepared psychologically for such a
possibility. They emphasize the "two-tactic policy" of Communism: military preparations by the Communist countries and the
"struggle for peace," diplomatic negotiations and national liberation wars, "coexistence" and "class struggle" should go hand in
hand.

The Chinese are not only prepared to risk "national liberation
wars," but also insist that the newly independent states be included
in the Communist bloc as soon as possible. In principle, they still
cling to Stalin's "two worlds theory" and simply speak of "countries
situated in the area between the United States and the socialist
camp." Even today in the Chinese world outlook there is no place
for a "third world": In their portrayal, two-thirds of the world population belongs to the capitalist world and one-third to the socialist
camp. The Chinese evaluation of the "third world" emerges clearly
in Anna Louise Strong's story about the Chinese leader:

> Chairman Mao laughingly illustrated his point with the teacups and
> little wine cups on the table, placing a big cup for American impe-
> rialism and surrounding it with a circle of little wine cups for the
> American people, with a long zigzag line filled up with match-boxes
> and cigarettes to represent other countries all separating American
> imperialism from the Soviet Union, a big cup at the other side.[13]

In the Chinese view it is not enough to separate the independent
countries from the capitalist camp, since the "U.S. imperialists" can

still use such an intermediate area as a "springboard and base." The Soviets, on the other hand, are more flexible in their willingness to accept a kind of independence of the "third world" between the blocs, with the qualifier that these non-aligned countries join with the Communist countries in a "vast peace zone" and follow a path that bypasses the capitalist stage of development.

Despite these differences of opinion on the "distribution of forces" and the attendant strategy and tactics, Moscow and Peking remain in accord on the goal of world revolution and on the use of the "national liberation movement" and the non-aligned countries in the effort to achieve this goal. Lenin's prognosis that "in the coming decisive battles of the world revolution the movement of the majority of the world's population, initially directed toward national liberation, will turn against capitalism and imperialism and may play an even greater revolutionary role than we expected"[14] is still regarded as valid. According to Marxist dialectic, this is not only a prophecy of the future, but a directive to all Communists to bring this "majority" to the battle front against "imperialism." The debate between Moscow and Peking has made it clear that in Communist calculations the "third world" is considered primarily a weapon against the West—a weight in the balance of forces and a pawn in the chess game of international politics. Khrushchev expressed this judgment:

> The national liberation movement is an anti-imperialist movement. . . . Asian, African, and Latin American countries, supported by the socialist camp and the progressive forces of the world, are inflicting defeats upon the imperialist powers and coalitions more and more frequently. At present, Asia, Africa, and Latin America are the most important centers of the struggle against imperialism. . . . The successes of the national liberation movement, due in large measure to the victories of socialism, in turn strengthen the international positions of socialism in the struggle against imperialism.[15]

The Chinese demands are more rigorous and one-sided:

> Asia, Africa, and Latin America, which used to be the imperialist rear, have now come to the forefront in the fight against aggression and colonialism.
>   The African people's struggle for national independence is certainly not an isolated one. It is an important component part of the cause of the people of the whole world in opposing imperialism: first of all to oppose and end colonial rule, and end control and bondage by the imperialist forces of aggression and completely eliminate

their influence in every field before they could achieve a solution of the social problems facing them and make speedy social progress.[16]

Both the Soviet and the Chinese Communists evaluate the position of the non-aligned countries strictly from the standpoint that they must be either friends or foes, as expressed by Yu Chao-li: " 'Neither East nor West' is only a deliberate attempt to confuse friends with enemies."[17] Moscow as well as Peking is trying to prevent the newly independent countries from being concerned only with their own affairs, or acting "the role of a 'third force' in the international arena instead of opposing imperialism."[18] The "struggle against imperialism" is used by all Communists as a criterion (1) for evaluating all non-aligned countries in terms of the "characteristics of the epoch," (2) for evaluating each newly independent country in relation to the Communist bloc, and (3) for adapting Communist tactics to the situation in the "third world" and in individual countries.[19] Despite all the interest in the independence of the former colonies expressed in Communist oratory, the emphasis is not placed on their political and economic development as self-governing nations, but on their mobilization as "auxiliary troops" in the struggle against imperialism and on depriving the colonialist nations of their "source of cheap raw material and cannon fodder."[20]

The Communist Model for the Development of Non-Aligned Countries

Marxism-Leninism holds that it is not enough for former colonies to win national independence; they must embark on a "non-capitalist road" and sooner or later begin "socialist construction." This raises the question of timing and brings up the old, still unresolved question of how to relate the specific historical, national, social, economic, and cultural conditions of each country to the "general laws" of Communist transformation. On a more practical level, it must be decided whether the countries of the "third world" should adopt and imitate the Soviet or the Chinese model. The way this question is decided will determine not only whether a country or society is to be shaped in Soviet or Chinese fashion, but ultimately whether it will come under Soviet or Chinese hegemony. Thus, the competition between the rival Communist models casts the non-aligned countries in the role of hostages in the fight between Moscow and Peking over the "correct" road to Communism.

Mao Tse-tung had already stressed in *New Democracy* (1941)

the "world significance of the Chinese revolution," and Liu Shao-chi had declared in *Internationalism and Nationalism* (1948) that only by directing the national liberation movements on the basis of Mao's theories "can we liberate all the oppressed peoples in the world and solve the world's national question today." In 1959, Liu restated this claim in speaking about the "international signifi-cance" of the "Chinese experience," and Chen Yi embroidered it with a picturesque formula: "In the Chinese people they see their own tomorrow. . . . The Chinese people see their yesterday in all the oppressed nations."[21] The Chinese point to an identity between their own experiences and those of Asia, Africa, and Latin America under "prolonged imperialist oppression" and to an identical start-ing point for social and economic development. For them, the So-viet model is adaptable only to "revolutions in imperialist coun-tries"; "revolutions in colonial countries" must follow the Chinese way.

Moscow, for its part, has never abandoned its claim to provide the universal model. Soviet ideologists quote Lenin again and again to stress this point in their polemics against the Chinese "dogma-tists": "The Russian model teaches all countries something, and something very important, about their inevitable and none-too-distant future."[22]

The new Soviet Party program regards the "Communist con-struction in the U.S.S.R." as the "prototype of the new society, of the future of all mankind," and Khrushchev has referred to the fast industrial development of the "flourishing republics of Soviet Cen-tral Asia" as an example for the underdeveloped countries.[23] By following the Soviet model, other countries can indeed leap over a prolonged capitalist phase, but—Soviet theory maintains—can in no way omit the different stages of "socialist construction" developed in the Soviet Union. The Chinese propagate the possibility of pre-cisely such a "leap" over these stages and offer their "Great Leap" and the people's communes to other countries as "the best form of organization for the attainment of socialism . . . the practical road of transition to Communism."[24] They even claim that "new pro-duction relations can be developed faster in backward countries than in countries with a higher level of productivity," that in hu-man history "it has always been the weak who defeat the strong and the people deprived of material forces who defeat those pos-sessed of powerful material forces."[25]

These differences, of course, are not only concerned with the subtleties of Marxism-Leninism or the advantage of this or that tactic. They also reveal quite divergent interests, attitudes, and resentments. The "historical dialectics" of the Chinese are full of anti-Western, anti-white, racist, and chauvinist undercurrents, and their model is presented as the best counter to "worn-out Western civilization."[26] In wooing the underdeveloped countries they do not hide the "poverty and blankness" of China, but compare it with the identical state of the former colonies, advertise their creed as a gospel for have-nots, and preach that only by the concerted efforts of a united people will "a poor country be changed into a rich country." Last but not least, they teach other peoples to rely "on their own efforts" in their armed struggles and economic development and not to apply "mechanically and inflexibly certain experiences of the proletarian revolution in foreign countries."[27] Is it too far-fetched to surmise that these psychological aspects of the Chinese appeals to the peoples in Asia, Africa, and Latin America are as much directed against the white and relatively rich Russians as against the Western "imperialists"?

THE DIFFERENT METHODS FOR NATIONAL LIBERATION AND "TRANSITION TO SOCIALISM"

Inasmuch as the Communists regard the national liberation movement as a means and the newly independent countries as auxiliary forces in the "struggle against imperialism," Communist tactics must first find a way to win these countries over to Marxist-Leninist views and then prepare and carry out a Communist take-over within them. In the Communist blueprint, national liberation must be achieved in such a way as to create the best conditions for a "socialist revolution." In general, according to Communist doctrine, national liberation can only be attained through a revolution in which broad strata of the population participate under the leadership of Communists. Under present conditions this can "take the form of a prolonged guerrilla war, or of an army coup backed by the people."[28]

The developments since World War II have convinced the Soviet leaders that national liberation can also be achieved by "peaceful, constitutional means." Moscow now declares that civil war is not inevitable and advocates the "parliamentary method" as a legitimate Communist tactic. The main prerequisites for such a method are the transformation of the state machine of an independent country by the "extension of the state sector of the national economy"; introduction of state planning, "strict state control over foreign trade and currency operations"; establishment of regional economic federations, and formation of public organizations.[29] The Soviets also consider it possible that by "forcing the colonialists to make certain concessions the national liberation revolution might develop peacefully" or that the "transformation to socialism" might be advanced by "concessions to the bourgeoisie."[30]

Here again, Mao differs by pointing out that in most of these semi-colonial and semi-feudal countries that resemble China there is no parliament that can be utilized, and that therefore "the main form of struggle is war and the main form of organization is the army."[31] The road of "cooperation and peaceful development," the use of "Western parliamentary democracy" or the "transition to independence through elections" are for the Chinese nothing but an "opiate administered by the imperialists to benumb the colonial peoples." They see no evidence that the era of classic colonialism is dead. In their judgment, "genuine independence can be achieved only through resolute anti-colonial struggle; there is no other way."[32] Their own experiences force the Chinese to conclude that "national independence can be achieved only by the use of force, armed struggles, the complete destruction of the bourgeois state machinery," and finally the establishment of a "dictatorship of the proletariat."

United Front Tactics and "National Democracy"

The Communists cannot overlook the fact that liberation and independence in the "third world" march under the flag of nationalism. They hold that national development must be turned into a class struggle, since only the "class forces of the proletariat" and not "national forces" can bring about the final transition to Communism. The 1960 Moscow statement and the new Soviet Party program are proof that the Communist approach to all national problems remains dogmatic and full of contradictions. On the one hand, the Communists in power try to wipe out all national aspirations of the subjugated peoples; at the same time, they profess support for all manifestations of nationalism outside the Communist orbit, provided these are directed against the capitalist world.

The Communists realize that at present no "proletarian masses" exist in the Asian and African countries. The movement, therefore, must seek allies in the "national bourgeoisie" and among the peasantry. The organization and leadership of united fronts in backward countries as the main task of Communist tactics was long since discussed at the Second Comintern Congress, where Lenin, against the opposition of Roy and Serrati, favored Communist support of all "nationalist revolutionary movements." Today, in contrast to the heated discussions of the old Comintern days, the Communists are not so much concerned with a comprehensive sociological analysis of the "national bourgeoisie"; they simply accept in this category all the leading or governing groups in national liberation movements or independent countries, including even army cliques and religious castes. The main characteristic of a national bourgeoisie is that it stays "unconnected with imperialist circles," participates in the "struggle against imperialism" and finally shows a favorable attitude toward the local Communist Party and the "world socialist system." Should the national forces in a country become anti-Communist or follow a policy of "active coexistence," they are no longer regarded as a national bourgeoisie, but as "puppets of the imperialists."

In the first enthusiasm for national liberation movements after 1955, the Soviets even conceded to the bourgeoisie the "role of the leading force of any national movement," and were content as long as these bourgeois political leaders sided with the Soviet Union on important international questions.[33] For the Chinese, Mao's theories of "new democracy" have always been the guidelines for United front tactics. In accordance with these theories, the Communists must try to enlist allies from all sides and can even tolerate capitalist private property. But the Chinese press the concept of "uninterrupted revolution" with no "intervening stage of bourgeois dictatorship." They call for "hegemony in the democratic revolution by the proletariat through the Communist Party," requiring the "establishment of political control of the state by the proletariat."[34] They advise giving the national bourgeoisie only conditional support and still share Stalin's view of the leaders of the newly independent states as "lackeys of imperialism." There is some evidence that the Communist attitude toward the national bourgeoisie in non-aligned countries has been somewhat affected by recent outbreaks of national sentiment in their own realm—the Chinese experiences with the so-called "rightists" during the "Hundred Flowers" troubles, for example, or the repercussions aroused in the Central Asian Union Republics by Soviet propaganda on "bourgeois nationalism" intended for the Middle East.

In Soviet politics, there has lately been a perceptible shift of emphasis from unqualified support for "national independence" to demands for "economic independence" in non-aligned countries, as expressed in the new Party program: "As long as they [the young sovereign states] do not put an end to their economic dependence on imperialism, they will be playing the role of a 'world countryside' and will remain objects of semi-colonial exploitation."[35]

The prerequisite for "economic independence," according to the Soviet definition, is a "developed economy with many branches and a certain industrial basis . . . radical changes in the social and economic spheres . . . agrarian and other urgent reforms."[36] The purpose is, of course, to awaken "the differences in class interests" and to carry the class struggle into the new countries. At the same time, the Soviets are turning their interests more and more away from the "national bourgeoisie" and toward the "working class" in Africa, Asia, and Latin America. There are also more and more condemnations of all attempts to develop a "socialism of the national type" and of all steps taken by non-aligned countries toward federations and alliances among themselves.[37] A stiffening of the Soviet attitude can be seen in Khrushchev's recent outbursts and threats in Sofia:

> Many of the leaders of the countries that have won their national independence are trying to pursue a kind of fence-sitting policy which they call non-class, are trying to ignore the class structure of society and the class struggle which are matters of fact in their countries. . . . Those leaders will sooner or later have to realize that only by leaning on the working class as the most consistent, most revolutionary class of society, in alliance with the peasantry and with support of all progressive forces, can they bring about victory and the correct solution of fundamental social problems. They will either grasp this fact or they will be followed by others with a better understanding of life's demands.[38]

The "alliance with the peasants" occupies a special place in the Communist plans for national liberation movements. "It is impossible for the peasants to become an independent political force during modern revolutions";[39] the Communists must, therefore, prevent all "spontaneous" tendencies among the peasants, drive a wedge between the national bourgeoisie and the peasants, and win over the rural population with promises of a solution of the peasant problem and agrarian reforms. On the basis of their own experience, the Chinese advocate combining agrarian reform with the "liberation struggle"—that is, abolishing the feudal land system, organizing "peasant associations," setting up Party nuclei, arming the peasants, and establishing rural revolutionary base areas, the final purpose being to "surround the cities from the countryside and then take the cities." "To bestow land upon the peasants"[40] is vehemently rejected as erroneous. The Soviets, on the other hand, believe that effective agrarian reforms can only take place after there has been a distribution of land and technological development of agriculture.[41]

In order to give Communist efforts in Asia, Africa, and Latin America a firmer theoretical basis, the meeting of the eighty-one parties in Moscow in 1960 endorsed the concept of the "independent state of national democracy."[42] This was defined as the "dictatorship of the really national-patriotic forces (the working class, the peasantry, and the national bourgeoisie)" and, in effect, as a stage in the "transition to socialism." Even though certain features of this "national democracy" were taken from Mao's concept of "new democracy," the Chinese viewed this Soviet model for newly independent countries with some reservation and remained faithful to Mao's somewhat different formula of "people's democratic dictatorship."[43]

THE ROLE OF COMMUNIST PARTIES AND FRONT ORGANIZATIONS

It is not surprising that Communist parties in the non-aligned countries at present play only a secondary role in Communist tactics. Their social and political base is weak and their membership small. In most countries they have no trained, reliable cadres and are compelled to work underground. Moscow and Peking are both training agitators, organizers, and other specialists in an all-out effort to organize cores of Communist parties in the newly independent countries. Peking, however, stresses that a steeled and experienced Party can emerge only in the course of "struggle," while Moscow favors gradual and careful organizational work with due concern for "legality." The Soviets, moreover, give precedence to dealings with non-aligned countries on a state-to-state basis, even if this means conducting diplomatic activities that conflict with the political line of the local parties.

The Chinese seem to have some basis for their complaint that Moscow's "coexistence" with national leaders has been unable to prevent the persecution of Communists in the new countries and does not strengthen the position of the local Communists at all. The Soviets counter that the Communist parties in the new countries are still too weak for a take-over and that too radical actions by leftists could only drive the national leaders into the arms of the West. These differences in the evaluation of Communist parties in the newly independent states have already produced a schism in some of the parties themselves, although the Chinese attack on India has done much to undercut Peking's previous gains.

Communist tactics in non-aligned countries concentrate at present on the use of various front organizations that cover the broad spectrum between the state relations and Party connections of Communist countries with the "third world." All these organizations serve as transmission belts for influencing governments and peoples, and as a vast reservoir for recruiting Communist cadres and promoting illegal activity. One must not underestimate such techniques of Communist infiltration, particularly those employed by Communist trade unions. But a realistic evaluation must recognize the discrepancies between appearance and effectiveness. Moreover, these fellow-traveling front organizations do not have the centralized, disciplined organization and leadership of the Communist parties, and their memberships are more prone to be affected by such actions as Moscow's in Hungary, Peking's in Tibet, and the Soviet resumption of nuclear testing. Sino-Soviet differences have come out into the open at meetings of these organizations, as at sessions of the World Peace Council, the World Federation of Trade Unions, and the Afro-Asian People's Solidarity Organization.

SOVIET BLOC INTERFERENCE IN NATIONAL AFFAIRS

Communist theory holds that the national liberation movement cannot succeed without the direct support of the "proletariat of the most advanced countries" (Lenin) or the "socialist world community" (Khrushchev). In other words, oppressed peoples are in general unable to obtain their independence by themselves. No avowals of "non-interference in the internal affairs of young national states" and no denials of the "export of revolution" have really changed this principle of Communist strategy and tactics directed against the "third world." As Khrushchev has remarked, "our world outlook . . . the interests of all working people for which we are fighting, impel us to insure that the peoples take the right road to progress."[44] The only crucial question for the Communists, then, is how to succeed without giving the impression of outside interference and without endangering Communist goals.

In line with its view of the present epoch, the Soviet Union puts the emphasis on economic aid. Moscow may claim to grant aid without strings, in contrast to the Western aid that perpetuates "colonial exploitation," but its aid in fact is far from selfless. Khrushchev conceded as much in declaring: "It does not follow that socialist aid exerts no influence on the prospects of the further development of newly independent countries." Economic aid granted by the Soviet Union, China, and the satellites to twenty-three former colonies takes the form chiefly of direct trade, credits, construction of plants, and training of personnel. It is concentrated primarily on a few spectacular heavy industry projects, with little consideration for the economic realities and the urgent needs of the people. In the end, by providing this kind of aid, Moscow hopes to create conditions for the emergence of a broad working class, thereby paving the way for a "socialist transformation" and providing the substructure for a later Communist take-over.

At the same time, as a by-product of economic aid, Soviet planning methods could come to exert a distinct influence on the state apparatus of the partner governments. The technical assistance programs allow for sending Communist-trained technical personnel to these countries and open up opportunities for agitation and infiltration; moreover, the training of specialists from these countries in bloc institutions can be utilized to indoctrinate a future Marxist-Leninist elite. The delivery of weapons and the training of military personnel open up new possibilities for fanning international tensions, as well as for winning over segments of the armies. Last but not least, there is what Lenin called the "unselfish cultural aid" rendered by Communist academic institutions, and there are the uses made of the press and other communications channels.

The economic aid given by Communist states is certainly exaggerated in their propaganda, and is insignificant compared with Western assistance. It burdens the economies of the Communist donors, and it puts the Soviet Union in a field of competition where the West enjoys clear superiority. Khrushchev has granted that the "imperialists" have powerful economic levers. It is therefore not surprising that the Soviet Union cynically advises the non-aligned countries to use Communist aid proposals as a weapon to extort still more from the rich capitalist countries.

The Chinese argue that the Soviet policy on economic aid to the underdeveloped countries does not help the cause of Communism. In their view, the scarce economic means available could better be utilized by the Communist countries—that is, by China. For them, the paramount task of Communism is not the expansion of foreign trade, but the promotion of revolution—an attitude that may well be conditioned by the practical consideration that they are not yet in a position to compete with the Soviet economic penetration of the non-aligned countries. In any event, they offer Mao's strategy of guerrilla warfare as China's principal export, and they underscore the fact that the Chinese example has had greater success than what they regard as Khrushchev's giveaway program in such countries as Indochina, Cuba, and Algeria:

> The revolutionary theories, strategy, and tactics that the Chinese people have summed up from their revolutionary practice, and that are expressed in a nutshell in Comrade Mao Tse-tung's writings, are attracting ever greater attention among the people of various countries who long to find in them something that will benefit their own struggles for liberation. To put it frankly, all oppressed nations and peoples will sooner or later rise in revolution, and this is precisely why revolutionary experiences and theories will naturally gain currency among these nations and peoples and go deep to their hearts. This is why such pamphlets as those expounding guerrilla warfare in China have had such a wide circulation in Africa, Asia, and Latin America and are looked upon as precious things even after they are worn and the print has become illegible through much use.[45]

The essence of Mao's military doctrine is that "the deficiencies in the field of armaments and equipment are of secondary importance and can and must be made up for by a political mobilization of the masses"; he teaches a "piecemeal solution, smashing the enemy bit by bit."[46] It cannot be denied that this kind of advice, widely distributed in many languages, can have a special attraction for backward countries and poor peoples.

But the Chinese do not content themselves with teaching revolutionary tactics. They also advocate direct military intervention in national liberation wars by the Communist powers "to end imperialist unjust war by just war" and to establish Communism through military action: "When the armed forces of the socialist countries . . . have to go beyond their borders . . . it is only natural that they should exert an influence and have an effect wherever they go."[47] Khrushchev, on the other hand, cautions that "local wars" could grow into a world thermo-nuclear and missile war; at the same time, he has recognized "national liberation wars, popular uprisings, and guerrilla wars" as justifiable and inevitable and has promised to support them wholeheartedly and without reservation.[48]

All these differences relate ultimately to the issue of the correct methods for a Communist take-over in newly independent states. According to Soviet doctrine, a certain social, economic, and political transformation is the prerequisite for a take-over without risks and sacrifices. The Chinese maintain that power must first be seized by Communists as a pre-condition for successful transformation of the country. For the Chinese Communists, this seizure of power is not so much a political and social process as a military action. In Mao Tse-tung's words: "Whoever wants to seize state power and keep it must have a strong army. . . . All political power grows out of the barrel of a gun."[49] Also connected with these questions are the growing differences between Moscow and Peking about the effect total disarmament would have on young sovereign states. Khrushchev has again and again put forward the argument that disarmament would release huge funds that could be channeled into aid to the underdeveloped countries: "If a program of universal and complete disarmament were adopted, the peoples of the countries needing economic assistance would be able to receive it in considerably larger amounts."[50] The Soviets add that disarmament would deprive the police, the army, and the state apparatus of imperialist countries of the opportunity to use weapons against the revolution and would "pull the colonial shark's teeth." For the Chinese, disarmament is a snare and a delusion. They call for "armed national liberation struggles" as a means "to disperse, tie down, and deplete imperialism's armed forces" and thereby secure world peace. The Chinese delegation put the case with remarkable frankness at the Stockholm session of the World Peace Council in December, 1961:

> It is erroneous to believe that general and complete disarmament is the only road to peace. To impose this view upon the oppressed nations will inevitably impair their national liberation struggle. The most important issue for the oppressed nations and newly independent countries is definitely not disarmament, but to build up, expand, and strengthen their armed forces.[51]

Thus the differences in evaluation of the "characteristics of our epoch" influence the Soviet and the Chinese tactics toward non-aligned countries, and each side's choice of tactics in turn affects its ideological and political positions on major international questions.

Some Conclusions

1. The differences of opinion between Moscow and Peking on Communist tactics in non-aligned countries can by no means be regarded as "antagonistic." The Chinese criticism of Khrushchev's "revisionist" policy does not preclude Peking's use of Khrushchev's methods; for example, Peking, like the U.S.S.R., gives economic aid and recognizes governments that persecute Communist parties. Nor is Moscow exclusively an advocate of peaceful solutions.

2. In assessing the Soviet and Chinese attitudes toward the non-aligned countries, one cannot but remark on the egocentric approach of the Soviets. They like to exaggerate their "confidence in the superiority of the socialist system" and regard the socialist camp (with or without the "leading role of the Soviet Union") as the center of the world that, sooner or later, all non-aligned countries must join. Khrushchev's remark to Egyptian visitors, "History will teach you" is almost as great a threat to non-aligned countries as his famous "We will bury you" is to Western countries. The Soviet leader is convinced that Communism can win only by "force of the example of the world socialist system." His slogan "We shall win minds" seems to reveal his creed of world revolution through propaganda and public relations. Something like Victorian enthusiasm appears in the Soviet approach to the "third world," expressed in Kuusinen's exclamation: "We have entered the time of a striking technical revolution." In a sense, the Soviet attitude toward the young states looks like a reincarnation of the nineteenth-century European attitude of superiority over other races and continents.

The Chinese pride themselves no less, but they concentrate on stirring up hatred for the "enemy"—"U.S. imperialism"—rather than enticing people with pictures of a utopian future. Where the Soviets are enamored of their own technical achievements, the Chinese believe in the "forces of the people" with a kind of puritanical fervor. They do not close their eyes to modern developments everywhere in the world, but they follow the teaching of Marx more fanatically than the Russians do.

3. The reasons for Soviet-Chinese differences are deeply rooted: (a) different historical, national, economical, social, and cultural developments in Russia and China will for a long time result in different positions and may even affect loyalties to the Communist goals; (b) the structure of the Communist totalitarian system and the problems of so-called "democratic centralism" must always af-

fect the relationship of the center to the components and produce frictions between them; (c) as long as Communist ideology claims to express absolute and total truth, Marxism-Leninism must prove that it can adapt itself to all realities without sacrificing dogma. It follows that in every case the "correct" interpretation of the dogma establishing policy has to be decided by power struggles.

4. There is no doubt that some of the ground gained by Communism in Asia, Africa, and Latin America has been lost by the controversy between Soviet and Chinese leaders. We cannot expect these troubles to disappear in the near future, and there are grounds for believing either that Sino-Soviet contradictions will produce a paralysis of Communist activities in the "third world" or that they will heighten the chances of rash actions. Nevertheless, both the non-aligned countries and the West would be in error if they were to count on profiting from these frictions.

Communist Polycentrism and the Underdeveloped Areas

—WILLIAM E. GRIFFITH

The Sino-Soviet rift has ushered in a new epoch of polycentrism in the international Communist movement.[1] The recent acquisition of independence by almost all underdeveloped countries opened a new epoch in the history of the Southern Hemisphere. This paper considers the interaction of the two.

Communist polycentrism has primarily arisen from the organizational and policy differences between the Soviet and Chinese Communist parties. The organizational difference arises out of the world-wide Chinese challenge to the historic claim of the Soviet Union to ideological, policy-making, and organizational supremacy in the international Communist movement. The policy differences encompass all domestic and foreign policy issues within and between the two countries; in them, the Soviet Union takes the more moderate, China the more extreme position.

For our purposes, perhaps the most important point about the Sino-Soviet differences is that the resultant line-up among the various Communist parties and in fellow-travelling or sympathetic parties or organizations is not necessarily the same over all issues. On the organizational question, most if not all smaller parties sympathize with the Chinese; on the policy issues, most of them clearly support the Soviet Union. Furthermore, on some specific policy issues such as the relative priority of disarmament and the "national liberation struggle," leftists from underdeveloped countries generally support the Chinese position,[2] while on the question of widely rather than narrowly defined organizational and policy limits for trade-union and peace activities, they tend to support the Soviet Union.[3]

In the course of its development toward polycentrism the Sino-

Soviet rift has produced a rightist trend as well as a leftist (Chinese-Albanian) deviation from the Soviet "centrist" position. The rightist trend has been perhaps most clearly present in the leadership, and even more in the rank and file, of the Italian Communist Party;[4] but it also exists, less strongly and more on the domestic than on the international level, in the Polish[5] and Hungarian parties.[6] It has arisen because the Sino-Soviet rift has given other Communist parties the chance of gaining more domestic autonomy, and has therefore enlarged opportunities for their potential domestic deviations by making it possible for them to choose among several differing organizational courses of action: (1) strong support of either the Soviet Union (e.g., Poland) or of China (e.g., Albania); (2) balancing between the two (e.g., North Vietnam); and (3) possibly even mediating between the two (perhaps North Vietnam). The rightist deviation tends to produce a more favorable attitude toward the Yugoslav position, the more so because one of the main issues in the Sino-Soviet dispute has been the proper attitude to be taken toward the Yugoslav "nationalist" and "rightist" deviation.

The purpose of this paper is to suggest some tentative hypotheses concerning the inter-relationship between the polycentric tendencies in international Communism, on the one hand, and leftism and Communism in general in underdeveloped areas, on the other. Specifically, it attempts to isolate the factors of attraction and repulsion of the various trends in Communist polycentrism and to estimate their effectiveness in various social groups and geographic areas in the underdeveloped world.

First, however, something must be said briefly about the general attraction of Communism for the people of underdeveloped areas: the specific categories below primarily represent intensification or diminution of these general ones. Generally speaking, Communism obtains support primarily from a certain part of the newly educated elites in underdeveloped areas; these people believe that they have been alienated from their traditional society and frustrated in the use of their talents and in the acquisition of power primarily by present or former "imperialist colonizers,"—in fact, the traditional society itself is just as much responsible for their position.[7] Communism's mass support comes primarily from a dissatisfied, landless peasantry and from the new working class, itself of peasant origin, that develops during the beginnings of industrialization and is economically and sociologically alienated from its new and strange surroundings.[8] There is one important caveat in this categorization, however; Communism in underdeveloped societies frequently tends to recruit both its elite and mass members primarily from alienated ethnic, religious, and economic minorities.[9] Within all these groups, the attraction of Communism is that of a tried and tested prescription for rapid social change and economic development, characterized by the use of force by a new elite, by an uncompromising policy of opposition to Western "imperialism," and, more recently, by the natural desire of members of weak nations to be on what they consider the winning side—that is, because of Soviet military and space power, on the Communist side.

The factors which inhibit the development of Communist strength in underdeveloped areas may briefly be summarized as those of nationalism, traditional religion, the effects or aftereffects of Western culture, fear of Communist power and the desire to avoid getting in its grip, ethnic, color, or historic rivalries that make the area concerned traditionally hostile toward one or more Communist powers, and in general (a category which subsumes and combines most of the other foregoing ones) a kind of isolationism: the desire to opt out of the East-West power struggle and *cultiver son jardin*—a policy characteristic of the United States of America in the early decades of its independence and of India, Indonesia, and other underdeveloped countries today.

What is the likely impact of Communist polycentrism upon these general categories of attraction and repulsion? In the first place, it is greatly influenced by the controversies over various issues, important in the Sino-Soviet rift and therefore in the current phase of polycentrism, that directly affect underdeveloped areas. The primary one is the controversy over the role of the "national bourgeoisie," i.e., of the leftist, nationalist, non-Communist rulers of underdeveloped areas—Nehru, Nasser, Kassem, Sukarno, Nkrumah, Sékou Touré, Betancourt. On this issue, first debated by Lenin and M. N. Roy at the beginning of the twenties, the Soviet position has remained remarkably consistent from Lenin to Khrushchev: the "national bourgeoisie" is initially an "objectively progressive force" that is to be supported and used before it is eventually thrown away. Mao takes Roy's position: the national bourgeoisie, if aided, will only consolidate its objectively anti-Communist position and thus make the transition to socialism more difficult; it must therefore be unmasked and attacked, and only Communists and their totally reliable allies supported.

The issue of the national bourgeoisie directly involves the Communist left wing (China, Albania, and some of the Asian parties) in conflict not only with the Soviet Union but even more with the rightist tendencies in the polycentric framework: specifically, with the Yugoslavs[10] and the Italian Communists. (The Poles are still domesticists[11]—they deliberately eschew international ambitions in favor of retaining and expanding domestic autonomy.) Since his break with the Soviet Union in 1948, Tito has built up extensive contacts with leaders of underdeveloped countries, initially with Asians but by now quite as much with Africans as well.

The appeal of the "Yugoslav model of socialism" to leftist underdeveloped states should not be underestimated. Its economic policies both offer more success and require less change than do Moscow's or Peking's: agriculture remains private, and its decentralized market economy and workers' self-management combine flexibility with "social ownership." Furthermore, within the last few years Yugoslavia's economy has grown more rapidly than that of any other country in the world except Japan. On the domestic political scene, Yugoslavia is a multi-ethnic state that combines rapid economic growth and much cultural autonomy with rigidly centralized mono-party political controls, headed by a charismatic leader. In foreign policy, Yugoslavia, like almost all the underdeveloped states, is relatively without military power and is therefore no threat to their independence. It carries on extensive political activity within the non-aligned nations; it is very active, in alliance with the Afro-Asians, in the United Nations; it successfully practices what the underdeveloped states dream of: getting extensive economic aid from West and East, both "with no strings attached." Furthermore, for Moslems Yugoslavia is a partly Moslem country, where the Islamic faith is not only tolerated but subsidized, and where the Moslem areas of Bosnia-Herzegovina, Macedonia, and the Kosmet are in the midst of a very rapid economic development program subsidized by the regime. Finally, Tito's long personal experience in dealing profitably with both Moscow and Washington, while remaining independent of both, makes him a very useful adviser in this delicate but indispensable art for heads of newly independent states. Yugoslavia's weaknesses are the weaknesses not of its leader or of its policy, but rather of its physical and human resources. It is still a half-developed, small Balkan country, and economically it is increasingly squeezed between the growing European Economic Community to the west and the Council for Mutual

Economic Assistance to the east. The prospects of its foreign trade with underdeveloped areas, which is in large part financed by Yugoslav credits, are not good and it cannot hope to provide the diversified markets and the capital investments that the new states need. What it can do, what Tito can and does do so well personally, is to act as a catalyst and adviser in such international groups as the United Nations and the Afro-Asian bloc; to interpret Moscow and Peking, as well as Washington to underdeveloped areas; and to provide an economic and political model that is strikingly similar to but much more productive than those so laboriously being developed by the leftist leaders of the new countries.

Of the Italian and Polish Communists, the "semi-rightists," much less need be said. Poland's dependence on Soviet support of its western boundaries and its vulnerability to superior Soviet physical power require that it follow Soviet foreign policy closely; and Gomulka, unlike Tito, has no international ambitions. It seems likely, therefore, that Polish deviations will continue to be primarily domestic in character, and that Polish economic trade and aid activities in underdeveloped countries, which are in any case far less extensive than those of Czechoslovakia and East Germany, will remain closely coordinated with Moscow's.

The Italian Communists are not in power, and not likely to gain power in the near future. The only way they can have any significant influence on underdeveloped countries is through their activities in such international Communist or Communist-led organizations as the World Federation of Trade Unions (WFTU). At the WFTU Congress held in Moscow in December, 1961, the Italian delegation strongly favored the WFTU's relaxing its policy of noncooperation with other trade union organizations; the Italians particularly mentioned the All-African Trade Union Federation, which is closely connected with the Casablanca powers, as an example of a trade union organization with which cooperation should be established. They have consistently taken the same position since.[12] The Chinese position, on the contrary, was one of rigid non-cooperation and rather overt hostility toward non-Communist organizations; the Soviets have been following an indecisive, centrist policy. The Italian Communists themselves are rent with dissension, and it is unlikely that they will play any seriously significant role in affairs of underdeveloped countries in the near future.

So much for the external polycentric Communist currents acting on the underdeveloped areas; we must now turn to the tendencies of attraction and repulsion which exist there. These may be most conveniently divided into national and Communist factors; each will be considered in turn, some illustrative examples being given in each case.

The national factors may be divided into the geopolitical ones: distance, boundaries, common enemies, partition-irredenta; and the cultural ones: ethnic groups, color, and religion.[13] It is evident from this list that they are largely geographical and historical in character; it is not surprising, therefore, that their nature is usually specific to any one country.

Ideology often conceals but seldom if ever dissolves national interests, particularly those of geographic origin. The present Sino-Soviet rift has in part certainly been caused by the long history of Russo-Chinese enmity. It was hardly coincidental that the countries of Eastern Europe where anti-Russian feelings are the most intense and historically the oldest, Poland and Hungary, were the scene in 1956 of the Polish October rising and the Hungarian Revolution.

To turn to less developed areas, it is equally clear that the Albanian revolt against the Soviet Union in 1960 arose primarily out of the intense Albanian hatred for and fear of the Yugoslavs, with whom Hoxha feared Khrushchev was again about to come to terms. Outer Mongolia's current pro-Soviet position probably results primarily from its fear of reabsorption by China, of which it was a part under the Manchu. Such countries as Turkey and Iran, historically areas of Russian expansionism, remain strongly anti-Soviet; it might be expected, therefore, that the Chinese would be more successful there. India has, of course, become strongly anti-Chinese.

All the above cases are of countries where a variety of Communist polycentrism, either Soviet or Chinese, suffers handicaps in traditionally hostile border nations. It must be added that the anti-Soviet attitude of these countries is made possible only by American support, while Outer Mongolia has presumably been protected from Chinese influence by Soviet backing. When such powerful support by a great power is not present, the result may well be not so much a greater tendency toward the Communism of the powerful and feared neighbor, as less hostility to it: one thinks here of Finland, Cambodia, Burma, and Afghanistan.

In contrast to the mutual hostility of some countries with common boundaries are cases of a friendly attitude caused by noncontiguous boundaries with intervening common enemies. In Europe, the pro-Russian tendencies of the Czechs and Bulgars are excellent examples; in the Middle East, the even relatively pro-Soviet (because anti-British) attitude of Nasser and Kassem, and of large parts of the leftist, nationalist, anti-Western Egyptian and Iraqi intelligentsia. The Sino-Indian border feud has led to signs of a Chinese-Pakistani rapprochement; not surprisingly, since both have two common hostile neighbors: India and Russia.

There is also at least one Communist country whose geographical position makes it inclined to attempt to balance between the Soviet Union and China: North Vietnam. Its independence is historically and actually menaced by neighboring Chinese power, to counterbalance which it needs Soviet support. The leaders of North Vietnam therefore probably wish the Sino-Soviet rift to continue, since it gives them advantages of maneuver; they presumably do not want a break, which would force them to choose between China and the Soviet Union. The same is to a lesser extent true of some groups within the Cuban Party and of some Communist parties not in power, notably the Japanese and the Indonesian: each has less geographical but just as much Party reason for maintaining a neutral position between Moscow and Peking. Until the Chinese attack on India in October, 1962, the Indian Party was a special case: if it were to remain united, it had also to try in some fashion to balance between the two great Communist powers, and hope that a break would not occur.[14]

In the case of North Vietnam this balancing is complicated by another geographical factor arising from World War II and its aftermath: partition. For the North Vietnamese Party, as for Ulbricht in East Germany, the non-Communist part of the country is an irredenta under the "control" of a hostile great power, the United States. This irredentism drives it toward extremism and thus closer to the present Chinese policy position; its balancing is thus modified by its extremism. Parenthetically, the large Albanian irredenta in the Kosmet (southwest Yugoslavia) has had much the same extremist, anti-Yugoslav, and more recently anti-Soviet effect on Albanian policy. Such geographical hostilities can frequently be subsumed in what an Austrian professor once called *Das Gesetz der Gegengrenzlichkeit*, or, to put it another way, "the enemy of my enemy is my friend."

Cultural hostilities are those not necessarily contiguous with national boundaries; they are often involved in nationalistic or religious irredenta; and they are usually particularly violent in underdeveloped areas. As has already been indicated, ethnic minorities suffering from discrimination or persecution are among the most fertile fields for Communist propaganda. This was true of Eastern Europe between the world wars, and it is equally true in South Africa, in India, and of the ethnic Chinese throughout Southeast Asia. When the minority becomes, as in the last case, economically prosperous, then their very susceptibility and the prevalence of Communism among them is another factor creating or reinforcing anti-Communist sentiment on the part of the majority of the population; the Jews of Eastern Europe were in a similar position between the wars.

Closely akin to the ethnic factor, but in African and Asian (and in many Latin American) underdeveloped countries much more important, is that of color. This is certainly one of the greatest advantages of the Chinese Communists in dealing with underdeveloped areas: they, like Africans, Asians, and the Indians and Negroes in Latin America, are non-white. With the Chinese, the color factor is also closely allied with two others that also tend to work in their favor rather than that of the Russians: their non-Western and non-affluent characteristics. To many intellectuals from underdeveloped countries in Africa and Asia, the Soviets are both European (i.e., Western) and well-off; they have nothing of the complete underdog symbolism, in color, geography, and poverty, from which the Chinese benefit.

Finally, there is the religious factor. This is particularly important when a religion has become identified with the history, traditions, and new nationalism of an area; one thinks of Pakistan, of the newly independent Arab states, and of countries with relatively important Christian elements, such as Senegal, South Vietnam, and many of the Latin American countries. Religion and nationalism make a potent brew, as the histories of Ireland, Poland, and Croatia demonstrate; in underdeveloped areas the mixture is equally potent and greater than the sum of its parts. Pakistan is here an excellent example. A state whose only *raison d'être* is religious, where Islam and statehood are co-equivalent, its population composed of a former, now deposed elite that once ruled the whole Indian sub-continent, anti-Indian and therefore anti-leftist, traditionally anti-Russian, Pakistan can hardly help but be largely anti-Communist.

The religious factor acts even more strongly against Communism when, as with Nasser's "Arab socialism," it can be successfully combined with nationalism, anti-colonialism, some variety of international "mission" (in this case pan-Arabism), and modernization: the combination deprives Communism of most of its gospel, while substituting for it a much more effective one of its own. (This factor is not nearly as effective in respect to Yugoslavia.)

The past history of Communist parties, and in particular their relations with the Soviet Union, with China, and with Yugoslavia, has much more influence than is usually realized upon their strength and their tendencies in the present polycentric situation. It is unlikely, for example, that a party whose leadership was ruthlessly decimated by Stalin during the nineteen thirties or forties will be totally pro-Soviet; the Polish and North Korean parties are excellent examples. The same is true where the Russians or Chinese have long been involved in factional struggles within the leaderships of small underdeveloped parties: Vietnam, Korea, and India are examples here. It should be added, however, that in most of the underdeveloped areas the history of Communist parties is so far relatively brief; the factor of past purges, therefore, does not play a major role in most of them.

We have already discussed the racial factor; this is of particular importance in the case of the ethnic Chinese, who reportedly make up most if not almost all of the leadership and membership of the Burmese, Thai, and Malayan parties. (Thus the traditional fear of the Chinese in these countries has been augmented by the ethnically Chinese character of the local Communist parties.) The South African Communist Party has been largely made up of people not of Afrikaans or English stock—its members are either other Europeans, Indians, or, mostly, Africans. Although Soviet or Chinese activities in many underdeveloped countries, particularly in Africa, are not yet advanced enough for much material to be available on this point,[15] it would be surprising if they had not already taken advantage of ethnic and tribal hostilities. Such artificial boundaries as those created in Africa by the colonial powers probably have even more potentialities than did those in Central and Eastern Europe drawn at Versailles, as far as Communist exploitation of disaffected elements is concerned.

One other distinguishing characteristic among Communist parties in power is the method by which they attained it, that is, whether it was by their own efforts or by total or major assistance from the Soviet Union or (in part for North Vietnam and North

Korea) from China. Those parties which have come to power by their own feats of arms tend to be more extremist in policy and proud in posture; they all have shown much more independence vis-à-vis Moscow. This pride and self-confidence derive largely from the self-assurance, group loyalty, and *esprit de corps* that arose during their partisan struggles. Developing Communist polycentrism will probably further such tendencies, since it will inhibit Soviet or Chinese attempts to impede them by pressure or force; furthermore, the examples it presents of advantages to be gained by more independence from Soviet or Chinese control will certainly become contagious. Finally, the extremism of intellectuals of underdeveloped countries, particularly when added—as in some cases it is likely to be—to the even greater extremism arising from partisan warfare will tend to make some of them pro-Chinese rather than pro-Soviet.

It may seem from the above that the Chinese, or even the Soviets, have large-scale, indeed perhaps irresistible prospects in the underdeveloped areas, particularly for the frustrated intellectuals and the new working class. Yet this, in the writer's view, is far from the truth. Fundamentally, all underdeveloped areas want to be left alone: aided but not controlled, and gaining the advantages but carrying none of the burdens of playing a role on the international scene, particularly in the United Nations. Only the shortness of memory and the lack of historic perspective of too many Westerners, particularly of Americans, can explain why this should seem strange or engender Western protests; what else, after all, was nineteenth-century America but isolationist and moralist? Exactly in this area, however, in my view lies the major weakness of the Soviet Union, and less surely and less soon but still probably as seriously, of the Chinese. Communist polycentrism will demonstrate to the underdeveloped areas that Communism does not mean centralized control from Moscow or from Peking; that, as in the case of Yugoslavia, it can combine national independence, a market economy, ethnic harmony, rapid economic growth, and centralized, personalized authority; that, as in the case of the Italian Communist Party, it can advocate the parliamentary transition to socialism and attempt to adjust to the increasingly affluent society of Western Europe.

Yet it may be questioned whether this will aid Communism in the East-West race for the favor of the underdeveloped areas. The Soviet Union has increasingly tried to adjust to the fact of the world-wide diffusion of power. It has also attempted, with so far not too great success, the more difficult adjustment to polycentrism in the Communist camp. However, if only because of its anti-pragmatic and anti-nationalistic ideology Moscow is unlikely to be able to adjust to it so rapidly as can, if they will, the pluralistic and increasingly post-nationalist Western societies. In this respect, the very continued dynamism of Soviet expansion will get in the way of its success. For underdeveloped states that want to go their own way, profiting much but losing little from the cultivation of them by East and West, the Soviet Union is likely still to appear as a big power, a strong power, and therefore a dangerous power, one that wooes them too openly, that refuses to accept pan-Africanism, pan-Arabism, or pan-Asianism, and that too clearly wishes to in-fluence and above all to involve them—that, in a word, will not let them alone and cannot really understand why they should want to be let alone. When one adds to this the ethnic, historic, geo-political, religious, and color hostilities that Moscow in any case encounters, Khrushchev's problems do indeed look difficult. He can hope to profit more from the West's blunders than from his own achievements.

Communist China's problems are quite different. To extremist intellectuals in many underdeveloped countries "Maoism" certainly has some appeal. But these intellectuals are too completely alien-ated even from the new indigenous ruling elite, itself still largely encircled with the nimbus of having fought for and gained inde-pendence. They are certainly more anti-Chinese than anti-Soviet, for obvious reasons; the Chinese openly proclaim the necessity for their liquidation. In underdeveloped countries near to China, ethnic and historic hostilities gravely limit Peking's influence, while the Sino-Soviet rift ensures that Khrushchev will hardly help Mao restore it. In other areas, China's economic, military, and political weakness, its lack of a modern industrialized economy, in contrast with the Soviet panoply of space and missile successes, inhibits the Chinese Communists still further. Chinese successes are still to come, and probably not in the near future.

As to the right-wing tendencies in Communist polycentrism, only the Yugoslavs need be seriously considered. (As already stated, the Italian Communists are not in power, the Poles are securely do-mesticist.) Tito's Yugoslavia has considerable appeal to many underdeveloped countries, both to extremist leaders in power and extremist factions striving for it. Nevertheless, the Yugoslavs suffer from one fatal weakness, even more serious than those of the Chinese—they are too small, too weak, and too limited in their freedom of movement on the international scene. Impressive as their rate of economic growth has been, it has recently outrun their means, and the resultant domestic economic crisis has intensified Tito's already existing tendency again to seek a rapprochement with the Soviet Union, hoping to profit from the Sino-Soviet rift. This, in turn, may well somewhat inhibit Yugoslav influence in underdeveloped areas, by discrediting that very independence of view which has until now been one of Tito's major assets. Most importantly, however, his country's permanent economic weakness prevents the formation of a massive and secure economic base for its policy toward underdeveloped areas, of the sort that the United States and the Soviet Union enjoy.

The divisive tendencies in the international Communist movement described above were greatly intensified by the two major international crises of October and November, 1962—the Chinese attack on the northern border of India and the major Soviet-American confrontation over Cuba.[16] As a result of the former, India was driven rapidly toward the West once it realized that it could no longer depend on Soviet pressure on China to prevent the latter from attacking it, and after its army had been swept aside by the invading Chinese. Fear of the onrushing Chinese further cowed some of their neighbors (Burma, Cambodia), while Peking lost much of its credit with more distant and less endangered neutralists.[17] Soviet indecision probably lost Moscow some support in underdeveloped areas, but the Kremlin's failure to support the Chinese held this within bounds. Indian dependence on the West in fact deprived the neutralist bloc of its most populous power and its former leader, while Western prestige in the underdeveloped world rose as it became clear that the West would give aid against the Chinese aggressor without requiring the formal abjuration of Indian non-alignment.

The Cuban crisis was the most serious Soviet-American confrontation since 1945, and Moscow clearly came out the loser. Since power is the primary instrument of influence in underdeveloped areas, this inevitably meant that Washington won. Moreover, the Soviet defeat was magnified by the U.S.S.R.'s public and almost total disregard for Castro's wishes in the crisis. During the emergency, Soviet requests for air transit rights in Africa to Cuba were turned down in all instances. Finally, the role of the United Nations, a forum in which hitherto the underdeveloped world had played a role far greater than the sum of its power, was cut back to that of a convenient center for discussion between the two superpowers. The efforts of Nasser, Sukarno, and Sékou Touré to impress their populations and their associates with their "decisive" role in the crisis were in crass contrast with their actual impotence.

The Cuban affair, coming on top of the Sino-Indian encounter, drastically accentuated the Sino-Soviet conflict; the Sino-Indian crisis itself had already divided the neutrals according to their geographic propinquity to China. Even should an open break be avoided and some form of "divergent unity"[18] be preserved, it may well be questioned whether this will serve either Soviet or Chinese interests in the underdeveloped areas; the contrary will more likely be the case. "Divergent unity" necessarily produces lack of ideological clarity; and those alienated intellectuals in underdeveloped areas to whom Communism appeals tend to be men with an abnormal concern about theory. The Sino-Soviet ideological clash will be accompanied by drastically increased organizational disunity, thus inhibiting the operations of all parties concerned, and enabling actual or potential Communists or fellow-travellers in underdeveloped areas to play the Soviets off against the Chinese and vice versa —a game in which they will easily learn to excel. Should they need any coaching, the Yugoslavs will always be available.

In brief, then, polycentric tendencies in international Communism probably will increase and become institutionalized; they will further inhibit Communist success in underdeveloped areas; but this hindrance will neither be uniform, decisive, nor, probably, a major factor in the further development of the Sino-Soviet rift itself.

Communist China's Economy and Its Impact on Afro-Asia

—CHOH-MING LI

I

The non-aligned countries of Asia and Africa are all underdeveloped countries. To them, the rise of the Communist regime on the Chinese mainland is significant on two counts. The first is China's widely publicized industrialization effort, which stands as an example for all the non-aligned countries of what one type of political regime and economic system can do. This subject has received a good deal of attention from economists and other social scientists and will not be the primary concern here. The second is the emergence of China as a power with whom the non-aligned countries have had to readjust their relations and, therefore, also their relations with the rest of the world. The crucial problem is the assessment of China's power status.

For the first time in modern history, China has been operating as a world power, extending its political and economic influence as far away as Cuba in the Western Hemisphere, Albania in Eastern Europe, and Guinea and Ghana in Africa, not to mention its military adventures in the Far East and in South and Southeast Asia. While its huge area and population, the effective political control of the regime over the people, the strategic location of the country, and its military alliance with the Soviet Union, all have to do with China's world-power status, perhaps the most important factor is the industrialization effort, which aims at developing its military potential. Without economic growth, China's claim to world-power status would be pretentious and unreal. For this reason the severe agricultural crisis and economic setback on the mainland since 1958 has raised the pertinent question of the reality of this power, and led many observers to scale down considerably their appraisal of China's present and potential role in world politics. This paper attempts to gauge the economic basis of China's power status.

II

The first three years of the new regime were devoted to rehabilitating the economy, which had been ravaged by eight years of Japanese aggression and four years of civil war. The chief effort during this initial period consisted in restoring the iron, steel, and coal complex in southern Manchuria. This complex was built up by the Japanese during their occupation, but was dismantled by the Soviet Union in 1945; yet it still represented the only major industrial base of the country. The Soviet credit of $300 million, negotiated in February, 1950, and meant to be drawn upon at 20 per cent a year for 5 years against the supply of industrial machinery, was in fact exhausted in 3 years for the equipment of 50 new or renovated large-scale enterprises, most of which were located in Manchuria. No sooner had the base been thus strengthened than deliberate industrialization began in 1953 with the first five-year plan.

For many decades, the Chinese people had increasingly come to realize that industrialization was the effective means of developing the resources of the country and enhancing its defensive strength against foreign encroachment. The central government started a national effort in the nineteen thirties, only to be interrupted by the Japanese invasion. The end of World War II found in the country a general and strong desire for a relatively rapid industrialization program, with a growing consensus on the demarcation between public and private sectors and on the priority rating of different categories of industry, if not on individual projects. When the Communist regime, having established itself on the mainland in October, 1949, announced the policy of "socialist industrialization" in late 1952, it was not so much the objective as the method of industrialization that represented the sharpest break from the past.

As its name signifies, the policy was concerned with both socialization and industrialization; and it anticipated mutual reinforcement between the two processes. By socialization is meant the conversion from private to collective or state ownership of all means of production, while industrialization refers to the development of the capacity to produce all the machinery and equipment the country needs for further economic growth. Originally scheduled to be achieved in fifteen years, socialization of the different sectors of the economy was virtually completed by the end of 1956, when the country was officially declared to have become a socialist state. Industrialization, however, would take at least fifteen years, according to official thinking, and it is the development in this sphere that has excited world-wide attention.

Because of the lack of experience of the Chinese and the absence of adequate statistical information, the first five-year plan was not finalized until early 1955. The draft of the second five-year plan, on the other hand, was released in outline form in September, 1956. Each plan consists of an investment program and a series of production targets for major commodities. Socialization resulted in increasing the number of industrial and mining enterprises operating within the state plan from 3,145 in 1949, and 11,600 in 1952, to over 60,000 in 1957.

Concentrated development of heavy industry—a special feature of the Soviet pattern of growth and for a long time an article of faith in Communist ideology—was accepted without reservation by Peking in its first five-year plan. The principle was given expression in the state investment program in which nearly 70 per cent of the funds were allocated to producer goods industries, and railroads, with a mere 6 per cent for agriculture, water conservation, and forestry. The program called for a total basic construction investment of 42,740 million yuan for the five years.[1] As it turned out, 49,270 million yuan were invested within the state plan, and there was non-planned investment of 5,730 million yuan. Of the combined total of 55,000 million, 56 per cent went into heavy industry and railroads, as against 4.6 per cent for water conservation and 3 per cent for agriculture, forestry, and meteorological services. Light industry received 6.7 per cent of the investment funds, compared with the 6.9 per cent that was planned.[2]

Investment is planned in terms of "projects." A project is an investment unit that involves both integrated planning for all its parts and a complete, unified budget. It may be a completely new construction, or an old enterprise restored or renovated. The size of a project is defined not only according to the amount of investment but also to the type of industry; large projects each require an investment of 5 to 10 million yuan in heavy industry and 3 to 5 million in light industry. During the period of the first five-year plan, 10,789 industrial and mining projects of all sizes were undertaken, including 921 large ones, of which 537 (428 fully, and 109 partially, completed) were already engaged in production by the end of 1957. Among the large projects were 166 engineering units provided by Soviet aid; these formed the backbone of the industrialization program, and 135 of them were under construction and in operation at the end of the period. East Germany, Czechoslovakia, Poland, Hungary, Rumania, and Bulgaria had contributed aid for 68 projects, of which 64 were under construction during the period in question, with 27 in operation at the end of 1957. In the following two years, an additional 125 large enterprises were contracted with the Soviet Union and over 40 with the six Eastern European Communist countries.[3]

As a result of the massive investment program, fixed industrial assets had increased from 15,800 million yuan (at original purchase prices) in 1952 to 35,200 million in 1957—an increase of 123 per cent in five years. This enabled each producing worker in industry and mining to work, on the average, with 49 per cent more fixed assets, 79 per cent more mechanical power, and 80 per cent more electric power in 1957 than in 1952. The industrial labor force had increased from 4,939,000 in 1952 to 9,008,000 in 1957, while over the same period the number of industrial engineers and technicians grew from 58,000 to 175,000.

The end of the first five-year plan found China operating, for the first time in its history, airplane, automobile, modern machine tool, electric generating equipment, foundry and mining equipment, high grade steel alloy refining, heavy chemicals, and other such industries. In the space of five years self-sufficiency had increased from 50 per cent to over 60 per cent in machinery and equipment, and from 61 per cent to 86 per cent in rolled steel.

That many of the gains were real was attested by the difference in the way Soviet-aid projects were conceived between the two five-year plan periods. During the first five years, Soviet assistance with regard to the 156 projects comprised detailed planning and surveying, the supply and installation of machinery and equipment, the operation, if necessary, of the plants when completed, and the training of personnel both on the job and in the Soviet Union. As the work on these projects progressed, China actually manufactured about 42 per cent of the complete sets of equipment required in 1957, and planned to raise the ratio to 60 per cent in 1958. For example, the First Tractor Manufacturing Plant at Loyang, one of the Soviet-aid projects initiated in 1955, had major construction completed and machinery installed in 1958; it has been estimated that 90 per cent of all its equipment was made in China.[4] Hence, when Soviet aid for the additional group of 125 large industrial projects was agreed upon in August, 1958, and February, 1959, it was decided that not only the surveying and planning was to be done mostly by the Chinese, but also that a considerable proportion of the equipment was to be made in China from specifications supplied by the Soviet Union.[5]

Nevertheless, much of all this spectacular progress was confined to heavy industry. According to official statistics, industry led all other sectors (except construction) in growth. And in the industrial sector itself, the average annual rate of growth over the period of the first five-year plan was 25.4 per cent in producer goods industries, as against 13 per cent in consumer goods industries. Although there are many serious technical problems in connection with the official data, the wide discrepancy in growth rates is not unexpected because of the nature of the investment program. It should be realized that while 85 per cent of the industrial investment funds went to heavy industry during the period of the first five-year plan, leaving only 15 per cent for light industry, it took the large projects in heavy industry many years longer than those in light industry to reach their planned operating capacity. Thus, a good deal of the progress in heavy industry during the period was due to the development of the production potential of the existing enterprises— through raising the rate of utilization of productive equipment, increasing the actual working hours of the labor force, improving planning and management, and introducing emulative drives. A rough calculation by the State Statistical Bureau shows that in factory industry, if the increase in the value of production derived from the newly added productive capacity was 100 in 1954, then it was 103 in 1955, 184 in 1956, 179 in 1957, and 449 in 1958.[6]

Agriculture, however, lagged very much behind industry in development. By 1957, Peking had begun to realize that agricultural output profoundly affects the economic health of the country. A good harvest would be followed by a substantial increase in state revenue, basic investment, internal and external trade, industrial output (consumer goods in particular), and employment. The reverse was true after a poor crop year.[7] The regime had pinned its faith in raising agricultural productivity on rural reorganization that had gone through several stages. Land redistribution, which took place during the years of rehabilitation up to the spring of 1953, was followed by the organization of mutual-aid teams and preliminary producer cooperatives; these in turn led to collectivization during the fall of 1955 and in 1956. Contrary to the expectations of the Party leaders, however, collectivization did not bring about any improvement in agricultural output in 1957. Something would have to be done. The leaders of the regime, ever taking special pride in their skill in handling agrarian problems, probably did not anticipate any serious difficulties arising from putting into effect the twelve-year agricultural development program (1956–67), the amended draft of which was published in October, 1957. After all, in spite of the drag of agriculture, and with merely moderate Soviet aid, heavy industry had sustained continuous and spectacular growth during the period. There is little doubt that toward the end of 1957 Peking was at the peak of its self-confidence, both internally and externally, and its status as a major world power was widely conceded by the Afro-Asian countries.

III

In contrast to the first five-year plan, which was finalized only in the third year of the period it covered, the second five-year plan was drawn up and released in outline form fifteen months before its start.[8] To continue the development of heavy industries was regarded as the first and basic task under the second five-year plan. National income was to maintain the same rate of increase as in the first five years, but the plan anticipated a higher rate of savings and, therefore, a larger investment program for both industry and agriculture. The increase in the value product for industry during the entire second five-year period was expected to be 100 per cent, as against 129 per cent in the first five years, and for agriculture 35 per cent, as against 25 per cent. Thus, the growth rate in the second five years was expected to be lower for industry and higher for agriculture than in the first five years.

But the operation in the second five years was destined to be vastly different. Toward the middle of 1957, two problems of major importance came to the forefront of Peking's attention. One was the excessive centralization of control over planning and operation of various economic enterprises. Heretofore, virtually all the large enterprises, wherever located, were centrally controlled and operated, leaving the local governments to run the medium-sized and small enterprises. Local authorities, thus debarred from looking into the operations of the centrally-controlled units located in the area, were not in any position to exercise unified authority over the planning and operations of the local economy. Locally-controlled enterprises might be critically short of certain materials that the centrally-controlled enterprises in the same city found redundant and were prepared to send away to other areas; yet the local authorities concerned had neither the information nor the authority to make any readjustments. Excessive centralization was also evident in the field of investment. Local revenues that were placed at the disposal of local governments were very limited; practically all the basic investments had to be approved and allocated by the central authorities. Local initiative was not allowed to develop at all.

Thus, on the eve of the second five-year plan, Peking—probably also influenced by developments in the Soviet Union—introduced an extensive decentralization program, relegating a great number of the large enterprises to local control, and authorizing local governments to retain a good proportion of the annual profits made by the various enterprises, as well as of the local taxes collected.[9] This unleashed local initiative and set the stage for the "Great Leap Forward" of 1958, in which all the major output goals were revised upwards continuously and competitively by factories, mines, farms, communes, and cities.

The other problem, as indicated above, concerns agriculture. Recognizing the crucial role of agriculture in industrialization, the regime mobilized its working population in the countryside after the autumn harvest of 1957 to engage in the construction of small waterworks and the collection of fertilizers. Soon this merged with the "Great Leap" movement in industry and construction, and, as far as rural areas were concerned, also led to the development of people's communes in August, 1958.[10]

A great deal of fanfare was given to the results of the "Great Leap." It was at first claimed that it had produced a 103 per cent increase in the output of food grains (rice, wheat, potatoes, and other grains), and a 65 per cent increase in the agricultural value product during the year.[11] Late in August, 1959, however, Peking had to admit that these claims had been exaggerated and should be reduced to an increase of 35 per cent and 25 per cent, respectively.[12] The value of output of producer goods industries and consumer goods industries was reported to have increased 104 per cent and 33 per cent during 1958, giving a combined rate of 66 per cent increase for industry as a whole. All these growth rates—even after all exaggerations have been adequately allowed for—represent significant achievements, particularly when compared with the corresponding rates during the preceding five-year period. Since 1958, the growth rates have on the whole declined. For industry, the annual rate of increase had returned, by 1960, to the first five-year level of 18 per cent per year—an increase that was in fact far behind the planned 29 per cent. Peking claimed, however, that China had achieved 85 per cent self-sufficiency in production of machinery and equipment by the end of 1959.[13] For agriculture, the planned rate of increase in the value of output for 1960 was 12.4 per cent, but it has recently been disclosed that the actual performance failed to reach the goal.[14] Much worse than this is the fact that in 1961 the regime was confronted with the third successive year of poor crops and found it necessary to purchase abroad foodstuffs worth several hundred millions of American dollars.

IV

It is important to realize that the continuous deterioration of the total economic situation on the mainland was due to the introduction of the people's commune system. Coming into existence in the summer of 1958, these rural communes were conceived to be the basic political, economic, and social unit, ushering the socialist society to the first stage of Communism. The commune, consisting on the average, in the winter of 1958, of three administrative villages (*hsiang*) was to take—and has taken—the place of the *hsiang* as the primary level of government. This modification of the administrative structure would not affect people's lives in any significant way. But to operate the commune as one integrated socioeconomic unit for a number of *hsiang* was a different matter. Economically, the activities of industry, agriculture, trade, education, and the military were all to be welded together in a commune. Socially, the institution of the common mess halls and the organization of housework into cooperative projects were intended to "socialize private living." This, plus the incessant deployment of the peasants away from their home villages to other parts of the commune and the payment of wages to individuals instead of to the heads of families (as was the case in the agricultural collectives), would weaken the family institution as the basic social unit. But the people were being persuaded at the time that communal life was far more enriching than family life. Even Liu Shao-chi emphasized the role of the commune instead of the family as the unit for passing on cultural heritage from generation to generation.

Under this system, private property was no longer to exist. Not only were all agricultural land and draft animals that belonged to the agricultural collectives communized, but also all other means of production that had been left to private ownership during the stage of collectivization, such as private plots (which, in 1958, accounted for 5 per cent of all cultivated acreage in Szechuan province), small agricultural implements, handicraft tools, poultry, and trees around homesteads. Cadres were given the understanding that, with proper education of the peasantry, such items as private bank deposits, furniture, cooking utensils, watches, and extra bedding might also be confiscated in favor of the commune.

The severe psychological adjustments thus entailed were expected to be greatly eased by the serving of free meals at the mess halls. The consequent leveling effect in personal food consumption would, of course, produce dissatisfaction among those peasants who were relatively better off, but at the same time invite strong support from those who were relatively worse off and were now given security and a better diet for the first time in their lives. In exchange for this security, peasants were expected to work to the full extent of their physical capacity, usually from fourteen to eighteen hours a day. The millennium was soon at hand, as people were provided for according to their needs while working at their maximum endurance.

All these ideas and measures were put into effect in the first few months following August, 1958. Although there may have been excesses due to the zeal of the cadres, the whole program was so new in conception that it had to conform to what was centrally conceived. The public reaction, however, must have been anything but "enthusiastic," as was officially claimed; corrective measures had to be taken. The commune system was, therefore, revised in December, 1958, when the Central Committee of the Party met in Hankow. This marks the beginning of a series of revisions that have finally reduced the commune to a collection of small, independent agricultural collectives.

Many advantages have been claimed for the commune system by Peking. The first was that the system assured rational use of land, particularly by eliminating the notoriously low-yielding "island lots," which were bits of property belonging to one agricultural collective, but located deep in the domain of another; such lots occupied as much as 9 per cent of the cultivated acreage in the Soochow region of Kiangsu. The second was the rational use of labor resources, which could now be effectively and flexibly deployed, for various productive and service activities, between seasons, between sectors, and between special tasks (such as fighting drought).[15] Third was the claim that unified planning and management of the human, natural, and material resources of a commune made it possible to develop diversification and balanced growth of the rural economy.[16]

The first advantage claimed for the commune has in fact little to do with the system, since the island lots could have been exchanged between agricultural collectives with as much ease or difficulty as between production brigades within one commune. The second and third so-called advantages were precisely the factors that greatly contributed to the failure of the system. The flexible deployment of the agricultural labor force for the development of a balanced rural economy meant much more than the effective utilization of labor during non-agricultural seasons, for it entailed a more or less permanent withdrawal of a substantial part of the labor force from agriculture for such other activities as industry and transportation—at the cost of lowering agricultural output. The extent of this withdrawal is indicated by the fact that in the autumn of 1960, when the Party leadership ordered a permanent deployment of the maximum amount of labor for food grain production, the proportion of the rural labor force so engaged was immediately raised from 59 to 80 per cent. According to an editorial of November, 1961, the reallocation of sufficient labor for agriculture from other economic departments and activities was then considered "one of the strategic links in the implementation of the policy of simultaneous development of industry and agriculture."[17]

Similarly, the alleged advantage of unified planning turned out to be disastrous to production. Up to 1961, what to produce and how to farm were determined by the authorities of the commune or of the production brigade, instead of by the production team, which was the only group actually engaged in production. The techniques of farming and farm management, evolved locally out of thousands of years of experience, and necessarily widely divergent even among different pieces of land within a village, were summarized in the so-called eight-word charter for agriculture in the summer of 1958. The eight words were "soil" (deep ploughing), "fertilizer" (accumulation), "water" (conservation), "seed" (selection), "denseness" (in cropping), "protection" (from pests), "implement" (improvement), and "farm" (management). A specific content for each measure was uniformly applied by the cadres over large areas, inevitably resulting in violation of local farming customs and practices. The damaging effects on production were officially admitted in late 1960 and early 1961.[18]

The egalitarian feature of the commune system has been particularly detrimental to any initiative to increase output. At the beginning, each commune, comprising some 4,600 households divided into a number of production brigades and a much larger number of production teams, was regarded as one single accounting unit; the profits and losses from the operations of different brigades were pooled together. An efficient brigade would automatically subsidize a less efficient one. The result was to equalize the income of all the members in the commune. The first year of experience brought home the lesson that "equalizing the distribution among the brigades of different efficiencies is not conducive to internal solidarity of the commune and to the development of production."[19] Thus, the so-called "three-level system of ownership" was introduced in October, 1959; ownership of land and other means of production was shifted from the level of the commune commission to that of the production brigade (which corresponded to the agricultural collective of 1957). The ownership at the level of the brigade was "basic"; but the ownership of communal properties still retained by the commune and of the assets of the production team (income from plots belonging to the team and retained portion of output exceeding the quota) were "partial."[20] The brigade thus became the accounting unit in place of the commune. The equalizing effect was eliminated between brigades, but it remained very much alive between the production teams of a brigade.

Under the commune system, the lack of incentive to work was greatly accentuated by the institution of the common mess halls, which developed into a nation-wide phenomenon in 1960.[21] It has long been established in family budget studies that, in China as elsewhere, about 70 to 80 per cent of the family expenditures of the poor are generally spent on food. If the peasants were freely provided with food and if all fruits of personal toil had to be shared by hundreds of others, there was no reason for anyone to exert himself more than was necessary to gain access to the mess hall. This holds true even if the production of payment in cash for work done was raised, as was actually the case—unless consumer goods were made available to the peasants in increased amounts, which could not have happened in view of the declining agricultural output.

Thus, the commune system could only result in a continuous fall in agricultural output, irrespective of weather conditions. It was toward the end of 1960, when Peking, in contrast to previous pronouncements, officially acknowledged "two years of unprecedented bad weather" that the central authorities of the Party drew up "Sixty Articles for Agriculture" for the purpose of reforming the whole agricultural system. The document, not published, was disseminated orally to the peasantry by the cadres through mass meetings held all over the countryside in the spring and summer of 1961. In essence, it provided for the return of private plots to individual peasant households, reopening of free markets on the village level,[22] voluntary participation in common mess halls, and a further downshift of the "basic" level of ownership from the brigade to the production team. The last measure was of particular importance, because it assured the production team of fixed quantities of cultivated land, labor, draft animals, and agricultural implements, all of which could no longer be deployed by the commune or brigade without compensation and without the team's consent.[23] Now production plans and arrangements for farming activities were to be left to cadres and members of production teams, while the *hsien* (county), commune, and brigade cadres would confine their work to ideology, policies, training of cadres, and giving assistance to production teams in improving their production conditions.[24] It is significant that the production team, consisting of some 35 households on the average, was much smaller in size than that of the elementary type of agricultural producer cooperative (48 households) in 1956. According to an account given in the April, 1962, issue of the *People's Daily*, one of the production teams in Hunan province had no more than 20 households, which was the average size of an agricultural cooperative in 1954.[25]

These radical revisions are tantamount to scrapping the whole commune system. How completely the system has been discarded may be explored from a different angle. As early as March, 1958, in preparation for the development of communes, a nation-wide movement was initiated to "merge collectives, combine *hsiang*, eliminate *ch'u*, and enlarge *hsien*" in rural areas.[26] What was the effect of the breakup of communes into production teams on the structure of local government? A close examination in this respect reveals that the number of *hsien* in the country (Tibet excepted), having steadily declined from 2,063 in April, 1958, to 1,728 at the end of that year and having fallen further to 1,651 by September, 1960, increased to 1,884 toward the end of 1961, and was back almost to the pre-commune level (1,994) by December 31, 1962.[27] The increase in the number of *hsien* would not have taken place if communes had not themselves been reduced into smaller units. The restoration of both the number of *hsien* and the size of production teams to the pre-1955 level strongly suggests that even as an administrative device the commune has failed.

V

Thus, 1962—the end of the second five years of planning—was, in terms of total and per capita output of food grains, industrial employment, the rate of capital formation, speed of industrialization, popular support of the regime, and self-confidence of the Party leadership, a much less satisfactory year than 1957, the end of the first five years. It is true that, for the first time since 1958, the late summer of 1962 saw a definite turn for the better in agriculture as a result of the abandonment of the commune system, but agricultural recovery thus far has been evident mainly in the production of subsidiary food (vegetables, eggs, poultry) on the private lots. The new policy of giving top priority to agricultural development over industrial growth will take a good deal of time to produce the desired effect. This is so because the dismantling of the commune system has severely demoralized the Party cadres at the primary level. Party discipline among cadres will take a long time to be reestablished and may never be able to return to the effective level prevailing during the first five years. This period of recovery before further expansion takes place may of course be considerably shortened if long-term economic aid or medium-term trade credit becomes available from abroad. This probably is what Peking must be seeking in earnest.

The impact of all these developments on the non-aligned countries has been many-sided—cultural, diplomatic, political, commercial, economic, and military. All these manifestations have one characteristic in common; that is, they are all deliberate, carefully considered actions of policy. And the objective of the policy consists not so much in enhancing China's role in world politics as in attempting to influence the non-aligned countries to side with it against the so-called colonial and imperialist powers.

In economic matters, the most important impact has been found in trade and economic aid. China began both in its relations with the non-aligned countries in Asia in 1954. In that year, barter and payments agreements were entered into with Burma, Indonesia, Ceylon, India, and Pakistan; since then, trade with many other non-aligned countries in Asia and Africa has been developed. Over the same period, economic grants and long-term loans at low interest rates have been made by Peking to such countries outside the Communist bloc as Cambodia, Ceylon, Indonesia, Burma, Yemen, Cuba, Guinea, Ghana, and Egypt. Probably, the development of trade relations has been motivated more by economic than political objectives. For, as the writer has stated elsewhere, "the possibility of netting a heavy export surplus as well as the changing composition of exports [in favor of light-industry and mineral products] goes a long way to explain Communist China's export drive in her trade with the free world."[28] But the volume of trade with each foreign country remains a political decision on the part of Peking, in view of China's limited available exports. Economic aid given by Communist China is, however, clearly dominated by political considerations, although the development of a market for China's heavy-industry products may also be one of its objectives.

The weakening of the economy in recent years might lead one to conclude that the Chinese economic offensive would be slowed down. But the contrary has been the case. We must remember that the new policy is designed to develop agriculture—not for the sake of improving the farm economy as such, but for the sake of strengthening the base for further rapid development of heavy industry. The slackening of the pace of industrialization has led to multiplication of effort. The fact that Peking has almost trebled its economic aid commitments to the non-aligned countries from $55.8 million in 1958 to $143.1 million in 1961, indicates clearly that Communist China is determined to live up to its status as a world power, even at the great sacrifice of its people.[29] Perhaps Communist China will be bolder and more conspicuous in its role as a world power during a period of internal difficulty than it was during a period of economic growth and self-confidence, and in much of this development, the non-aligned countries, especially in Asia, may have to bear the brunt.

Notes

Introduction
(*pp. vii–xii*)

1. Kurt London (ed.), *Unity and Contradiction: Major Aspects of Sino-Soviet Relations* (New York: Frederick A. Praeger, 1962).

Colonialism Yesterday and Today
(*pp. 3–18*)

1. Sir Surendranath Banerjea, *A Nation in Making* (London: Oxford University Press, 1925), p. 308.
2. *Legislative Council Debates*, Sierra Leone Colony, No. III of Session, 1938–39.
3. *Ibid.*, No. III of Session, 1939–40.
4. Raymond Leslie Buell, *The Native Problem in Africa* (New York: The Macmillan Company, 1928), II, 81.
5. *Speeches and Press Conferences*, No. 85 (*Ambassade de France, Service de Presse et d'Information*). That independence has brought no great change to Houphouet-Boigny's views is indicated by a story in *The New York Times*, March 25, 1962, headed "Ivory Coast's Economy Remains under French at Leader's Wish."
6. Sékou Touré, *La Guinée et l'Emancipation Africaine* (Conakry: Impr. Nationale, 1959), p. 78.
7. Margery Perham, *The Colonial Reckoning* (New York: Alfred A. Knopf, 1962), p. 16. John Strachey writes that if "these startling fourteen years between 1945 and 1959 can possibly mark the end of the imperialist epoch . . . then they will constitute one of the most extraordinary turning points in history. For never since the dawn of civilisation has there existed an even partially non-imperialist world." John Strachey, *The End of Empire* (London: Victor Gollancz, 1959; New York: Random House, 1959–60), pp. 137–38.
8. John S. Mill, *Utilitarianism, Liberty, and Representative Government* (Everyman ed.; New York: E. P. Dutton and Co., 1926), p. 382.
9. The standards that are likely to be drawn on for this purpose are subject to the cogent argument of John Plamenatz that these standards, which also imply European superiority, have come to more or less universal acceptance only because the Europeans have, in one way or another, imposed them on other peoples. John Plamenatz, *On Alien Rule and Self-Government* (London: Longmans, 1960), p. 3.
10. See Rupert Emerson, *From Empire to Nation* (Cambridge, Mass.: Har-

vard University Press, 1960). More than a century ago Karl Marx saw England as "the unconscious tool of history" in causing a social revolution in India. (Written by Marx on June 10, 1853; printed in *The New York Daily Tribune*, June 25, 1853, in an article entitled "The British Rule in India.")

11. In the December, 1960, United Nations debate on colonialism, David Ormsby-Gore stated that 29 British non-self-governing territories had populations of less than 1 million each, and that 14 of these had populations of less than 100,000. *United Nations Review*, VIII, No. 1 (January, 1961), 38.

12. The liquidation of colonialism has produced a number of other actual or potential conflicts, such as those between the Netherlands and Indonesia over Western New Guinea, between India and Pakistan over Kashmir, and, in the Chinese borderlands, between the Communist powers and the West over Korea and the Indochinese countries.

13. "South Africa and the Portuguese colonies exhibit the unyielding supremacy of white over black. While these situations exist they can be condemned utterly, and all colonialism, past and present, can, when occasion demands, be associated with their condemnation. And all Western policy will also be condemned for tolerating them, while Communist propaganda is given its maximum opportunity." Perham, *op. cit.*, p. 181.

The Communist Attitude Toward Colonialism (to 1941)
(pp. 19–33)

1. K. Marx and F. Engels, *On Colonialism* (Moscow: Gospolitizdat, 1960), p. 37.

2. K. Marx and F. Engels, *Letters to Americans 1848–95* (New York: International Publishers, 1953), pp. 77–80.

3. V. I. Lenin, *Imperialism* (London: Martin Lawrence Ltd., 1934), p. 68.

4. *Ibid.*, p. 72.

5. *Ibid.*, pp. 72, 77, 89.

6. Quoted from J. Degras (ed.), *Soviet Documents on Foreign Policy* (London: Oxford University Press, 1957), I, 16.

7. Quoted from E. H. Carr, *The Bolshevik Revolution 1917–1923* (London: Macmillan, 1953), III, 235.

8. *Ibid.*, p. 236.

9. Quoted in X. J. Eudin and R. C. North, *Soviet Russia and the East 1920–1927* (Stanford, Calif.: Stanford University Press, 1957), p. 17.

10. J. Degras, *op. cit.*, I, 257.

11. J. Degras (ed.), *The Communist International 1919–1943: Documents* (London: Oxford University Press, 1956), I, 42. Subsequent quotations from proceedings of the Communist International, unless otherwise stated, are taken from this source, or from Vol. II (1960).

12. *Ibid.*, p. 66.

13. Second Halle Congress of the USPD (Unabhaengige Sozialdemokratische Partei Deutschlands): *Protokoll ueber die Verhandlungen des ausserordentlichen Parteitages in Halle* (October 12–17, 1920) (Berlin: Buchhandlung "Freiheit," 1920).

14. See Degras, *The Communist International*, I, 368.

15. J. Stalin, *Works* (1952–56) (Moscow: Foreign Languages Publishing House, 1953), VI, 143.

16. Second Congress of the Communist International: *Protokoll der Verhand-lungen* (Petrograd, July 19, and Moscow, July 23–August 7, 1920) (Hamburg: Bibliothek der Internationale, C. Hoym Nachf, 1921), VII.

17. J. Stalin, *Works* (Moscow: Foreign Languages Publishing House, 1954), VII, 135.

18. J. Stalin, *Marxism and the National and Colonial Question* (London: Lawrence and Wishart, 1942), p. 127.

19. Quoted in Degras, *The Communist International*, II, 527.

20. *Protokoll des 6. Weltkongresses der kommunistischen Internationale* (Protocol of the VI. World Congress of the Communist International [Moscow, 1928]) (Altona: C. Hoym Nachf, 1928), IV, 154.

21. *Ibid.*

22. Quoted in Degras, *The Communist International*, II, 527.

23. *Protokoll des 6. Weltkongresses* (. . . theses).

24. *Ibid.* (program), p. 45.

25. *Fifteen Years of the Communist International* (New York: 1934).

26. B. Basak, article in the periodical *Rundschau* (Basel), October 6, 1933.

27. *The Communist International* (periodical) (London), November 20, 1934.

28. *Ibid.*, January 5, 1935, p. 18.

29. *Seventh World Congress of the Communist International: Resolutions and Decisions* (Moscow: Foreign Languages Publishing House, 1935), p. 29.

"Neo-Colonialism" — the Soviet Concept
(pp. 34–44)

1. Turgot, *Réflexions sur le progrès de l'esprit humain* (Oneires ed.; Paris), I, 141.

2. Comte, *Système de la politique positive* (1st ed.; Paris, 1852–54), II, 463. Probably the best survey of French anti-colonialist thought over the centuries is René Maunier, *Sociologie coloniale* (Paris: Domat-Montchrestien, 1932).

3. Karl Kautsky, *Sozialismus und Kolonialpolitik* (Berlin: Vorwörts, 1907), and "Aeltere und Neue Kolonialpolitik," in *Neue Zeit*, XVI, No. 1; Otto Bauer, *Der Balkankrieg und die deutsche Weltpolitik* (Berlin: P. Singer, GmbH., 1912); see also the writings of Parvus (*Die Kolonialpolitik und der Zusammenbruch*), Hilferding, and Rosa Luxemburg.

4. I have dealt in some detail with these changes in the middle 1950's in Chap. 6 of my *The Soviet Union and the Middle East* (New York: Frederick A. Praeger, 1959).

5. V. Ia. Avarin, *Raspad kolonial'noi systemi* (*The Disintegration of the Colonial System*) (Moscow: Gospolitizdat, 1957), p. 7.

6. L. A. Fituni and V. D. Shchetinin, *Problemy pomoshchi ekonomicheski slaborazvitym stranam* (*Problems of Economic Aid to Underdeveloped Countries*) (Moscow: Institute of International Relations, 1961), chap. i.

7. The following account of "Western neo-colonialism" is based on Avarin, *op. cit.*, E. D. Modrzhinskaia, *Ideologiia sovremennogo kolonializma* (*The Contemporary Ideology of Colonialism*) (Moscow: Izd. Vostoch. Rit-I, 1961), K. N. Brutents, *Protiv ideologii sovremennogo imperializma* (*Against the Contemporary Ideology of Imperialism*) (Moscow: Sotsekgiz, 1961), and others.

8. *Mirovaia ekonomika i mezhdunarodnye otnosheniia* (Moscow: 1962), VI, 104.

9. G. E. Skorov (ed.), *Sotsial-reformizm i kolonialny vopros* (*Social Reformism and the Colonial Question*) (Moscow: Akademia Nauk SSSR, 1961, p. 290.

10. Brutents, *op. cit.*, p. 60.

11. N. S. Khrushchev, "Schast'e i mir–narodam," p. 68. An English translation has been published under the title "Happiness and Peace for the Peoples, N. S. Khrushchev's Visit to India, Burma, Indonesia and Afghanistan, February 11–March 5, 1960" (Moscow: Foreign Languages Publishing House, 1960), p. 65.

12. *Pravda*, May 20, 1962. Speech in Sofia.

13. Cf. the discussion in *Mirovaia ekonomika i mezhdunarodnye otnosheniia*, 1962, *passim*, particularly No. 5.

14. L. Labedz, in *Survey*, No. 43 (August, 1962); Brutents, *op. cit.*, pp. 183–232.

15. Cf. Ia. Bochkarev, "Kolonializm pod flagom O. O. N." ("Colonialism under the Flag of the U.N."), in *Pravda*, September 13, 1960.

16. Modrzhinskaia, *op. cit.*, pp. 160–61.

17. Cf. A. Ia. Popov, "Sovremennoe Mal'tuzianstvo–chelovekonenavistnicheskaia ideologiia imperialistov" ("Contemporary Malthusianism–Man-hating Ideology of Imperialists") (Moscow: Gospolitizdat, 1953), *passim*; see also, Modrzhinskaia, *op. cit.*, pp. 115–25.

18. Modrzhinskaia, *op. cit.*, p. 145.

19. Brutents, *op. cit.*, p. 197.

20. *Sotsial-reformizm i kolonial'nyi vopros, passim.*

21. *Ibid.*, p. 286.

22. *Ibid.*, p. 278.

23. *Ibid.*, p. 283.

24. "Politicheskii Slovar" (Moscow: Gospolitizdat, 1958), p. 254; the "Diplomaticheskii Slovar" (2d ed.; Moscow: Gospolitizdat, 1961), II, 82, gives a more cautious definition, speaking about a system of oppression and exploitation by foreign monopoly capitalism.

The Communist View of Colonialism — An African Interpretation
(pp. 45–55)

1. V. I. Lenin, *Imperialism* (preface to the French and German eds.; New York: International Publishers, 1939), p. 10.

2. Jack Woddis, *Africa: The Lion Awakes* (London: Lawrence and Wishart, 1961), p. 274.

3. O. Kuusinen (ed.), *Fundamentals of Marxism-Leninism* (Moscow: Foreign Languages Publishing House, 1961).

4. K. Marx and F. Engels, "The Communist Manifesto," *Selected Works* (New York: International Publisher, 1933), I, 210.

5. Colin Legum, *Pan-Africanism* (London: Pall Mall Press, 1962), p. 78.

6. Mamadou Dia, *The African Nations and World Solidarity* (New York: Frederick A. Praeger, 1961), especially chap. v.

7. John Eaton, *Political Economy* (New York: International Publishers, 1949), p. 136.

8. R. Palme-Dutt, *The Crisis of Britain and the British Empire* (rev. ed; London: Lawrence and Wishart, 1957), p. 69.

9. A. C. Pigou, *Socialism Versus Capitalism* (London: Macmillan and Company, 1937).

10. Quoted approvingly by Soviet Africanist Professor I. I. Potekhin at the Plenary Session of the First Congress of Africanists at Legon, Ghana, in December, 1962.

11. Palme-Dutt, *op. cit.*, pp. 172–74.

12. This is the argument of R. Robinson and J. Gallagher in *Africa and the Victorians* (New York: St. Martin's Press, 1961) with respect to British imperialism in tropical Africa.

13. This justification was offered by the Fabian socialist George Bernard Shaw. See Norman Mackenzie, *A Short History of Socialism* (London: Hutchinson's University Library, 1949), p. 89.

14. Of course, the "liberalized" Soviet attitude toward the national liberation movements that has been developed under Khrushchev places particular emphasis on the assertion that each society will pass through the various stages according to its own pace and experience. This, however, is not meant to imply any change in the historical materialist overview of the historical process.

15. G. W. F. Hegel, *The Philosophy of History* (rev. ed.; New York: John Wiley, 1944), p. 14.

16. *Ibid.*, p. 53.

17. S. N. Dyde (trans.), G. W. F. Hegel's *Philosophy of Right* (London: Bell and Sons, 1896), Sec. 347, p. 343.

18. In this connection, recall Hegel's statement that "Europe is absolutely the end of History, Asia, the beginning," *The Philosophy of History*, p. 103.

19. Hegel, *op. cit.*, p. 99.

20. Legum, *op. cit.*, p. 13.

21. Kwame Nkrumah, *I Speak of Freedom* (New York: Frederick A. Praeger, 1961), p. 219.

"National Democracy" and the Post-Colonial Revolution
(pp. 56–74)

1. *Pravda*, December 6, 1960.

2. B. Ponomarev, "O gosudarstve natsionalnoi demokratii" ("Concerning the National Democratic State"), *Kommunist*, No. 8, 1961.

3. *Politicheskoe Samoobrazovane*, No. 9, 1961.

4. A. Arzumanyan, "Novyi etap obshchego krizisa kapitalizma," ("New Stage of the General Crisis of Capitalism"), *Mirovaia ekonomika i mezhdunarodnye otnosheniia*, No. 2, 1961; "Krizis mirovogo kapitalizma" ("The Crisis of World Capitalism"), *Pravda*, December 17, 1961.

5. Official English text issued by Tass, July 30, 1961.

6. Thus Donald Zagoria, "Sino-Soviet Friction in Underdeveloped Areas," *Problems of Communism*, X, No. 2 (March–April, 1961).

7. In his Commission Report on the National and Colonial Question to the Second Congress of the Comintern.

8. See Mao Tse-tung "The Chinese Revolution and the Chinese Communist Party," *Selected Works* (London, 1954), Vol. III.

9. Cf. the reprinting of the corresponding passages of Liu Shao-chi's address

to the Peking conference of the WFTU in *Pravda*, January 4, 1950, and *For a Lasting Peace* . . . , December 30, 1949, and the editorial repetition of its key arguments in *For a Lasting Peace* . . . , January 27, 1950.

10. *Problems of Peace and Socialism*, Nos. 8 and 9, 1959.

11. By the spring of 1960, all these elements of the new strategy, including the "national democratic" label, had been fully developed by the Indonesian Communists; see the quotations from speeches and essays of their leader, D. N. Aidit, in J. M. van der Kroef, "Lenin, Mao and Aidit," *China Quarterly*, No. 10, April–June, 1962, pp. 25–27. This largest and most influential Communist Party in any ex-colonial country thus seems to have acted as pioneer and model for the new concept. Yet its clearly pro-Chinese stand in the public controversies that followed the Twenty-second Congress of the CPSU makes one wonder whether it is satisfied with the results.

12. *World Trade Union Movement*, No. 7, 1960.

13. *World Marxist Review* (Prague ed.), XI, No. 1 (January, 1961).

14. Arzumanyan, *op. cit.*

15. Ponomarev, *op. cit.*

16. *Pravda*, October 19, 1961.

17. See in particular the repeated attacks of I. I. Potekhin, the leading Soviet Africanist, on the concept of a special "African Socialism," in *World Marxist Review* (Prague ed.), XI, No. 11 (November, 1961), and *Narody Azii i Afriki*, No. 1, 1962, and the Khrushchev speech quoted in note 24 below.

18. *Peking Review*, IX, No. 4 (1961).

19. Li Wei-han, "The Chinese People's Democratic United Front: Its Special Features," *Red Flag*, No. 12, 1961, reprinted in *Peking Review*, August 18, 25, and September 1, 1961.

20. Ponomarev, *op. cit.*

21. See in particular the comments on the publications of the fourth volume of the works of Mao Tse-tung in *People's Daily*, October 6, 1960, and *Red Flag*, November 2, 1960.

22. Wang Chia-hsiang in *Red Flag*, October 1, 1959.

23. See particularly, in addition to the program and Khrushchev's speech, M. G. Kirichenko, "O nezavisimom gosudarstve natsionalnoy demokratti" ("Concerning the Independent National Democratic State"), in *Sovietskoe Gosudarstvo i Pravo*, No. 11, 1961, and J. Tsedenbal, "From Feudalism to Socialism," *World Marxist Review* (Prague ed.), IV, No. 3 (1960).

24. In an article on "Soviet Aid and Its Critics," in the Soviet journal *International Affairs*, No. 6, 1960.

25. See in particular Khrushchev's speech in Sofia, on May 18, 1962, reported in *Pravda*, May 20, 1962.

26. I am aware that the above argument applies mainly to Asia and Africa, and that the situation in Latin America is rather more favorable to the Communists. This seems to be due to at least three different factors. Firstly, the long association between most of the caudillo regimes and foreign, particularly U.S., business interests has tended to make Latin American revolutionary nationalists see themselves as champions of a "democratic revolution." Secondly, while Asian and African nationalists are inclined to deny the relevance of European political ideas and models to their problems and to distrust Communism as an "alien"—because European—ideology, Latin American revolutionaries, owing to their different cultural heritage, incline to think about their problems in Euro-

pean terms borrowed from the French Revolution and the Marxist and syndical-
ist intellectuals of Latin Europe, and to accept the Communists at their own
valuation as the extreme left of the democratic revolutionary movement.
Thirdly, the still recent experience of U.S. diplomatic support for anti-democratic regimes of the conservative oligarchy and the absence of Soviet involvement with such regimes in Latin America (in contrast to Soviet aid for, say,
Afghanistan or Ethiopia) favors the Communist effort to identify the struggle
for national independence, economic development, and social reform with an
"anti-Yanqui" and pro-Soviet attitude. To that extent, the case of Cuba, where
"national democracy" fulfilled its destiny as a transitional slogan more rapidly
than the Communists themselves expected, was made possible by factors of a
symptomatic rather than an exceptional character.

Soviet Doctrines on Developing Countries: Some Divergent Views
(pp. 75–89)

1. V. Rymalov, "Economic Competition of the Two Systems and the Problem of Aid to Underdeveloped Countries," *Mirovaia ekonomika i mezhdunarodnye otnoshenie (World Economics and International Relations)*, No. 2, 1960,
p. 35.
2. G. Mirskii and V. Tiagunenko, "The Tendencies and Outlook of the
National Liberationist Revolutions," *Mirovaia ekonomika i mezhdunarodnye
otnoshenie*, No. 11, 1961, p. 24.
3. Rodney Arismendi, "Latin America Comes to the Front of the Stage,"
Kommunist, No. 5, 1961, p. 72.
4. E. Bragina and O. Ul'rikh, *Gosudarstvennyi kapitalizm v promyshlennosti
stran Vostoka (State Capitalism in the Industry of the Countries of the East)*,
(Moscow: Izd-vo vostochnoi Lit-ry, 1961), p. 24.
5. V. Rymalov, "Economically Underdeveloped Countries in the World
Capitalist Economy," *Mirovaia ekonomika i mezhdunarodnye otnoshenie*, No.
5, 1962, pp. 42, 44.
6. V. M. Kollontaí, *Inostrannye investitsii v ekonomicheskii slaborazvitykh
stranakh (Foreign Investments in Economically Underdeveloped Countries)*
(Moscow: Academy of Sciences, 1960, p. 190.
7. R. Abakov and G. Mirskii, "On the Class Structure in Underdeveloped
Countries," *Mirovaia ekonomika i mezdunarodnye otnoshenie*, No. 4, 1962,
p. 80.
8. *Ibid.*
9. The classic view is expounded, with India as the example, in L. I. Reis-
ner and G. K. Shirokov, "Foreign Private Capital in India," *Problemy vos-
tokovedeniia (Problems of Oriental Research)*, No. 1, 1960, pp. 52–54; the
new view can be found in L. Stepanov, "The Problem of Economic Independence," *Mirovaia ekonomika i mezhdunarodnye otnoshenie*, No. 5, 1962, p. 91.
10. S. I. Tiul'panov, "On the Question of State Capitalism in Underdeveloped Countries," *Vestnik Leningradskogo universiteta (Leningrad University
Herald)* (Series in Economics, Philosophy, and Law), No. 5, 1961, p. 17.
11. Bragina and Ul'rikh, *op. cit.*, p. 21.
12. Mirskii and Tiagunenko, *op. cit.*, pp. 28–29. Emphasis in original.
13. D. N. Aidit, Chairman of the Central Committee of the Communist
Party of Indonesia, "The Program of the Communist Party of the Soviet Union

and the Struggle of the Peoples for Full National Liberation," *Kommunist*, No. 1, 1962, p. 94.

14. R. Ul'ianovskii, "Economic Independence—The Immediate Task of the Liberationist Movement in Asia," *Kommunist*, No. 1, 1962, p. 96.

15. Abakov and Mirskii, *op. cit.*, p. 78.

16. B. Ponomarev, "On the National Democratic State," *Kommunist*, No. 8, 1961, p. 45.

17. Stepanov, *op. cit.*, pp. 92–94.

18. "A Short Review of Discussion," *Mirovaia ekonomika i mezhdunarodnye otnoshenie*, No. 6, 1962, p. 105.

19. V. Tiagunenko, "The People Are against the Capitalist Path," and R. Abakov and R. Andresian, "The Progressive Role of the State Sector," *Kommunist*, No. 13, September, 1962, pp. 89–96.

20. Ponomarev, *op. cit.*, p. 47.

21. Aidit, *op. cit.*, p. 94.

22. Mirskii and Tiagunenko, *op. cit.*, p. 31.

23. Abakov and Andresian, *op. cit.*, p. 93; V. Tiagunenko, "Tendencies of the Social Development of the Liberated Countries in the Modern Epoch," *Mirovaia ekonomika i mezhdunarodnye otnoshenie*, No. 3, 1962, pp. 29–33.

24. Ponomarev, *op. cit.*, p. 43.

25. V. Tiagunenko, "Tendencies of the Social Development of the Liberated Countries in the Modern Epoch," *Mirovaia ekonomika i mezhdunarodnye otnoshenie*, No. 3, 1962, p. 33.

26. Arismendi, *op. cit.*, pp. 75, 76.

27. "The Challenge of Soviet Foreign Policy and the Defense of the Status Quo," address at the American Political Science Association, St. Louis, Missouri, September 6–9, 1961.

28. G. Akopian, "On the Role and Character of the National Bourgeoisie of the Countries of the East," *Mirovaia ekonomika i mezhdunarodnye otnoshenie*, No. 6, 1962, pp. 100–103; Abakov and Mirskii, *op. cit.*, pp. 81–82.

Some Factors in the Communist View of Neutrality
(*pp.* 90–98)

1. V. I. Lenin, *Works* (4th Russian ed.; Moscow: Marx-Engels-Lenin Institute, 1950), XXIX, 144.

2. V. I. Lenin, *Selected Works* (Russian ed.; Moscow, 1943), VIII, 297.

3. V. I. Lenin, *Works* (4th Russian ed.; Moscow: Marx-Engels-Lenin Institute, 1950), XXIX, 46 ff.

4. Mao Tse-tung, *Works* (Japanese ed.; Kyoto: San-ichi-shobo, 1959), I, 13–14.

5. *Ibid.*

6. V. I. Lenin, *Selected Works* (English ed.; Moscow: Foreign Languages Publishing House, 1952), II, Part II, 178.

Notes on Democracy and Leadership in the New Afro-Asian States
(*pp.* 101–120)

1. Thus for instance, the remarks of Léopold Senghor, President of Senegal:

All of us in Africa are fully aware of our "situation" in Sartre's sense of the word. Our countries need developing. . . . We are living in an unsettled age, in which man's passion for violence seems in the ascendancy. Never in our history has mankind been in such danger of annihilation. . . . These countries . . . are simply . . . aware of their situation and of the part they can play in bringing back a greater sense of humanity and greater peace to the rest of the world ("Some Thoughts on Africa," *International Affairs* [London], XXXVIII, April, 1962, p. 190.)

2. For this and the following see, for instance, N. S. Khrushchev's "Report on the Program of the CPSU," (October 17, 1961), in *Documents of the 22nd Congress of the CPSU* (New York: Crosscurrents Press, 1961), II, 18, 134, 143.

3. See Kwame Nkrumah's address on opening the Accra Assembly, June 21, 1962 (New York: Ghana Information Service, Press Release No. 185).

4. Shortly before his death, a leading Indian Communist, Ajoy Ghosh, in an article on "Some Features of the Situation in India" (*World Marxist Review*, V, No. 2 [February, 1962], pp. 17 ff., pp. 23 ff.), suggested that the sound development of India requires that it be governed by a coalition in which the Communist Party occupies a strong position. Similarly, a Communist report on a recent book by the English Communist Jack Woddis (*Africa: The Lion Awakes* [London: Lawrence and Wishart, 1961]) stresses that the "national bourgeoisie" has had its merits, but that after independence the struggle in Africa demands that the working class take over the leadership of the nationalist movement. See *World Marxist Review*, V, No. 3 (March, 1962), p. 84.

5. Kwame Nkrumah, "The Place of Students in the Present Gold Coast," speech delivered in Accra on October 24, 1953 (circular [m. d., m. p.]), p. 8.

6. *86th Congress, 2nd Session, U.S. Foreign Policy, Economic, Social and Political Change in the Underdeveloped Countries and Its Implications for United States Policy*. A study prepared at the request of the Committee on Foreign Relations of the U.S. Senate by the Center for International Studies, Massachusetts Institute of Technology, March 30, 1960, pp. 9, 10.

7. *Ibid.*, p. 10.

8. Since another paper in this collection is devoted to national democracy, the subject cannot be pursued here. The writer has examined it in a paper presented to a conference on "The Soviet Bloc and the Developing Areas," held under the auspices of the Friedrich Ebert Foundation in March, 1962. The Foundation will publish the conference proceedings in German. See also H. Seton-Watson, "The Communist Powers and Afro-Asian Nationalism," in Kurt London (ed.), *Unity and Contradiction* (New York: Frederick A. Praeger, 1962), p. 187, and Walter Z. Laqueur, "Toward National Democracy," *Survey* (London), No. 37, July-September, 1961, pp. 3 ff.

9. As an eminent Indian put it a few years ago:

. . . [it] was undoubtedly the desire of the political leadership of these [new] countries to be considered modern and progressive, and in view of the fact that democracy has regained its prestige as a result of the Second World War, there was no immediate attempt to set up new monarchies or to experiment with semi-Fascist regimes, as had been the case in the Asian countries during the period of Japanese-sponsored independence.

He hastened to add, rather bluntly, that it was "clear that in most cases the full implications of this system of government have not been understood—not only by the people but by the leaders themselves." See K. M. Pannikar, *The Afro-Asian States and Their Problems* (London: Allen and Unwin, 1959), pp. 16 ff. See also the observations of Chief H. O. Davies, a leading Nigerian, in his article "The New African Profile," *Foreign Affairs* (New York), XL, No. 2 (January, 1962), pp. 293 ff.

10. R. Aron, "Democracy in the New States," *Manchester Guardian Weekly*, October 23, 1958. (A report of a conference held in 1958 on the problems of representative government in the new states.)

11. Rupert Emerson, *Representative Government in Southeast Asia* (Cambridge, Mass.: Harvard University Press, 1955), p. 157. See most recently the same author's *From Empire to Nation* (Cambridge, Mass.: Harvard University Press, 1960), chap. xv, "Erosion of Democracy in the New States," which provides a concise survey of the principal problems. One might take issue with the chapter title, since it suggests "democracy" existed in the first place. Henry L. Bretton has contributed a pessimistic case study in his *Power and Stability in Nigeria* (New York: Frederick A. Praeger, 1962), while some contributions to R. O. Tilman and T. Cole (eds.), *The Nigerian Political Scene* (Durham, N.C.: Duke University Press, 1962), strike a guardedly hopeful note. S. S. Harrison, *India, The Most Dangerous Decades* (Princeton, N.J.: Princeton University Press, 1960), throws much light on these problems in another context. See the present writer's comments in *Science*, CXXXI, 1662 (January 3, 1960). See also R. Butwell, *Southeast Asia Today and Tomorrow* (New York: Frederick A. Praeger, 1961), pp. 72 ff. and 166 ff.

12. Quoted from C. Legum, *Pan-Africanism* (New York: Frederick A. Praeger, 1962), pp. 121–22.

13. This was brought into focus in R. McKeon (ed.), *Democracy in a World of Tensions: A Symposium Prepared by UNESCO* (Chicago: University of Chicago Press, 1951).

14. M. Cranston, "Liberty, Equality, Fraternity," *The Listener* (London), September 3, 1959, p. 348.

15. Thus Herbert J. Spiro, "New Constitutional Forms in Africa," *World Politics* (Princeton, N.J.), XIII, No. 1 (October, 1960), p. 76; see also the same author's recent *Politics in Africa* (Englewood Cliffs, N.J.: Prentice-Hall, 1962), *passim*, especially his concluding pages entitled "The Vice of Imitation," pp. 164 ff. Among the most suggestive recent reflections on this whole problem, one might mention T. Hodgkin, *African Political Parties* (London: Penguin, 1961), pp. 155 ff., and the recent provocative essay by Sir Stephen King-Hall, "What Is Parliamentary Democracy?", *Parliamentary Affairs*, XVL, No. 1 (Winter, 1962–63), pp. 13 ff.

16. Mohammed Ayub Khan, "Pakistan Perspective," *Foreign Affairs*, XXXVIII, No. 4 (July, 1960), pp. 547 ff.

17. See Seymour M. Lipset, *Political Man* (Garden City, N.Y.: Doubleday, 1960), chap. ii, "Economic Development and Democracy," pp. 45–76.

18. James S. Coleman, "Conclusion: The Political Systems of the Developing Areas," in Gabriel A. Almond and James S. Coleman (eds.), *The Politics of the Developing Areas* (Princeton, N.J.: Princeton University Press, 1960), pp. 532 ff.

19. In 1957, a group of social scientists from the Massachusetts Institute of Technology, composed of the members who were later responsible for the 1960 report cited in n. 6 above (including W. W. Rostow, the present Chairman

of the Policy Planning Staff of the State Department), was charged with defining the objectives of U.S. economic assistance programs. The group described as the "chain of reasoning" underlying its recommendations the following points, each of which was developed at some length in the body of the statement. (*85th Congress, 1st Session, The Objectives of United States Economic Assistance Programs*, January, 1957, pp. 19 ff; italics added.)

1. That American assistance *can* lead to economic growth.
2. That American assistance and consequent economic growth *can* be made to lead to politically mature and democratic societies.
3. That if a majority of the underdeveloped countries, notably those of Asia, demonstrate over a 10- to 20-year period that they are able to meet and progressively resolve their internal problems without resort to totalitarian solutions, are given, still, sustained Western deterrence to military adventure, then the only rational option remaining to the Soviets will consist in a negotiated settlement with strong built-in safeguards against international violence.
4. That it is an essential American interest, even apart from the cold war, that the emerging nations of Asia and Africa achieve economic growth and social maturity within a democratic framework.

We cannot comment here on the rather heavily speculative point 3. Manifestly, these social scientists regarded it as likely but by no means assured that economic growth would indeed result in "politically mature and stable democratic societies." This provoked George Liska's irritated questions (*The New Statecraft* [Chicago: University of Chicago Press, 1960], p. 16) as to whether the writers assumed spontaneous connection between economic growth and political maturation toward democracy, whether they were committed to automatism or paternalism, optimism or pessimism—or were just unable to make up their minds. Most recently, Hans Morgenthau's astringent analysis of the whole problem appeared in "A Political Theory of Foreign Aid," in *American Political Science Review*, LVI, No. 2 (June, 1962), pp. 301–9. On the one hand, he sees the correlation in the American popular mind between aid, economic development, social stability, democratic institutions, and a peaceful policy as stemming from the American folklore of politics; on the other hand, he considers it a "moot question" whether economic development is actually conducive to the advancement of democratic institution and practices. "The political results of successful foreign aid . . . may be either unpredictable or counterproductive in terms of the political goals of the giving nation" (p. 307). For a shrewd classification of policy viewpoints see C. B. Marshall, "On Understanding the Unaligned," in L. W. Martin (ed.), *Neutralism and Nonalignment* (New York: Frederick A. Praeger, 1962), pp. 13 ff.

20. David Apter, "The Role of Traditionalism in the Political Modernization of Ghana and Uganda," *World Politics*, XIII, No. 1 (October, 1960), pp. 45 ff.

21. In a review article, "Communist Strategies and Asian Societies," *World Politics*, XI, 1 (October, 1958), p. 125, Lucian W. Pye ascribed the Communist appeal to its success

. . . in bringing a degree of order and structure to human relations in the wake of the revolutionary changes originated by the West. In breaking down the faiths and myths that gave order to the traditional Asian communities and in disrupting the old distribution of power . . . the Western impact has been extraordinarily efficient. . . . But in regard to the crucial problem of establishing the organizational bases necessary for mobilizing effort and giving purposeful direction to action, the West has been conspicuously less successful . . . the Communists, on the other hand, have had remarkable success in building what are often, aside from the formal offices of government, the most elaborate and certainly the most efficient organizations in some of these societies.

22. Cf. Almond and Coleman, *op. cit.*, pp. 53 ff., who refer to an apparently unpublished study by Edward Shils. The most recent approach (which could no longer be properly considered here) is Herbert J. Spiro's ingenious analysis of the problems of comparative politics, "Comparative Politics: A Comprehensive Approach," *American Political Science Review*, LVI, No. 3 (September, 1962), pp. 577–95. It constitutes one of the most interesting efforts to minimize ethnocentric and cold-war biases in the systematic study of political systems. While emphasizing a functional analysis ("policy flow"), he declares the "norm of individual responsibility" to be his highest normative criterion.

23. Immanuel Wallerstein, *Africa—The Politics of Independence* (New York: Vintage Books, 1961), p. 94.

24. From the Lagos *Sunday Express*, February 26, 1961, as reported by Reuben Frodin in *Nigeria and the World Outside* (American Universities Field Staff: Reports Service, "West Africa Series," IV, No. 4 [New York: May 25, 1961]). For a suggestive grouping of African leaders in terms of their public style, see Wallerstein, *op. cit.*, p. 98. For an informative survey of emerging African leaders see, e.g., Ronald Segal, *African Profiles* (Baltimore: Penguin, 1962).

25. This and the following quotation are cited by D. Apter and R. A. Lystad in "Bureaucracy, Party, and Constitutional Democracy," in G. N. Carter and W. O. Brown (eds.), *Transition in Africa* (Boston: Boston University Press, 1958), p. 26.

26. This appears to be one of the broader implications of L. W. Pye, *Politics, Personality, and Nation Building: Burma's Search for Identity* (New Haven, Conn.: Yale University Press, 1962).

27. This phrase is from C. Legum, *op. cit.*, p. 96, and occurs in an enlightening chapter on "Culture and Politics." On the role of the intellectuals in the emerging nations, see the remarkable essay by Edward Shils, "The Intellectuals in the Political Development of the New States," *World Politics*, XIII, No. 3 (April, 1960), pp. 229–68; H. Seton-Watson, *Neither War nor Peace* (New York: Frederick A. Praeger, 1960), pp. 182 ff.; N. R. Keddie, "Western Rule Versus Western Value," *Diogenes*, No. 26, Summer, 1959, pp. 71–96; H. J. Benda, "Non-Western Intelligentsias as Political Elites," in John H. Kautsky (ed.), *Political Change in Underdeveloped Countries* (New York: John Wiley, 1962) pp. 235 ff.; F. Oladipo Onipede, "African Nationalism: A Critical Portrait," *Dissent* (New York), Summer, 1956, pp. 276 ff. Onipede speaks of an attitude both "emulous and resentful towards Western mores," which tends to impose a "painful schizophrenia on the emergent 'moral being' of the new Africans." See the self-examination of their role by members of the Ceylonese Westernized elite, in "The Role of the Western-Educated Elite," *Community* (Colombo) IV, No. 1.

28. On the occasion of the alleged discovery of a member and supporter of

the defunct Togoland Congress illegally dressed as a Ghanian soldier who had sought to join troops. See *Ghana Today*, VI, No. 4 (April 25, 1962).

29. Based on C. Legum's figures, *op. cit.*, p. 127. A helpful contribution to the subject is Gwendolyn M. Carter (ed.), *African One-Party States* (Ithaca, N.Y.: Cornell University Press, 1962); very rewarding is Martin L. Kilson's "Authoritarian and Single-Party Tendencies in African Politics," *World Politics*, XV, No. 2 (January, 1963), pp. 262 ff.; also C. H. Moore, "The Neo-Destour Party of Tunisia—A Structure for Democracy?", *World Politics*, XIV, No. 3 (April, 1962), pp. 461ff., and Elie Salem, "Emerging Governments in the Arab World," *Orbis*, VI, No. 1 (Spring, 1962), pp. 102 ff.

30. Thus Wallerstein, *op. cit.*, pp. 95 ff.

31. Thus Sékou Touré of Guinea stresses that all responsible leaders are democratically chosen by members who are totally free, that there is free discussion of policy until it is adopted, that the leadership has sole responsibility from then on, and that no violation of discipline is permissible. See for these and other cited views, C. Legum, *op. cit.*, pp. 122 ff. For Sékou Touré's style of leadership, his deliberateness, and his political skill see Victor D. DuBois, *Problems of Independence* (American Universities Field Staff: Reports Service, "West Africa Series [Guinea]," VII [New York: November, 1962]).

32. Charles-Henri Favrod, *Poids de l'Afriques* (Paris: Éditions du Seuil, 1958), cited in unpublished paper "Notes on African Leadership," by Mercer Cook.

33. Ruth Schacter, "Single-Party Systems in West Africa," *American Political Science Review*, LV, No. 2 (1961), pp. 304 ff. On the other side, Lucy Mair, the social anthropologist, urges the need for securing minorities in her *Safeguards for Democracy* (London: Oxford University Press, 1961).

34. See R. Frodin, *Political Potpourri* (American Universities Field Staff: Reports Service, "West Africa Series [Nigeria]," IV, No. 3 [April 24, 1961]). pp. 6 ff.

35. D. E. Apter, "Some Reflections on the Role of a Political Opposition in New Nations," *Comparative Studies in Society and History*, IV, No. 2 (January, 1962), pp. 154 ff. By contrast, in a different setting, D. H. Bailey explores why and when repression of public demonstrations in India becomes disfunctional; see his "The Pedagogy of Democracy," *American Political Science Review*, LVI, No. 3 (September, 1962), pp. 663 ff.

36. Davies, *op. cit.*, pp. 301, 302. In 1962, Ghana officially declared itself to have a one-party system.

37. J. Nyerere, *Africa Digest* (London), October, 1961, quoted from Legum, *op. cit.*, p. 114.

38. This is an important part of J. H. Kautsky's conclusion in "An Essay in the Politics of Development," in J. H. Kautsky (ed.), *Political Change in Underdeveloped Countries: Nationalism and Communism*, (New York: John Wiley, 1962), pp. 13–119. Cf. Richard Lowenthal's remarkable review article in *Problems of Communism*, XI, No. 6 (November-December, 1962), pp. 37–44, with which the present writer is in agreement.

39. See Neal Riemer, *The Revival of Democratic Theory* (New York: Appleton-Century-Crofts, 1962), especially pp. 140 ff. See also the essays by Stephen King-Hall and Spiro (*Comparative Politics*) cited above. Spiro relates the norm of personal responsibility to the opportunity of contributing to the central decisions that affect one, to the need for the system to provide the ingredients of

foreknowledge of the probable consequences of such decisions, choice among alternatives, requisite resources, and a commitment on the part of the system to the norm of responsibility.

The Social and Political Role of the Intelligentsia in the New Countries
(pp. 121–133)

1. For background, see Edward Shils, "The Intellectual Between Tradition and Modernity: The Indian Situation," in *Comparative Studies in Society and History* (The Hague: Mouton and Company, 1961), Supplement I, *passim*. See also "The Intellectuals in the Political Development of the New States," in *World Politics* (Princeton, N.J.), XII, No. 3 (April, 1960), pp. 329–68.

2. Fritz Schatten, *Afrika-Schwarz oder Rot?* (Munich: R. Piper and Company, 1961), p. 94.

3. Albert Feuerwerker, *China's Early Industrialization: Sheng Hsuan-huai (1844–1916) and Mandarin Enterprise* (Cambridge, Mass.; Harvard University Press, 1958).

The Role of a Constitution in Developing
Political Systems: The Nigerian Example
(pp. 134–145)

1. Sir Ivor Jennings, *Some Characteristics of the Indian Constitution* (Oxford: Oxford University Press, 1953), p. 56.

2. Max Beloff, "The Federal Solution in Its Application to Europe, Asia, and Africa," *Political Studies* (London), I, No. 2, 122.

3. Charles McIlwain, *Constitutionalism and the Changing World* (Cambridge: The University Press, 1939), p. 123.

4. Charles Issawi, "Economic and Social Foundations of Democracy in the Middle East," *International Affairs*, (London), XXXII, No. 1 (January, 1956), 28.

5. The Central African Federation is the other area where the concept of federalism has been adopted. But the African majority regards it as an imposition designed to perpetuate white supremacy and is demanding its dissolution.

6. R. B. McCallum (ed.), John Stuart Mill's *On Liberty and Considerations on Representative Government* (Oxford: B. Blackwell, 1946), p. 305.

7. *The Nigeria (Constitution) Orders in Council*, 1960, Part II of the Schedule.

8. Chief F. R. A. Williams, Q. C., "The Division of Legislative and Executive Power Between Federal and Regional Governments," *Constitutional Problems of Federalism in Nigeria*, Record of Proceedings of a Seminar held in Lagos, August 8–15, 1960, p. 35.

9. Nigeria, though independent, still has Her Majesty, the Queen of England, as Head of State. The Federation's Governor-General and the three regional Governors are her representatives. Hence, such appeals could still be sent to the Queen whose signature alone is technically valid on all state and constitutional documents. This anomalous situation has frequently been cited as the strongest argument of the advocates of a republican constitution for Nigeria.

10. The Action Group Party was at the same time in power in Western Nigeria and in opposition in the federal legislature, where a coalition of the NCNC and the NPC is in control.

The Idea of African "Neutralism" and "Non-Alignment":
An Exploratory Survey
(pp. 146–160)

1. In this connection, note what the Africanist E. W. Blyden said in 1862, and compare it with Nkrumah's words today:

> An African nationality is the great desire of my soul. I believe nationality to be an ordinance of nature; and no people can rise to an influential position among the nations without a distinct and efficient nationality. . . . We need some African power, some great center of the race . . . whence such an influence may go forth in behalf of the race as shall be felt by the nations. WE ARE NOW SO SCATTERED AND DIVIDED, WE MAY EXPECT IMPOSITIONS. SO LONG AS WE LIVE SIMPLY BY THE SUFFERANCE OF THE NATIONS, WE MUST EXPECT TO BE SUBJECT TO THEIR CAPRICES. . . . We must build up Negro states . . . we must have governments; we must have legislation of our own; we must build ships and navigate them; we must ply the trades, instruct the schools, control the press, AND THUS AID IN SHAPING THE OPINIONS AND GUIDING THE DESTINIES OF MANKIND. . . . (*Liberia's Offering* [New York: J. A. Gray, 1862], pp. v, vi, 74–76.)

Cf. Nkrumah's words:
> It is only when a people are politically free that other races can give them the respect that is due them. It is impossible to talk of equality of races in any other terms. No people without a government of their own can expect to be treated on the same level as peoples of independent sovereign states. . . .
> (Nkrumah, *Ghana* [New York: Nelson, 1957], p. xiv.)

2. C. Legum, *Pan-Africanism* (New York: Frederick A. Praeger, 1962), p. 111.

3. See the author's "Sierra Leone: The Pattern of Constitutional Change, 1924–1951" (Unpublished doctoral dissertation, Harvard University, 1959), chaps. v and vi. See also other references to Azikiwe, below.

4. Nnamdi Azikiwe, *Liberia in World Politics* (London: A. A. Stockwell, 1934).

5. Azikiwe was forced to leave the Gold Coast (Ghana) as a consequence of a sedition and libel case in which he had been involved as editor-in-chief of the *African Morning Post.*

6. Azikiwe, *Renascent Africa* (privately printed; Accra, Gold Coast, 1937), pp. 8–10, 120 ff.

7. Azikiwe, letter to Ladipo Solanke, a Nigerian Yoruba lawyer and Secretary-General of the West African Students Union, which has its headquarters in London, 1929, cited in Azikiwe's "My Odyssey," an unpublished manuscript that first appeared in a series of articles in his Lagos newspaper, the *West African Pilot,* beginning October 16, 1938. The series runs to more than 300 typewritten pages and is found in his private library at Nsukka, Nigeria.

8. Azikiwe, *Renascent Africa,* pp. 45–47.

9. *Ibid.,* pp. 42–45.

10. See, for example, J. E. Casely-Hayford, *Gold Coast Native Institutions*

(London: Sweet and Maxwell, Ltd., 1903), and *The Truth About the West African Land Question* (London: C. M. Phillips, 1913). See also George Padmore, *The Gold Coast Revolution* (London: D. Dobson, 1953).

11. For a biographical sketch of Aggrey, see W. M. Macartney, *Dr. Aggrey: Ambassador for Africa* (London: SCM Press, 1949).

12. Cited in Smith, *op. cit.*

13. See Martin Wight, *Gold Coast Legislative Council* (London: Faber and Faber, 1947), p. 26, n. 4.

14. For example, Casely-Hayford, in 1913, declared:

I bid you shake hands across the waters over your *common* need, your *common* trouble, your *common* anxiety . . . smoke the peace pipe together. It is a sacrament to be received on bended knees. AND UNITED WEST AFRICA rises chastened and stimulated by the thought that in UNION IS HER STRENGTH, HER WEAKNESS IN DISCORD. (*The Truth About the West African Land Question*, p. 103.)

15. *Gold Coast Native Institutions*, pp. 246, 247.

16. Both Hayford and Aggrey believed in the goal of a Gold Coast that would be free and independent but jointly administered by Africans and the Europeans. Hence the term "cooperationist" to describe them in this essay. In fact, Hayford went even farther and advocated in both his earlier and later writings the goal of an "Imperial West Africa," thus making his brand of nationalism (considered radical by contemporaries, both European and African) appear conservative, if not reactionary, today. Hayford wrote of "the imperialisation of the Gold Coast and of Ashanti [but] on purely aboriginal lines, leading ultimately to the imperialisation of West Africa" (*ibid.*, p. ix); of the "Imperial West Africa that shall be," that "Nature has decreed . . . shall be . . ." (*ibid.*, p. 246); of the "Gold Coast and Ashanti . . . and the several States . . . federated together in one UNION . . . FLYING THE UNION JACK, not by coercion . . ." (*ibid.*, p. 254).

17. For Sékou Touré's "Doctrine of Africa," see his *L'Expérience Guinnéénne et L'Unite Africaine* (Paris: Presence Africaine, 1959); *L'Action du Parti Démocratique de Guinée et la Lutte pour L'Emancipation Africaine* (Conakry: Impr. Nationale, 1959); and *Rapport D'Orientation et de Doctrine* (Conakry: Congrès Général de L'UGTAN), January 15–18, 1959.

18. See Nehru, "Report on Bandung" (Statement in the Lower House of the Indian Parliament, April 30, 1955), p. 293.

19. *Ibid.*, pp. 288–91.

20. Since this paper was presented in Athens, Sékou Touré has offered yet another definition or interpretation of the idea of "African neutralism." He writes:

African Neutralism, then, is not shameful indifference, a sort of political demobilization. On the contrary, it *is the expression of a lively faith in a happy future for mankind. It is something active, a participating force, an active agent in the struggle for the achievement of a world society—emancipated, fraternal and united* . . . [a] *historical movement.* . . . "Africa's Future and the World," *Foreign Affairs* [New York], XLI, No. 1 [October, 1962], pp. 141–51).

21. Nehru, *op. cit.*, pp. 508 ff.

22. Kwame Nkrumah, *My Plan for Africa* (Enugu: Anno Printing Press, 1962), p. 22; cited in Legum, *op. cit.*, p. 276.

23. *Ghana Today* (Accra: Ghana Ministry of Information Bulletin [March 20, 1957]).

24. Unless otherwise indicated, this and other citations or references to statements by African leaders on the subject of neutralism and non-alignment may be presumed to be drawn from *Africa Report* and/or *West Africa*, as well as from the press of the country whose leaders or spokesmen are being quoted. Legum, *op. cit.*, also contains extensive citations on the subject from the speeches and other statements by African leaders.

25. "We are neither for East nor West, neither for Communism nor Democracy; we are for Africa." [Sékou Touré in a television interview in New York in November, 1959.] "When I went to school, I was taught that there were four cardinal points of the globe—East, West, North, and South." [*Ibid.*]

26. *Documents and Resolutions*, Conference of Independent African States, Accra, 1958.

27. *Information Bulletin* (Guinea Mission to the U.N. [New York, 1959]).

28. Nnamdi Azikiwe, *Nigeria in World Politics* (London: Diplomatic Press and Publishing Co., 1959), p. 11.

29. The author has encountered this approach to the writing (or, rather, rewriting) of American revolutionary history at several conferences in the U.S. during the past few years and has repeatedly heard the argument urged, sometimes in very assertive terms. One such instance was at a symposium held at Mount Holyoke College during the spring of 1960 on the subject "Non-Alignment in a Divided World," at which the delegates to the U.N. from Ceylon, India, and the U.A.R., together with the present writer, were pitted against a spokesman of the U.S. State Department. Even in retrospect, it is hard to go along with historians and political analysts who would see in the maneuvers of Samuel Adams, John Hancock, and others, acts that could be dignified with the epithet "moderate."

30. Henry Steele Commager and Richard B. Morris, *The 'Spirit of '76'* (2 vols.; Indianapolis, Ind.: Bobbs-Merrill, 1958). Note the use of such ugly epithets as "rebels," "scoundrels," "pimps and parasites," etc., employed by responsible British statesmen of the day, both in and out of the House of Commons (and, probably, Lords?) to describe the American colonial nationalists engaged in *their* struggle for independence.

31. A. M. Schlesinger, Sr., *Prelude to Independence: The Newspaper War on Britain, 1764–1776* (New York: Alfred A. Knopf, 1958).

32. Dumas Malone, "Paradox of the American Revolution," *The New York Times Magazine*, February 21, 1960, p. 22.

33. E. Borchard, *American Foreign Policy from 1776 to 1946* (Indianapolis, Ind.: National Foundation Press, 1946).

34. *Ibid.*

35. For his views on "Socialism" for new African states, see his *The African Nations and World Solidarity* (New York: Frederick A. Praeger, 1961).

The Soviet Union Seeks a Policy for Afro-Asia
(*pp.* 163–179)

1. A study of Communist activities in Asia during the 1920's indicates that the problem is not only a current one, and that even under Lenin and his im-

mediate successors, Communist statements about the colonial question and national liberation were no more than slogans and did not represent an agreed policy.

2. De-Stalinization and the failure of the regime to come up with an answer to the agricultural problem may be undermining the "infallible science of Marxism" on the domestic scene as well.

3. The one infallible law of the West, about which the Communists have been so confident, is that the Marxist laws of capitalism point to the inevitable demise of that system. But the continued resurgence and development of the capitalist world undermines even this confidence.

4. "Wars of national liberation" would include limited wars because, although the Communists would deny that they were intervening from outside; "volunteer aid," as in the Spanish Civil War, Korea, and Laos, would be permissible.

5. It may also be argued that the trend away from violence is a typical reaction of a mature power and of a leadership that has much to lose, externally and internally, by war.

6. The following account is given of the foundation of the Communist Party in Angola:

> The Communist Party of Angola was created in 1955. In 1956, on the initiative of the Communist Party of Angola and joined to it, the United Party for the Struggle of Africans in Angola was established as the basic party of the People's Movement for the Freedom of Angola. In 1959, the People's Movement for the Freedom of Angola and the African Party of Independence (illegal political party of Portuguese Guinea) created a coordinating center of the African Revolutionary Front struggling for the national independence of Portuguese colonies. (*Afrika Segodnia* [*Africa Today*] [Moscow: Gospolitizdat, 1962], p. 119.)

7. A. Beliakov and F. Burlatski, "The Leninist Theory of Socialist Revolution and Our Times," *Kommunist*, No. 13, 1960, p. 13. In effect, the authors imply that the dilemma, presented by an alliance with the national bourgeoisie, of whether the struggle against the bourgeoisie was to be abandoned for the moment or merely disguised, was decided in favor of the former. This was in part a renewal of the 1926–27 dispute between Stalin and Trotsky over China, and the opposite decision from that of the Popular Front of the 1930's.

8. Cf. G. Mirskii, "The Banner of Bandung," *Azii i Afrika Segodnia*, (Moscow), No. 4, 1961, pp. 5–6.

9. See treatment by the Soviet press of the attempted coup against Haile Selassie in 1960, the military coup in Thailand in 1960, and the government changes in Turkey and South Korea.

10. E.g., *Pravda*, August 27, 1959, and October 26, 1959, and *World Marxist Review*, IV, No. 4 (1961), 59–63, and V, No. 5 (1962), 36 ff.

11. I. I. Potekhin, the chief of Soviet African studies, recently laid down the Soviet law of African history:

> It is necessary to show that the victory of the national revolution in Africa was the result of the connected activities of three factors: popular movement in the colonies themselves, growth of influence and power of the world socialist system, and the class struggle of the proletariat in capitalist countries. ("Some

Problems of Africanists in Light of the Resolutions of the Twenty-second Party Congress," *Narody Azii i Afriki* [Moscow], No. 1, 1962, p. 8.)

12. Soviet propaganda sometimes hints at this theme in condemning the new imperialism of the United States. The United States, it is claimed, supports political independence for the colonies but at the same time is making every effort to expand its economic imperialism. The implication is that such a policy undermines the United States' imperialist competitors of Western Europe, is used to dupe the native population, and is less costly.

13. This argument is not meant to imply that the popular national liberation struggle and the presence of the socialist bloc are not also important contributing factors. The native elites were also inclined to exaggerate their country's value to Western Europe, but are now afraid they will be left out of the growing prosperity of the Common Market.

14. Statement by G. N. Sheviakov, Member of the State Committee of the Council of Ministers of the U.S.S.R. on the External Economic Relations, *International Affairs* (Moscow), No. 3, 1962, pp. 74–75.

15. E.g., *Narody Azii i Afriki*, No. 5, 1961, pp. 9 ff.

16. The more acute leaders also wonder about the inconsistencies of Communist propaganda: the crisis of capitalism and the growing threat of capitalist penetration, the threat of collective colonialism, and the competition between imperialist states. But the most disturbing inconsistencies to the Asian and African leaders are Communist support for both the national bourgeoisie and the proletariat, and the Communist parties as part of both the so-called nationalist and international movements. For a Communist attempt to rationalize these inconsistencies see Aziz Al-Hajj, Abdelkader El Ouahrani, and Adnan Safi, "The True and False Friends of the Arab Peoples," *World Marxist Review*, V, No. 5 (1962), 36–43.

17. The settlement of the Western New Guinea crisis also deflated Soviet allegations of continued Dutch and American imperialism in Southeast Asia.

18. It can also be argued that Soviet support of the ambitions of such leaders as Nkrumah, and formerly Nasser, aroused the suspicions of many groups.

19. Cf. "Statement by the Honorable Frank M. Coffin, Deputy Administrator for Program Agency for International Development Before the Senate Foreign Relations Committee, April 12, 1962" (mimeographed), p. 16.

20. In forcing peaceful coexistence on capitalism, the Socialist countries are reaffirming the basic Marxist-Leninist thesis that revolution—be it socialist, democratic or a national-liberation revolution—cannot be "exported." A revolution can succeed only if it is in accord with the objective process maturing in the country concerned, if it is carried out by the people of that country. Needless to say, the Socialist states are not indifferent to popular revolutions in other countries. (Mamum, "Peaceful Coexistence and the National-Liberation Struggle," *World Marxist Review*, V, No. 10 [1962], p. 4.)

See also N. S. Khrushchev, "The Vital Question of Developing a World Socialist System," *Kommunist*, No. 12, 1962, p. 9.

21. E.g., front page editorial on Africa in *Pravda*, December 1, 1962.

22. The Soviet Union also appears concerned about Yugoslavia and its attempt to act as a leader of the neutralist bloc. André Gromyko's trip to Belgrade during the latter part of April, and Tito's visit to the U.S.S.R. in 1962, appear

to have been part of a new effort to win over, or at least neutralize, Tito.

23. Cf. Milton Kovner, "Trade and Aid," *Survey* (London), No. 43, August, 1962, p. 54, and Richard Lowenthal, " 'National Democracy' and the Post-Colonial Revolution," pp. 56 ff. above.

24. The Soviet Union appears to be seeking markets by use of its political position rather than by economic competition.

25. Criticism of leaders of the underdeveloped countries is more prevalent in journals not associated directly with the Soviet Government, but it is still restrained. For a good example of the restraint shown in criticizing repressive actions of governments against Communists, see L. N. Chernov, "Communists in Countries of Asia and Africa in the Vanguard of the Struggle for Freedom and National Independence," *Narody Azii i Afriki*, No. 5, 1961, pp. 15–31.

26. Cf. I. I. Potekhin, *Afrika smotrit v budushchee* (*Africa Looks to the Future*) (Moscow: Izd-vo vostochnoi Lit-ry, 1960). One of the primary purposes of this little volume seems to be to refute the statement often repeated by African leaders: "We are not Communists but that does not signify that we are anti-Communists; we are socialists." The argument runs that there is only one true socialism and that is Soviet socialism. Therefore, the African leaders working for socialism are working in fact with the U.S.S.R.

27. I. I. Potckhin, "Some Problems of Africanists in Light of the Resolutions of the Twenty-second Party Congress," *Narody Azii i Afriki*, No. 1, 1962, p. 10.

28. At Sofia in May, 1962, Khrushchev implied criticism of the "socialism" of some African and Asian leaders, and stressed that only the working class can lead their countries to socialism:

> It is also revealing that many of the leaders of the newly free countries are nowadays talking of socialism as offering the chance to overcome their age-old backwardness within a short space of time.
>
> But what kind of socialism do they have in mind? What do they mean by it? Which are the forces they would lean on in building socialism?
>
> We are convinced of one thing—time and trend of historical development will face the former colonial countries with the choice of taking either the capitalist or the noncapitalist path of development. Which path to choose will be decided by the peoples themselves. And those leaders who really have the best interests of the people, the working masses, at heart will sooner or later have to realize that only by leaning on the working class as the most consistent, most revolutionary class in society, in alliance with the peasantry and with the support of all progressive forces, can they bring about victory and the correct solution of fundamental social problems. (*The Current Digest of the Soviet Press*, XIV, No. 20, 7.)

29. The Declaration of the Eighty-one Communist Parties in November, 1960, paid scant attention to the role of the party organization, but from 1961 comments on the declaration began to stress the positive role of the Party organs.

30. *World Marxist Review*, V, No. 5 (1962), 68.

31. Curt Gasteyger, "The Soviet Union and the *Tiers Monde*," Survey, No. 43, August, 1962, p. 16.

32. Discussing a recent meeting organized by the *World Marxist Review*, the *New Times* reports:

> On the question of the social nature of the state sector in the nonsocialist

countries of Asia, Africa and Latin America participants warned against a blanket definition of it as a form of state capitalism. Such a definition applies only to countries where the national bourgeoisie is in power. It obviously does not apply to certain African countries where the bourgeoisie is weak, or where there is virtually no bourgeoisie. In such countries power is exercised by a bloc of the democratic and patriotic forces, in which the working masses are in the dominating element. But even in these countries the state sector cannot be described as socialist.

What is its nature? Marxist literature distinguishes three types of productive relations: exploitation in societies with antagonistic classes; comradely cooperation in socialist societies, and relations of a *transitory nature*. Proceeding from this, the forum participants suggested that the latter type applies to African countries in which there is practically no native bourgeoisie. And if that is so, then the state sector in their economics is neither capitalist nor socialist, but transitory. (*New Times* [Moscow], No. 41, October 11, 1961, pp. 14 ff.)

33. E.g., M. V. Lavrichenko, *Ekonomicheskoe sotrudnichestvo SSSR so stranami Azii, Afriki i Latinskoi Ameriki* (*The Economic Collaboration of the U.S.S.R. with the Countries of Asia, Africa, and Latin America*) (Moscow: Gospolitizdat, 1961), and *SSSR i strany Vostoka* (*The U.S.S.R. and the Countries of the East*) (Moscow: Gospolitizdat, 1961).

34. *World Marxist Review*, V, No. 5 (1962), 69.

35. Cf. R. Avakov and R. Andreacian, "The Progressive Role of the State Sector," *Kommunist*, No. 13, 1962, p. 92.

36. From the author's own personal experience in the U.S.S.R., the experiment has thus far proven far from satisfactory. The outbreak of racial disputes and the heavy and not very subtle pressure of the Komsomols has led to negative results.

37. "One thing that distinguishes African trade unions is that, as a rule, they do not limit their struggle to purely economic demands but regard active participation in the national liberation movement as their number one task." (*New Times*, No. 27, 1961, p. 18.)

38. The African working people are right in insisting that the trade unions must be independent and neutral. But independence and neutrality do not preclude fraternal ties (based on equality and non-interference in each other's internal affairs) with the international working class movements; and specifically with such trade union centers as the WFTU, the French General Confederation of Labor, the Italian Confederation of Labor and the Central Trade Union Organization of Indonesia (SOBSI). (*World Marxist Review*, V, No. 12 [1961], 21.)

39. "Hence to strengthen the Communist parties in those African countries where they already exist and to form such parties where none existed before is a perfectly natural and logical process. . . ." (Ali Yata, "New Weapons for Embattled Africa," *World Marxist Review*, IV, No. 12 [1961], 21.) See also *Afrika Segodnia* (*Africa Today*), pp. 52 ff. This group also attacks the thesis advanced by Sékou Touré and other African leaders of a classless society. See differences in tone of William MacLorin, "The Bourgeoisie in Senegal and Neo-Colonialism," *World Marxist Review*, V, No. 10 (1962), 14–19; Jack Woddis, "Role

of the African Working Class in the National Liberation Movement," *World Marxist Review,* V, No. 7 (1962), 49 ff.; G. Starishenko, "Via General Democratic Reforms to Socialism," *Kommunist,* No. 13, 1962, pp. 104–9; and N. Numade, "The Working Class and the African Revolution," *The African Communist,* II, No. 1 (October–December, 1962), pp. 66–85.

40. Recently, many Soviet analysts have also been stressing the class struggle after independence. See I. I. Potekhin, "Some Problems of Africanists in Light of the Resolutions of the Twenty-Second Party Congress," *Narody Azii i Afriki,* No. 1, 1962, p. 10.

The U.S.S.R. and Ethiopia: A Case of Traditional Behavior
(*pp. 180–192*)

1. Leo Silberman, "Why the Haud Was Ceded," in *Cahiers d'Études Africaines* (Paris, 1961), II, 51 ff.

2. *Pravda,* July 1, 1959, p. 2.

3. Alexander, Grand Duke of Russia, *Always a Grand Duke* (Garden City, N.Y.: Garden City Publishing Company, 1935), pp. 170, 174.

4. *Pravda,* July 1, 1959, p. 2.

5. *Second Conference of Independent African States,* Addis Ababa, June 14–26, 1960 (Addis Ababa: Ministry of Information of the Imperial Ethiopian Government, 1960), p. 3.

6. "Selassie to Moscow," *The New Republic* (New York), XIV, No. 15 (April 13, 1959), p. 6.

7. Paul Underwood, "Selassie Fears Big-Nation Pact," *The New York Times,* August 28, 1959.

8. Paul Wohl, "Ethiopian Support Wooed by Moscow," *Christian Science Monitor,* July 23, 1959.

9. *Soviet Economic Relations with Middle East and African Countries,* Supplement to *Mizan Newsletter* (London), No. 2, February, 1962, p. 8.

10. Jeanne Contini, "The Winds of Change and the Lion of Judah," *The Reporter,* XXIV, No. 11 (May 25, 1961), 31–34.

11. *Soviet Economic Relations . . . ,* p. 8.

12. *Christian Science Monitor,* July 23, 1959.

13. *Afrika Segodnia (Africa Today)* (Moscow: Gospolitizdat, 1962), p. 308.

14. A. Abramov, *Efiopiia—strana, ne ystavshaia na koleni* (Moscow: Gospolitizdat, 1961), pp. 106 ff.

15. M. Dobrynin, "U brat'ev—khristian Efiopii," *Zhurnal Moskovskoi Patriarkhii* (Moscow), April, 1959, p. 74.

16. Liviu Stan, "Novyi patriarkhat—tserkov' Efiopii," *Zhurnal Moskovskoi Patriarkhii,* May, 1961, p. 72.

17. Leo Silberman, "Ethiopia: Power of Moderation," *Middle East Journal* (Washington, D.C.), XIV, No. 2 (Spring, 1960), p. 144.

Soviet Economic Policies Toward Afro-Asian Countries
(*pp. 193–204*)

1. *Pravda,* November 4, 1960. The receiving countries covered by this announcement are India, Pakistan, Indonesia, Burma, Nepal, Ceylon, Cambodia, United Arab Republic, Iraq, Yemen, Guinea, Ghana, Ethiopia, and Turkey.

2. *Economic Report of the President* (1960) (Washington, D.C.: U.S. Government Printing Office, 1960), p. 238; *Economic Report of the President* (1962) (Washington, D.C., U.S. Government Printing Office, 1962), p. 296; *Statistical Abstract of the United States, 1960* (Bureau of the Census [Washington, D.C., 1960]), pp. 871 ff. Excludes military assistance.

3. *Hearings, Foreign Assistance Act of 1962* (Committee on Foreign Affairs, U.S. House of Representatives: [Washington, D.C., 1962]), Part II, p. 336; *The Communist Economic Offensive Through 1960* (U.S. Department of Defense [Washington, D.C., November, 1961]), p. 11.

4. *Ibid.*, p. 332.

5. *Narodnoe Khoziaistvo SSSR v 1960 godu* (*The National Economy of the U.S.S.R. in 1960*) (Moscow: Gosstatizdat, 1961), p. 744.

6. The export balance of the Soviet Union has apparently been due to one or several of the following conditions: (1) in relations with underdeveloped countries, net lending by the Soviet Union offset by net borrowing by other members of the bloc; (2) in relations within the bloc, net lending by the Soviet Union; or (3) in relations with remaining countries outside the bloc, net lending (negative borrowing) by the Soviet Union.

7. *Economic Survey of Europe in 1960* (Geneva: Economic Commission for Europe, 1960), p. V-10.

8. *Ibid.*, pp. V-6 and V-10.

9. *The Communist Economic Offensive Through 1960*, p. 13.

10. Table 1, and Joseph Berliner, *Soviet Economic Aid* (New York: Frederick A. Praeger, 1958), p. 38.

Soviet Economic Aid to Non-aligned Countries and the Soviet Program in South and Southeast Asia

(*pp. 205–221*)

1. J. Berliner, *Soviet Economic Aid* (New York: Frederick A. Praeger, 1958), p. 57.

2. Hiroshi Kurimoto, "Recent Economic Development of the Underdeveloped Countries," *Imperialism and the Development of Newly-Growing Countries* (*International Economics Series*, Vol. V), Tokyo: YUSIKAKU, 1962), p. 194.

3. O. Ulirikh, "Economic Policy of Underdeveloped Countries, *Mirovaia Ekonomika i mezhdunarodnye otnosheniia*, No. 4, April, 1962, p. 95. The author emphasizes the importance of establishing the public sector in the underdeveloped countries, because of its "anti-imperialistic" and "anti-feudalistic features." According to him:

As a result of the establishment of the new nationalized enterprises, the more "progressive" form of ownership of the means of production will appear, and under a certain condition it will become the basis of non-capitalistic development of those countries. Foreign monopoly makes every effort to maintain its position in the underdeveloped countries and strikes strong blows at the public sector and protective tariff policies.

An article by Y. Panfilov, "On Certain Peculiarities of Non-Capitalist Development," *Politicheskoe Samobrazovanie*, No. 6, 1961, p. 67, cites further advantages of the "public sector":

Under conditions of noncapitalist development, the formation of the working class occurs in the main on the basis of the development of the public sector in the national economy, where this class from the very start is virtually free from exploitation by private capital. In these conditions the tasks of consolidating and developing the new, noncapitalist system of economic life and its gradual transformation into socialism stands before the working class and its revolutionary vanguard.

4. *Foreign Ministry Monthly Research Bulletin* (Tokyo: Japanese Foreign Office), II, No. 3 (March, 1961), p. 58.

5. I. Kapranov, "The U.S.S.R.'s Technical Assistance to Foreign Countries," *Vneshnaia Torgovlia*, No. 6, 1961. (See *Problems of Communism*, April, 1962, p. 44.)

6. Suzanne Labin, "The Activities of the Soviet Union in the Underdeveloped Countries," *Studies on the Soviet Union*, I, No. 2 (1961), 163.

7. Samuel Pisar, *A New Look at Trade Policy Toward the Communist Bloc* (Subcommittee on Foreign Economic Policy of the Joint Economic Committee [Washington, D.C., 1961]), p. 28.

8. Alec Nove, *Communist Economic Strategy* (Washington, D.C.: National Planning Association, 1959), p. 54.

9. I. Kapranov, *op. cit.* (See *Problems of Communism*, April, 1962, p. 51.)

10. "Southeast Asia Handbook" (unpublished Japanese Government compilation, 1962), pp. 269–71.

Note—Data on economic aid to Southeast Asia were taken from *Economic Assistance from Major Powers to Southeast Asia—Present & Future* (Japanese Industrial Structure Research Institute, February 15, 1962); "Tabulated Data on Communist Bloc Assistance to Newly Developing Countries" (unpublished compilation by the Economic Cooperation Division, Ministry of Foreign Affairs, March, 1962, and Taijiro Ichikawa, "Sino-Soviet Economic Assistance & Trade in South Asia" (unpublished compilation).

Leadership Cohesion in Communist China and Underdeveloped Asian Countries

(*pp. 222–235*)

1. For instance, in Liu Shao-ch'i's advocacy of the Chinese model of revolutionary struggle for the rest of Asia in a speech before the Asian-Australasian Trade Union Conference in 1949 (for a discussion of this, see A. M. Halpern, "The Foreign Policy Uses of the Chinese Revolutionary Model," *The China Quarterly* [London], No. 7, July–September, 1961); in Mao's speech on collectivization, July 31, 1955 (translated in *For a Lasting Peace, For a People's Democracy*, October 28, 1955); in the Central Committee's resolution on the communes of December 10, 1958 (translated in *Contemporary China*, III, 1958–59).

2. India sent delegations to study various aspects of the Chinese scene; see, for instance, the *Report of the Indian Delegation to China on Agricultural Planning and Techniques* (New Delhi: Government of India, Ministry of Food and Agriculture, 1956). For a Western analysis, see Werner Klatt, "Chinese Agriculture as a Model for Asian Countries," a paper presented to the symposium on "Economic and Social Problems of the Far East," at the University of Hong Kong Golden Jubilee Congress.

3. For an extended discussion of these points, see Maurice Zinkin, *Development for Free Asia* (London: Chatto & Windus, 1956), pp. 63–92.

4. H. F. Schurmann, "Organizational Principles of the Chinese Communists," *The China Quarterly*, No. 2, April–June, 1960.

5. For a discussion of charismatic leadership, see Max Weber's article "The Sociology of Charismatic Authority," in H. H. Gerth and C. Wright Mills (eds.), *From Max Weber: Essays in Sociology* (London: Routledge & Kegan Paul, 1948), and Arthur Schlesinger, Jr., "On Heroic Leadership," *Encounter* (London), XVI, No. 6 (December, 1960).

6. Kao Kang was the first Chairman of the State Planning Commission and Party leader in the vital Northeast Region (Manchuria); Ch'en Yun was senior Deputy Premier and holder of various ministerial posts connected with economic affairs; Marshal P'eng Teh-huai was Deputy Premier, Defense Minister (until disgraced), the Communists' most respected civil war veteran after Chu Teh, and the leader of the "volunteers" in Korea; Lin Po-ch'ü was one of the Party's respected "elder statesmen"; Chang Wen-t'ien was Party secretary-general before Mao during the 1930's, a one-time ambassador to Moscow, and Deputy Foreign Minister at the time of his disgrace.

By the core of the leadership, I mean the Standing Committee of the Politburo. This was set up in 1956 and was initially made up of Mao Tse-tung, Liu Shao-ch'i, Chou En-lai, Chu Teh, Ch'en Yun, and Teng Hsiao-p'ing, to whose number Lin Piao was added in 1958. There can be no doubt that if this body had been in existence from 1949, Kao Kang would have been a member of it.

7. See Leonard Schapiro, *The Communist Party of the Soviet Union* (London: Eyre & Spottiswoode, 1960), Appendix III, "Members and Candidate Members of the Politburo and Praesidium 1917–1958," for information on most of the period that my figures cover.

8. See Michael Brecher, *Nehru: A Political Biography* (abr. ed.; London: Oxford University Press, 1961), p. 236.

9. There obviously is a problem of definition here. What is a "substratum of stability"? In China, whole sections of the economy and the society have been disrupted from time to time by largely political "campaigns" such as the "three-anti," "five-anti," the suppression of counter-revolutionaries, the anti-rightist struggle, etc., to a degree which would probably be regarded as intolerable in, say, India. But there was never any question of the regime losing its grip on the country, and this must be the essential criterion for deciding whether the "substratum of stability" exists.

10. It is interesting to note that those occasions during the twentieth century on which a British Prime Minister has been removed from office as a result of pressure from colleagues who no longer had confidence in him have been times of extreme crisis—Asquith during World War I, Chamberlain during World War II; Eden might well have been forced to resign after the Suez expedition even if he had not been taken ill; and Macmillan's position was threatened in 1962 when Britain had to make the crucial decision on whether or not to go into Europe, and in 1963 after the Profumo affair had rocked the Conservative party.

11. Mao's triumph was in part due to the fact that he had been building up a "machine" in the Kiangsi Soviet (see Tso-liang Hsiao, *Power Relations Within the Chinese Communist Movement, 1930–1934: A Study of Documents* [Seattle, Wash.: University of Washington Press, 1961, pp. 156–59]), and in part to the unswerving personal loyalty of Chu Teh, the chief military leader. But the fact

that Mao was able to build up a machine when not in the supreme organizational position (unlike Stalin) and was able to command the respect of Chu Teh would indicate recognition of his abilities by his colleagues.

12. See Richard Walker, "Chairman Mao and the Cult of Personality," *Encounter*, XV, No. 6 (June, 1960).

13. See Chao Kuo-chün, "Leadership in the Chinese Communist Party," in Howard L. Boorman (ed.), "Contemporary China and the Chinese," in *The Annals of the American Academy of Political and Social Science*s (Philadelphia), CCCXX, January, 1959, 1–147.

14. Liu Shao-ch'i, Chou En-lai, Chang Wen-t'ien in the present Politburo, and Li Wei-han, Li Li-san, Ch'en Shao-yu (Wang Ming) in the present Central Committee. See Robert C. North, *Kuomintang and Chinese Communist Elites* (Stanford, Calif.: Stanford University Press, 1952), Appendix C, Table 3.

15. There has been some dispute among Sovietologists in recent years as to whether or not Khrushchev is "threatened" from the right or the left. Without wishing to theorize in an unfamiliar field, the writer thinks it fair to say that if Khrushchev felt he was so pre-eminent that his colleagues could not even consider removing him, he would have had little need to scythe so merrily among his own protégés when things went wrong. Presumably Aristov, Furtseva, and the rest were efficient Khrushchev-type officials or they would not have risen under him. Could so many of them really have been found wanting in so short a period after so many years of loyal service? Certainly Mao has had no similar need to find top-level scapegoats.

16. Brecher, *op. cit.*, pp. 153–56, 237. Brecher, it seems to me, rather underestimates the chances that a split between Nehru and Patel might have occurred —at any rate, on the basis of the evidence he presents. As this book goes to press, New Delhi is still agog at the news of the dismissal of several senior cabinet ministers, although no one seems certain whether their dismissal was a genuine attempt to reinvigorate the Congress party or a way of getting rid of Morarji Desai and other right-wingers. At any rate Mr. Nehru's position seems stronger than ever.

17. See Boyd Compton, *Mao's China: Party Reform Documents, 1942–44* (Seattle, Wash.: University of Washington Press, 1952).

18. See George McTurnan Kahin, *Nationalism and Revolution in Indonesia* (Ithaca, N.Y.: Cornell University Press, 1952), pp. 90–212.

19. Ben Bella's most ardent opponent in the dispute among the Algerian leaders that followed the achievement of independence was apparently Mohammed Boudiaf who had been his fellow prisoner in a French gaol.

20. These men make up six of the seven members of the ruling Standing Committee of the Politburo; see note 6 above.

21. The number includes Tibet.

22. This analysis is based on Chao, *op. cit.*

23. Not all the other Chinese leaders had taken part in every one of these episodes, of course.

24. The Northeast Region was in fact set up before the central government.

25. For an extensive analysis of the Kao Kang affair, see Harold Hinton, *The "Unprincipled" Dispute Within the Chinese Communist Top Leadership* (Washington, D.C.: U.S. Information Agency, December, 1955).

26. See David A. Charles, "The Dismissal of Marshal P'eng Teh-huai," *The China Quarterly*, No. 8, October–December, 1961.

27. *Ibid.*

28. Even so, it must be remembered that it was Khrushchev who brought the dispute truly into the open with his attack on the Albanians at the Twenty-second Congress of the Communist Party of the Soviet Union.

29. For a discussion of Chou's probable attitude, see the writer's "Communist China's Intra-Party Dispute," *Pacific Affairs* (New York), XXI, No. 4 (December, 1958), 323–35, and "The Leadership in China," *The World Today* (London), XV, No. 8 (August, 1959), 310–23.

Communist China and the Non-Committed Countries: Motives and Purposes of Communist China's Foreign Policy

(pp. 236–255)

1. The comments quoted are taken from statements made in 1959 by Ch'en Yi, Foreign Minister of Communist China, and the editor of the *People's Daily*, as cited in R. G. Boyd, *Communist China's Foreign Policy* (New York: Frederick A. Praeger, 1962), pp. 40–42. Innumerable parallels could easily be given.

2. See Walter Laqueur, "The Schism," *Survey* (London), No. 42, June, 1962.

3. See Boris Levitski, "Coexistence Within the Bloc," *Survey*, No. 42, June, 1962, pp. 28–38.

4. The aid given to Guinea amounted to $25 million in 1960, plus 20,000 tons of rice in 1959 and 1960; to Ghana, $20 million in August, 1961; to Cambodia, $22.4 million in 1956 and $26.5 million in 1960; to Ceylon, $15.75 million between 1958 and 1962; to Nepal, $12.6 million in 1956; to Burma, $84 million in 1961; and to Indonesia, $11.2 million in 1962.

Communist Tactics in Non-Aligned Countries and the Ideological Quarrel Between Moscow and Peking

(pp. 256–273)

1. V. L. Tiagunenko, *Krushenie kolonial'noi sistemy imperializma* (Moscow: Izdatel'stvo "Znanie" [All-Union Society for Dissemination of Political and Scientific Knowledge], 1961), pp. 9 ff., gives an interesting Soviet periodization of these changes: (a) the "first or Asian phase" after World War II is characterized by the "preponderance of the armed form of national liberation struggle"; (b) the "second phase," beginning in the middle 1950's, spreads national liberation to Africa and Latin America and expresses the "preponderance of peaceful methods for building independent states in former colonies."

2. D. S. Zagoria, *The Sino-Soviet Conflict* (Princeton, N.J.: Princeton University Press, 1962), pp. 245 ff.; E. Kux, "Peking and Moscow at Ideological Odds," *Swiss Review of World Affairs* (Zürich), June, 1960; "Recent Chinese Foreign Policy," *Swiss Review of World Affairs*, July, 1961; "Peking and Moscow," *Swiss Review of World Affairs*, February, 1962.

3. N. S. Khrushchev, "For New Victories of the World Communist Movement; on Results of the Conference of Representatives of Communist and Workers Parties," an address delivered on January 6, 1961, at a joint meeting of the Party organizations of the Higher Party School, the Academy of Social Sciences, and the Party Central Committee's Institute of Marxism-Leninism

(*Pravda*, January 25, 1961). There is some reason to believe that this is a revised version of Khrushchev's speech at the Moscow meeting of the eighty-one Communist parties in November, 1960. Nowadays, the scholastic definition of Communist strategy and tactics as given by I. V. Stalin, "Ob osnovakh leninizma" (1924), *Sochineniia* (Moscow: 1952), VI, 132 ff. is replaced in *Osnovy Marksizma-Leninizma* (Moscow: 1959), pp. 363 ff. by a vaguer formulation: "Tactics are mostly considered as the political line for a relatively short period, determined by certain concrete conditions. . . . Strategy is meant as the line for a whole historical period."

4. For instance, the Moscow statement of the eighty-one parties (*Pravda*, December 6, 1960), puts forward as the main task for all Communist parties: "*The struggle for peace, national independence, democracy and socialism.*" The Chinese interpretation of the Moscow statement (*Hongqi* [*Red Flag*] December 15, 1960) altered the definition of the main tasks as follows: "*struggle against imperialism and for a world peace*, for *national liberation*, democracy and socialism on a world wide scale."

5. N. S. Khrushchev, "Report on the Program of the Communist Party of the Soviet Union," delivered to the Twenty-second Congress of the CPSU, October 18, 1961 (abbreviated report; London: Soviet Booklet No. 81, 1961).

6. *Peking Review*, November 22, 1959, p. 15.

7. *Hongqi*, No. 6, 1958; *Peking Review*, March 29, 1960, p. 12.

8. *Peking Review*, February 9, 1960, p. 7.

9. *Peking Review*, November 8, 1960, p. 19.

10. *Peking Review*, June 14, 1960, p. 14.

11. Mao Tse-tung, quoted by Yu Chao-li in *Hongqi*, No. 6, 1958, and No. 7, 1960; *Peking Review*, December 15, 1961, p. 9.

12. Y. Frantsev, "Problemy voiny i mira v sovremennykh usloviiakh" ("Problems of War and Peace under Modern Conditions"), *Pravda*, August 7, 1960; A. Beliakov and F. Burlatskii, "Leninskaia teoriia sotsialisticheskoi revoliutsii i sovremennost" ("The Leninist Theory of Socialist Revolution and Modern Times"), *Kommunist*, No. 13, September, 1960, pp. 10 ff.

13. Mao Tse-tung, address, Moscow, November 6, 1957; *Peking Review*, December 15, 1961, p. 7; *Peking Review*, November 29, 1960, p. 15.

14. V. I. Lenin, "Doklad o taktike, July 5, 1921, III. Kongress Kommunisticheskogo Internatsionala," *Sochineniia* (2d ed.; Moscow, 1930), XXVI, 453.

15. N. S. Khrushchev, address, January 6, 1961.

16. Chou En-Lai, address, April 18, 1959, *Peking Review*, July 5, 1960, p. 12; *Peking Review*, April 19, 1960, p. 13.

17. *Hongqi*, No. 4, 1959.

18. N. S. Khrushchev, address, January 6, 1961; I. Plyshevskii, "Nekotorye problemy bor'by za nezavisimost' v Afrike" ("Some Problems on the Struggle for Independence in Africa"), *Problemy mira i sotsializma*, No. 7, 1961, pp. 33 ff.

19. *Osnovy Marksizma-Leninizma*, pp. 437 ff.; *Program of the Communist Party of the Soviet Union*, adopted by the Twenty-second Congress of the Communist Party of the Soviet Union, October 31, 1961, (abr. ed.; Moscow: Foreign Languages Publishing House, 1961) pp. 43 ff.

20. At the Sixth Comintern Congress, in 1928, Losovskii spoke of colonial peoples as "allied, colored auxiliary troops against imperialism . . . the world countryside, the world periphery that we lead towards socialism," *Protokoll des*

Sechsten Weltkongresses der Kommunistischen Internationale (*Protocol of the Sixth World Congress of the Communist International*) (Hamburg, 1928), III, 358. Compare also the evaluation of colonial peoples as "main reserves," I. V. Stalin, *op. cit.*, p. 137.

The new Party program states: "As long as [the young sovereign states] do not put an end to their economic dependence on imperialism, they will be playing the role of a 'world countryside,' and will remain objects of semi-colonial exploitation." (*Program* . . . , p. 43.)

21. *Peking Review*, October 6, 1959, p. 21.

22. V. I. Lenin, "Detskaia bolezn' 'levizny' v Kommunizme (1920)" ("Infantile Disease of Leftist Communism"), *Sochineniia* (2d ed.), XXV, 170.

23. *Program* . . . , pp. 7 ff.; N. S. Khrushchev, "Report . . . ," p. 25.

24. *Peking Review*, September 16, 1958.

25. Radio Peking, November 26, 1961; *Peking Review*, November 22, 1960, p. 15.

26. For example: "The myth about 'Western civilization' has gone bankrupt" (Peng Chen, *Peking Review*, January 27, 1959, p. 12); "The 'civilized men' of Europe fattened on the blood of Negroes to mature the 'civilization' of Western capitalism" (*Peking Review*, July 5, 1960, p. 14); and Liu Shao-chi's attacks against "superiority of the white race," *Internationalism and Nationalism* (Peking: Foreign Languages Press, s.a.), pp. 5, 23.

27. Mao Tse-tung, *On the Correct Handling of Contradictions among the People*, February 27, 1957 (Peking: Foreign Languages Press, 1957); *Peking Review*, August 23, 1960, pp. 11, 15; *Peking Review*, March 23, 1962, p. 8; Zagoria, *op. cit.*, p. 264.

28. M. Dzhunusov, *Nekotorye voprosy teorii sotsial'noi revoliutsii v svete krushenia kolonial'noi sistemy imperializma* (*Some Questions Concerning the Theory of Social Revolution in the Light of the Downfall of the Colonial System of Imperialism*) (Frunze, 1961).

29. Y. Iudin, "Nekotorye problemy stanovleniia natsional'noi gosudarstvennosti v nezavisimykh stranakh Afriki" ("Some Problems on the Formation in the National State Structure in the Independent Countries in Africa), *Sovetskoe gosudarstvo i pravo* (Moscow), No. 2, 1961.

30. Dzhunusov, *op. cit.* The draft of the new Party program (*Pravda*, July 30, 1961) included the formula "concessions of the bourgeoisie," which was left out in the definitive text. Liu Shao-chi, on the other hand, did agree "that in certain conditions the proletariat may adopt a policy of buying out the bourgeoisie." (*Peking Review*, July 7, 1961, p. 8.)

31. *Peking Review*, November 8, 1960, p. 18. Khrushchev took this Chinese criticism into account by using the formula "by utilizing parliament and in other countries by utilizing institutions conforming to their national traditions." (Address, January 6, 1961.)

The controversies about the "legal" or "revolutionary" way date back at least to Lenin's polemics with Karl Radek and Rosa Luxemburg in October, 1916, when Lenin criticized the "right for self-determination of nations" and advocated "revolutionary mass-struggle of the proletariat against the capitalists." (*Sochineniia* [2d ed.], XVIII, 323 ff., and XIX, 239 ff.)

In their veiled attacks on the new Soviet Party program, the Chinese accuse so-called "Bernsteinian opportunists" who have "disseminated the illusion of pursuing only a peaceful road and only a legal road, while accusing all those who talked about armed revolution and civil war of being anarchists and Proud-honist." (*Hongqi*, No. 3/4, 1962.) The apparent differences of "dictatorship of the proletariat" versus "all-peoples-state," of smashing or reforming the state machine, etc., are, of course, mainly connected with the "transformation from socialism to Communism," but also have some influence upon Soviet and Chi-nese tactics in the "Third World." The Chinese argument in *Hongqi*, No. 8/9 and 10, 1962, seems to be that by abolishing the "dictatorship of the proletariat" in favor of an "all-peoples-state" in the new Soviet Party program the Soviet leaders have given a bad example for the nonsocialist countries, that may en-courage them to renounce "dictatorship of the proletariat" even as a means for "transformation from capitalism to socialism."

32. *Peking Review*, July 5, 1960, pp. 15 ff.

33. E. Zhukov, "Znamenatel'nyi faktor nashego vremeni" ("A Significant Factor of Our Times"), *Pravda*, August 26, 1960.

34. *Peking Review*, January 20, 1961, p. 10, and October 1, 1959, p. 7.

35. *Program* . . . , pp. 35 ff.

36. *Ibid.*, p. 45.

37. See Khrushchev's attacks on Pan-Arabism, "Address at a reception of an Iraqi delegation," *Izvestiia*, March 17, 1959; and Plyshevskii, *op. cit.*, p. 33. On the other hand, Iudin, *loc. cit.*, is more in favor of a federation of African coun-tries and points to the dangers of a "balkanization of the African continent."

38. N. S. Khrushchev, "Address at a Meeting for the Soviet Party Delegation in Sofia, May 19, 1962," *Pravda*, May 20, 1962.

39. *Peking Review*, March 31, 1962, p. 8.

40. *Peking Review*, March 16, 1962, pp. 13 ff.; March 31, 1961, pp. 9 ff., and December 27, 1960, p. 26.

41. *Program* . . . , pp. 45 ff.; G. Kim, "Puti razvitiia stran, zavoevavshikh natsional'nuiu nezavisimost'" ("The Path of Development of Countries that Have Won National Independence"), *Problemy mira i sotsializma*, No. 4, 1962, pp. 77 ff., stresses the necessity of a structural change of agricultural pro-duction and of the development of agrotechnics (use of tractors, fertilizers, etc.) as prerequisites for agrarian reforms.

42. B. Ponomarev, "O gosudarstve natsional'noi demokratii" ("On the Na-tional Democratic State"), *Kommunist*, No. 8, May, 1961, pp. 33 ff., calls the "thesis of building an independent state of national democracy a creative devel-opment and enrichment of the Marxist-Leninist theory of national liberation revolutions." The model of "national democracy" is partly an adaptation of the concept of "people's democracy" for "peoples of economically underdeveloped countries." According to the theoretical definition, a "people's democracy" is on the "road to socialism" on the basis of a "dictatorship of the proletariat"; a "national democracy" develops on a "non-capitalist road" on the basis of the "dictatorship of the really national-patriotic forces" (Dzhunusov, *op. cit.*).

This concept of "national democracy" is in certain points a revival of Kuusi-nen's definition of "bourgeois-democratic revolution" in the "Theses on the Revolutionary Movement in Colonial and Semi-colonial Countries Adopted by the Sixth Comintern Congress," in J. Degras (ed.), *The Communist Interna-tional, 1919–1943: Documents* (London: Oxford University Press, 1960), II, 536.

43. *Peking Review*, June 16, 1961, p. 20.

44. N. S. Khrushchev, address, January 6, 1961.

45. *Peking Review*, December 15, 1961, p. 10.
46. Mao Tse-tung, *Collected Works* (Russian ed.), II, 263.
47. *Peking Review*, April 26, 1960, p. 16.
48. N. S. Khrushchev, address, January 6, 1961.
49. *Peking Review*, December 15, 1961, p. 9.
50. N. S. Khrushchev, *O vneshnei politike Sovetskogo Soiuza 1960 (On the Foreign Policy of the Soviet Union)* (Moscow, 1961), II, 182; N. S. Khrushchev, "Address at a Meeting of the Congress for Total Disarmament and Peace, Moscow, July 10, 1962," *Pravda*, July 11, 1962.
51. Liu Chang-sheng, *Peking Review*, June 14, 1060, p. 14; Liao Cheng-chih, "Address at a Meeting of the World Peace Council, Stockholm, December 16, 1961," *Jen-min Jih-pao (People's Daily)*, December 21, 1961.

Communist Polycentrism and the Underdeveloped Areas
(pp. 274–286)

1. See Donald S. Zagoria, *The Sino-Soviet Conflict, 1956–1961* (Princeton, N.J.: Princeton University Press, 1962); Alexander Dallin, "Long Divisions and Fine Fractions," *Problems of Communism*, XI, 2 (March–April, 1962), 7–16 and, with Jonathan Harris, his *Dissension in International Communism* (New York: Columbia University Press, 1963); the present writer's *Albania and the Sino-Soviet Rift* (Cambridge, Mass.: Massachusetts Institute of Technology Press, 1963).
2. See *Albania and the Sino-Soviet Rift*, pp. 125–29.
3. *Ibid.*, pp. 122–25.
4. See Giorgio Galli on Italy, in W. Laqueur and L. Labedz (eds.), *Polycentrism: The New Factor in International Communism* (New York: Frederick A. Praeger, 1962), pp. 127–40; see also his chapter in a forthcoming volume on rightist tendencies in European Communism that the writer is editing for the MIT Center for International Studies, to be published by the MIT Press.
5. See K. A. Jelenski on Poland, in Laqueur and Labedz (eds.), *op. cit.*, pp. 59–71, and Jerzy Ptakowski, "Politics in Poland," *East Europe*, XI, 12 (December, 1962), 18–25.
6. See George Urban on Hungary, in Laqueur and Labedz, *op. cit.*, pp. 72–80, and a chapter by François Fejtö in the forthcoming volume cited in note 4, above.
7. R. V. Burks, *The Dynamics of Communism in Eastern Europe* (Princeton, N.J.: Princeton University Press, 1961).
8. See Adam B. Ulam, *The Unfinished Revolution* (New York: Random House, 1960).
9. See Burks, *op. cit.*, and Lucian Pye, *Guerrilla Communism in Malaya* (Princeton, N.J.: Princeton University Press, 1956).
10. See the writer's chapter on Yugoslavia and Africa, to be published by Stanford University Press in a collective volume edited for the Hoover Institute by Professor Zbigniew Brzezinski.
11. See Z. K. Brzezinski, *The Soviet Bloc* (Cambridge Mass.: Harvard University Press, 1960), pp. 52–53.
12. See note 3, above. For persistence of this CGIL attitude prior to the WFTU conference held at Leipzig in December, 1962, and especially as regards

the European Economic Community, see Luciano Lama in *L'Unità*, October 14, 1962 (JPRS 15, 986, November 1, 1962).

13. See Z. K. Brzezinski, "Deviation Control: A Study in the Dynamics of Doctrinal Conflict," *American Political Science Review*, LVI, 8 (March, 1962), 7, n. 9.

14. For the Sino-Soviet dispute and Asian Communist Parties, see Robert A. Scalapino, "Moscow, Peking, and the Communist Parties of Asia," *Foreign Affairs* (New York), XLII, 2 (January, 1963), 323–41; Doak Barnett (ed.), *Communism in Asia* (New York: Frederick A. Praeger, 1963); for the Democratic Republic of Vietnam, see P. J. Honey, "The Position of the DRV Leadership and the Succession to Ho Chi Minh," *The China Quarterly*, No. 9 (January–March, 1962), pp. 24–36.

15. See Walter Kolarz, "The West African Scene," *Problems of Communism*, X, 6 (November–December, 1961), 15–23; Fritz Schatten, *Afrika— Schwarz oder Rot?* (Munich: Piper Verlag, 1961).

16. See the writer's *Albania and the Sino-Soviet Rift*, pp. 158–66.

17. See "The Colombo Line," *The Economist* (London), pp. 1208–10.

18. See Z. K. Brzezinski, "Patterns and Limits of the Sino-Soviet Dispute," *Problems of Communism*, IX, 5 (September–October, 1960), 1–7.

Communist China's Economy and Its Impact on Afro-Asia
(pp. 287–300)

1. Since March, 1955, the official rate of exchange has been 2.46 yuan to an American dollar, but it has no real meaning. According to a report published in the *Christian Science Monitor*, May 16, 1961, the Peking currency reached an all-time high in the exchange markets in Southeast Asia—4.39 yuan to an American dollar—in March, 1959, but exactly two years later it had dived to the low of 11.7.

2. The best source of official data for the period 1949–58 is *Wei-ta ti Shih-nien* (*The Great Ten Years*) (Peking: State Statistical Bureau, September, 1959). An English translation was issued by the Foreign Languages Press, Peking, in October, 1959, under the title *Ten Great Years*. For a study of the operation of the statistical services in China, see the writer's *The Statistical System of Communist China* (Berkeley, Calif.: University of California Press, 1962).

3. Chou En-lai, "The Great Ten Years," *Jen-min Jih-pao* (*People's Daily*, henceforth cited as *JMJP*), October 6, 1959; and the editorial "Long Live the Great Solidarity among the Socialist Countries under the Leadership of the Soviet Union," *JMJP*, October 3, 1959.

4. See dispatch in *JMJP*, November 3, 1959, p. 3.

5. Sun Shang-ching, "Shining Achievements and Selfless Assistance," *Ching-chi yen-chiu* (*Economic Research*), No. 11, November, 1959, pp. 1–10; also Hu Shih-chieh, "On the Economic Relations among Socialist Countries," *Ts'ai-ching yen-chiu* (*Financial and Economic Research*), No. 8, November, 1958, pp. 41–44.

6. Fang Chung, "High Speed and the Wavy Course," *Chi-hua yu t'ung-chi* (*Planning and Statistics*), No. 10, July, 1959, pp. 10–12, 15.

7. See discussion in the writer's *Economic Development of Communist China* (Berkeley, Calif.: University of California Press, 1959), pp. 109–10.

8. "Draft Proposal of the Second Five-Year Plan for the Development of the National Economy," (Chinese Communist Party), in *JMJP*, September 29, 1956.

9. There is quite an extensive literature on this important policy shift. Among the documents that should be consulted is the editorial, "Improve the Control Structure for Industries, Trade, and Public Finance," *JMJP*, November 18, 1957.

10. See discussion in the writer's article, "Economic Development," *The China Quarterly*, No. 1, January–March, 1960, pp. 35–50.

11. "Communiqué on the Results of the 1958 Plan" (State Statistical Bureau), *JMJP*, April 15, 1959.

12. Chou En-lai, "Report on Revision of the Major Targets in the 1959 Plan and on Stepping Up the Movement for Increasing Output and Economizing," *JMJP*, August 29, 1959; "Communiqué on Correction of the 1959 Agricultural statistics" (State Statistical Bureau), *JMJP*, August 27, 1959.

13. Fan Mu-han, "Technological Reform in the National Economy Speeds Up," *Chi-hua yu t'ung-chi (Planning and Statistics)*, No. 2, February, 1960, pp. 7–9.

14. Li Fu-ch'un, "Report on the Results of the 1960 Plan and on the Plan for 1961," *JMJP*, January 21, 1961.

15. Sun Chia-no, "What the Communes Did for Kiangsu," *China Reconstructs*, IX, February, 1960, 24–26.

16. Tan Hsi-yao, "The 12-Year Program—Blueprint for China's Modern Agriculture," *China Reconstructs*, IX, August, 1960, 8–11.

17. Editorial, "Simultaneous Development of Industry and Agriculture Is an Important Law in China's Socialist Economy," *Hung-ch'i (Red Flag)*, No. 22, November, 1960, pp. 1–6.

18. For example, *JMJP*, November 12, 1960, January 11, 1961, and February 3, 1961.

19. Chen Cheng-jen, "On the System of Ownership and of Distribution in People's Communes," *JMJP*, October 18, 1959.

20. *Ibid.*

21. New China News Agency release, *JMJP*, October 1, 1960, p. 6.

22. "Communiqué of the Ninth Plenary Session" (Chinese Communist Party, Central Committee), *JMJP*, January 21, 1961.

23. Editorial, "Uphold and Improve Continually the System of Three Guarantees and One Bonus," *JMJP*, December 29, 1960.

24. Editorial, "Production Plans for People's Communes Must Be Rooted in the Masses," *JMJP*, January 23, 1961; Chao Jen, "Each Has His Own Duties," JMJP, August 3, 1962.

25. *JMJP*, April 2, 1962.

26. Yi Nung, "People's Commune the Inevitable Product of China's Historical Development," *Ching-chi yen-chiu (Economic Research)*, No. 11, November, 1959, pp. 21–33. *Hsiang* corresponds to an administrative village, whereas *ch'u* (district) was an extension of the *hsien* government (county) for the purpose of exercising direct control over a number of *hsiang*. For details, see my *Statistical System of Communist China*, pp. 16–18.

27. An estimate based primarily on data given in the annual issues of *Jen-min shou-ts'e (People's Handbook)* for 1958, 1959, 1960, 1961, and 1962.

28. Choh-Ming Li, *Economic Development of Communist China*, p. 190.

29. The writer is indebted to Mr. Chin Si-hai of the Union Research Institute of Hong Kong for supplying a careful tabulation of Communist China's economic grants and loans to other countries in recent years.

Notes on the Contributors

EDWARD W. BLYDEN, III is the head of the Department of Political Science and Diplomacy at the University of Nigeria, Nsukka, Eastern Nigeria.

DAVID T. CATTELL is Associate Professor of Political Science at the University of California, Los Angeles.

JANE DEGRAS is a senior research specialist on Soviet affairs at the Royal Institute of International Affairs, London.

HERBERT S. DINERSTEIN is a specialist on the Soviet Union on the staff of the RAND Corporation, Santa Monica, California.

RUPERT EMERSON is Professor of Government and Research Associate at the Center for International Affairs, Harvard University, Cambridge, Mass.

KALU EZERA is a Senior Lecturer in Political Science, and Dean of the Faculty of Social Studies at the University of Nigeria, Nsukka. He is also a member of the Nigerian Parliament.

B. G. D. FOLSON is a Lecturer in Political Science at the University of Ghana, Legon, Ghana.

WILLIAM E. GRIFFITH is a Research Associate at the Center for International Studies, Massachusetts Institute of Technology, Cambridge, Mass.

WOLFGANG H. KRAUS is Professor of Political Science and a member of the Institute for Sino-Soviet Studies at the George Washington University, Washington, D.C.

ERNST KUX is a Lecturer in Communist Affairs at the Handelshochschule of St. Gallen, Switzerland, and an editorial writer on Sino-

Soviet questions for the *Neue Zürcher Zeitung*, Zürich, Switzerland.

CHOH-MING LI is Professor of Business Administration and Chairman of the Center for Chinese Studies at the University of California, Berkeley.

WALTER Z. LAQUEUR, an expert on Soviet and Middle Eastern affairs, is the editor of *Survey*, London.

KURT LONDON is the Director of the Institute for Sino-Soviet Studies and Professor of International Affairs at the George Washington University, Washington, D.C.

RICHARD LOWENTHAL is a Professor of International Relations at the Otto-Suhr Institut, Free University of West Berlin, Germany.

RODERICK MACFARQUHAR, a specialist on Chinese and Asian affairs, is the editor of *The China Quarterly*, London.

KLAUS MEHNERT is Professor of Political Science at the Institute of Technology, Aachen, and editor of *Osteuropa*, West Germany,

FRANZ MICHAEL is Professor of Chinese History and Government and Chairman of the Modern Chinese History Project at the Far Eastern and Russian Institute, University of Washington, Seattle.

G. WARREN NUTTER is Professor of Economics and Chairman of the James Wilson Department of Economics, University of Virginia.

MASAO ONOE is Professor of Diplomatic History and International Relations at Kobe University, Kobe, Japan.

SERGIUS YAKOBSON is Chief of the Slavic and Central European Division at the Library of Congress and Senior Specialist in Russian Affairs in the Library's Legislative Reference Service, Washington, D.C.

TETSUJI YASUHIRA is an economist specializing in the economy of the U.S.S.R. and Professor at the Tokyo Metropolitan University, Tokyo, Japan.